AF839551

Stoning as Punishment in Early Islam

Stoning as Punishment in Early Islam

SYED ATIF RIZWAN

OXFORD
UNIVERSITY PRESS

OXFORD
UNIVERSITY PRESS

Oxford University Press is a department of the University of Oxford.
It furthers the University's objective of excellence in research, scholarship,
and education by publishing worldwide. Oxford is a registered trade mark of
Oxford University Press in the UK and in certain other countries.

Published in the United States of America by Oxford University Press
198 Madison Avenue, New York, NY 10016, United States of America.

© Oxford University Press 2026

All rights reserved. No part of this publication may be reproduced, stored in a retrieval system, transmitted, used for text and data mining, or used for training artificial intelligence, in any form or by any means, without the prior permission in writing of Oxford University Press, or as expressly permitted by law, by license or under terms agreed with the appropriate reprographics rights organization. Inquiries concerning reproduction outside the scope of the above should be sent to the Rights Department, Oxford University Press, at the address above.

You must not circulate this work in any other form
and you must impose this same condition on any acquirer.

CIP data is on file at the Library of Congress

ISBN 9780197823743

DOI: 10.1093/9780197823774.001.0001

The manufacturer's authorized representative in the EU for product safety is
Oxford University Press España S.A. of Parque Empresarial San Fernando de Henares,
Avenida de Castilla, 2 – 28830 Madrid (www.oup.es/en or product.safety@oup.com).
OUP España S.A. also acts as importer into Spain of products made by the manufacturer.

Brief Contents

Detailed Contents

Acknowledgments

All praise and gratitude belong to God Almighty—the Everlasting, the More Compassionate. Nothing can be better applied to this project than the adage "it takes a village." I am humbled by the sheer number of people who have guided me, supported me, and influenced me on the path of writing this book. I would like to thank Khaled Abou El Fadl, who was my doctoral dissertation adviser and remains my lifelong teacher. He has taught and shown me what it takes to be a true scholar. I can only hope that one day I might be able to display a modicum of his scholarly acumen. I would like to thank Ahmad Atif Ahmad, who, along with sharing a middle name with me, has not only been a mentor but also an incredibly dear friend. I thank Behnam Sadeghi for generously giving his time to help me with methods in hadith analysis. Someone who has become nothing short of a big brother is Scott C. Alexander, and words cannot capture what his support has meant for me both personally and professionally. I am also deeply thankful to my friend and colleague Benjamin E. Sax for helping me with rabbinic studies and for giving me the space to ask the most remedial questions without making me feel bad. I want to acknowledge the support of my family and my in-laws, though, for the latter, the label feels like a disservice. I thank all my friends for providing me with the levity that served as a reminder about the important things in life, such as laughter. I am not even sure how to express my gratitude to my wife, Seema, the smartest person I know and who, as a federal criminal defense attorney, became my personal teacher of criminal law. Her dedication to pursuing justice *and* compassion is awe-inspiring and remains a constant model for me. She is the cornerstone of our family whose singular drive and focus make our lives one of pure joy. Speaking of joy, I could not fully be who I am without our son, Jibreel, a true angel sent from God just for us. His disarming smile, big brown eyes, and sense of humor continue to be the light of our lives and the perfect antidote to the stresses of life. His keen awareness of justice as an eight-year-old is a perfect reminder that every human, no matter their age, has a sense of fairness and equity. May God Almighty protect you, Jibreel, and bless you with a long, happy, and healthy life. Āmīn.

Syed Atif Rizwan

Q16:11 Indeed, in this is a sign for those who reflect.
Q16:12 Indeed, in this are signs for those who use their reason.

Notes on Transliteration and Translation

I use the *International Journal of Middle East Studies* transliteration system.

I do not transliterate the *ta'marbūṭa* (ة) into English with an 'h.' For example, instead of *sharī'ah*, I use *sharī'a*.

All translations of Arabic into English are mine unless indicated otherwise.

I have transliterated the names of most locale. For example, instead of Iraq, I use 'Irāq. My reason for doing so is with the intent of producing an image in the mind of a reader that is not conflated with what may be a natural present-day understanding of the same place.

Introduction

> I [Abū Isḥāq al-Shaybanī] asked 'Abd Allāh b. Abī Awfā: Did the Prophet ever order someone to be stoned?
> Ibn Abī Awfā said: Yes.
> I asked: Was it before or after *sura al-nūr* (Q24:2 - 100 lashes)?
> He said: I do not know.

The exchange between the Companion of the Prophet Muḥammad, 'Abd Allāh b. Abī Awfā (d. *c.* 86/705),[1] and the latter's Kūfan student, Abū Isḥāq al-Shaybanī (d. 139/756), is actually quite startling. Ibn Abī Awfā was not just any Companion. He was a key figure in early Islamic history, known for his close association with the Prophet. He witnessed the Treaty of Ḥudaybiyya (20/630), gave his allegiance to the Prophet at the Bay'a of Riḍwān (6/628), and fought in crucial battles such as at Khaybar (7/628) and at Ḥunayn (8/630), among others. He remained in Medina until the Prophet's death and later moved to Kūfa, where he continued to be a respected authority.[2]

The significance of this exchange is further underscored when one keeps in mind that Ibn Abī Awfā was frequently sought out precisely for how well he remembered his time with the Prophet. For instance, he was once asked whether it was permitted to eat locusts. He replied that he had fought six battles alongside the Prophet, where locusts were often all they had to eat.[3] This depth of experience and his close proximity to the Prophet make his testimony particularly weighty. If even he, with his direct connection to the Prophet and his participation in these pivotal moments, is portrayed in the

[1] I use a dual dating system: one based on the start of the *hijra*, emigration of the Prophet Muḥammad from Mecca to Medina, and the other based on the common era. Note that the *hijrī* year can overlap with two consecutive years in the Gregorian calendar. For the sake of simplicity, I only provide one Gregorian year. On the *hijra* and its relationship to the dating of the Islamic calendar, see Marshall Hodgson, *Venture of Islam*, vol. 1, 20–2.

[2] Ibn Sa'd, *Kitāb al-ṭabaqāt al-kubrā*, 5:206–7 and 8:144; al-Dhahabī, *Siyar a'lām*, 3:428–30; Ibn al-Athīr, *Usd al-ghāba*, 641.

[3] Ibn al-Athīr, *Usd al-ghāba*, 641.

Stoning as Punishment in Early Islam. Syed Atif Rizwan, Oxford University Press. © Oxford University Press 2026.
DOI: 10.1093/9780197823774.003.0001

report as being unsure about the timing and context of the stoning punishment for *zinā*, then what does this say about our own certainty regarding its provenance and applicability to Muslims?

Ibn Abī Awfā's student, Abū Isḥāq al-Shaybanī, had this exchange with his teacher sometime before the latter's death in 86/705. Abū Isḥāq then passed it on to no less than eight of his own students: Shuʿba b. al-Ḥajjāj (d. 160/776),[4] Khālid b. ʿAbd Allāh al-Wāsiṭī (d. 179/795),[5] ʿAbd al-Wāḥid b. Ziyād al-ʿAbdī (d. 179/795),[6] Hushaym b. Bashīr al-Sulamī (d. 183 AH/799),[7] ʿAlī b. Mushir al-Qurashī (d. 189/805),[8] ʿUbayda b. Ḥumayd al-Laythī (d. 190/806),[9] ʿAbd al-Raḥmān b. Muḥammad al-Muḥāribī (d. 195/811),[10] and Muḥammad b. al-Fuḍayl b. Ghazwān (d. 195/811).[11] Each of these, in turn, transmitted this narrative to a wide range of students until it found its place in several collections of hadith[12]—defined as reports, accounts, or narratives-ensuring its preservation for posterity.

If we are to trust the numerous hadith stipulating that the stoning punishment is Islamic as early as during the Prophet's lifetime, that is, the very accounts used to justify its lawfulness, then how are we to explain the above report on the authority of Ibn Abī Awfā? How can we be sure about the application of such a severe punishment if a close Companion to the Prophet is depicted as harboring doubts? Why is Ibn Abī Awfā even asked about the matter by Abū Isḥāq as late as the end of the first/seventh Islamic century if the legitimacy of punishment is a settled question? Why do several students of Abū Isḥāq, as late as the middle of the second/eighth Islamic century, think this report worthy of preservation, unless they too saw the problem that it posed? Why do compilers as late as the third/ninth Islamic century-giants such as Ibn Ḥanbal (d. 241/855), al-Bukhārī (d. 256/870), and Muslim (d. 261/875)-deem it worthy of inclusion in their respective compilations? It is not usual that a Companion's hesitancy is preserved, unless it tells us that

[4] Abū ʿAwāna, *Musnad*, 13:371f, no. 6,761.
[5] al-Bukhārī, *Ṣaḥīḥ* (2002 ed.), 1,685, no. 6,813.
[6] al-Bukhārī, *Ṣaḥīḥ* (2002 ed.), 1,692f, no. 6,840; Muslim, *Ṣaḥīḥ*, 1,328, no. 1,702 (29).
[7] Ibn Ḥanbal, *Musnad* (1992 ed.), 31:471, no. 19,126.
[8] Ibn Abī Shayba, *al-Muṣannaf* (1989 ed.), 5:549, no. 28,775.
[9] al-Bukhārī, *Ṣaḥīḥ* (2002 ed.), 1,692f, no. 6,840.
[10] al-Bukhārī, *Ṣaḥīḥ* (2002 ed.), 1,692f, no. 6,840.
[11] Abū ʿAwāna, *Musnad*, 13:371, no. 6,760.
[12] The plural of hadith is *aḥādīth*, but I use the former to signify both the singular and the plural usage. According to Hodgson, translating hadith as 'tradition' retains a certain level of imprecision that ignores the (non-Islamic) usage of the term. See Hodgson, *Venture of Islam* vol. 1, 63–6.

uncertainty is warranted. In the present case, this uncertainty is not only the justification for my project, but it is also its starting point.

This book aims to explore this tension—the gap between early ambiguity and later legal rigidity—by examining some of the contingencies that developed and contributed to the beginnings of the historical process by which the stoning punishment for illicit sexual intercourse (*zinā*) came to be normalized in the Islamic tradition.[13] I accomplish this inquiry by examining particular hadith that I argue are central to justifying the use of the stoning punishment upon Muslims. I conduct a close study of such reports' respective transmission chains, *isnād* (s. *sanad*),[14] to situate their initial circulation during the first/seventh century of Islam and, corresponding text content(s), *matn* (pl. *mutūn*), to demonstrate their significance in the process of legitimating the capital punishment. I also illustrate how such hadith and others on stoning are used by Muslim legal authorities to develop *zinā* laws. I argue that the stoning punishment was retrospectively projected into the Islamic legal tradition, rather than being a normative practice

[13] Any references I make to the Islamic legal tradition are to be understood as a broad corpus that includes not only the Qur'ān, Islam's sacred text, but also the compendiums of reports (hadith) that purport to document the edicts and teachings of the Prophet Muḥammad and other early legal authorities (e.g., the Prophet's Companions), as well as legal works composed by Muslim legal authorities, comprising both works of legal theory and works devoted to explicating positive law. See Wael Hallaq, *Introduction to Islamic Law*, 14–30.

Zinā is the definite form whereas *zinā'* (or *zinan*) is the indefinite form. The former has come to represent both in scholarship. For a general overview on the meaning of *zinā*, see *Encyclopaedia of Islam*, 2nd ed., s.v. "Zinā" or "Zinā'," by Rudolph Peters; for recent insightful discussions on the meaning of *zinā* in the Qur'ān, see Holger M. Zellentin, *Law Beyond Israel*, 184–91, 203f and 206; also see Karen Bauer and Feras Hamza, *Women, Households, and the Hereafter*, 191–3, including footnote 17; in the classical Islamic legal tradition, Muslim authorities also recognized the lawfulness of concubinage, and verses of the Qur'ān referring to ownership of slaves (*mā malakat aymānukum*, e.g., Q23:6) were interpreted as permission for Muslim men to engage in sexual relations with their unmarried female slaves even in the absence of a marriage contract. The term usually employed to describe this form of relationship is *waṭi'a bi-milk al-yamīn* (sexual intercourse based on ownership). See, e.g., the opinion of the Mālikī jurist Saḥnūn (d. 240/854), *al-Mudawwana*, 2:26, 56f, and 381. Importantly, while Muslim jurists deemed it lawful for free Muslim women to own male slaves and even relaxed the ordinary rules pertaining to proper dress (*'awra*)—which usually required free Muslim women to cover their entire body when in the presence of unrelated men—so as to facilitate the mistress-slave relationship, the same jurists were uncompromising in their insistence that only Muslim men may enjoy the right to take concubines. See, e.g., 'Abd al-Razzāq, *al-Muṣannaf*, 7:209f:12, 816–21; for an insightful discussion on the matter of licit sexual intercourse with slaves, see Kecia Ali, *Sexual Ethics and Islam*, 50–71 and 77.

[14] Though the singular is *sanad*, I will use *isnād* to signify both the singular and the plural. *Isnād* is the technical term used by Muslim compilers of hadith to designate a chain of authorities for each individual report rendered in successive chronological order stretching back to the Prophet himself or another authority, such as a Companion. Each authority within the *isnād*, including the authority from whom the compiler himself received the report, was to be identified by name. Thus, the compiler would state that A told him, that B told him (i.e., A), that C told him (i.e., B), that the Prophet told him (i.e., C). Only once a full list of authorities was rendered could the alleged statement of the authoritative figure, e.g., the Prophet, be produced.

during the twenty-three-year revelatory period (610–32 CE) of the Prophet Muḥammad.

I am aware of the fact that I am not the first to assert this argument. Both in popular culture and in the academy, one can find this opinion.[15] In fact, Muslim sources reveal the existence of certain groups immediately after the death of the Prophet, including those pejoratively labeled the *Khawārij*, who rejected the claim that the Prophet ordered lapidation upon certain categories of Muslim offenders of illicit sexual intercourse.[16] Accordingly, I may be charged with the accusation that I am not bringing anything new to light. My project, however, diverts from both public opinion and scholarly works by way of a critical analysis of specific historical material that I submit is central to the beginnings of the process of formalizing the legitimacy of the capital punishment.

As is well known, there are four verses in the Qur'ān ('Uthmānī codex) that furnish earthly punishments for those convicted of illicit sexual intercourse. In Chapter Four, *al-Nisā'* (The Women):

> 15 Concerning those of your women who [may have] committed a sexual transgression, first bring four witnesses to testify against them. If the testimony of witnesses [confirms their wrongdoing], confine the [convicted women] to [their] houses until death overtakes them or God provides another way.
>
> 16 Concerning the two [transgressors] from among you that [are confirmed] to have committed a sexual transgression, discipline them. However, if they repent and reform, then leave them alone. Indeed, God is more forgiving and merciful.[17]

And in Chapter 24, *al-Nūr* (The Light):

[15] For example, see Hartwig Hirschfeld, *New Researches into the Composition and Exegesis of the Qoran*, 137.

[16] For a reference to this opinion, see, e.g., the work of the Ḥanafī jurist al-Sarakhsī (d. 483/1090), *al-Mabsūṭ*, 9:36; see also the work of the Ḥanbalī jurist, Ibn Qudāma (d. 620/1223), *al-Mughnī*, 12:309; on the disparaging nature of the term *khawārij*, see Adam Gaiser, *Shurāt Legends*, esp. the "Introduction."

[17] Zellentin writes that "the two from among you" has two possible interpretations: a heterosexual or homosexual encounter. On the latter, see Zellentin, *Law Beyond Israel*, 192–9; on these verses and their financial and social implications, see Bauer and Hamza, *Women, Households, and the Hereafter*, 260–4.

> 2 As for the woman and man who commit illicit sexual intercourse (*al-zāniya* and *al-zānī*), flog each of them 100 times. If you [sincerely] believe in God and the Last Day, do not compassion lead you to have pity on them such that you undermine God's directives. And have a group of believers watch the punishment being carried out.

Finally, Q24:33 stipulates that a particular class of slave girls convicted of illicit sexual intercourse is subject to half of the punishment applicable to non-slave women convicted of the same type of transgression. Given that there is no mention of lapidation for sexual transgressions in the Qur'ān, how is it then that the stoning punishment for certain kinds of Muslim offenders became firmly anchored in the Islamic legal tradition?

Muslim legal and exegetical authorities—quite a few scholars were both—drew on source material about early key figures in Islamic history and utilized various jurisprudential methodologies to justify the stoning punishment for certain types of Muslims convicted of illicit sexual intercourse.[18] This source material would be preserved in hadith that purport to describe events from the life of the Prophet Muḥammad and his Companions. It is according to a subset of such hadith that the Prophet or other authoritative individuals prescribed the stoning punishment upon Muslims.

The quandary about the legitimacy of death by lapidation is exacerbated by the ambivalence toward the capital punishment in the history of Islamic law and jurisprudence—an ambivalence that appears to date back to the earliest stages of Muslim history.[19] It is very poignant, then, to question why Muslim jurists consciously sought to limit the legal system's ability to make use of lapidation, even as they justified it as a religious obligation. To be sure, an answer to this question is important. But in the present project, I look to investigate the foundation upon which the question can even be asked. The bulk of this book focuses on examining the provenance and transmission history of certain reports that, I submit, play a key role in juristic opinions that sought to justify the legality of the stoning punishment.

The reader would be quite justified in asking: if it is not *because* of hadith or a purported Qur'ānic verse about stoning that necessitated Muslim jurists to legalize the stoning punishment, then what did? Sometimes the

[18] On jurisprudential methods, see details in Chapter 1.

[19] Intisar Rabb, "Crime and Punishment in Medieval Islamic Societies;" Muslim jurists made the evidentiary requirements for conviction so high so as to render the implementation of the punishment nearly impossible. See Khaled Abou El Fadl, "Shari'ah," 18.

law follows cultural practices—a legal position does not lead, but instead lags.[20] At times, jurists provide a legal basis for laws already thoroughly entrenched by social realities.[21] The reader's skepticism about this claim of mine might be tempered by the fact that this phenomenon is observable even in the contemporary American context. For example, there existed a time when interracial marriages were unlawful in the United States. But social realities—including the fight against racism—could not be ignored indefinitely, and this state of affairs informed the U.S. Supreme Court to overturn the rule. In the Muslim case, during the first two centuries of Islam, jurists could and did formulate legal judgments that reflected local practices of non-Prophetic provenance, such as tribal laws or laws instituted by other key figures, such as the Prophet's Companions.[22] In short, the development of Islamic law and jurisprudence is an intricate process that draws upon various sources of authority and other considerations. My argument is that the process by which the stoning punishment became part of the Islamic criminal law would eventually necessitate the emergence of a legal discourse that made use of certain hadith as a way to substantiate an already-existing legal regiment that had entered into force—a *fait accompli*—but for which there had not yet been a firm Islamic basis.

Before proceeding any further, it would be useful for the reader if I provide a brief overview of how the Qur'ān defines the parameters of *zinā* (illicit sexual intercourse), as compared (and contrasted) with how such parameters emerge in Muslim legal writings of the third/ninth and fourth/tenth Islamic centuries. In the case of the legal discourse, I will also provide a brief account of what Muslim jurists thought constituted the legal elements for the transgression for which death by stoning becomes, in their view, the stipulated punishment.

In many cases, the Qur'ān uses *zinā* in the general sense to connote illicit sexual relations:

Q17:32 Do not go near *zinā*. It is a *fāḥisha*. It is an evil path.[23]

[20] Khaled Abou El Fadl, *Rebellion & Violence*, 102 and 107.

[21] On an explanation of this process within the purview of law-making with respect to rebellion, see Abou El Fadl, *Rebellion & Violence*, 107–11.

[22] One example is regarding women's participation in group ritual prayers. See generally Behnam Sadeghi, *The Logic of Law Making*.

[23] *Fāḥisha/faḥshā'* connotes a sexual transgression in all its forms, with one being *zinā*. See Zellentin, *Law Beyond Israel*, 184–6; *fāḥisha* can also signify homosexual relations. See, e.g., Q7:80 and Zellentin, *Law Beyond Israel*, 190; Bauer and Hamza define *fāḥisha* as lewdness/sexual indecency and conceptualized as the antithesis of modesty and morality. See Bauer and Hamza, *Women,*

Q25:68 Those are the ones who do not associate anything with God, nor take a life except for a [legal reason] because God has made all life sacred, nor engage in *zinā* (*lā yaznūna*)

Q60:12 Prophet, when believing women come to you and pledge that they will not associate anything with God, nor commit theft, nor engage in *zinā* (*lā yaznīna*)

As noted previously, it is in Q24:2 that one finds the meaning of *zinā* to signify sexual relations between a male and a female conducted outside the context of a licit relationship.[24] Note, again, that the offender's marital status remains unspecified.[25] This ambiguous aspect of the term *zinā* contributed to divergent interpretations of the term's meaning.

In the Islamic legal tradition, Muslim jurists agreed that the punishment for heterosexual *zinā* depended on the particular status of the accused, whether male or female. Never-married males and females found guilty of engaging in sexual intercourse outside of wedlock were liable to one hundred lashes, as per the Qur'ān. The jurists also mandated the punishment of flogging for male and female *zinā* offenders who had entered into a marriage contract but *did not* consummate it. On the other hand, males and females who had entered into and consummated a legal marriage, and were later found guilty of engaging in unlawful sexual intercourse, were deemed by Muslim jurists to have committed an offense of such gravity that the only appropriate punishment for such offenders was to suffer death by stoning. Moreover, for Muslim jurists, an offender's current marital status had no bearing on whether or not they could be found guilty of this more severe form of *zinā*. In other words, a person could be found guilty of having committed this more severe form of *zinā* even if the offender was no longer married to their spouse at the time they committed the offense. As far as Muslim jurists were concerned, a guilty verdict would result in a mandatory sentence of death by stoning for such an offender, so long as it could be shown that the offender in question had *once* consummated a marriage.[26]

Households, and the Hereafter, 114. For their broader discussion on the term, see pp. 114–6, 175f, and 197.

[24] Zellentin, *Law Beyond Israel*, 203.

[25] Zellentin, *Law Beyond Israel*, 203–6; Bauer and Hamza, *Women, Households, and the Hereafter*, 193.

[26] One possible exception is if a Muslim converts away from Islam. See, e.g., al-Sarakhsī, *Kitāb al-mabsūṭ*, 5:151.

Going forward and for the sake of efficiency, I employ the term '*zinā*-stoning' to refer to the capital punishment mandated for persons found guilty of illicit sexual intercourse based on having *iḥṣān*, the central legal element that triggers the applicability of the capital punishment. In Chapter 1, I review in detail the conceptual development of *iḥṣān* and the various implications that arise for understanding the purported normativity of *zinā*-stoning. *Iḥṣān* acquires various meanings as it develops in the Islamic legal and exegetical literature, but can generally be understood as a legal status gained by a free Muslim person *after* consummation in a lawful marriage.[27] By developing and incorporating *iḥṣān* as the necessary element for *zinā*-stoning, Muslim authorities rendered the Qur'ān's use of *zinā* decidedly unique to their own usage of the term.[28]

In the chapters that follow, I use the term 'fornication' to refer to the lesser form of *zinā* that is punishable by flogging, while I will reserve the term 'adultery' to refer to the more severe form of *zinā* that is punishable by lapidation. I caution readers to bear in mind, however, that my usage of these two respective terms will often not coincide with their linguistic meanings in the Islamic legal tradition. Moreover, it must always be remembered that I am using the designations in a strictly technical sense. Most English speakers, for instance, will likely find it odd that, according to *zinā* laws, a married person who has yet to consummate their marriage is technically not guilty of 'adultery', just as they are likely to find it odd that an unmarried person who engages in sexual relations outside of wedlock can technically still be found guilty of 'adultery', even if many years have passed since the offender was last married.

The place of *zinā*-stoning in the Islamic legal tradition has certainly garnered the attention of modern scholarship (and not only in the English language). For instance, Rudolph Peters provides a general historical overview of the subject matter as part of a broader discussion on pre-modern and modern Islamic criminal law.[29] John Wansbrough,[30] John Burton,[31]

[27] For a study on the development of *iḥṣān*, see John Burton, "The Meaning of '*Ihsan*'"; Burton's analysis is based on sources after 200/800 century, by which time the concept of *iḥṣān* had already received considerable attention among Muslim jurists. I examine earlier sources that lead me to different conclusions than those of Burton. See Chapter 1, p. 64.

[28] For a summary of the different ways in which pre-modern Muslims understand Q4:15 and its relationship to Q24:2, see, e.g., John Burton, *The Sources of Islamic Law*, 123–7.

[29] Rudolph Peters, *Crime and Punishment in Islamic Law*, 37f, 55f, and 60f.

[30] John Wansbrough, *Quranic Studies*, esp. 70f and 193–6.

[31] John Burton, *The Collection of the Qur'ān*, esp. Chapter Three, "The Sub-Science of Naskh;" Burton, *The Sources of Islamic Law*, esp. Chapter Seven, "The Third Mode of *Naskh*;" and in many of his other publications, some of which are cited throughout the present work.

and Christopher Melchert[32] study the jurisprudential theory of abrogation (*naskh*) and demonstrate the methods by which Muslim jurists draw on it to legalize *zinā*-stoning.[33] Intisar Rabb examines the historical development of the "doubt canon"[34] and the ways in which jurists deploy it to determine the applicability of, for example, *zinā*-stoning.[35] Sarah El Tantawi looks at various contextual circumstances in modern Nigeria that contributed to a demand for the implementation of the stoning punishment as a specific representation of the *Sharīʿa*.[36] In a series of highly technical articles, Pavel Pavlovitch employs a combination of methods current in the field of hadith studies to investigate certain Prophetic reports on *zinā*-stoning. In "The Islamic Penalty for Adultery in the Third Century AH and Al-Shāfiʿī's *Risāla*," Pavlovitch attempts to date an epistle on legal theory attributed to the famed Muslim jurist Muḥammad b. Idrīs al-Shāfiʿī (d. 204/820) by evaluating debates in Muslim legal literature as to whether those convicted of severe *zinā* ought to, in addition to being stoned to death, suffer the flogging punishment typically reserved for those convicted of the lesser form of *zinā*. In "The Stoning of a Pregnant Adulteress from Juhayna," Pavlovitch employs his methods for analyzing the transmission of hadith to argue that a report about the Prophet ordering the stoning punishment upon a female self-confessor emerges as a response to a report about the Prophet ordering the stoning punishment upon a male self-confessor.[37] In "The ʿUbāda b. al-Ṣāmit Tradition at the Crossroads of Methodology," Pavlovitch also incorporates non-hadith sources (e.g., works on Qur'ānic exegesis) to establish the manner in which the emergence of particular aspects of the hadith under investigation become possible. The possible ways in which the narratives fit into the beginnings of the process of legitimizing *zinā*-stoning are largely tangential to Pavlovitch's extensive studies, which, to (re)summarize, are more

[32] Christopher Melchert, "Qur'ānic Abrogation Across the Ninth Century."

[33] Also see Joseph Lowry, *Early Islamic Legal Theory*, 93–104.

[34] *idra'ū 'l- ḥudūd bi'l-shubuhāt*, "The fixed punishments should not be applied when there is doubt about one's guilt." This legal maxim became central in discussions of Islamic criminal law from a very early period. See generally, Intisar Rabb, *Doubt in Islamic Law*.

[35] Rabb, *Doubt in Islamic Law*, 41–3, 52, 111, and 276.

[36] Sarah El Tantawi, *Shari'ah on Trial*; Sarah El Tantawi, "Ṭūsī Did not 'Opt Out;' " more recently, El Tantawi writes about the role of ʿUmar b. al-Khaṭṭāb in the legalization of the stoning punishment. See El Tantawi, "Mysterious Legislation;" on ʿUmar's role and the analysis of reports involving his ruling on stoning as a punishment for certain classes of Muslims convicted of sexual transgressions, see Chapter 4 in this book.

[37] The hadith about the self-confessing woman is the focus of Chapter 3 in this book. My socio-historical contextualization of the transmission process and the analytical methods I employ lead me to different conclusions than Pavlovitch, with one being that the self-confessing woman report emerges in the first/seventh century of Islam and as an antecedent to the self-confessing man version.

focused on the results from methods of source criticism. Ersilia Francesca has made an important intervention in the state of scholarly research on the topic of *zinā*-stoning. She notes the value of including the long-neglected Ibāḍī legal and theological traditions in the study of early Islamic legal history in general and, Ibāḍī *zinā* laws including those related to *zinā*-stoning in particular, to make her case.[38] Recently, Seyfeddin Kara examines various hadith to establish the integrity of the Qur'ān, and among the topics he uses to support his argument are specific reports about the stoning verse.[39] Other scholarly works on *zinā*-stoning and the manner in which the punishment serves as a fulcrum for various types of studies in Islamic law, jurisprudence, and historiography are also available.[40]

Discussions relating to the *origins* of *zinā*-stoning have been particularly contentious. One claim, for instance, is that the practice of *zinā*-stoning is a carryover from pre-Islamic times.[41] Indeed, many legal traditions designated adultery as a capital offense.[42] In Ancient Egypt (3,100 BCE–332 BCE), for instance, a legal complaint that involved an accusation of adultery by a man against his wife was primarily resolved by allowing the humiliated husband to get his vengeance in the form of death.[43] Laws drafted by Draco, the Athenian lawgiver, guaranteed immunity to a husband who killed another man caught "next to" his wife.[44] The Hammurabi Code, written in *c.* 1760 BCE, mandated that a married woman caught by her husband having intercourse with another man should be bound along with her paramour and thrown into a river.[45] Finally, during the Mosaic period (tenth–sixth century BCE), biblical sources indicate that adultery was an offense punishable by death, with stoning being the primary method used to inflict death on the

[38] Ersilia Francesca, "Flogging, Banning, and Lapidation."

[39] See generally Seyfeddin Kara, *The Integrity of the Qur'an*. Among the hadith he examines, one focuses on the incident involving the Prophet's order to stone a Jewish couple who commit *zinā* and the other on ʿUmar b. al-Khaṭṭāb's claim that the stoning verse was part of the Book of God. I examine these two reports in this book. The discontinuity between some of his conclusions and my own is partly attributable to the wider aperture I apply to the available historical sources.

[40] E.g., see Patricia Crone, "Two Legal Problems Bearing on the Early History of the Qur'an;" Hossein Modarressi, "Early Debates on the Integrity of the Qur'ān;" Scott C. Lucas, "Perhaps You Only Kissed Her?"

[41] On attempts to resolve the origins of the stoning punishment, see, e.g., the various publications by John Burton, including "The Origin of the Islamic Penalty for Adultery."

[42] E.g., see Raymond Westbrook, "Adultery in Ancient Near Eastern Law;" Walter Young, "Stoning and Hand-Amputation," Chapter Three, "Sexual Offense and Theft in Ancient Near Eastern Law."

[43] See C.J. Eyre, "Crime and Adultery," 92.

[44] Eva Cantarella, "Gender, Sexuality, and Law," 239. Such laws date back to 621 BCE.

[45] G.R. Driver and John C. Miles, *The Babylonian Laws*, 281; for a historical background and legal introduction about the Hammurabi Code, see Driver and Miles, *The Babylonian Laws*, 1–26.

offender.[46] The evidence thus shows that, while certain legal cultures did treat adultery as a capital transgression, all such legal cultures had become obsolete well before the emergence of Islam in the seventh century CE.

Was *zinā*-stoning the predominant customary punishment for adultery on the eve of Islam and, on this basis, absorbed into the Prophetic practice (*sunna*) and consequently into the Islamic legal tradition? The short answer is no. In the Christo-Byzantine Empire, from Augustus to Justinian, adultery was neither wholly treated as a capital offense, nor was lapidation the primary form of punishment mandated for it.[47] Augustus in 18 CE enacted *lex Julia de adulteriis*; according to its provisions, a husband had to divorce his adulterous wife before she could be prosecuted.[48] Following her divorce, she was exiled, prohibited from remarrying, and a portion of her property and inheritance was confiscated.[49] A convicted husband was also subject to exile and loss of property, in addition to a possible sentence of hard labor if he belonged to a lower social class than his paramour.[50] Conversely, a married man was not guilty of adultery when having an extramarital affair with someone of lower social status.[51] Constantine (r. 306–337 CE) maintained much of *lex Julia*.[52] After Constantine's conversion to Christianity, the religion ostensibly became that of the Roman state.[53] Although Constantine's Law of 326 CE includes death by sword for adulterers, the provision was likely an interpolation by later commissioners of Justinian's law.[54] The Church Council in Rome allowed for the possibility of appeal and pardon to convicted *Christian* fornicators and adulterers through various forms of penitential penance.[55] All non-Christian Romans continued to have *lex Julia* applied to them.

[46] For additional details on the Torah's prescription, see Chapter 2, p. 84; a key difference here, however, is that while Islamic law stipulates stoning as a mandatory sentence for those guilty of severe *zinā*, it appears that the Jewish legal tradition had at times allowed the death penalty for adultery to be inflicted by means other than stoning, such as strangulation. See Samuel Mendelsohn, *Criminal Jurisprudence*, 51, n.97; Goldin argues that the Talmud permitted the use of strangulation as punishment and at no time does it appear in the Scripture as a lawful punishment. See Hyman E. Goldin, *Hebrew Criminal Law*, 37.

[47] For a general overview, see Juan Cole, "Late Roman Law," 209–14.

[48] Judith Evans Grubbs, *Women and the Law*, 84.

[49] Judith Evans Grubbs, *Law and Family*, 204.

[50] Grubbs, *Law and Family*, 204; Paul du Plessis, *Roman Law*, 130.

[51] Grubbs, *Law and Family*, 204.

[52] James A. Brundage, *Law, Sex, and Christian Society*, 104f.

[53] Brundage, *Law, Sex, and Christian Society*, 77f.

[54] Grubbs, *Law and Family*, 216f.

[55] Grubbs, *Law and Family*, 220ff.

In the rare situations that adultery could be punished with death, the judgment was a function of particular circumstances, such as the rank of the offender(s) and related charges.[56] In his codification of the law, Justinian (r. 527–565 CE) makes clear his intention to continue to publicly regulate sexual mores. Under the new code, the standard punishment is death for upper-class male adulterers or, depending on the situation, confiscation of property and confinement for either male or female adulterers.[57] But judges had considerable discretion over the form of punishment applied in cases of a conviction (beyond the aforementioned two), meaning death was not a given.[58] This was especially the case for those provinces of the Roman Empire which would have been immediate neighbors to the peninsular Arabs.[59] In sum, adultery was not, strictly speaking, treated and punished as a capital offense, in the regions to the west of Arabia.

To the east of Arabia, the Sasanians emerged from an area previously occupied by various ancient Mesopotamian communities, so it would be reasonable to expect Sasanian legal treatment of sexual morality to have some semblance to predecessor legal systems. But the available evidence points to material changes. The Sasanians did not entirely conceive of sexual relations outside of marriage as offenses subject to punishment. In fact, the Sasanian king Kavad I (r. 488–531 CE) supported the doctrine of Zoroaster that "no man was united to one woman to the exclusion of another."[60] In cases Sasanian law did penalize heterosexual improprieties, it did so with monetary sanctions only. Penalties in the form of compensatory fines were restricted, moreover, to specific males, which would indicate that the Sasanians viewed illicit sexual relations as property damage to either a husband or a father.[61] For example, adultery with another man's wife resulted in a fine of 300 *saters*.[62] If a man abducts a married woman and has sexual relations with her, then the fine is 700 *drahms* for the offense of adultery and 500 *drahms* for the offense of abduction.[63] Sasanians, in short, did not treat adultery as a capital offense.

[56] According to Grubbs, related offenses were typically magic and treason. See Grubbs, *Law and Family*, 219–21.
[57] Brundage, *Law, Sex, and Christian Society*, 119; on adultery as a capital offense, see David J.D. Miller and Peter Sarris, *The Novels*, 2:897f.
[58] Grubbs, *Law and Family*, 216–8.
[59] Grubbs, *Law and Family*, 222–5; Cole, "Late Roman Law," 222f.
[60] Victoria Erhart, "Development of Syriac Christian Canon," 120.
[61] Erhart, "Development of Syriac Christian Canon," 120.
[62] Anahit Perikhanian, *Book of a Thousand Judgements*, 181:73.7.
[63] Perikhanian, *Book of a Thousand Judgements*, 73.8–9.

As for pre-Islamic Arabia, it is difficult to surmise from the current state of available sources that lapidation was a (common?) punishment for adultery or that adultery itself was considered a capital transgression. Now, there does exist a legal maxim attributed to the Prophet from which one could *infer* that he adopted an existing pre-Islamic practice of death by stoning for adultery. The legal maxim is *al-walad lil-firāsh wa lil-ʿāhir al-ḥajar*. This can be translated as, "a child will be presumed to be the offspring of the man who lawfully shares the bed of the child's mother whereas the lecher (*ʿāhir*) is entitled to nothing but a rock (*ḥajar*) [i.e., death by lapidation]."[64] In my view, this saying attributed to the Prophet is not borne out of a customary practice of pre-Islamic Arabia. Among the reasons for my assessment is that in some pre-modern Muslim sources, *ḥajar* is not understood to signify the stoning punishment. Rather, it serves as a metonym for a man's complete lack of entitlement under the law to raise a claim of paternity when a child is born to a woman with whom he contends to have engaged in illicit sexual relations.[65] Therefore, a more idiomatically accurate reading of the Arabic would be "a child belongs to the man who shares a bed with the child's mother whereas the lecher (*ʿāhir*) gets nothing." Another reason I contend that the legal maxim is not reflective of a pre-Arabian context is because of the term *ʿāḥir*. As referenced in the saying, *ʿāḥir* means someone who commits *any* type of illicit sexual intercourse.[66] Accordingly, if *ḥajar* signifies the stoning punishment, then any form of sexual transgression would be subject to the capital punishment. This position would be at odds with the Qur'ān, the purported practices of the Prophet, and the eventual Islamic legal tradition. Accordingly, it is implausible that the legal maxim initially supported the use of the stoning punishment. And extant sources on pre-Islamic Arabia do not convey that adultery was a capital offense or punished with death by lapidation. These observations mean we do not have probative evidence to claim that, at the advent of Islam, adultery was strictly understood as a capital offense, much less that stoning was the primary form of punishment.[67]

It would not be accurate to describe the transition from the pre-Islamic period into the Islamic period as heralding a sharp dichotomy in terms of the structure and content of legal systems between the pre-Islamic and the

[64] See generally, Uri Rubin, "'al-Walad li-l-Firāsh.'"
[65] Rubin, "'al-Walad li-l-Firāsh,'" esp. at 6, n. 4; E.W. Lane, *Arab-English Lexicon*, 516 under *ḥ-j-r*.
[66] Lane, *Arab-English Lexicon*, 2184 under *ʿ-h-r*.
[67] Francesca, "Flogging, Banning, and Lapidation," 172 and 198; for a different opinion, see Young, "Stoning and Hand-Amputation," 179–84.

Prophet's revelatory periods.[68] Indeed, the Qur'ān serves as a witness to a high degree of ethnic and religious heterogeneity in its immediate environment.[69] The Qur'ān, at times, carries forward certain aspects of a long past legal culture (e.g., biblical), modifies certain elements, or promulgates something new altogether.[70] Nevertheless, we have to consider the fact that there is simply no evidence that the Qur'ān or the Prophet adopted an already-existing practice. One might claim that while cultures in the immediate environment of Arabia in the first/seventh century did not treat adultery as a capital offense, the Qur'ān could have done so. In my view, the evidence is not there. Even if the focus of our inquiry were to shift to the Prophetic practice (*sunna*), we are no better off to positively assert continuity because it would, in effect, ignore that it was only later on that the punishment would be officially consecrated in the Islamic legal tradition.[71] That adultery was not generally treated as a capital offense in the legal cultures in and around first/seventh century Arabia raises important questions about stoning as the preferred punishment for sexual transgressions and its purported continuity from pre-Islamic socio-historical contexts.[72]

I.1. Methodological Considerations

To take on the task of analyzing the source material means to bring into conversation the question of historicity—that is, the extent to such material can be said to convey history accurately. Academics refer to the inquiry I engage in here as 'source criticism'. By now, it is well established in the field of Islamic studies that probing into the accuracy of the sources currently in our possession is complicated by the fact that, though today we access by means of

[68] Francesca, "Flogging, Banning, and Lapidation," 167.
[69] Salaymeh writes that "much scholarship employs a periodization of Islam that is wholly based on events internal to Islamic history, without reference to other global historical periods." Accordingly, she employs the term "Islamic late antiquity," which is delimited to the end of the second/eighth century CE. See Lena Salaymeh, *The Beginnings of Islamic Law*, 7–9.
[70] See Zellentin, *The Qur'ān's Legal Culture* and esp. 56–9; also see, generally, Zellentin, *Law Beyond Israel*.
[71] As Zellentin notes regarding the Qur'ān's approach to sexual transgressions, it "stands in direct continuity with many of the legal and cultural norms attached to the notion of illicit sexual intercourse throughout late antiquity." See Zellentin, *Law Beyond Israel*, 184; Zellentin also provides an informative overview of the different ways in which the Qur'ān's treatment of sexual transgressions aligns with or differs from Christian and rabbinic traditions. See Zellentin, *Law Beyond Israel*, 203–18.
[72] I use the phrase "legal culture" as deployed by Zellentin, who describes it as "the continuation of culture and law." See Holger M. Zellentin, *The Qur'ān's Legal Culture*, 19 and esp. footnote 29.

formal written material, for the first 150 years or so after the Prophet's death, the means by which this material was preserved was *not* primarily through writing.[73] For example, G.R. Hawting, a historian specializing in this period, writes that, in light of what he describes as "the relatively late stabilization of the tradition in literary form," it would appear that "attempts to define what Islam was . . . when none of the Islamic texts available to us existed, must be fragmentary, speculative and impressionistic."[74] On the premise that principles of normativity are well established by the time oral traditions begin to take written form, Jonathan Berkey, whose research interests center on Islam in the medieval period, clarifies that this entails "the sources [at our disposal] inevitably reflect later attitudes and interests as much as, if not more than, those of the earlier Muslims, and project those attitudes and interests *back* upon the people and events they describe."[75] Stephen Humphreys, another historian of the formative period of Islam, puts the problem rather bluntly when he says, "If our goal is to comprehend the way in which Muslims of the late 2nd/8th and 3rd/9th centuries understood the origins of their society, then we are very well off indeed. But if our aim is to find out 'what really happened,' . . . then we are in trouble."[76]

Fred Donner, a historian of early Islam who is in no way sanguine about the problems that the early written sources pose for historical reconstruction, nevertheless contests the *a priori* assumption expressed above that takes the entirety of the Islamic tradition as having been reshaped in accordance with later dogma.[77] This is partly because the sources, despite the existence of much disagreement among them in matters of detail, appear to be in agreement on the central features of the traditional narrative of the origins of the Islamic faith.[78] While some key beliefs may have experienced change at some time during Islam's first fifty years, traditional Islamic sources still contain "sufficient material to reconstruct at least the main issues debated

[73] G.R. Hawting, *The Idea of Idolatry and the Emergence of Islam*, 3; Jonathan Berkey, *The Formation of Islam*, 58; Note that Donner defines literary sources in a way that excludes documentary evidence, such as inscriptions and papyri, that are contemporary to the events that they purport to describe. See Fred Donner, *Narratives of Islamic Origins*, 2, fn. 1.

[74] Hawting, *The Idea of Idolatry and the Emergence of Islam*, 13. In my view, Hawting is not suggesting that the issue at stake here is uniquely Islamic.

[75] Berkey, *The Formation of Islam*, 58. Emphasis mine.

[76] R. Stephen Humphreys, *Islamic History*, 68; on history and historiography, see Humphreys, *Islamic History*, 69–98; see also Chase F. Robinson, *Islamic Historiography*, 18–82; for an informative summary of scholarship regarding the issue of reliability of Islamic sources with a particular focus on the biography of the Prophet, see Gregor Schoeler, *The Biography of Muḥammad*, 3–19.

[77] Donner, *Narratives of Islamic Origins*, 26.

[78] Donner, *Narratives of Islamic Origins*, 26f.

by Believers in the early Islamic period and the basic attitudes of the main parties to those debates."[79] Moreover, in the communities of Muslims, there was no singular authority "who had the power to impose a uniform dogmatic view."[80] In fact, skeptics who support the tradition-revision framework never "identify a group or people who are supposed to have [implemented] a uniform view on the entirety of the community."[81] One might even question what abilities a group would have had to impose a uniform view, assuming that such a group did exist. Indeed, "[t]he early Islamic community was not integrated in a tightly knit hierarchical structure, but consisted rather of a mosaic of small sub-communities and sub-sects."[82] For Donner, the lack of contemporaneous material from Islamic late antiquity, or the possibility of source modifications, does not disqualify their use; at least not *ipso facto*.

How is a historian, then, to think about and to deal with the slippages, inconsistencies, and/or other distorting elements that invariably crept into the transmission and preservation processes designed to remember the past? There are at least two ways to answer this question. One is by employing methods of source criticism, and, on this, see below.

The second way I wish to address the question is by offering a personal story that I hope, at some level, can be helpful to the reader in understanding the process I refer to here—one that we all, as humans, use to make sense of the world in which we live. Growing up, my wife's family had two refrigerators—the primary unit in the kitchen and the secondary unit in the garage. For nearly thirty years, the family, including my wife, would refer to it as the "garage refrigerator." Fast forward to the present, my wife and I recently moved into our first home. My wife—pardon, I mean *we*—decided that we needed a second refrigerator. *We* purchased one at the earliest opportunity and thought long and hard about where to place our proud new possession, and *she*—I assure you, it was her—decided that we should place it in the basement. That is where it happens to be today. Many months have passed since we purchased our second fridge, and neither I nor my wife has, at any time, been under the illusion that we have been miraculously blessed with a garage in the interim. Yet, without fail, my wife, persistently and without

[79] Donner, *Narratives of Islamic Origins*, 29.
[80] Donner, *Narratives of Islamic Origins*, 27.
[81] Donner, *Narratives of Islamic Origins*, 27.
[82] Donner, *Narratives of Islamic Origins*, 27. On the tradition-revision framework, see Donner, *Narratives of Islamic Origins*, 23, 35, and 287.

batting an eye, regularly directs me to procure things from our nonexistent "garage refrigerator."

Our eight-year-old son finds it comical that his mother keeps calling what is clearly our basement refrigerator the "garage refrigerator." Can it be that my wife, a highly educated woman and an astute, sharp criminal defense attorney, has not yet learned the difference between a "basement" and a "garage?" Could she be expressing a hidden desire for a garage? Or is she just trying to mess with us? My son may perhaps find any one of these explanations eminently plausible. But I, along with most reasonable adults, intuitively understand a much simpler and far more plausible explanation for his mom's strange turn of phrase. By calling the basement refrigerator the "garage refrigerator," my wife is doing *exactly* what psychology reveals about how we, as humans, process, make sense of, and *preserve* the information we glean from our experiences.

Memory is needed to establish the meaning of a human experience, to deepen its understanding, and to make various connections with other experiences.[83] Humans deal with information through meaning.[84] Whenever someone attempts to make sense of something, memory is involved. Memory is used for contextualization and association and is vital for thought and understanding.[85] In fact, contextualization and association help to consolidate memories in much more stable ways.[86] Thus, memory is in dialogue with contextualization and association, which in turn helps with the stabilization of memory.

Some scholars assert that written history and memory are two distinct things. Donner explains: "... there is a difference between history, which is a collective undertaking, and memory, which is borne by individuals."[87] Rainer Brunner also seems to make a similar argument when he writes that cultural memory helps with the continuity of identity and, thus, helps to preserve a sense of community. This type of memory, according to Brunner, "is different from any kind of 'scientific' *historiography* that lacks the characteristics of memory, that is, the relation to a collective self-

[83] Rodrigo Q. Quiroga, *The Forgetting Machine*, 96.
[84] Steven P.R. Rose, "How Brains Make Memories," 138.
[85] Quiroga, *The Forgetting Machine*, 94.
[86] Quiroga, *The Forgetting Machine*, 100.
[87] Donner, *Narratives of Islamic Origins*, 138. For additional ways in which Donner makes a distinction between history and memory, also see 147ff, 204, and 206; in Jewish studies and historiography, Yerushalmi makes a similar distinction: "Memory and modern historiography stands, by their very nature, in radically different relations to the past." See Yosef Hayim Yerushalmi, *Zakhor: Jewish History and Jewish Memory*, 94.

image."[88] But do history and memory stand in such sharp contrast? It appears to me that memory and the *writing* of history are necessarily coeval.

To make sense of the world and to stabilize memories, humans primarily preserve concepts.[89] As I note above, this is done through an interdependence between contextualization, association, and memory.[90] Here, returning to the enigma of my wife's "garage refrigerator" remains instructive. Growing up, she conceptualizes the fact that she has a second refrigerator and that this appliance is in the garage. Despite the change in environments (moving to a new house) and even the difference in time—one that spans more than a decade—my wife continues to recall the overlap between the *concepts* of a "second fridge" and the primary identifying spatial location of her first "second fridge" in the garage. In some ways, she is held hostage to such a deep association-perhaps due to fond memories of her time living in the home in which she was raised-that engenders amusement and slight befuddlement in our eight-year-old when she tells me to grab something from the "garage fridge" in a house that we all know has no garage. It is likely that, over time, my wife will adapt to our new domestic situation. Indeed, we can develop new concepts and associations quite rapidly, even from a single experience.[91] But for now, our son continues to be entertained by his mother's supposed *ikhtilāṭ* (confusion).

In my view, one must emphasize, as part of any historical analysis, the influence of concepts in the stabilization of memory-it is only inevitable that humans employ concepts to make sense of their experiences. This is also true when investigating the provenance and transmission history of Islamic source material. Research in the field of psychology shows that during a series of transmissions between individuals, the material can change both in length and in detail, even if the overall gist remains intact.[92] A person can also substitute one particular detail with another that is more familiar.[93] The process of making mental changes to particular details and anchoring newly acquired data with pre-existing knowledge is part and parcel of what we mean when we say someone is "remembering" something: it is, indeed, primarily a (re)constructive mechanism and *not* one of replication.[94] Ultimately, brains

[88] Brunner does admit "that the line separating the two cannot always be drawn properly through the ages." See Rainer Brunner, "The Role of Ḥadīth," 327.
[89] Quiroga, *The Forgetting Machine*, 123.
[90] Quiroga, *The Forgetting Machine*, 124–6.
[91] Quiroga, *The Forgetting Machine*, 128.
[92] Alex Mesoudi and Andrew Whiten, "The Multiple Roles of Cultural Transmission," 3,491.
[93] Mesoudi and Whiten, "The Multiple Roles of Cultural Transmission," 3,491.
[94] Mesoudi and Whiten, "The Multiple Roles of Cultural Transmission," 3,491.

do not make memories and meaning; it is people who use their brains to do so.[95] I believe that drawing on the interrelationship between and among experiences, concepts, and memory can sensitize the analysis of source material from and about early Islam in meaningful ways—the kind I aim to convey in the current project. What does this mean for my investigation into hadith on *zinā*-stoning, practically speaking? It means that differences in textual contents in two or more versions of a report do not *a priori* signify nefarious intent on the part of a transmitter. Rather, such differences constitute a unique contribution on the part of the transmitter, even if only because they signify a transmitter has honestly misremembered details while trying to make sense of a bygone person or event.

Even if several individuals witness the same event and attest to the basic contours of this event, the subjective contextual experience can impact how memory is shaped and preserved.[96] This seeing, hearing, and (re)conveying of information can be understood as a constructive and selective exercise in group authorship. Khaled Abou El Fadl remarks:

> other than the possibility of fabrication, there is also the issue of *creative selection and recollection* [my emphasis]. Those who experienced the life of the Prophet [or other individuals], interacted, and talked to him, did not experience the Prophet in some ideal objective medium. The Companions and others experienced the Prophet in a subjective fashion, and this subjectivity influenced what they saw or heard, how they saw or heard it, and what they ultimately remembered and conveyed to others.[97]

In fact, as Sebastian Günther remarks, the unconscious mind can help to shape a narrative during the transmission process.[98] Thus, one selects from an event according to various hierarchies of the senses in which our values also play a role.[99] For example, social relationships could be an important factor because sometimes individuals or groups "remember in ways that are more relatable to [an] audience."[100] Not only does each individual's

[95] Rose, "How Brains Make Memories," 134.
[96] Quiroga, *The Forgetting Machine*, 56.
[97] Khaled Abou El Fadl, *Speaking in God's Name*, 88. Emphasis mine.
[98] Sebastian Günther, "Fictional Narration," 464 and 466.
[99] Thomas Butler, "Memory: A Mixed Blessing," 15.
[100] Alistair Thompson, "Memory and Remembering in Oral History," 88; there are numerous studies in the field of Islamic history that examine the different ways in which individuals or groups remember the past as a function of particular contextual circumstances. E.g., see Najam Haider, *The Rebel and the Imām*; Aaron M. Hagler, "Repurposed Narratives;" Aaron M. Hagler, "Sapping the

interpretive contribution to a report yield information about an intended subject, it also reveals information about the transmitter and their historical context. The personality of a transmitter must be viewed as a visible watermark, indicating that the identity of the transmitter is directly related to the nature and substance of the narrative's textual content. To paraphrase Abou El Fadl, a full acknowledgment of the subjectivity of the transmitter's report necessitates that we interpret reports not exclusively as establishing authoritative precedent for the elaboration of a particular issue, but as pieces of a complex, multilayered, multifaceted, and frequently inchoate historical metanarrative.[101]

Indeed, at the beginning of Islam, knowledge was predominantly retained and transmitted by memory.[102] However, evidence indicates that in pre-Islamic late antiquity, the use of memory as the primary method for learning was supplemented with writing.[103] The central epistemological principle of the nascent Muslim communities reflects many prior millennia in that oral/aural transmission is deemed superior to written transmission alone.[104] By oral/aural transmissions, I intend the concept as developed by Gregor Schoeler: instruction under the direct supervision of the teacher, often involving audition (*samāʿ*) or reading material aloud (*qirāʾa*) in the presence of the teacher. The teacher would then either listen for mistakes or confirm the material as accurate based on their own recollection of the material or, occasionally, by relying on their own personal written notes. Errors would be corrected during such instruction sessions.[105] Ann Rigney notes that the use of mnemonic devices, such as rhyming, tends to be rare in purely oral societies and is rather something utilized by literate cultures in which vowel and consonant rhyme is more significant.[106] Her evaluation of literate cultures is reflected in, for example, the text of the Qur'ān. It signifies that the

Narrative;" Tayeb El-Hibri, *Reinterpreting Islamic Historiography*; Ayman S. Ibrahim, *Conversion to Islam*; Nancy Khalek, *Damascus After the Muslim Conquest*; Jacob Lassner, *Islamic Revolution and Historical Memory*; Uri Rubin, *The Eye of the Beholder*; Suleiman Mourad, *Early Islam Between Myth and History*.

[101] Abou El Fadl, *Speaking in God's Name*, 88.
[102] I employ here Schoeler's definition of knowledge: scholarly forms ("sciences") and literary forms, including poetry. See Gregor Schoeler, "The Relationship of Literacy and Memory in the Second/Eighth Century," 121; on pre-modern Muslims' multivalent conceptualization of knowledge, see generally Jonathan Brown, "Did the Prophet Say It or Not?"
[103] Birger Gerhardsson, *The Reliability of the Gospel Tradition*, 9f and 54.
[104] Tarif Khalidi, *Arabic Historical Thought*, 27.
[105] See Schoeler, *The Oral and the Written in Early Islam*, 30f; Gregor Schoeler, *The Genesis of Literature in Islam*, 36f and 122f; Schoeler, *The Biography of Muḥammad*, 21f.
[106] Ann Rigney, "Scales of Postmemory," 74.

transmission of knowledge in Islamic late antiquity was oral/aural. Writing was part of the culture; the practice did not emerge suddenly.[107] After the death of the Prophet, transmitters, including the historian kind, utilized notes to "jog their memory."[108] The use of notes indicates that Muslims belonging to the first/seventh century of Islam did employ writing as a means to preserve information of a historical character. Accordingly, there is reason and evidence to believe that written collections of hadith emerge quite early, perhaps even immediately after the Prophet's death.[109] Over time, the customary method of learning through a teacher's dictation and the pupil's recitation primarily from memory "gave way to dictation and recitation from manuscripts."[110]

Lena Salaymeh notes that in conventional historiography dealing with early Islam, some methodologies of source criticism employ distinctions between "documentary" and non-documentary (i.e., what Salaymeh refers to as "narrative-historical") sources, identifying only the former as original and therefore uniquely reliable.[111] But for the reasons noted above, it would be unfruitful to dismiss the efficacy of oral/aural modes of transmission. To this end, Salaymeh emphasizes a framework with respect to source criticism in Islamic studies by partly introducing Mark Bevir's postfoundational methodology, which "pursues heuristics that [*generate*] *historical truth*."[112] Salaymeh endorses an approach that posits a deep structural 'complementarity' between documentary and narrative historical sources whereby both genres "offer [complementary] layers of historical evidence."[113] She further asserts that "contemporaneous sources are not inherently more reliable than later sources; there is no general rule that can be applied to all sources or that can guarantee the reliability of a particular kind of source.[114] As Salaymeh correctly notes, there are inconsistencies, slippages, and contradictions in

[107] Schoeler, *The Genesis of Literature in Islam*, 2–80, esp. 16.

[108] Schoeler, *The Oral and the Written in Early Islam*, 30–43; Schoeler, *The Genesis of Literature in Islam*, 8–40; Harald Motzki, "The Prophet and the Cat," 30.

[109] Nabia Abbott, "*Ḥadīth* Literature," 289-91; Khalidi, *Arabic Historical Thought*, 19.

[110] Abbott, "*Ḥadīth* Literature," 295; Schoeler, *The Oral and the Written in Early Islam*, 29f.

[111] Salaymeh, *Beginnings of Islamic Law*, 24.

[112] Salaymeh, *Beginnings of Islamic Law*, 16, my emphasis. I take the liberty of using "[discover]" for Salaymeh's original "[generate]" in order to emphasize the contrast between positivist claims to 'find *the* real Truth (writ large)' and a postfoundationalist approach that attempts to produce any number of plausible interpretations of complex and variegated historical processes; on historical truth versus literal truth in Sunnī hadith criticism, see Brown, "Did the Prophet Say It or Not?," 264 and 272–5.

[113] Salaymeh, *Beginnings of Islamic Law*, 27.

[114] Salaymeh, *Beginnings of Islamic Law*, 32.

Islamic narrative historical literature.[115] But these features are hardly unique to such sources and thus not grounds for treating them as *a priori* unreliable for information on the historical development of Islamic beliefs, customs, institutions, and laws. Importantly, such inconsistencies, slippages, and contractions are not sufficient, in and of themselves, to be used to level a charge of dishonesty against transmitters. They may simply have had a second refrigerator and misremembered its location.

It cannot be doubted that ambiguities, contradictions, and other glaring issues raise a degree of questionability about the historicity of the reports investigated in this book. In the chapters to follow, we will encounter, for example, the presence of marked anachronisms in the reports of Muslim scholars belonging to at least the first several centuries of Islam, adduced as evidence for the validity of the stoning punishment upon certain classes of Muslim men and women convicted of *zinā*. It will become apparent that the legal practices of their days were, at times, being retroactively projected back into the past via insertions into the textual content of a report, likely in order to convey the appearance that the jurists were simply complying with normative precedents set by the Prophet himself or some other authoritative figure. To shed light on the part of the process by which Muslim authorities successfully persuaded their coreligionists that their legal arguments rested on unquestionable Prophetic authority, I will examine the transmission chain, *isnād* (s. *sanad*) and corresponding text content, *matn* (pl. *mutūn*) of the relevant hadith cited by Muslim scholars that purportedly secure the precedents of the Prophet and Companions.

Even if there is disagreement about when writing as a means of preservation emerges for the early Muslim communities, I believe we still need to address the underlying premise when discussing the transmission of knowledge by memory, that is, orally/aurally, versus by writing. The presumption is that the preservation of knowledge by writing is distinctly more "accurate" and "reliable" than preservation by memory. But whether one attempts to preserve by memory, writing, or a combination thereof, very few humans "have the ability to capture a complex sensory event in such a way that they can later reproduce it in all its complexity...."[116] It is because "[w]e have learned to process experiences so quickly that we usually are not even conscious of what we are doing."[117] In general, humans absorb only a fraction

[115] Salaymeh, *Beginnings of Islamic Law*, 33.
[116] Butler, "Memory: A Mixed Blessing," 15.
[117] Butler, "Memory," 15.

of the "information" they receive.[118] In fact, the limitation starts at the level of sight, that is, even *before* the brain actually processes the information it receives. "There is a three-order-of-magnitude reduction between the information that could, in principle, be transmitted by the eyes and the information that reaches the brain."[119] Therefore, the ability of a person to make sense of and preserve something by writing versus orality/aurality is not sharply distinct. The contrast between how much can be understood and preserved by memory versus writing is not represented by a light switch, but rather a dial. It is a matter of degree and not a difference in kind.[120] Whatever due diligence an individual may exert in their attempts to preserve something by memory and/or writing, the result will only be part of the story. It is also worth mentioning here that the insistence on documentary evidence as a means of ensuring the objectivity of information fails to account for the fact that the producers of such documentary evidence are just as human as the humans who cannot be trusted to tell the story in written sources from a later period.

That in the first 150 years or so of Islam, the oral/aural medium was the dominant form of preserving and transmitting knowledge also raises important questions about the concept of "textuality." Can an oral/aural transmission be designated as a "text?" Among Islamicists, this remains an open-ended yet unresolved question. Looking at disciplines in similar fields, we may find tools and methods that are useful for our own purposes. In the field of New Testament textual criticism, for instance, Eldon Jay Epp notes that a "text" can reflect elements representing the formation and transmission of pre-literary content.[121] Recently, Hany Rashwan observes that hadith were conceived by Muslims as literary text and accordingly integrated into the Islamic literary culture.[122] As noted above, Schoeler explains the transmission process at the beginning of Islam comprised a mix of lectures and memorization, occasionally with limited use of notes as a memory aid. These are then 'published' by others.[123] Rashwan argues that, because hadith emerged first as an oral/aural tradition, Muslims believed that the

[118] I do not turn here to an elaborate definition of what is meant by the term "information," which is a complex question that is beyond the scope of this study. An entire body of work has been produced on information theory that sets out standards on how to define and measure "information." For the application of information theory, see, e.g., Quiroga, *The Forgetting Machine*, 20f.
[119] Quiroga, *The Forgetting Machine*, 25.
[120] Thompson, "Memory and Remembering in Oral History," 88.
[121] Eldon Jay Epp, "Multivalence," 246.
[122] See generally Hany Rashwan, "Hadith as Oral Literature."
[123] Gregor Schoeler, "Die Frage der schriftlichen oder mündlichen," 218 and 224f.

"textual" content "could be altered according to the writing process[,] the literary skills of writers," even spontaneously improved during oral/aural transmissions[124]—in line with my above comments about what psychology teaches us about the transmission process between humans. Such transmission flexibility is recognized by hadith critics when they categorized oral/aural reports into three distinct types: (1) transmissions focusing on precise wording (*al-riwāya bi al-lafẓ*), (2) transmissions focusing on the meaning irrespective of the vocal form (*al-riwāya bi al-maʿnā*), and (3) transmissions that combine both methods.[125] Epp's, Schoeler's, and Rashwan's respective observations should expand the scope of "texts" and, by extension, "books," as meaning something much *broader* than the way these two terms are understood today. After all, whether in the case of "the philosophical heritage of classical Greece, the rhetorical tradition of Greece and Rome . . . or the scriptures of Israel," books were not so much read as they were heard, recited, and listened to during speeches, lectures, and public readings of various kinds.[126] Accordingly, it would be inaccurate to apply the narrow concept we have today of texts and books and the ways they are "transmitted" to a time period wherein it would not apply.

As has been intimated, the issue of historicity comes into sharp focus when dealing with hadith literature. For the purposes of clarity, I consider the term historicity in two ways. The first relates to determining whether a transmission process did take place as reflected in a transmission chain. For instance, is it reasonable that two individuals shared the contents of a hadith based on, for example, their respective birth dates, death dates, or places of travel? The second concerns the content of a report. Can a historian reasonably postulate that a report does in fact preserve the occurrence of an event along with the involved individuals? For example, what is the likelihood that the person in a hadith did in fact say "x" or that event "y" did occur? In the present work, I employ both expressions of historicity and convey the usage as needed.

There have been countless studies published in many languages about the methodologies for addressing the thorny and contentious question about the historicity of hadith.[127] Many of the more influential studies and the various spectra of debates are so well reviewed that there is no need to rehearse them

[124] Rashwan, "Hadith as Oral Literature," 66.
[125] E.g., see al-Khaṭīb al-Baghdādī, *al-Kifāya*, 1:503–84.
[126] Wayne A. Meeks, *The Moral World of the First Christians*, 40.
[127] E.g., see Ignaz Goldziher, *Muslim Studies*; Joseph Schacht, *The Origins of Muhammadan Jurisprudence*; Michael Cook, *Early Muslim Dogma*; Gautier Juynboll, "Some *Isnād*-Analytical Methods;" Gautier Juynboll, "Nāfiʿ, the *mawlā* of Ibn ʿUmar;" Harald Motzki, *The Origins of Islamic Jurisprudence*; Harald Motzki, "Dating Muslim Traditions;" Jonathan Brown, *Ḥadīth*; A. Kevin Reinhart, "Review: Juynbolliana, Gradualism, the Big Bang, and ḥadīth Study;" Pavel Pavlovitch,

all here.[128] Rather, I make note of certain methodological points that hold the most promise.

Over the last several decades, the *isnād-cum-matn* analysis (ICMA) technique has greatly advanced the field of hadith source criticism. One of the guiding principles of ICMA is that any claim to historicity for a particular narrative depends on a correlation between the transmission chain and the corresponding textual content across numerous versions of the report.[129] The level of correlation is derived by cross-checking textual content variations of the same story cycle among different transmission lines as well as establishing the historical character of the transmission chains themselves.[130] Here is a transmission map of an imagined hadith:

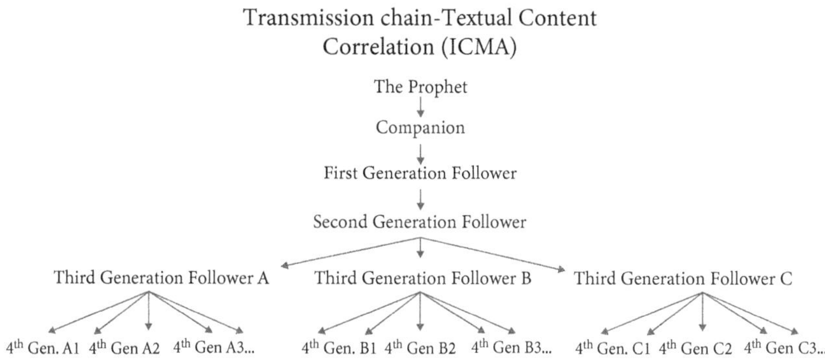

Starting from the bottom of the chart, which would represent the "youngest" or "latest" transmitter, if there is a strong textual correlation between and among the versions recorded on the respective authorities of Fourth Generation persons A1, A2, and A3, then on the basis of textual consistency, we could assert that the Fourth Generation is drawing from a common source. In this case, the common source would be the Third Generation Follower A. We would then conduct a transmission chain analysis to determine if a relationship can be established between the Third Generation

The Formation of the Islamic Understanding of Kalāla; Hiroyuki Yanagihashi, *Studies in Legal Hadith*; Abu-Alababas et al., *Modern Hadith Studies*.

[128] Both Reinhart's and Motzki's respective articles are especially helpful for a summary of these studies and debates. See A. Kevin Reinhart, "Review: Juynbolliana;" See Harald Motzki, "Dating Muslim Traditions."

[129] On the use of locality as a supplement to ICMA for determining the provenance of a particular aspect of a hadith, see Behnam Sadeghi, "The Traveling Tradition Test."

[130] Motzki, "Dating Muslim Traditions," 250–2.

Follower A and each of their students, that is, Fourth Gen. A1, Fourth Gen. A2, and Fourth Gen. A3. If we can establish the relationships, then on the basis of the transmission chain and textual content analysis (ICMA), we could argue with a high degree of confidence that the fourth generation did receive the report from their noted teacher, Third Gen. Follower A. We would repeat this examination with the Third Gen. Follower B and Third Gen. Follower C. If we find high degrees of similarities among the textual contents of the versions on the respective authorities of the Third Gen. Followers, then we could state that *they* had a common source, that is, the Second Gen. Follower. As Harald Motzki argues, it is highly unlikely that correlations found among different versions of a hadith across numerous transmission lines are the result of a systematic forgery because "the phenomenon of correlation is so widespread that almost every hadith transmitter (*muḥaddith*) must have [otherwise] participated in forgery."[131] Accordingly, ICMA can help to determine the provenance of a hadith, that is, its transmission history and the circulation of specific textual elements by particular transmitters.[132] The method can also help to establish a reasonable degree of confidence about the historicity of the event(s) referenced in the textual content.[133]

Of important consideration are those transmitters identified as the partial common links (PCLs) or the common links (CLs).[134] CL is the transmitter who is responsible for the circulation of the (general) form of a report as found in a hadith collection.[135] The CL phenomenon is not something that has been identified exclusively within modern hadith studies. Ali Aghaei provides critical insights into the different ways in which Muslim hadith scholars identified and designated transmitters known to be responsible for the predominant dissemination of narratives.[136] As per ICMA, PCLs and/or CLs are typically identifiable by first bringing together numerous transmission chains of a hadith—the *isnād* bundle—and determining the individuals upon whom these lines of transmission converge. The CL (or PCL) can then

[131] Motzki, "Dating Muslim Traditions," 250.

[132] Essentially the same method is applied in the field of psychology to understand cultural transmission as a fundamental component of cultural evolution. See Mesoudi and Whiten, "The Multiple Roles of Cultural Transmission," 3, 491.

[133] On the development of textual criticism of hadith by pre-modern Muslim scholars, see Jonathan Brown, "The Rules of Matn Criticism," 360–6 and 376–81.

[134] For an overview of the scholarly debates regarding the role of the Common Link, see Motzki, "Dating Muslim Traditions," 216–30, 237–42, and 251–2.

[135] Andreas Görke, "Eschatology," 190.

[136] Ali Aghaei, "The Common Link."

be confirmed with a comparative analysis of the applicable textual contents. Here is the same diagram as the previous one, but this time, I label the applicable generation as a CL or PCL:

Transmission chain-Textual Content Correlation (ICMA)

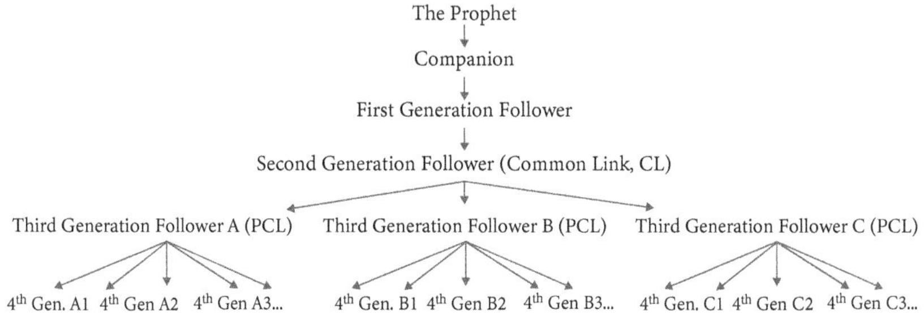

The extent to which there exists a correlation between the transmission chains and the textual content, that is, the higher the correlation, the more a CL (or PCL) becomes lucid.

ICMA, as a comparative method, is also helpful in resolving some single-strand transmission lines, of which there are various types. A single-strand hadith can come in a form wherein a portion of the *isnād* has only one *recorded* chain of transmission between two transmitters. This single line of transmission can occur at any level. It can originate with an initial authoritative figure, be it the Prophet, a Companion, or within subsequent generations.

Single-strand and Multi-strand Transmission Lines

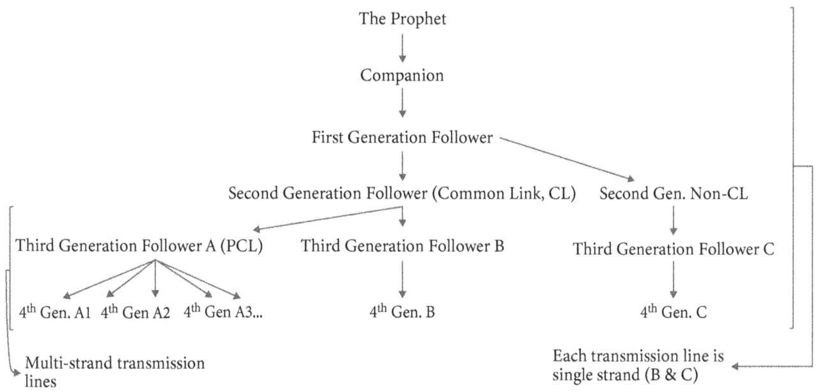

One group of single-strand transmissions occurs earlier than the PCL or CL. This variety is important for the study of early Islam because most recorded accounts about the earliest Muslim communities begin as single-strand transmission chains.[137] CLs were also the first collectors and professional teachers of events and persons living in the first century of Islam.[138] Because these CLs were the first systematic collectors/teachers of hadith, they were predominantly the first to provide transmission chains in addition to the historical material.[139] In study circles, these collectors/teachers would cite their sources if they could remember them or to the extent they deemed it important to do so. In other words, the CL could and did correctly name their source(s) when discussing a particular matter.[140] It is also entirely possible that other persons knew of a report, but the CL did not cite them.[141] By not naming the person, a CL's source may appear to be single-stranded when in actuality it was not. Broadly, the lack of need to name a source reflects a time period when there was no standard for having to cite the exact and/or numerous source(s).[142] The single-strand portion earlier than the CL can thereby reflect a historical communication.[143] Outside evidence would have to demonstrate whether an error in transmission occurred. With the help of ICMA, scholars have been able to address the single-strand portion earlier or later than the PCL or CL and date hadith transmissions and/or their contents to various historical moments, including from the end of the first/seventh century all the way to the time of the Prophet.[144]

One of ICMA's challenges lies with the fact that its deployment is more difficult in cases involving single-strand reports. These transmission lines exist in various configurations. One kind I described above, wherein a single-strand transmission occurs earlier than the CL. In another scenario,

[137] Reinhart, "Review: Juynbolliana," 415f and 440; the hadith critic al-Khaṭīb al-Baghdādī (d. 463/1071) writes the single-strand reports (*khabar al-wāḥid*) cannot be used to establish matters on religion but can be used for matters on law. See al-Khaṭīb al-Baghdādī, *al-Kifāya*, 1:557; on debates about the use of single-strand reports to confirm theological positions, see Brown, "Did the Prophet Say It or Not?," 265–71.

[138] Harald Motzki, *Analysing Muslim Traditions*, 51.

[139] Motzki, *Analysing Muslim Traditions*, 51.

[140] Schoeler, *The Biography of Muḥammad*, 16f.

[141] Motzki, *Analysing Muslim Traditions*, 52.

[142] Motzki, *Analysing Muslim Traditions*, 52 and 137.

[143] Herbert Berg, *Method and Theory*, 270; Schoeler, *The Biography of Muḥammad*, 16f.; Motzki, *Analysing Muslim Traditions*, 53 and 137.

[144] See, e.g., Motzki, "The Prophet and the Cat;" Mohammed Shahab Ahmed, "The Satanic Verses Incident;" Schoeler, *The Biography of Muḥammad*; Andreas Görke, "Remnants of an Old *Tafsīr* Tradition;" e.g., see Andreas Görke, Harald Motzki, Gregor Schoeler, "First Century Sources for the Life of Muḥammad?"; Ahmed El Shamsy, "The Curious Case;" Nicolet Boekhoff-van der Voort, "Untangling the 'Unwritten Documents.'"

numerous independent single-strand transmission lines converge onto a single source. For this type of phenomenon, scholars have developed techniques for assessing their historicity both in transmission and in content. For instance, Motzki argues that the single-strand narratives recorded by ʿAbd al-Razzāq (d. 211/829) in his *al-Muṣannaf* are likely historical and that the transmission chains and textual contents are not forged.[145] He comes to this conclusion by examining the variations in the language, that is, style and vocabulary, of the transmissions. Motzki argues that, were there to be forgeries, one would find a significantly higher consistency in the textual content of the reports.[146] His tests show that the transmissions are "strongly differentiated from each other."[147] The results also allow Motzki to contend that there is a high probability of historical transmissions between ʿAbd al-Razzāq's informants—Ibn Jurayj (d. 150/767), Maʿmar b. Rāshid (d. 153/770), and Sufyān al-Thawrī (d. 161/778)—and the individuals from whom these informants received both prophetic and non-prophetic legal opinions and judgments.[148] In another example on establishing the historicity of single-strand reports, Behnam Sadeghi analyzes the *Kitāb al-āthār* of the jurist Muḥammad al-Shaybānī (d. 189/805). He opines that the text "has a single redactor who heard and recorded al-Shaybānī's lectures, except for the equivalent of a one-hour lesson amounting to six pages of the printed text. . . ."[149] According to Sadeghi, al-Shaybānī often notes points of disagreement with his teacher Abū Ḥanīfa (d. 150/767) and even with the latter's teacher, Ibrāhīm al-Nakhaʿī (d. 96/714), which indicates al-Shaybānī did not project his views back onto his sources.[150] To be sure, both Motzki's and Sadeghi's respective approaches involve single collections, meaning each corpus is ascribed to one author and his sources. Their methodology could not be used for works where the author is collecting narratives on the authority of numerous sources with a plethora of transmitters. Nevertheless, taken together, Motzki's and Sadeghi's respective works illustrate that the historicity of single-strand reports can be established and dated to the last quarter of the first century, if not earlier, without the use of ICMA.

145 Motzki, "The *Muṣannaf* of ʿAbd al-Razzāq," 1–21.
146 Motzki entertains the possibility that in some cases the textual content may have undergone changes by one or more transmitters.
147 Motzki, *The Origins of Islamic Jurisprudence*, 59f.
148 Motzki, "The Development of Islamic Jurisprudence in Mecca to the Middle of the Second/Eighth Century," in *The Origins of Islamic Jurisprudence*.
149 Sadeghi, *The Logic of Law Making*, 177–99.
150 Sadeghi, *The Logic of Law Making*, 192–4.

In the present work, I utilize ICMA and supplement it with precisely those hadith that the method cannot incorporate, that is, independent attestations for a given hadith complex (subject matter).[151] I am employing a term of art when using the phrase "hadith complex." By this, I mean a group of reports that share a distinctly common subject matter but that do not converge on a single authority at any of the levels. Here is one example:

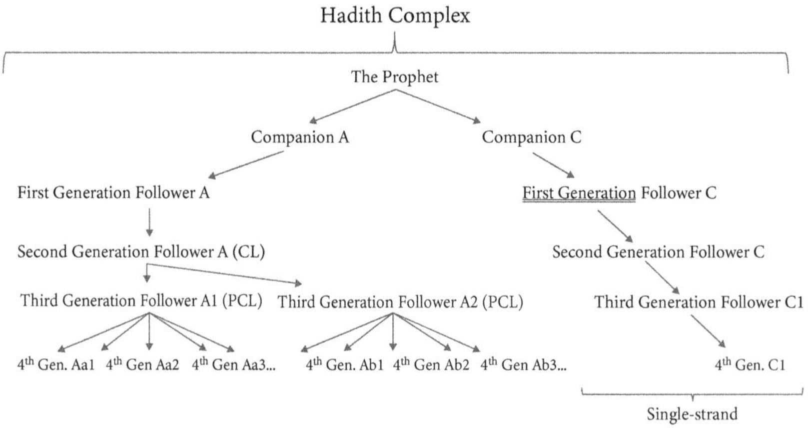

These solitary variants originate with different authorities entirely but are nevertheless part of the same hadith complex. In my view, these related single-strand hadith can help to shed light on the transmission history and the provenance of the textual content of a hadith complex. Among my considerations is that what is identified as a single-strand transmission may appear to be so only because other recensions with different transmission chains were lost or not recorded.[152] As unedited and unpublished manuscripts become more widely available through print publication and/or online texts, we may discover new transmission chains of a report that is currently limited to a single strand.[153] Though it is reasonable to consider that multi-strand hadith have higher historical veracity in terms of both transmission and content, it may not always be the case. Consider the scenario in which A, B, and C versions of a hadith have high degrees of similarity as compared to version D. It would follow that narratives A, B, and

[151] For one example, see Sean W. Anthony, "Crime and Punishment," 426–32.
[152] Motzki, *Analysing Muslim Traditions*, 52–8.
[153] On the impact of unedited and unpublished Arabic papyri on available documentary material, see Salaymeh, *The Beginnings of Islamic Law*, 26.

C are more likely to be historical. But we can also imagine a case in which narrative D contains the historical material, not the A, B, and C complex. Moreover, a transmitter may have favored one teacher or student over another, and a report was shared in accordance with the teacher's preference.[154] By citing or disregarding specific sources of information or by allowing only certain individuals into study circles, a historical transmission that originally had multiple recipients appears as a single-strand transmission chain in canonical and/or non-canonical sources. A report may appear to be single-stranded because certain collectors of hadith deliberately avoided using it by designating it as a weak transmission on the basis of evolving hadith verification standards that began to take root in the first quarter of the second/eighth century.[155] Certain versions were disqualified because, for example, the biographical profiles did not meet the eventual standards that Muslim hadith scholars established, for example, individuals thought to be of weak memory. At the risk of being charged with developing speculative possibilities, the point I am trying to make is that it is unhelpful to make generalizations about the transmission history of hadith.[156] Indeed, multiple attestations can serve as evidence of a historical transmission. Nevertheless, each case demands its own assessment while remaining aware of the hadith criticism trends and evaluative methods.[157]

I also give weight to those single-strand hadith that contain within the transmission chain an unidentified transmitter.[158] As the sciences of hadith criticism develop, such narratives progressively fall out of favor.[159] Transmission chain criticism begins to formalize during the second half of the first/seventh century and was even then adopted to varying degrees in different regional centers of learning.[160] To be sure, narratives with defective transmission chains do not "always accompany earlier forms of a [report] than a more complex or perfect [one]."[161] The opposite can and did

[154] Motzki, "Dating Muslim Traditions," 226f; Motzki, *Analysing Muslim Traditions*, 52–8 and 235.
[155] Jonathan Brown, *Hadith*, 69–122; Motzki, *Analysing Muslim Traditions*, 91 and 137.
[156] I recognize this is a generality in itself.
[157] It would be reasonable to consider a narrative as a potential fabrication if it is transmitted by only one person in the entire world.
[158] See Chapters 2 and 3.
[159] For the opinion of Shu'ba b. al-Ḥajjāj (d. 160/776), see al-Khaṭīb al-Baghdādī, *al-Kifāya*, 11:367; for the standardization of the evaluation of hadith with unknown transmitters, see, e.g., Ibn Ṣalāḥ, *'Ulūm al-ḥadīth*, 375–9; Ibn Ḥajar, *Nuzha al-naẓar*, 136.
[160] Khalidi, *Arabic Historical Thought*, 22; Pavlovitch, "The Origin of the *Isnād*," 19–32; Aghaei, "The Common Link," 112.
[161] Sean Anthony, "Crime and Punishment," 450.

occur.[162] The point is that it would be imprudent to make qualifying or disqualifying generalizations about hadith with defective transmission chains. As to why hadith with defective/incomplete transmission chains exist in the first place, they may reflect uncertainty about sources or sincere lack of recollection, especially in the early part of the transmission history, when later standards of hadith transmission do not exist or are systemic. Instead of adding a name of a known transmitter, the gap is "resolved" by simply acknowledging the inability to recall by whom and by what manner the report is received. In sum, reports with defective transmission chains have value, and they were not always a problem. Why else preserve them? An analysis of defective transmission chains and corresponding textual content can reveal important information about a hadith. I test their efficacy in Chapters 2 and 3 with promising results.

I.2. Final Considerations

Harald Motzki is not the first or only historian to assert that historiographical methods depend "on certain premises and subjective considerations which everyone does not necessarily share."[163] In fact, as Carmen Nanko-Fernández notes:

> too often methods are imposed in ways that preempt questions, content, and context, forcing sources and engagement into preconceived categories and patterns with contrived correlations.[164]

Nanko-Fernández further argues that methods are inherently subjective, even as they are often presented with assumptions of normativity and objectivity.[165] In other words, while methodologies serve as essential frameworks for systematically engaging with a subject or object of inquiry, they are ultimately constructed by individuals for specific instrumental purposes. Normativity and objectivity are imagined. Acknowledging this reality is crucial to democratizing methodological approaches and making explicit that

[162] Anthony, "Crime and Punishment," 450.
[163] Motzki, *Analysing Muslim Traditions*, 3.
[164] Carmen Nanko-Fernández, "Held Hostage by Method?," 39.
[165] Nanko-Fernández, "Held Hostage by Method?," 42.

any given method is employed with a particular aim in mind. In this study, I have endeavored to maintain transparency in this regard.

The very questions a historian asks about a point of interest shape the results and, thereby, the "facts" about the point of interest under observation.[166] In other words, statements about the past should not be presumed to "'correspond' to some preexistent body of 'raw facts.'"[167] The historian draws on a methodology to understand in one particular way "what constitutes the facts themselves."[168] For example, suppose I am attempting to determine whether Samsung makes the best refrigerators. I go to an appliance store and come across marketing information from Whirlpool that states, "Our refrigerators are as reliable as those by Samsung." Now, one way of interpreting Whirlpool's message is that Samsung is indeed the gold standard. Why else would Whirlpool reference its competitor? But the conclusion is premised on my question of determining whether Samsung is the best manufacturer of refrigerators. If I asked a different question or had other considerations in mind, for example, which refrigerator is the most energy efficient of the bunch, then Whirlpool's marketing ploy would simply be irrelevant or an anomaly. What I attempt to keep in mind is that people of the past had their own ways of asking questions and, on this basis, developed historical narratives with particular concepts, arcs, and wording. The same applies to me. I am first constructing a story based on whatever narrative models are familiar to me and then filling in the gaps using "data" that have been, like a diamond, cleaved, sawn, cut, and polished to fit a particular purpose. Therefore, there is a double lens operating that needs to be kept in mind—one relating to the narrativization of bygone individuals and another of the researcher.

In the present work, I want to explicitly create space for a kind of critical historical inquiry that does not disparage, ignore, or adopt otherwise approaches to the inescapable complexities of efforts to preserve and stabilize what is inherently unstable: memory. I advocate the necessity and legitimacy of inferring modalities of oral/aural transmissions prior to and within the context of written transmissions. When read through a hermeneutic that takes into account that efforts to teach a lesson, and/or to make sense of one's experiences of the past and present, necessitate a connection between concepts and the stabilization of memory, the literature I investigate remains

[166] Hayden White, *Tropics of Discourse*, 43.
[167] White, *Tropics of Discourse*, 47.
[168] White, *Tropics of Discourse*, 47.

the most promising source material available for 'generating historical truth' about the earliest periods of Islamic history, to use Salaymeh's apt phrase. In my view, efforts to stabilize memory can be viewed as historiography's "logical extension,"[169] or better still, an extremely fruitful means for achieving this end. This is because "[m]emory is anchored in facts even while it colors them."[170]

I would also like to briefly remark on the concept of authenticity. What does it mean to assert that the content of a report is authentic? Maiken Umbach and Mathew Humphrey make a convincing case that the concept of authenticity can be (re)defined, (re)appropriated, and (re)deployed for a variety of purposes.[171] By claiming something to be authentic, the claimant presents a particular view as stable and natural even when, historically speaking, the perception itself is fleeting and unstable.[172] Over the course of their work, Umbach and Humphrey also demonstrate the different ways in which the development of an idea—a connection to a past—reveals the context against which the development was taking place. Their presentation shows how authenticity can be manufactured and deployed for instrumental ends.

For instance, Umbach and Humphrey examine authenticity in relation to consumption.[173] One example deals with advertising in the global market for "food authenticity." Advertisements position corporations as entities poisoning individuals with processed and denatured food.[174] People are encouraged to seek out "authentic" ways of eating. This goading drives the need for "organic foods," and stores such as Whole Foods have a windfall. But then others, such as Walmart and Target, also get into the organic foods business, the result being that corporations such as Whole Foods no longer have the glamour they once did. To reassert its position as the arbiter between authentic and inauthentic, these businesses then begin to market food authenticity anew, turning toward notions of "farm fresh" or "from farm to table." In all of these instances, the concept of authenticity is reimagined and operates with an underlying framework in which there is an "understood standard to determine what is or is not genuine."[175] But in reality, the idea of authentic food is subjective.

169 Maiken Umbach, "Memory and Historicism," 28.
170 William Spohn, *Go and Do Likewise*, 17.
171 Maiken Umbach and Mathew Humphrey, *Authenticity*, 2.
172 Umbach and Humphrey, *Authenticity*, 7.
173 Umbach and Humphrey, *Authenticity*, 95–121.
174 Umbach and Humphrey, *Authenticity*, 96.
175 Umbach and Humphrey, *Authenticity*, 96.

The aforementioned is to say that the notion of authenticity requires nuance.[176] As with subjectivity, there is a double lens at work. One relates to the possible ways in which the individuals under investigation perceived things to be authentic. The other is what an outsider may deem to be authentic.[177] Recall from above my discussion about the fact that humans make sense of, and remember their experiences in the world, by generating concepts. This operation is not one of replication such as when a person innocently takes a selfie in front of a hungry lion. Because the formulation of concepts is constructive, it is important, as I just noted above, to acknowledge variances in the idea of authenticity. Accordingly and in light of creating and stabilizing memory, there are three considerations with regard to authenticity that are relevant for the current project. One has to do with the potential of didactics in the formation of certain hadith and the corresponding impact on authenticity. The anthropologist and historian Jan Vansina remarks that didactic formulae can readily be understood by insiders while being incomprehensible to outsiders.[178] This insider/outsider positionality is weight-bearing in determining whether something is authentic or inauthentic. Importantly, Vansina asserts that didactic commentaries "sometimes contain historical information" and are instructive about values and ideas.[179] His observation is noteworthy because it means that didactic elements that generate concepts within a narrative can be authentic for both the narrator and the listener, as well as contain historical information.

The two other considerations about the interlink between concepts, the stabilization of memory, and authenticity draw on the frame of reference of an observer. For instance, a Companion may remember something about the Prophet and consider it to be authentic even if the facts do not line up. Two Companions could be a party to an experience with the Prophet yet describe it differently and believe each to be authentic. A twenty-first-century (CE) example can help to further illustrate my point. On January 6, 2021, supporters of then-defeated U.S. President Donald J. Trump entered the U.S. Capitol Building in Washington, DC, without proper authorization.

[176] Schoeler, "Die Frage der schriftlichen oder mündlichen," 226f.

[177] As part of my discussion on authenticity, Brown's remarks on notions of truth in relation to hadith are also helpful. See Jonathan Brown, *Misquoting Muhammad*, 218–20.

[178] Jan Vansina, *Oral Tradition*, 146.

[179] Vansina, *Oral Tradition*, 146, 154, and 157; on non-legal hadith within the framework of didactic commentaries, see, e.g., Sebastian Günther, "Fictional Narration"; on the different ways in which hadith critics debated the merits of didactic elements in hadith, see Brown, *Misquoting Muhammad*, 223–33 and 247–53.

These supporters authentically believed that the U.S. presidential election was stolen from Mr. Trump and that their actions were justifiable in the spirit of upholding the U.S. Constitution. But another group describes such supporters and the events differently. This second group depicts Mr. Trump's supporters as rioters, a mob, or terrorists, who seditiously stormed the Capitol. Now, which group's understanding of the event is authentic? Is one group going to be convinced of the other's claim? And all of this says nothing about the fact that there is *video* evidence, that is, not oral/aural, capturing the events of the day. Presently, we have reporting that describes the events of January 6 in contrasting terms. What would be an appropriate way for a historian to describe, evaluate, and interpret the incident as a function of authenticity one hundred, two hundred, or a thousand years from now? How would such a historian make sense of the divergent views of the event? Whatever methodology is deployed—perhaps ICMA plus video evidence?—would require nuance about the meaning of authenticity. To state what may be obvious, what I designate to be authentic about persons and/or events can stand in contrast to their perceptions, that is, the view of the subject(s) under investigation.[180]

To be sure, I critically explore the relevant reports and, doing so, only serves to reinforce my belief that the methods of textual criticism are invaluable. In this study, I employ ICMA with certain modifications. But the method is only partially helpful in determining whether a person said X or an event Y occurred in some shape or form. A comprehensive methodological approach requires the application of all available tools, including reasoned intuition, to reconstruct the past. I operate under the presumption that the transmission of a report, as indicated by its chain, is historical at each transmitter level unless external evidence suggests otherwise. With regard to the textual content of the different versions of a hadith, I evaluate its historical nature on a case-by-case basis. As Motzki observes, the mere possibility of forgery does not necessarily imply that it occurred, nor that it was a frequent practice.[181] In my view, the highly contested nature of discussions in and about various aspects of early Islam, as reflected in the sources, indicates that early Muslims themselves did not passively accept a purported status quo or transmitted reports. My methodological approach underscores the necessity

[180] For an insightful discussion on the development of the concept of reliability in relation to hadith, see Brown, "Did the Prophet Say It or Not?"

[181] Motzki, "Dating Muslim Traditions," p. 209.

of a balanced and critical engagement with historical sources to avoid unwarranted skepticism or uncritical acceptance.

Indeed, the center of the percussion of sound historical analysis lies somewhere in the inescapable tension between the pursuit of ultimate objectivity (read: authenticity) and a careful identification of the limits that come with a fulsome embrace of the creative potential of the ultimate inescapable subjectivity. The danger to be assiduously avoided is trying to pass off as quality historical analysis either the worthless absolutism that is the byproduct of a supposed objectivity or the equally worthless relativism that is the byproduct of the celebration of unaccountable subjectivity. Understanding and preserving our experiences through the attempt to stabilize individual and collective memory is not only unavoidable, it is also necessary for our very survival and flourishing as the social, self-aware species that we are as humans. As we reckon with how the processes of understanding and preserving the past unfold as a first-order human activity, our second-order attempts to do the same as critical historians can be all the better for it.[182]

The problem of historicity—the degree to which textual sources accurately reflect actual events—is not unique to the study of early Islamic history. As argued by Ricoeur and Gadamer, the problem stems from the dialectic of "alienating distanciation" (from speaking to writing) and "belonging" (the extent to which the context of the speaker, listener, and/or writer is shared) that lies at the heart of the hermeneutical project.[183] As Ricoeur asserts, the gap between the objectification of something written about the past and its interpretation is not dichotomous but complementary.[184] One needs to bear in mind the significance of the ways the oral/aural and the written transmissions were shaped and reshaped by their contexts. As Mark Bevir writes, "historical distance—the gap between past and present, or between fact and narrative"—is not a problem because facts are not certain truths; they are always intertwined with narratives, which means that an analysis reveals more about the character of facts than a supposed objectivity.[185] Something such as chronology is significant only to the extent that, in addition to any number of witnesses interpreting and remembering an event differently, "memory is a creative process, and that the consolidation of a memory, far from being the etching on wax envisioned by Plato, reinforces

[182] Schoeler, *Biography of Muḥammad*, xiii–xv.
[183] Paul Ricoeur, "The Hermeneutical Function of Distanciation," 93–106.
[184] Ricoeur, "The Hermeneutical Function of Distanciation," p. 102.
[185] Mark Bevir, "Why Historical Distance Is Not a Problem," 24–37, esp. 31–4.

a schema—a subjective representation that often changes the memory itself."[186] As Ricoeur and others affirm, the oral/aural shares a context that may be absent in written modes of discourse but is nevertheless productive in the quest to acquire a reasonable sense of the past.[187]

To recap my project, I investigate certain aspects of Islamic law and jurisprudence as well as particular hadith to provide insights into the beginnings of some of the contingencies that inform the process by which *zinā*-stoning comes to be deemed normative in Islam. I apply various methods of source criticism and draw on broader considerations about the different ways in which humans understand their world, stabilize memories, and preserve knowledge. In the bulk of this book, I analyze the transmission history of three specific reports and explain how various aspects of their respective textual contents are critical for helping to naturalize the applicability of the stoning punishment upon certain classes of Muslims. The results of my analysis raise important questions about the provenance of these hadith and, by extension, the provenance of *zinā*-stoning. It is my contention that during the twenty-three revelatory years of the Prophet's life, death by lapidation was not normative in Islam.

I.3. Sources

The hadith collections I investigate are:

- *Muwaṭṭa'* of Mālik b. Anas (d. 179/795)
- *Musnad* of Abū Dāwūd al-Ṭayālisī (d. 203)
- *al-Muṣannaf* of ʿAbd al-Razzāq al-Sanʿānī (d. 211/827)
- *Musnad* of al-Ḥumaydī (d. 219/834)
- *al-Muṣannaf* of Ibn Abī Shayba (d. 235/849)
- *Musnad* of Ibn Ḥanbal (d. 241/855)
- *Ṣaḥīḥ* of al-Bukhārī (d. 256/870)
- *Ṣaḥīḥ* of Muslim (d. 261/875)
- *Sunan* of Ibn Majah (d. 273/887)

[186] Quiroga, *The Forgetting Machine*, 58; besides, for early Muslim transmitters, chronology was not of primary concern, which is in fact a reflection of oral traditions. Unclear chronology does not *a priori* make a hadith problematic. See Schoeler, *Biography of Muḥammad*, 91.

[187] Ricoeur, "Hermeneutical Function of Distanciation," 21f.

- *Sunan* of Abū Dāwūd (d. 275/889)
- *Jāmiʿ al-kubrā* of al-Tirmidhī (d. 279/892)
- *al-Sunna* of al-Mawarzī (d. 294/906)
- *al-Sunan al-kubrā* of al-Nasāʾī (d. 303/915)
- *Musnad* of al-Mawsilī (d. 307/919)
- *Sunan al-kubrā* of al-Bayhaqī (d. 458/1066)

I employ pre-canonical and post-canonical sources because they include relevant versions of *zinā*-stoning reports that do not make their way into the six canonical books. I examine the six canonical works because of their authority within the larger hadith corpus. Of special interest are the *Muṣannafs* of ʿAbd al-Razzāq and Ibn Abī Shayba, respectively, because they also record opinions of legal authorities from the late first/seventh and early second/eighth Islamic centuries, a time period in which legal orthodoxy was notably absent. These are the hadith sources I investigate systematically. They provide a sufficiently diverse cross-section of material on *zinā*-stoning reports for conducting ICMA. I incorporate additional material as needed and will identify it accordingly.

An indispensable supplement to hadith compilations is the *rijāl* literature, which includes biographical dictionaries (*kutub al-rijāl*) among others. Muslim scholars of hadith in time composed multivolume works in the disciplines known as *jarḥ wa al-taʿdīl* and *kutub al-ḍuʿafāʾ* dedicated to certifying the reliability (*ḍabṭ*) and probity (*ʿadāla*) of individual authorities that turned up in the transmission chain or problems in a corresponding textual content.[188] Not infrequently, authors of such works would also warn about transmitters of Prophetic material who made it a habit to deceive (ar., *tadlīs*) unsuspecting listeners by citing a highly respectable authority for a report that they were narrating, all the while neglecting to mention or even actively concealing the fact that they did not receive the report directly from their named source. Indeed, some authors of this genre could be motivated to elevate the status of certain transmitters while dismissing the prestige of others. Scott C. Lucas demonstrates how this process of classifying and promoting certain transmitters over others helped to stabilize particular

[188] For an overview of these genres, see Brown, *Ḥadīth*, 66–89 and 95–100; Muhammad F.B.M. Yusoff, "On Biographical Dictionaries of Ḥadīṯ Transmitter;" on the origins of Shīʿī biographical dictionaries, see Liyakat Takim, "The Origins of and Authentications in Shiʿi Biographical Literature."

aspects of Sunnī orthodoxy.[189] But as Abou El Fadl notes, "branding a particular transmitter . . . as reliable or unreliable is helpful but not conclusive."[190] A person's life is complex, and it is imprudent to judge the entirety of a transmitter's output on the basis of such evaluations.[191] Used judiciously, sources on transmitter appraisal are an invaluable and necessary tool for ICMA in particular and research in general.

There are certain limitations to the present study. The project centers on select primary sources that gain relevance in the eventual Sunnī Islamic legal tradition. Research needs to be conducted on why there appears to have been no effort on the part of *some* early non-proto-Sunnī or the eventual non-Sunnī communities to debate the legitimacy of *zinā*-stoning. It may be that the early communal fractures emerging along political lines did not extend to legal matters during the historical moment when *zinā*-stoning found its anchoring in various Muslim communities. At least with the Ibāḍī and Shīʿī cases, I do not conduct a distinctive investigation, leaving for future study the compelling question about how *zinā*-stoning came to be established in these legal traditions.[192]

I.4. Chapter Overview

In Chapter 1, I provide several examples of reports on *zinā*. Some include a reference to stoning or an order to stone an offender for unlawful sexual intercourse. I also illustrate the different ways in which Muslim legal authorities utilized such stoning narratives to justify *zinā* laws. Lastly, I survey opinions reflecting the different ways in which some Muslims conceived of the Prophet's involvement in stoning.

In Chapter 2, I examine an incident involving Medinan Jews, their purported *zinā* case, and the Prophet's order to have the transgressors stoned to death. The report conveys that the rabbis were lying about a stoning command in the Torah. I investigate numerous transmission chains and their corresponding textual content to shed light on their likely

[189] See generally Scott C. Lucas, *Constructive Critics*; for a summary of scholars who identify issues to keep in mind when using biographical dictionaries, see the helpful comments by Pavlovitch, *The Formation of the Islamic Understanding of Kalāla*, 41.

[190] Abou El Fadl, *Speaking in God's Name*, 87.

[191] Abou El Fadl, *Speaking in God's Name*, 87.

[192] For one review on the acceptance of *zinā*-stoning in the Shīʿī legal tradition, see Sarah El Tantawi, "Ṭūsī Did Not 'Opt Out,'" 312–32, esp. 323–8.

provenance and the significance of specific motifs and transmitters. I also examine exegetical commentaries and the ways in which Muslims used the report in their understanding of certain Qur'ānic verses. I contend that the narrative emerges during the second half of the first/seventh century. The significance of the report for the present study is that (1) the Prophet's involvement in the adjudication of the case involving Jewish *zinā* offenders forges a relationship between stoning and *zinā* in the historical memory of early Muslims, and (2) it serves as a lesson for Muslims to maintain fidelity to *zinā*-stoning. Accordingly, it is in these ways that the hadith contributes to the beginnings of the process by which stoning is legalized in the Islamic tradition.

In Chapter 3, I examine a report according to which the Prophet orders the stoning punishment upon a Muslim woman who confesses to the act of *zinā*. I analyze the chains of transmission and the corresponding textual variations of recensions attributed to three Companions. My analysis reveals several characteristics suggesting that the event did not occur during the Prophet's lifetime. I demonstrate that it has an early provenance dating to the mid-first/seventh century. The narrative holds significance because, unlike the case involving the Jewish offenders of *zinā*, it places the Prophet's authority in the context of administering death by lapidation for a Muslim who has committed illicit sexual intercourse. Accordingly, the report becomes another element for the mechanism by which to justify *zinā*-stoning.

In Chapter 4, I focus on the figure of ʿUmar b. al-Khaṭṭāb and the different ways in which he is portrayed in *zinā* reports. I begin by providing several narratives that depict ʿUmar as having a predisposition toward imposing the stoning punishment upon Muslims. Thereafter, I turn to an examination of the transmission chains and the corresponding textual content of a report in which ʿUmar delivers a sermon claiming that the Book of God and the Prophet mandate *zinā*-stoning. In my view, ʿUmar's authority is used in attempts to normalize the punishment, when Muslims, after the death of the Prophet, reject the capital punishment precisely because it is neither Qur'ānic nor a practice of the Prophet. I further contend that this report of ʿUmar delivering a public sermon about *zinā*-stoning is the "Islamic version" of the narrative involving the Prophet and Jewish *zinā* offenders. Finally, I argue that those Muslims who support *zinā*-stoning connect the matter to an issue that already garners its own *communal* controversy: the selection of Abū Bakr as caliph after the death of the Prophet. In other words, a sermon ʿUmar delivers about the legitimacy of Abū Bakr's caliphate is later remembered as the setting for a dictum according to which he attempts to legitimize the use of the stoning punishment upon Muslim *zinā* offenders.

To help the reader navigate this book, I offer the following brief guide on how to approach its chapters. Chapter 1 is essential reading, as it provides a comprehensive review of extant hadith on the stoning punishment and relevant interconnected topics. The chapter establishes a foundational understanding for the discussions that follow. In Chapters 2 to 4, I have generally structured the analysis into two distinct sections. One focuses on the transmission history of different versions of a hadith and the other on their corresponding textual content. Depending on their interests, readers may choose to engage with only one aspect or explore both for a more complete perspective.

1

Zinā-Stoning, Hadith, and Law

Introduction

The primary objective of this chapter is to familiarize the reader with reports pertaining to *zinā*-stoning and to provide an overview of the different ways in which these accounts help to shape *zinā* laws. I also survey legal opinions about the relevance of non-virginity and the concept of *iḥṣān*—the legal state that devolves upon a person after having consummated a lawful marriage—as preconditions necessitating lapidation for those found guilty of the more severe form of *zinā*. I examine the different ways in which the Qur'ān employs derivatives of the verb *ḥ-ṣ-n* in relation to sexual mores, and I compare such usages to how Muslim authorities develop and utilize *ḥ-ṣ-n* in relation to *zinā*-stoning. Tracing the details of how Muslim authorities formulated specific hermeneutical, jurisprudential, and typological methodologies show the integration of various hadith related to *zinā*-stoning into the Islamic legal tradition.

1.1. Prohibition of *Zinā*

In this section, I review hadith in which *zinā* is prohibited and, in some cases, deemed as a capital offense. A narrative on the authority of the Companion ʿAbd Allāh b. Masʿūd (d. 32/652) states:

> (No. 1) ʿAbd Allāh b. Masʿūd asked the Prophet: What is the greatest sin?
> The Prophet answered: [The greatest sin is] to affirm that there are beings other than God that are worthy of worship, when it is He [alone] that created you!
> Then Ibn Masʿūd asked: And after that?
> The Prophet answered: To [selfishly] take the life of your child because you are loathe to share [with him] the food on your plate.

Stoning as Punishment in Early Islam. Syed Atif Rizwan, Oxford University Press. © Oxford University Press 2026.
DOI: 10.1093/9780197823774.003.0002

Then Ibn Masʿūd asked: And after that?

The Prophet answered: Committing *zinā* with your neighbor's wife.[1]

By virtue of her marital status, the neighbor's wife would be committing adultery, assuming she is a willing partner. For her partner, however, the classical Islamic legal tradition would deem the type of *zinā* for which he is guilty unclear. If he is unmarried, then he commits fornication. But if married, he is guilty of adultery and, as per the Islamic legal tradition, deemed to have *iḥṣān*. Hence, this narrative bears two potential meanings for unlawful sexual intercourse. But one thing remains clear: *zinā* is a grave transgression.

The following two reports involve the third Sunnī caliph after the Prophet's death, ʿUthmān b. ʿAffān (d. 35/656). One variant reads:

(No. 2) We were at the entrance of ʿUthmān b. ʿAffān's house at the time he was surrounded by his enemies [shortly before his assassination]. We heard him yell something at someone while they were standing at the paved courtyard of his residence. ʿUthmān came out looking pale (lit., he left changed in color, *kharaja mutaghayyir al-lawn*).

We asked him: Commander of the Faithful, what is wrong?

ʿUthmān replied: I always knew some people wanted to take my life, but now it is clear to me that those who are outside definitely want to!

We responded: May God protect you from them, Commander of the Faithful!

ʿUthmān then said to us: On what basis do they want to kill me? I remember the Messenger of God saying that the blood of a Muslim can be spilled only under three conditions: When a man leaves Islam after becoming Muslim, or when he commits *zinā* after he has *iḥṣān*, or when he commits homicide! By God, I have never committed *zinā*, nor have I ever wished to change my religion, nor have I ever committed murder! I do not understand how they could justify killing me.[2]

[1] "*an tazniya bi ḥalīlati jārika*." al-Ṭayālisī, *Musnad*, 1:212, no. 262; Ibn Ḥanbal, *Musnad* (1992 ed.), 7:200f, no. 4,131 and 7:429, no. 4,423; al-Bukhārī, *Ṣaḥīḥ* (1976 ed.), 1626, no. 4,207, 2236, no. 5,655 and 2497f, no. 6,426; Muslim, *Ṣaḥīḥ*, 90, no. 141; Abū Dāwūd, *Sunan*, 3:617f, no. 2,310; al-Tirmidhī, *al-Jāmiʿ*, 5:245f, no. 3,182f; al-Nasāʾī, *al-Sunan al-kubrā*, 3:425f, no. 3,462f, 6:399, no. 7,086, 10:9, no. 10,920 and 10:204, no. 11,305; al-Mawṣilī, *Musnad*, 9:64, no. 5,130; al-Bayhaqī, *al-Sunan al-kubrā*, 8:33, no. 15,840f.

[2] al-Ṭayālisī, *Musnad*, 1:71f, no. 72; ʿAbd al-Razzāq, *al-Muṣannaf*, 10:167, no. 18,703; on the authority of the Companion ʿAbd Allāh b. Masʿūd (d. 32/652), see al-Ḥumaydī, *Musnad*, 1:219, no. 119; on the authority of ʿĀʾisha (d. 57/677), see Ibn Abī Shayba, *al-Muṣannaf* (1989 ed.), 5:452:, no. 7,902 and 5:453, no. 27,905; Ibn Ḥanbal, *Musnad* (1992 ed.), 1:491, no. 437; Abū Dāwūd, *Sunan*, 6:408f, no. 4,353 and 6:552f, no. 4,502; al-Tirmidhī, *al-Jāmiʿ*, 4:33, no. 2,158; al-Nasāʾī, *al-Sunan al-kubrā*, 3:427, no. 3,466; al-Bayhaqī, *al-Sunan al-kubrā*, 8:34, no. 15,843; in other versions, the term *thayyib*

In another version, which does not mention the Prophet, ʿUthmān remarks that stoning is the applicable punishment:

> (No. 3) The blood of a Muslim can be spilled only under three conditions: When a person commits *zinā* and has *iḥṣān*, they are to be stoned. When a person kills another person, they are to be executed. When a person leaves Islam after becoming Muslim, they are to be executed.[3]

The accounts pertaining to ʿUthmān closely resemble the narrative circulated by Ibn Masʿūd in that they meticulously outline three major offenses, with one of them being *zinā*. The specificity of these three major transgressions tracks with the way in which the Qur'ān speaks of the types of acts that constitute three particularly vile transgressions of which a person can be guilty:

> Q25:68 Those are the ones who do not associate anything with God, nor take a life except for cause—as God has made all life sacred—nor engage in *zinā* (*lā yaznūna*)

The Ḥanbalī jurist Ibn Qudāma (d. 620/1223) himself saw the interconnection between the verse and the hadith, as he referenced both to convey the gravity of the *zinā* offense.[4] The hadiths referenced above highlight three of the most significant transgressions that a Muslim can commit and provide valuable insight into the gravity of *zinā*. They serve to affirm the divine proscriptions as described in Q25:68. But unlike the Qur'ān, the hadiths go a step further and convey that *zinā* (unclear which type) could be a capital offense. This shift enabled the juristic discourse to take steps toward affirming lapidation as punishment for forms of *zinā* deemed particularly severe.

is employed in place of *iḥṣān* to signify the status of the *zinā* offender. E.g., on the authority of the Companion ʿAbd Allāh b. Masʿūd, see Ibn Abī Shayba, *al-Muṣannaf* (1989 ed.), 5:452, no. 27,901 and 5:321, no. 36,492; Ibn Ḥanbal, *Musnad* (1992 ed.), 6:119f, no. 3,621; al-Bukhārī, *Ṣaḥīḥ* (1976 ed.), 2521, no. 6,484; Muslim, *Ṣaḥīḥ*, 1302, no. 25 and 1303, no. 26; Ibn Mājah, *Sunan*, 847, no. 2,534; Abū Dāwūd, *Sunan*, 6:408, no. 4,352; al-Tirmidhī, *al-Jāmiʿ*, 3:74f, no. 1,402 and 3:114f, no. 1,444; al-Nasāʾī, *al-Sunan al-kubrā*, 3:426, no. 3,456; al-Mawṣilī, *Musnad*, 8:136, no. 4,676 and 9:128, no. 5,202; al-Bayhaqī, *al-Sunan al-kubrā*, 8:35, no. 15,844.

[3] ʿAbd al-Razzāq, *al-Muṣannaf*, 10:167, no. 18,702; Ibn Ḥanbal, *Musnad* (1992 ed.), 1:502, no. 452; Ibn Mājah, *Sunan*, 847, no. 2,533; al-Nasāʾī, *al-Sunan al-kubrā*, 3:438, no. 3,497 and 3:440, no. 3,506; al-Ṭabarī, *Jāmiʿ*, 10:261, no. 11,843.

[4] Ibn Qudāma, *al-Mughnī*, 12:307.

1.2. *Zinā*-Stoning Cases and Laws

The reports presented in this section are examples of the different ways in which the Prophet or a Companion of his is remembered to have ordered the stoning punishment upon Muslims. I also illustrate the different ways in which Muslim jurists utilized *hadith* to formulate substantive *zinā*-stoning laws. Through debate and negotiation, Muslim jurists created stability around what otherwise appear to be conflicting, inconsistent, and unclear reports about stoning for Muslim *zinā* offenders.

1.2.1. Cases in which the Prophet mandates *zinā*-stoning

According to several versions of a hadith, the Prophet is asked to adjudicate a case involving a Jewish couple accused of having committed *zinā*. In these variants, the stoning punishment is ordered on the basis of the Hebrew Bible. In one version, the Companion ʿAbd Allāh b. ʿUmar b. al-Khaṭṭāb (d. 74/693) purportedly stated:

> A Jewish group came to the Prophet and told him about a Jewish man and a Jewish woman who committed *zinā*.
>
> The Prophet asked: Do you find anything about stoning in the Torah?
>
> They responded: We humiliate and flog them.
>
> Upon hearing that, ʿAbd Allāh b. Salām[5] interjected: You lie! Stoning is in the Torah!
>
> So they brought the Torah and opened it. One of the Jewish men covered the stoning verse with his hand and read what was before and after it.
>
> ʿAbd Allāh b. Salām said to the reader: Lift your hand up!
>
> The man did and they saw the stoning verse.
>
> The Jewish group said: ʿAbd Allāh b. Salām has told the truth, Muḥammad.
>
> Thereafter, the Messenger of God gave the command and the Jewish *zinā* offenders were stoned.
>
> ʿAbd Allāh b. ʿUmar said: I saw the man leaning over to protect the woman from the stones.[6]

[5] ʿAbd Allāh b. Salām was a Jewish convert to Islam. He was considered a legal authority in both traditions. On his biography, see Chapter 2, page(s) pp. 126–127.

[6] Mālik, *Muwaṭṭaʾ*, 1195, no. 623/3,035.

I examine this and other versions of the narrative in Chapter 2 and argue for its centrality in the beginnings of the process by which stoning becomes part of the Islamic legal tradition. We can already see that the report connects the Prophet's authority to the punishment of stoning for *zinā* offenders, albeit non-Muslims on the basis of their own scriptural framework.

Another report, which came to be known in the Islamic tradition as the "Day-Laborer (*'asīf*)" hadith, the Prophet orders a woman to be stoned in accordance with the Book of God. The account is circulated on the combined authorities of the Companions Abū Hurayra (d. *c.* 58/677) and Zayd b. Khālid al-Juhaynī (d. 78/697). They comment:

> Two men brought their dispute to the Messenger of God and one of them said: Messenger of God, make a judgment for us based on the Book of God (*aqḍi baynanā bi-kitāb Allāh*).
>
> The other, who was the more knowledgeable of the two, said: Yes, Messenger of God, make a ruling based on the Book of God. But first, listen to what I have to say.
>
> The Prophet responded: Speak.
>
> The man said: My son was hired to work for this man and he committed *zinā* with his wife. This man informed me that my son needs to be stoned. In order to save my son from that punishment, I offered a ransom in the form of 100 sheep and a female slave. But then I asked people of knowledge about the matter and they told me that my son is subject to 100 lashes and banishment for one year and that the wife is subject to stoning.
>
> Upon hearing the man's comments, the Messenger of God said: By the One in whose hand is my soul, I will decide the matter between the two of you based on the Book of God. As for your sheep and female slave, they are to be returned to you. Your son is to be flogged 100 times and banished for one year.
>
> Then the Prophet ordered Unays al-Aslamī to go to the man's wife and to have her stoned if she confessed to *zinā*. The wife confessed and she was stoned.[7]

The textual content does not include an explicit reference to the religion of the man's son or his paramour. This ambiguity could be consequential, in that the woman may or may not have been Muslim. A reader (or listener)

[7] See, e.g., Mālik, *Muwaṭṭa'*, 1199f, no. 628/3,040.

of the reporter must infer the offender's religion to assert that the Prophet ordered the stoning of a Muslim. This supposition is in fact what Muslim authorities gravitate toward.

In Chapter 4, I discuss the significance of the term "The Book of God" and its relationship to *zinā*. But, presently, I would like to offer brief insights about the reference. Joseph E. Lowry has argued that the "Book of God" is likely a reference to the Heavenly Book (*umm al-kitāb*) or the Torah.[8] On the basis of certain hadith and pre-modern legal texts, John Burton concludes that the "Book of God" appears to have multi-valent meanings that include the Torah, the Qur'ān, the practice of the Prophet, or a general reference to God's law.[9] Indeed, to Burton's last point, it seems that the phrase was used as a general idiomatic reference to any divine law.[10] Regardless of what the Book of God here may have signified, Muslim legal authorities employed the "Day-Laborer" hadith to legitimize stoning for Muslim *zinā* offenders on the basis of the Prophet's authority.

One of the most widely cited *zinā*-stoning reports concerns a self-confessing male offender. This narrative has been transmitted in several forms. Below are a few examples, separated into three categories based on how the confessor is identified. In one group, he is simply known as 'a man':

> During the time of the Messenger of God, a man confessed four times to having committed *zinā*, so the Messenger of God ordered that he be stoned, and he was stoned.[11]

According to the Companion Abū Dharr Jundub b. Junāda (d. 32/652):

[8] Lowry, *Early Islamic Legal Theory*, 97 including n. 66. One understanding of "The Heavenly Book," as mentioned in the Qur'ān (Q13:39 and Q43:4), is understood by Muslims to be the book in the heavens comprised of the scriptures of Judaism, Christianity, and Islam.

[9] John Burton, *The Sources of Islamic Law*, 129ff; Burton, "The Penalty for Adultery in Islam," 123; and generally, Burton, "The Origin of the Islamic Penalty for Adultery."

[10] In the Qur'ān, the expression is used for ordinances in any scripture, including the Qur'ān. E.g., see Q2:79, Q2:101, and Q3:23.

[11] Mālik, *Muwaṭṭa'*, 1198, no. 626/3,038; 'Abd al-Razzāq, *al-Muṣannaf*, 7:319, no. 13,333f; Ibn Abī Shayba, *al-Muṣannaf* (1989 ed.), 9:353, no. 29,352; Ibn Ḥanbal, *Musnad* (1995 ed.), 9:328, no. 9,807, 13:77, no. 16,538, 13:94, no. 16,575, 15:374, no. 20,881, 16:20, no. 21,446, 16:236, no. 22,112, and 16:556, no. 23,104; al-Bukhārī, *Ṣaḥīḥ* (1976 ed.), 2,499, no. 6,430 and 2,502, no. 6,439; Muslim, *Ṣaḥīḥ*, 1318, no. 16 and 1319, no. 18; Abū Dāwūd, *Sunan*, 6:481, no. 4,432; al-Nasā'ī, *al-Sunan al-kubrā*, 6:421, no. 7,139, 6:423, no. 7,144, and 6:433, no. 7,162; al-Bayhaqī, *al-Sunan al-kubrā*, 8:371, no. 16,926, 8:392, no. 16,990, and 8:398, no. 17,003.

> We were traveling with the Messenger of God when a man approached him and said: I am the one who committed *zinā*. The Prophet sent him away for a third and a fourth time.[12] After the fourth confession the man remained in place because the Prophet did not send him away. The Messenger of God gave the command and the man was stoned. The Messenger of God appeared somber. Once his grief subsided, he said to me:
>
> Abū Dharr, do you not see that God forgives the man who was just here and grants him a place in Heaven?[13]

In both of these narratives, the offender confesses to *zinā* four times, after which the Prophet orders the stoning punishment. Recall that the Qur'ān stipulates the requirement of four witnesses for *zinā* cases involving independent prosecutions (Q4:15) or accusations leveled by members of the community (Q24:4). The (respective) textual content of the male *zinā* offender reports conveys that he confesses four times. It is on the basis of the four-fold confession that he is convicted and subjected to the capital punishment. Thus, it may be thought that the four-fold confession was meant to stand in place of the four-witness requirement as prescribed in the Qur'ān. Muslim jurists do stipulate a four-fold confession as one means of securing a conviction.[14] Also note that it is unclear from the text whether the man has *iḥṣān*, a necessary legal element for *zinā*-stoning in the Islamic legal tradition. It is only by inferring from his being subjected to the capital punishment—and having already assumed that *iḥṣān* is a precondition for eligibility for such punishment—that one can conclude that the requisite legal element has been met.

In the second grouping of the hadith, the self-confessor is identified as 'a man from the tribe of Aslam'. These variants are also used by Muslim jurists to substantiate legal procedures by which a *zinā* offender can be prosecuted, convicted, and, potentially, subjected to death by stoning. The textual content reads:

[12] The textual content does not make reference to a first or second dismissal.

[13] Ibn Abī Shayba, *al-Muṣannaf* (2008 ed.), 9:353, no. 29,352; Ibn Ḥanbal, *Musnad* (1995 ed.), 16:20f, no. 21,446.

[14] For a Ḥanafī opinion, see Abū Yūsuf, *Kitāb al-kharāj*, 162f; for a Mālikī opinion, see Saḥnūn, *al-Mudawwana*, 4:482; for a Ḥanbalī opinion, see Ibn Qudāma, *al-Mughnī*, 12:355; for a Shīʿī opinion, see al-Ṭūsī, *al-Mabsūṭ*, 8:4; al-Shāfiʿī argues that a single confession is permissible for a *zinā*-stoning conviction. See al-Shāfiʿī, *al-Umm*, 7:340; Schacht argues that the four-witness stipulation in the Qur'ān and the four-fold confession in *zinā* laws is one of the oldest examples of Iraqi *qiyās*. See Schacht, *Origins*, 106.

> A man from Aslam came to the Prophet and confessed to *zinā*. But the Prophet turned him away. The man returned and confessed to the Prophet again and the Prophet turned him away for a second time. This happened until the man confessed four times, after which the Prophet asked him: Are you sure you're okay (*a bi-ka junūn*)?
>
> The man responded: No.
>
> Then the Prophet asked: Do you have *iḥṣān*?
>
> The man responded: Yes.
>
> Based on the responses, the Prophet ordered that he be stoned. The man was stoned in the *muṣallā*.[15] When he felt the sharpness of the stones, he fled. But he was captured and stoned until he perished. The Prophet spoke well of him, but did not pray over him.[16]

In addition to the four confessions, the legal elements of *iḥṣān* and competency are explicitly mentioned in this narrative, whereas they are absent from the versions presented above.

In the third grouping of the report, the man is identified as Māʿiz b. Mālik al-Aslamī. In one iteration, the focus again is on the element of competency:

> Māʿiz b. Mālik al-Aslamī came to the Messenger of God and said: I have wronged myself because I committed *zinā*. I wish for you to purify me.
>
> The Prophet sent him away. The next day Māʿiz came back to him again and said: Messenger of God, I have committed *zinā*.
>
> The Prophet sent him away for a second time. The Prophet then sent for Māʿiz's people and asked: Do you know if Māʿiz is competent? Do you know if he has any deficiencies?
>
> They responded: We do not know anything like that about him. In fact, the only thing we do know is that when it comes to competency, he is the best among us.

[15] The room in the mosque where the ritual prayer is performed in congregation.

[16] ʿAbd al-Razzāq, *al-Muṣannaf*, 7:320, no. 13,337; for other versions, see Mālik, *Muwaṭṭa'*, 1196–8, nos. 624/3,036–626/3,038; ʿAbd al-Razzāq, *al-Muṣannaf*, 7:322, nos. 13,340 and 13,342; Ibn Ḥanbal, *Musnad* (1995 ed.), 11:456, no. 14,399 and 16:453, no. 22,773; al-Bukhārī, *Ṣaḥīḥ* (1976 ed.), 2498f, no. 6,429 and 2500, no. 6,434; Muslim, *Ṣaḥīḥ*, 1,320f, no. 20f; Abū Dāwūd, *Sunan*, 6:477f, no. 4,428 and 6:479f, no. 4,429f; al-Tirmidhī, *al-Jāmiʿ*, 3:99f, no. 1,429; al-Nasā'ī, *al-Sunan al-kubrā*, 6:415, no. 7,127, 6:418, no. 7,130, and 6:420–3, nos. 7,136–43; al-Bayhaqī, *al-Sunan al-kubrā*, 8:380, no. 16,955, 8:381f, no. 16,957, 8:393f, no. 16,991f, and 8:397, no. 16,999.

> Māʿiz came and confessed three times. Each time he confessed, the Prophet sent him away to his people. Three times the Prophet asked Māʿiz's people whether he was sane, and three times they informed him that there was nothing wrong with Māʿiz. When Māʿiz confessed for the fourth time in the presence of the Prophet, the Prophet ordered that a hole be dug up for him and that he be stoned, and Māʿiz was stoned.[17]

In a subgroup of Māʿiz narratives, the focus is on confirming whether the illicit sexual act did in fact occur. For example, in one report, the text reads:

> When Māʿiz b. Mālik came to the Prophet, the Prophet said to him: Perhaps you kissed her, or groped her (*ghamazta*), or maybe just stared at her with the intention [of having sex with her] (*naẓarta*)?
>
> Māʿiz responded: No, Messenger of God. I had sex with her.
>
> Māʿiz did not mince words about what he did. On the basis of his response, the Prophet gave the order for Māʿiz to be stoned.[18]

Mentioning the fact that Māʿiz did not speak metaphorically is not without purpose. Another report appears to clarify this particular remark:

> Māʿiz went to the Prophet and said: Messenger of God, I committed *zinā*.
>
> The Prophet sent him away, doing so repeatedly until Māʿiz confessed four times. Upon the fifth confession, the Prophet asked Māʿiz: Have you truly committed *zinā*?
>
> Māʿiz responded: Yes.
>
> The Prophet then asked: Do you know what *zinā* is?
>
> Māʿiz replied: Yes. I did something with her that is forbidden to me but permissible for a husband to do with his wife.
>
> The Prophet then asked: So what do you want me to do?
>
> Māʿiz replied: I want you to purify me.
>
> The Messenger of God asked: Did you enter her like the way a needle enters into a kohl jar, or a rod into something?

[17] al-Mawṣilī, *Musnad*, 10:352f, no. 29,350.

[18] al-Bukhārī, *Ṣaḥīḥ* (1976 ed.), 2502, no. 6,438; Lucas employs this hadith and others to argue that the Prophet's conduct in cases involving a judgment for illicit sexual intercourse demonstrates his reluctance to apply the stoning punishment. See generally Scott C. Lucas, "Perhaps You Only Kissed Her?"

> Māʿiz responded: Yes, Messenger of God.
>
> On the basis of Māʿiz's answers, the Prophet ordered that Māʿiz be stoned, and he was stoned.[19]

The Māʿiz versions helped Muslim jurists to affirm a legal basis for stipulating specific legal elements that triggered the laws on stoning. For example, confirming that witnesses saw the actual act of penetration constitutes one of the legal elements required to establish the *actus reus*. The Prophet's question, "Did you enter her like the way a needle enters into a kohl jar or a rod into something?" is the standard by which those confessing to the transgression confirm the occurrence of sexual intercourse.[20] The Prophet's inquiry about Māʿiz's mental state secured a precedent for establishing *mens rea* prior to the conviction of a potential offender.[21] In time, the case of the self-confessing male *zinā* offender came to be a standard Prophetic precedent for enumerating the legal elements that needed to be established in order to secure a conviction for *zinā* as well as to establish *zinā*-stoning as punishment upon conviction.

While a multitude of reports circulate in which the self-confessor is identified as a man, there exists another set of reports in which the self-confessor is identified as a woman. These variants are the focus of Chapter 3, but, presently, three versions are noted below. Similar to the case of the self-confessing man, the narratives are grouped together by the degree to which the woman is specifically identified. In one cluster, she is simply cast as 'a pregnant woman':

> A pregnant woman came to the Messenger of God and informed him that she had committed *zinā*.
>
> The Messenger of God said to her: Go away until you give birth.
>
> After she gave birth she returned to the Prophet.
>
> He said to her: Go away for as long as you are nursing him.
>
> Once she weaned the child, she returned to the Prophet.
>
> He said to her: Go and find someone to take care of him.
>
> Once she entrusted someone with her child, she returned to the Prophet and he ordered that she be stoned, and she was stoned.[22]

[19] al-Mawṣilī, *Musnad*, 10:524, no. 6,140.

[20] E.g., see Saḥnūn, *al-Mudawwana*, 4:486; al-Shāfiʿī, *al-Umm*, 7:391; Ibn Qudāma, *al-Mughnī*, 12:356.

[21] E.g., see al-Sarakhsī, *al-Mubsūṭ*, 9:39, 92, and 94; Ibn Qudāma, *al-Mughnī*, 12:309.

[22] Mālik, *Muwaṭṭa'*, 1199, no. 627/3,309.

In the second grouping, she is referenced as a woman of the tribe of Ghāmid:

> A woman from the tribe of Ghāmid came to the Prophet and said: Messenger of God, I have committed *zinā* and I am here because I want you to cleanse me [of this sin].
>
> The Prophet sent her away. She came back the next day and said: Prophet of God, why are you sending me away? Perhaps you are doing the same with me as you did with Māʿiz b. Mālik? [Or is it because], by God, I am pregnant?
>
> The Prophet responded: The reason I am sending you away is because you are pregnant. Go away until you have given birth.
>
> After she gave birth, she returned to the Prophet with a swaddled baby boy (*atathu bi-l-ṣabiyyī fī khirqa*) and said: Look here, I have given birth.
>
> The Prophet responded: Go and nurse him until he is weaned.
>
> Once she weaned the baby, she returned to the Prophet with the boy, who had a small piece of bread in his hand, and said: Look here Prophet of God, I have weaned him and he is now eating solid food.
>
> The Prophet placed the boy in the custody of Muslims and ordered that a chest-deep hole be dug up for her. Then he gave the order to the people and they stoned her. Khālid b. al-Walīd picked up a stone and threw it at her head and when her blood hit his face, he cursed at her. The Prophet of God heard him and said: Enough Khālid b. al-Walīd. By the One [God] in whose Hand is my soul, [the spiritual effects of] her repentance [are of such power] that even a tax collector (*ṣāḥib maks*) would be forgiven [by it]![23]
>
> Then the Prophet gave the order [for her to be stoned.] He and the others then conducted the funeral prayer for her, after which she was buried.[24]

Note the parallel themes shared by the Ghāmidiyya and Māʿiz reports. In fact, the version involving the woman from Ghāmid is directly connected to the variant about Māʿiz by virtue of her asking the Prophet if he is treating her in the same manner as he did Māʿiz.

Finally, in the third group, the female self-confessing offender is said to be instead from the tribe of Juhayna. The *matn* reads:

[23] On the significance of using the motif of a tax collector, see Chapter 3, pp. 228–229.

[24] Ibn Abī Shayba, *al-Muṣannaf* (2008 ed.), 9:361f, no. 29,388.

> A woman from Juhayna, who became pregnant after committing *zinā*, came to the Prophet. The Messenger of God ordered her guardian to take care of her and once she gave birth, to bring her to [him]. [Upon her return,] the Prophet ordered that she be bound up with her clothes and stoned, and then she was stoned. Thereafter, the Prophet led the congregation in reciting a funeral prayer for her, after which ʿUmar said to the Prophet: Messenger of God, [how could] you [have] prayed for her despite the fact that she committed *zinā*?
>
> The Prophet responded: Her [manner of] repentance [produced spiritual effects so powerful] that, were they spread over the people of Medina, it would be sufficient for all of them [to be forgiven their sins]. Do you not see how [noble] it is that she was willing to sacrifice her life in order to earn God's forgiveness?[25]

Similar to hadith versions about the self-confessing man, reports about the self-confessing woman also functioned as sources for legal precedent with respect to *zinā* laws.

In addition to the popularly narrated reports noted above, there are others that appear less frequently in the extant hadith and legal sources. For example, the Companion al-Lajlāj [Abū al-ʿAlāʾ al-ʿĀmirī] (d. first/seventh century) is recorded to have said:

> I was working in the market when a woman passed by with a young child. There was some hustle and bustle around her so I went to see what was going on. I reached the Prophet just as he was asking the woman: Who is this child's father?
>
> The woman remained silent. But then a young man opposite to her said: I am the father, Messenger of God.
>
> He then stood next to her.
>
> The Prophet asked the woman again: Who is this child's father?
>
> Again the young man responded: I am the father, Messenger of God.
>
> Then the Messenger of God looked to some of the surrounding people and asked them about the young man and they responded: We do not know anything bad about him.

[25] al-Ṭayālisī, *Musnad*, 2:182f, no. 888.

> The Prophet then asked the young man: Are you a *muḥṣan*?
>
> The young man responded: Yes.
>
> The Prophet gave the order that he be stoned and he was stoned. For the stoning, we dug up a hole that was sufficiently deep. Then we threw stones at him until he perished. After he died, a man came by asking about him so we took him to the Prophet. We said: This man was asking about the (fate of?) young man we stoned.
>
> The Messenger of God said: To God, his scent is more pleasant than musk.
>
> The inquirer turned out to be the young man's father and we helped him to wash the body, put it in a coffin, and bury it.
>
> Someone in the transmission chain said: I do not recall if al-Lajlāj said whether the Prophet prayed over him or not.[26]

The man in this report is identified as being a *muḥṣan*, that is, someone who has *iḥṣān*. This narrative serves to highlight once more that when someone with *iḥṣān* commits *zinā*, then they are to receive the punishment of stoning. It is also peculiar that, whereas in almost all *zinā*-stoning cases involving the Prophet, the transgressors come to him. But here, the Prophet is portrayed as abruptly asking a question and ostensibly *inviting* the confession. The following is another example of a less popular report on the authority of the Companion Abū Hunayda Wā'il b. Ḥujr (d. unknown):

> A woman who was on her way to the mosque during the dark part of the morning [was confronted by] a man [who] tried to sexually assault her. Having found herself in trouble, she screamed for help from a man who was walking by. Her [rapist] fled. A group of people was passing by her and she again called for help. [This group came to her] and they seized the man that was by her [-the same one who tried to help her-] when she called for help. They seized him and the [real culprit] got away. They took [the seized man] to [the woman] and the man said to her: I am the one who heard your call for help but [know that] the real culprit got away.
>
> [Abū Hunayda]: They went with him to the Prophet and told him that [the man they seized] tried to rape the woman. They also told him that they caught him [just when] he tried to run away.

[26] Abū Dāwūd, *Sunan*, 6:483, no. 4,435; Ibn Ḥanbal, *Musnad* (1992 ed.), 25:281f, no. 15,934; al-Nasā'ī, *al-Sunan al-kubrā*, 6:424f, no. 7,146f and 6:435, no. 7,165; al-Bayhaqī, *al-Sunan al-kubrā*, 8:379f, no. 16,954.

> This [innocent] man said: I was the one who heard her yelling for help when she was being sexually assaulted. But these people found me and grabbed me.
>
> The woman interjected: He is lying. He is the one who tried to rape me.
>
> The Prophet said: Take him and stone him.
>
> Then a man from among the people stood up and said: Do not go and stone him. Rather stone me. I am the one [who tried to rape her]. [By virtue of this statement,] he confessed.
>
> With the three gathered in the presence of the Prophet, the Prophet said: As for you [the woman], you are forgiven.
>
> He said something kind to the man who tried to help her.
>
> ʿUmar interjected: Are you going to order the stoning punishment upon the person who confessed?
>
> The Prophet responded in the negative by saying: No, [his confession is such that] he has repented to God.[27]

Note that in both of these reports, the Prophet orders the stoning punishment based on a single confession. In the second narrative, the Prophet orders the stoning punishment based on an *accusation* of *sexual assault* by *one* person, all of which fly in the face of both the Qurʾānic and the Islamic legal tradition requirements for a *zinā* conviction. Moreover, these narratives stand in sharp contrast to the hadith in which the Prophet either dissuades the person from confessing or has them do so multiple times. In my estimation, the two hadith just presented are early forms of *zinā*-stoning reports, given the manner by which the Prophet is portrayed as ordering the stoning punishment.

In one *zinā* case, the Prophet seemingly applies the dual penalty of stoning and flogging upon the offender. This report becomes central to legal and exegetical discussions on stoning. This narrative is circulated on the authority of the Companion ʿUbāda b. al-Ṣāmit (d. 34/654), and it is recorded that he said:

> The Prophet said: Listen to what I have to say. God has made a way for them (*la-hunna*). A non-virgin (*thayyib*) who has illicit sexual intercourse with a non-virgin (*thayyib*) is to receive 100 lashes and stoning. A virgin (*bikr*)

[27] al-Nasāʾī, *al-Sunan al-kubrā*, 6:474f, no. 7,270; al-Bayhaqī, *al-Sunan al-kubrā*, 8:494, no. 17,323.

> who has illicit sexual intercourse with a virgin (*bikr*) is to receive 100 lashes and one year's banishment.[28]

Note that part of the Prophet's statement is to be taken as an interpretation of verse Q4:15, which states, ". . . confine the [convicted women] to [their] houses until death overtakes them or *God provides another way*." The hadith conveys that "the way" God has shown the Muslims is a dual penalty for certain types of *zinā* offenders (e.g., non-virgins): 100 lashes, followed by stoning. Another narrative also incorporates the dual penalty on the authority of the Prophet. According to the Companion Jābir b. ʿAbd Allāh (d. 78/697):

> A man committed *zinā* with a woman, so the Prophet ordered that he be flogged. Then the Prophet was informed that the male offender was a *muḥṣan*, so then the Prophet ordered that he be stoned.[29]

It is, to be sure, open to question whether the offender would have been both flogged and stoned had the Prophet initially known about the offender's *iḥṣān* status. It may well be that this version of the report was circulated by jurists who supported the position that only one or the other of the punishments was to be implemented, as an attempt to explain the earlier report.

Reconciling *zinā* punishments on the basis of Qur'ān—flogging or house arrest—and death by lapidation based on hadith, necessitated particular jurisprudential methods. Commenting on Q4:15, Sulaymān Muqātil notes that the verse prescribes house arrest until death and specifies that confinement is for non-virgin women who commit illicit sexual intercourse.[30] For him, the subordinate clause of Q4:15, "or until God shows a way," is abrogated by the 100-lash prescription of Q24:2.[31] The ʿUbāda hadith then abrogates Q24:2, meaning that virgins are subject to flogging and banishment, whereas

[28] al-Ṭayālisī, *Musnad*, 1:478, no. 585; ʿAbd al-Razzāq, *al-Muṣannaf*, 7:310, no. 13,308 and 7:329, nos. 13,359f; Ibn Abī Shayba, *al-Muṣannaf* (2008 ed.), 9:357, no. 29,364; Ibn Ḥanbal, *Musnad* (1995 ed.), 12:369, no. 15,853 and 15:384, no. 22,565, 15:396, no. 22,602, 15:400, no. 22,614, 15:404, no. 22,628, and 15:406, no. 22,633; Muslim, *Ṣaḥīḥ*, 1316, no. 1,690; Ibn Mājah, *Sunan*, 852, no. 2,550; Abū Dāwūd, *Sunan*, 6:466, no. 4,415 and 6:468, no. 4,417; al-Timidhī, *al-Jāmiʿ*, 3:104f, no. 1,434; al-Marwazī, *al-Sunna*, 1:94, no. 338 and 1:95, nos. 343–5; al-Nasāʾī, *al-Sunan al-kubrā*, 6:405, nos. 7,104–6; al-Bayhaqī, *al-Sunan al-Kubrā*, 8:365f, no. 16,907; for an *isnād-cum-matn* analysis of this report, see generally Pavlovitch, "The ʿUbāda b. al-Ṣāmit Tradition at the Crossroads of Methodology."

[29] Abū Dāwūd, *Sunan*, 6:485f, no. 4,438; al-Bayhaqī, *al-Sunan al-kubrā*, 8:378f, no. 16,949f.

[30] Muqātil, *Tafsīr*, 1:371.

[31] Muqātil, *Tafsīr*, 371f.

non-virgins are subject to flogging and stoning.[32] For Muqātil, a two-step clarification process takes place to make stoning applicable to Muslims. First, the Qur'ān by the Qur'ān and, then, the Qur'ān by the Prophetic report. This procedure results in the justification for flogging and lapidation for particular types of *zinā* offenders.

Indeed, some Muslim legal authorities make use of various narratives to dispute the dual penalty—flogging then stoning—conveyed in the 'Ubāda hadith. While acknowledging the authenticity of the 'Ubāda report,[33] al-Shāfi'ī remarks that flogging is abrogated for a non-virgin (*al-jald mansūkh 'an al-thayyib*).[34] To support his argument, he brings into service the Mā'iz report, among others.[35] Al-Shāfi'ī writes that lashes are not mentioned in any of these reports, which means that the flogging mandate for the non-virgin is inoperative.[36] The Ḥanafī jurist al-Sarakhsī (d. 483/1090) alternatively opines that Q4:15 is abrogated by the Ubāda hadith, which in turn is abrogated by Q24:2. He then employs the Mā'iz and the Day-Laborer hadith, among others, to justify stoning only for someone with *iḥṣān*.[37] In fact, both he and al-Shāfi'ī argue that in the Day-Laborer report, the Prophet commands Unays to only stone the wife, not to flog *and* stone her. This directive affirms the abrogation of the 'Ubāda hadith.[38] Indeed, the Ḥanbalī judge Abū Ya'lā (d. 458/1066) writes that if the Prophet had intended both flogging and stoning, then he would have made it explicit to Unays.[39] But a later Ḥanbalī jurist, Ibn Qudāma, states that the proper punishment is both flogging and stoning.[40] He criticizes his predecessors by stating that the *ex silentio* argument—that the Prophet did not explicitly order lashes—is not sufficiently probative to eliminate the requirement of flogging.[41] Ibn Qudāma goes on to employ the reports attributed to

[32] Muqātil, *Tafsīr*, 372.
[33] al-Shāfi'ī, *al-Umm*, 8:461.
[34] al-Shāfi'ī, *al-Umm*, 7:336.
[35] al-Shāfi'ī, *al-Umm*, 7:336.
[36] In order to date al-Shāfi'ī's *Risāla*, Pavlovitch investigates the debates about the use of a single versus dual penalty for *zinā*. He concludes that Norman Calder's claim that the *Risāla* was composed toward the end of the third-century AH and Christopher Melchert's assertion that it was produced in 300 AH are not entirely correct. For Pavlovitch, some parts of the *Risāla* may have been redacted into the original text, but al-Shāfi'ī is the original author. Pavlovitch does not identify when the work was completed. See generally, Pavlovitch, "The Islamic Penalty for Adultery in the Third Century AH and al-Shāfiī's *Risāla*."
[37] al-Sarakhsī, *al-Mubsūṭ*, 9:36f.
[38] al-Shāfi'ī, *al-Umm*, 7:337.
[39] Abū Ya'lā, *Masā'il al-fiqhiyya*, 2:314. For another example of a Muslim legal authority arguing for stoning only, see the Mālikī jurist Ibn Abī Zayd, *al-Nawādir wa-l-ziyādāt*, 14:232.
[40] Ibn Qudāma, *al-Mughnī*, 12:308ff; the Ḥanbalī jurist al-Khiraqī provides both opinions but does not give his own position on the correct punishment. See al-Khiraqī, *Mukhtaṣar*, 190.
[41] Ibn Qudāma, *al-Mughnī*, 12:314.

particular Companions (see below) to affirm the dual sanction.[42] He asserts that Q24:2 is a general command, the Prophetic practice a specification (*takhṣīṣ*) of that command, and the practice of certain Companions evidence of the dual penalty's continued validity.[43]

Disputes about the single penalty versus the dual penalty, in my view, reveal the existence of uncertainty about the validity of *zinā*-stoning. In other words, the uncertainty appears to have been resolved by applying both forms of punishment. The fourth Sunnī caliph after the death of the Prophet and the first Shīʿī Imām ʿAlī b. Abī Ṭālib (d. 40/661) is also recounted to have based stoning on the Prophetic *sunna* and flogging on the Qur'ān. In other words, he upheld the dual punishment. The Kūfan jurist ʿĀmir al-Shaʿbī (d. *c.* 105/723) remarked:[44]

> ʿAlī said regarding the non-virgin (*thayyib*): I flog them based on the Qur'ān and I stone them based on the Prophetic *sunna*.[45]

In another report, also on the authority of al-Shaʿbī, ʿAlī's supposed reasoning is fleshed out with a detailed story about a self-confessing woman. The *matn* reads:

> A non-virgin pregnant woman from Hamdān was brought before ʿAlī. Her name was Shurāḥa and she had committed *zinā*. ʿAlī remarked: Perhaps the man forcibly had sex with you.
>
> She responded: No.
>
> ʿAlī then said: Perhaps the man had sex with you without you knowing it because you are a heavy sleeper.
>
> She responded: No.
>
> ʿAlī then said: Perhaps your husband is from among our enemies and you are trying to protect him.
>
> She responded: No.
>
> ʿAlī took the woman into custody until she gave birth. He then had her flogged 100 times on the fifth day and stoned on Friday. At the time of

[42] Ibn Qudāma, *al-Mughnī*, 12:309f.
[43] Ibn Qudāma, *al-Mughnī*, 12:310.
[44] The Syrian jurist Ibn Shihāb al-Zuhrī comments that al-Shaʿbī was the best legal authority in Kūfa. See al-Khaṭīb al-Baghdādī, *Tārīkh*, 14:144.
[45] ʿAbd al-Razzāq, *al-Muṣannaf*, 7:328, no. 13,356.

> stoning, he instructed people to dig a hole for her near the market. The people then surrounded her and struck her with whips. ʿAlī said: This is not the same as stoning. If you do this, then some of you will kill one another because you will hit each other. Rather, make straight lines the way you do when performing communal prayers. Remember people, when the offender self-confesses, the first person to stone them is the Imām. If four witnesses testify against the offender, then the first people to stone are the witnesses, then the Imām, and then everyone else.
>
> ʿAlī struck Shurāḥa with a stone, made the *takbīr*, and then instructed the first row of people: Throw stones at her and move away.
>
> He gave the same command to each successive line until she perished.[46]

The Iraqi Masrūq b. al-Ajdaʿ (d. *c.* 62/681) accordingly opines that those of venerable age (*shaykh*) are to be flogged and stoned.[47]

Many proponents of the single penalty can generally be found outside of Iraq, though not exclusively. The Meccan jurist ʿAṭāʾ b. Abī Rabāḥ (d. 115/733) opines that a person with *iḥṣān* receives stoning only.[48] The same opinion is given by another Meccan jurist, ʿAmr b. Dīnār (d. 126/744).[49] In the *Mudawwana*, the Mālikī jurist Saḥnūn asks his teacher Ibn Qāsim (d. 191/806) about Mālik's (a Medinan) position on the dual penalty:

> What was Mālik's opinion about combining the punishment of flogging (*al-ḥadd*) with stoning for *zinā* when committed by a non-virgin? Ibn Qāsim said: It is not permissible. The non-virgin receives stoning only (*al-thayyib ḥaddahu al-rajm bi-ghayr jald*).[50]

Inside Iraq, the Ḥanafī jurists Abū Yūsuf (d. 182/798) and Muḥammad al-Shaybānī prescribe stoning only (just as the Iraqi al-Sarakhsī noted above).[51]

[46] ʿAbd al-Razzāq, *al-Muṣannaf*, 7:326f, no. 13,350; ʿAlī's attempts to dissuade the offender from confessing become part of the judicial procedure when someone confesses to *zinā*. See, e.g., al-Qudūrī, *Mukhtaṣar*, 198; the report also conveys that a woman can be convicted on the basis of pregnancy alone—a legal standard generally accepted by the Malikīs. See, e.g., Abū Saʿīd al-Barādhiʿī, *al-Tahdhīb fī ikhtiṣār al-mudawwana*, 4:415–7.

[47] ʿAbd al-Razzāq, *al-Muṣannaf*, 7:329, no. 13,361; Ibn Abī Shayba, *al-Muṣannaf* (2011 ed.), 5:541, no. 28,787; al-Nasāʾī, *al-Sunan al-kubrā*, 6:407, no. 7,111; Masrūq also remarks that those who have sex with non-human animals should receive the dual penalty. See Ibn Abī Shayba, *al-Muṣannaf* (1989 ed.), 5:513, no. 28,515.

[48] ʿAbd al-Razzāq, *al-Muṣannaf*, 7:304, no. 13,276, 7:319, no. 13,334, 7:324, no. 13,345, and 7:337, no. 13,393.

[49] ʿAbd al-Razzāq, *al-Muṣannaf*, 7:304, no. 13,276 and 364, no. 13,489f.

[50] Saḥnūn, *al-Mudawwana*, 4:504.

[51] Abū Yūsuf, *Kitāb al-kharāj*, 162–4; al-Shaybānī, *Jāmiʿ al-ṣaghīr*, 279 and 286.

In the case of Aḥmad b. Ḥanbal (d. 241/855), both positions are attributed to him. It is possible that he held differing viewpoints on the matter or, alternatively, at a level of doctrinal uncertainty on his part or that of his students. For example, his son Ṣāliḥ (d. 265/878) argues that his father called for the *muḥṣan* to be stoned only.[52] But Ibn Ḥanbal's other son, ʿAbd Allāh (d. 290/902), claims that his father upheld the dual penalty for the non-virgin.[53] The debates surrounding the lawfulness of the single penalty versus the dual penalty accentuate the different ways in which Muslim authorities attempted to reconcile seemingly contradictory reports to develop laws on *zinā*-stoning.

1.2.2. Cases involving Companions and *zinā*-stoning

In addition to the aforementioned, other Companions are recorded to have adjudicated *zinā*-stoning cases or purportedly made statements about the lawfulness of *zinā*-stoning. For instance, ʿUmar b. al-Khaṭṭāb (d. 23/644) is often cited as someone who advocates for the stoning punishment. In Mālik's *Muwaṭṭa'*, one entry reads:

> ʿUmar b. al-Khaṭṭāb was brought a case involving a marriage contract that no one witnessed except a man and a woman.[54] ʿUmar said: This is a secret marriage (*nikāḥ al-sirr*) and I do not approve of it. Had I made mention of this before (*law kuntu taqaddamtu*), I would apply the stoning punishment.[55]

Another case involves a confession:

> A man brought a charge against his wife in the presence of ʿUmar b. al-Khaṭṭāb, while in al-Shām,[56] by alleging that he discovered his wife with another man. ʿUmar sent Abū Wāqid to the man's wife to ask her about the matter. When Abū Wāqid arrived at the accused's residence, he observed her socializing in the company of women. He told her about what her husband said to ʿUmar b. al-Khaṭṭāb and advised her not to [confess to] the

[52] Abū al-Faḍl Ṣāliḥ, *Masā'il al-Imām Aḥmad b. Ḥanbal*, 3:119, no. 1,469f.
[53] ʿAbd Allāh, *Masā'il al-Imām Aḥmad*, 348f, no. 1,284. I interpret the non-virgin here to signify a *muḥṣan*.
[54] It is unclear from the text whether the man and the woman are in fact the husband and wife.
[55] Mālik, *Muwaṭṭa'*, 767, no. 1,960; al-Bayhaqī, *al-Sunan al-kubrā*, 7:204, no. 13,726.
[56] Unclear from the report if it was ʿUmar or the man.

> accusation in order to avoid conviction. [Rather,] Abū Wāqid tried to make her [confess] to a lesser offense, one that would be similar to the original charge by her husband but not the same exact thing. She refused and instead confessed to the original charge. ʿUmar issued the ruling and she was stoned to death.[57]

ʿUmar is recalled to have proclaimed that stoning is prescribed for Muslims. In one version, he asserts that the capital punishment is mandated by the Book of God. The Companion ʿAbd Allāh b. ʿAbbās (d. 68/687) is recorded to have said:

> I heard ʿUmar b. al-Khaṭṭāb say: Stoning is in the Book of God and compulsory upon anyone who commits *zinā*, be it a man or a woman. The conditions needed to stone someone are *iḥṣān* and witness testimony, confession, or in the case of a woman, pregnancy.[58]

In another variant, ʿUmar is even reported to have referenced an elusive verse from scripture in support of stoning:

> ʿUmar said: I'm afraid that people will one day say, 'We do not find stoning in the Book of God.' Such people will be among those who will go astray and leave behind religious obligations mandated by God. Indeed, stoning is required for a man that is a *muḥṣan* and evidence such as pregnancy or a confession can convict him. I know I have read the stoning verse. It stated: 'The *shaykh* and the *shaykha*, when they commit *zinā*, stone them both.' The Prophet ordered the stoning punishment and we stoned after his death.[59]

In Chapter 4, I analyze several transmission chains and their corresponding textual content to argue that not only does the report reflect a likely historical moment when communal debates *writ large* existed about *zinā*-stoning's legitimacy, but that ʿUmar's authority (at least for Sunnī Muslims) was used to justify and stabilize the punishment for a specific category of *zinā* offenders. For example, the third-/ninth-century ascetic al-Ḥārith b. Asad

[57] Mālik, *Muwaṭṭa'*, 1202, no. 3,043.
[58] See, e.g., Mālik, *Muwaṭṭa'*, 1201, no. 630/3,042.
[59] Ibn Abī Shayba, *al-Muṣannaf* (2011 ed.), v. 9, 354:29,354.

al-Muḥāsibī (d. 243/857) argues that in accordance with 'Umar's proclamation, a verse existed that mandated stoning for *zinā* offenders. Al-Muḥāsibī then stipulates that while this verse is not part of the 'Uthmānī recension, the verse was memorized, thereby indicating its existence. Accordingly, its enforcement power remains.[60] For him, the verse's absence from the Qur'ān does not constitute its removal from the class of divinely revealed text or imply the suspension of the prescriptions given in it.[61] It is, however, worth mentioning that 'Umar's position is inconsistent with the hadith according to which 'Alī states that he orders the stoning punishment based on the Prophet's authority, not the Qur'ān.

'Uthmān is also recorded to have presided over cases in which he imposed the stoning punishment for *zinā*. One report reads:

> 'Uthmān b. 'Affān was brought a woman who gave birth after six months [of marriage], so he ordered that she be stoned. 'Alī b. Abī Ṭālib said to him: She is not subject to stoning. Indeed God says, "Pregnancy and care taking are for 30 months . . .[62]" and "Mothers may nurse their children for the entirety of two years if they wish to complete the nursing period.[63]" Since pregnancy was only six months of the total allotted time [of nursing], she is not subject to the stoning punishment.
>
> 'Uthmān nevertheless sought her out and once he found her, he had her stoned.[64]

It is clear from this narrative that 'Uthmān accepts stoning as part of Islam.

In sum, this section has provided several Prophetic and non-Prophetic reports involving cases of illicit sexual intercourse in which stoning is prescribed as a punishment. Several themes emerge throughout these narratives: *zinā* is prohibited, certain forms are punishable by stoning, and offenders are in fact stoned. In many of the cases involving the Prophet, the offender is also given several opportunities to recant their confession. The accounts raise questions about whether *zinā*-stoning's justification rests on the basis of the Qur'ān, the Prophet's authority, or both. The reports are of

[60] al-Muḥāsibī, *Fahm al-Qur'ān*, 1:256, 398, and 455.
[61] al-Muḥāsibī, *Fahm al-Qur'ān*, 1:398.
[62] Q46:15.
[63] Q2:233.
[64] Mālik, *Muwaṭṭa'*, 1204, no. 3,045; 'Abd al-Razzāq, *al-Muṣannaf*, 7:351, no. 13,447; al-Bayhaqī, *Sunal al-kubrā*, 7:727f, no. 15,551.

great utility to Muslim authorities in their arguments about the lawfulness of *zinā*-stoning.

1.3. Non-Virginity and *Iḥṣān* as Legal Elements for *Zinā*-Stoning

The review I provide in this section helps to shed light on the relationship between non-virginity and *iḥṣān* on the one hand and to flesh out some of the broader implications these elements have for *zinā*-stoning on the other. The survey is neither exhaustive nor within the primary scope of this book. However, understanding the different ways in which pre-modern Muslim authorities conceptualized non-virginity and *iḥṣān* as legal elements for the stoning punishment reveals a dynamic between legal doctrine and a practice that was not borne within that very system. To state it more directly, in my view, debates around the legal contingencies necessitating *zinā*-stoning reveal that a number of early Muslim jurists were attempting to justify a punishment about whose origins and normativity they may have been unsure of themselves.

1.3.1. Non-virginity

The term *thayyib* (non-virgin) is a hapax legomenon in the Qur'ān. In Chapter 66, *al-Taḥrīm* (Prohibition), it states:

> 5 . . . who turn to God in repentance and worship God, who fast, whether *thayyibāt* or *abkār*.

One can reasonably conclude that a *thayyib* (pl. *thayyibāt*) is a non-virgin, given its contrast to *bikr* (pl. *abkār*), virgin. According to *Lisān al-ʿArab*, a *thayyib* is also used to reference a divorcé or widow from a previously consummated marriage.[65] Recall the use of *bikr* and *thayyib* in the 'Ubāda hadith:

[65] Ibn Manẓūr, *Lisān al-ʿArab*, 1:248.

> The Prophet said: Listen to what I have to say. God has made a way for them (*la-hunna*). A non-virgin (*thayyib*) who has illicit sexual intercourse with a non-virgin (*thayyib*) is to receive 100 lashes and stoning. A virgin (*bikr*) who has illicit sexual intercourse with a virgin (*bikr*) is to receive 100 lashes and one year's banishment.

Some uses of *thayyib* exclude men, but in others, men are included.[66] The term is also used to connote a person of a mature age, regardless of their sexual status.[67] Mālik (d. 179/795) presumes that the term *shaykh*, used to refer to a person of venerable age, is synonymous with *thayyib*.[68] Ultimately, the legal opinion is that a *thayyib* is simply a non-virgin regardless of gender.

In the Islamic legal tradition, non-virginity (*thuyūba*) impacts a person's degree of legal responsibility in both civil and criminal matters. For instance, the Prophet is recorded to have said that a non-virgin woman is entitled to independence over her own affairs.[69] In another report, a non-virgin woman complained to the Prophet that her father had married her off without her consent, and the Prophet granted her the right to annul the marriage if she so chose.[70] The Meccan jurist ʿAṭāʾ b. Abī Rabāḥ (d. 115/733) opined that a father is permitted to marry his daughter without her consent only if she is a virgin.[71] Clearly, a correlation exists between non-virginity and autonomy/higher levels of responsibility. This interrelationship explains why someone like Mālik has an overlapping understanding of a *thayyib* and a *shaykh*.[72] Culturally, the older a person is, the more likely they are presumed to be autonomous in decision-making.

The connection between non-virginity as representing autonomy and responsibility is exemplified in instances of heterosexual *zinā* transgressions.[73] Specifically, it is a *thayyib* that is necessarily subject to lapidation. But with this qualification and ostensible clarity come more questions. Is a non-virgin

[66] Ibn Manẓūr, *Lisān al-ʿArab*, 1:248.
[67] Ibn Manẓūr, *Lisān al-ʿArab*, 1:248.
[68] Mālik, *Muwaṭṭaʾ*, 1204, no. 3,045; Mālik's opinion was within the purview of reports according to which a stoning verse existed. The purported verse stated that a *shaykh* and *shaykha* are to be stoned. Mālik said that a *thayyib* and *shaykh* are the same thing. For a more detailed examination of this report, see Chapter 4.
[69] ʿAbd al-Razzāq, *al-Muṣannaf*, 6:142, no. 10,284, 6:143, no. 10,286; al-Ḥumaydī, *Musnad*, 1:452, no. 527.
[70] ʿAbd al-Razzāq, *al-Muṣannaf*, 6:145, no. 10,305.
[71] ʿAbd al-Razzāq, *al-Muṣannaf*, 6:144, no. 10,294.
[72] Also see Chapter 4, pp. 297–298 on the relationship between *thayyib* and *shaykh*.
[73] Reportedly, ʿUmar b. al-Khaṭṭāb prohibited a non-virgin to designate someone on her behalf to act as her guardian for the purpose of marriage. See al-Shāfiʿī, *al-Umm*, 6:34.

divorcée or widow subject to stoning? Some Muslim authorities address these types of questions while others remain silent. The absence of consistent engagement does not imply a lack of consideration of the legal quandary. In my view, partly to mitigate the challenges that emerge out of the early ambiguities around non-virginity as an element for *zinā*-stoning, Muslim authorities turn to the legal principle of *iḥṣān*. It grants more legal flexibility and precision than non-virginity alone.

1.3.2. *Iḥṣān*

Iḥṣān is the verbal noun of the verb *aḥṣana*, which in turn is the transitive form of *ḥ-ṣ-n*. These verbs mean, among other things, to protect/guard, to make safe, to make something/someone unapproachable, or to make someone chaste.[74] The derivatives of *ḥ-ṣ-n* are used twenty times in the Qur'ān, though the term *iḥṣān* itself is absent.[75] As part of the process of stabilizing *zinā*-stoning, *iḥṣān* becomes one of the most critical legal qualifications. Only Muslims with *iḥṣān* are subject to lapidation if convicted of heterosexual illicit sexual intercourse. In what follows, I compare and contrast the uses of *ḥ-ṣ-n* in the Qur'ān and by Muslim jurists. It becomes clear that, in particular instances, there exists a disconnect between the ways in which the Qur'ān conveys a meaning of the verb or its derivative(s) on the one hand and the ways in which Muslim authorities understand and formulate *iḥṣān* on the other. Indeed, the term *iḥṣān* in Muslim juristic usage conveys an impression of legal precision when compared to the use of non-virginity alone as an element for a *zinā*-stoning conviction. However, the term also presents inherent technical and conceptual challenges. The legal debates about the meaning of *iḥṣān* reveal a confrontation with skepticism about the scriptural lawfulness of *zinā*-stoning and hermeneutical attempts to reconcile such doubt within a larger socio-historical context.

Among the many uses, it is apparent that the Qur'ān employs derivatives of *ḥ-ṣ-n* in connection to sexual relations with a particular focus on chastity, both in the context of abstinence and even of the licit kind.[76] In Chapter Four, *al-Nisā'* (The Women), the Qur'ān states:

[74] Ibn Manẓūr, *Lisān al-ʿArab*, 13:119.

[75] See verses Q4:24f, 5:5, 12:48, 19:20, 19:28, 21:80, 21:91, 24:4, 24:23, 24:33, 59:2, 59:13, and 66:12.

[76] For a survey of the ways in which the terms *muḥṣan* and *muḥṣana*, i.e., derivatives of *ḥ-ṣ-n*, are incorporated in Qur'ān verses different than the ones I use in this section, see Harald Motzki, "Wal-muhsanātu," 194–9 and 205.

> 23 Prohibited to you are your mothers, daughters, sisters
>
> 24 And *al-muḥṣanāt* from among your women except those your right hand possesses (i.e., slaves). This has been ordained for you by God. Lawful to you is any woman beyond the aforementioned categories that you seek [to marry] using your wealth with the aim of being chaste (*muḥṣinīn*), not libertine (*musāfiḥīn*).[77]

Verse 23 focuses on prohibitions for marriage as a function of consanguinity/quasi-kinship, and *al-muḥṣanāt*, in verse 24, represents an additional category to whom marriage is impermissible. Superficially, it is unclear as to who exactly constitutes this category: chaste unmarried or chaste married women.[78] The exegete Muqātil (d. 150/767) narrowly glosses *al-muḥṣanāt* (in Q4:24) as any woman with whom marriage is prohibited on the basis of blood relations.[79] The commentator al-Ṭabarī (d. 310/923) comments that the term is a reference to married women.[80] Moreover, the imprimatur to marry "any woman beyond the aforementioned categories" affirms that *al-muḥṣanāt* in verse 24 means chaste married women.[81] These married, that is, fortified/unapproachable women (*al-muḥṣanāt*), are distinguished from the carve out for "except those your right hand possesses," a formula indicating slaves and, in this case, *muḥṣanāt* slaves. This tracks with Southern Arabian inscriptions, according to which *ḥ-ṣ-n* signifies those under one's protection, including slaves.[82] Who exactly are *al-muḥṣanāt* slaves? The dominant gloss is that they are married non-Muslim women who are prisoners of war.[83] Accordingly, verses 23 and 24 for Muslim exegetes indicate that

[77] Using a *fatḥa* on the *ṣād* formulates the participle of *ḥ-ṣ-n*, i.e., *muḥṣanāt*, into the passive form. This is the form that first appears in v. 24. However, later in the verse, the vowel on the *ṣād* is a *kasra*, i.e., *muḥṣinīn*, thereby making it an active participle. Joseph Witztum believes the difference is not without consequence and, accordingly, vowels all appearances of the participle to exhibit it in the active form. See generally Witztum, "Q4:24 Revised."

[78] Karen Bauer and Feras Hamza, *Women, Households, and the Hereafter*, 264–6.

[79] Muqātil, *Tafsīr*, 1:366.

[80] al-Ṭabarī, *Jāmiʿ*, 8:155–8 and 161f; for al-Ṭabarī's own opinion, see al-Ṭabarī, *Jāmiʿ*, 165; al-Ṭabarī does provide a set of reports that support Muqātil's position. See al-Ṭabarī, *Jāmiʿ*, 8:158–60.

[81] Bauer and Hamza, *Women, Households, and the Hereafter*, 266.

[82] Zellentin, *Law Beyond Israel*, 216.

[83] For example, see Mujāhid, *Tafsīr*, 271; Ibn Wahb, *Tafsīr*, 1:80, no. 179; Ibn Abī Shayba, *al-Muṣannaf* (1989 ed.), 3:537f, nos. 16,888–96; *cf* al-Ṭabarī, *Jāmiʿ*, 8:151–5, wherein al-Ṭabarī provides opinions according to which the carve out signifies purchased married slaves; he also records a single report on the authority of Ibn ʿAbbās in which he reportedly said that he did not know who constitutes "except those your right hand possesses." See al-Ṭabarī, *Jāmiʿ*, 8:165, no. 9,013; Motzki argues that the beginning of Q4:24 is an interpolation into the pericope, likely by the Prophet himself. On this basis and intertextual analysis, he concludes that the carve out represents female slaves who can be taken as concubines. See Motzki, "Wal-muhsanātu," 215f; *cf* Witztum, "Q4:24 Revised," 10f.

al-muḥṣanāt—married women—constitute a part of a class of women with whom men may not enjoy sexual intercourse, with an exception for non-Muslim prisoners of war, who, on the basis of their slave status, can become accessible.

Even if the Qur'ān proscribes marriage to *al-muḥṣanāt* based on consanguinity/quasi-kinship or marriage, it also makes evident that the category can include unmarried women to whom marriage is permissible. In Chapter 24 *al-Nisā'* (The Women), it states:

> 25 Whosoever cannot afford to marry a believing chaste woman (pl., *al-muḥṣanāt al-mu'mināt*), then marry a believing slave girl [i.e., in the prime of life] from among your slaves (*mā malakat aymānukum min fatayātikum al-mu'mināt*).

Al-muḥṣanāt al-mu'mināt refers to women who uphold their chastity. Note that the verse is silent as to whether such women are virgins or non-virgins, which means the category constitutes both. These women are the ones to whom marriage is considered permissible. Together, a reading of verses 23–25 indicates that *al-muḥṣanāt* may refer to unmarried and married women, virgins and non-virgins, and non-Muslim married slaves.

The religious status of believing chaste women, *al-muḥṣanāt al-mu'mināt*, is not entirely clear in Q4:23–5. Verse five from Chapter Five of al-Mā'ida (The Feast) makes it plain that these women can be Muslim or non-Muslim:

> 5 Today, [God] has made all good things permissible to you. The [same] food that the People of the Book consume, you are permitted to consume. [Likewise,] *al-muḥṣanāt* from among the believing women and *al-muḥṣanāt* from the people that were given the Scripture before you.

The exegete Muqātil (d. 150/767) remarks that "*al-muḥṣanāt* from among the believing women" is a reference to chaste women with good public standing, and "*al-muḥṣanāt* of the people who were given the Scripture" means free, chaste Jewish and Christian women with good public standing.[84] The combination of Q4:23–5 and Q5:5 indicates that *al-muḥṣanāt* encompasses unmarried and married women, virgins and non-virgins, Muslims and non-Muslim, and non-Muslim married slaves.

[84] Muqātil, *Tafsīr*, 1:455.

Even though Q4:24 construes non-Muslim married slaves as part of *al-muḥṣanāt*, the Qur'ān conveys that other kinds of slaves can also comprise the category. In Chapter 24, we find:

> 33 Do not force your slave girls into illicit sexual relations (*al-bighā'*) if they wish to be chaste. You do so simply in pursuit of worldly gains. But if they are forced into such situations, God will be merciful and forgive them [but not to you].

According to al-Ṭabarī (d. 310/923), the general understanding of *bighā'* is *zinā*, illicit sexual intercourse.[85] There is, however, disagreement about the nature of this prohibited act. In that it is tied to coercion, some argue that it is for the purpose of prostitution, while others claim that it has to do with some kind of *zinā*.[86] Whatever the case may be, I wish to focus on the conditional clause: "if they wish to be chaste." The Arabic is *taḥaṣṣun*(*an*), the verbal-noun derivative of *taḥaṣṣana*, that is, to self-fortify/guard/make chaste. Muqātil (d. 150/767) comments that the term means a refusal to commit grave offenses (*fawāḥish*).[87] The exegete Ibn Wahb (d. 197/812) provides a specific occasion for the verse's revelation. Supposedly, an individual, upon getting drunk, would have sex with his two female slaves. One night, he desired to do the same, but was prevented from doing so because the slaves had converted to Islam and wished to maintain their chastity against illicit sexual relations.[88] The association of a derivative of *ḥ-ṣ-n* with a female slave indicates that they can be part of the *muḥṣanāt* class if they so choose. Therefore, the numerous uses of the term *al-muḥṣanāt* in the Qur'ān forge a rank that references unmarried and married women, virgins and non-virgins, Muslims and non-Muslims—presumably Jewish and Christian, free persons and slaves, and non-Muslim married slaves who are prisoners of war.

In a move necessary to make room for *zinā*-stoning within the Islamic rubric of punishments, the broad category of *al-muḥṣanāt* is redefined in the

[85] al-Ṭabarī, *Jāmi'* (ed. al-Turkī), 17:290.

[86] For the various opinions, see al-Ṭabarī, *Jāmi'* (ed. al-Turkī), 290–4; Zellentin, *Law Beyond Israel*, 186, n. 124 (cont.); *cf* Bauer and Hamza argue that *bighā'* likely does not mean prostitution because the act itself is morally wrongful and because elsewhere in the Qur'ān, the term does not connote prostitution. See Bauer and Hamza, *Women, Households, and the Hereafter*, 204f.

[87] Muqātil, *Tafsīr*, 3:198.

[88] Ibn Wahb, *Tafsīr*, 1:129, no. 297. This of course raises additional questions about Q4:24, Q16:71, and other verses according to which sex with slaves can be licit. A separate and more detailed analysis is necessary to determine how Ibn Wahb's comments may be reconciled with these verses.

post-revelatory period. The legal term *iḥṣān*, as well as the verbal noun of the participle *muḥsan/a* and the verb *aḥṣana*, becomes subject to co-optation, debate, and negotiation within the Islamic legal tradition. Eventually, only those Muslims with *iḥṣān* become subjected to lapidation if convicted of unlawful sexual intercourse.

What follows is a sample of legal discussions on *iḥṣān*. It covers opinions that emerged during the first two centuries of Islam to those of jurists belonging to the third/ninth century. In early juristic discussions, *muḥsan/a*, that is, someone with *iḥṣān*, is restricted to someone who consummates a lawful marriage. This opinion does not reflect the diversity of usages in the Qur'ān as discussed above. The Meccan jurist 'Aṭā' b. Abī Rabāḥ (d. 115/733) states:

> *Iḥṣān* is when a [married] man has sexual intercourse with [his wife]. Without [consummation] there is no *iḥṣān*, and there is no stoning until witnesses testify that they saw the male member disappear into her.[89]

The Syrian jurist Ibn Shihāb al-Zuhrī (d. 124/742) asserts:

> When a man marries a woman and commits *zinā* before consummating the marriage, he does not have *iḥṣān*.[90]

Recall from Q4:25 and Q5:5 that *al-muḥṣanāt* includes unmarried virgin or non-virgin women. For both 'Aṭā' and al-Zuhrī, virgins cannot have *iḥṣān*. It is only after consummation in an active marriage that a person acquires *iḥṣān* and, accordingly, becomes a *muḥṣan/a*.

Muslim legal authorities also considered cases involving non-Muslims and whether the latter could be considered (pl.) *muḥṣanūn/-āt*. The Iraqi-Baṣran jurist Qatāda b. Di'āma (d. *c*. 117/735) opines:

> If a man has *iḥṣān* as a non-Muslim and then converts to Islam, he does not have *iḥṣān* until he has sexual relations as a Muslim.[91]

[89] 'Abd al-Razzāq, *al-Muṣannaf*, 7:304, no. 13,276.
[90] Abd al-Razzāq, *al-Muṣannaf*, 7:305, no. 13,279.
A similar opinion is noted by the Companion Jābir b. 'Abd Allāh (d. 78/697) who is recorded to have said:
When a virgin man gets married and commits *zinā* before he consummates his marriage, he is flogged, not stoned. See 'Abd al-Razzāq, *al-Muṣannaf*, 7:304, no. 13,277.
[91] 'Abd al-Razzāq, *al-Muṣannaf*, 7:308f, no. 13,302.

For Qatāda, there are two kinds of *iḥṣān*. One exists for a non-Muslim and another after conversion to Islam and consummation. It is only after becoming Muslim and consummating a lawful marriage that the person becomes subject to *zinā*-stoning. An Iraqi-Kūfan jurist, Ibrāhīm al-Nakha'ī (d. 96/714), dismisses the notion of *iḥṣān* for non-Muslims altogether. For him, it can only be established after a person becomes a Muslim and has sexual intercourse.[92] Their positions modify Q5:5's expression of *al-muḥṣanāt*, wherein conversion and consummation are irrelevant. Al-Zuhrī (d. 124/742), on the other hand, remains consistent with the Qur'ān. He is recorded to have stated:

> If a non-Muslim gets married, consummates his marriage, converts to Islam, and commits *zinā*, he is stoned on the basis of his *iḥṣān* and because he is originally from among the People of Book. If he does not belong to the People of the Book, he is not stoned.[93]

The Iraqi jurist al-Ḥasan al-Baṣrī (d. 110/728) is in agreement since he is reported to have said that the *iḥṣān* of Jews and Christians carries over in the cases of conversion to Islam and is the same as *iḥṣān* of a Muslim.[94] It is possible that because they are Iraqis, Qatāda and Ibrāhīm are referring to non-Muslims who were Zoroastrians and thus not of the People of the Book (given al-Zuhrī's insistence that People of the Book are subject to lapidation). Qatāda's and Ibrāhīm's opinion might indicate excusing based upon ignorance of the ruling rather than *iḥṣān*. Whatever the case may be, the legal opinions of Qatāda, al-Nakha'ī, al-Zuhrī, and al-Ḥasan al-Baṣrī show that religious affiliation and consummation could determine *iḥṣān*. Accordingly, the definition of *iḥṣān* is potentially more restrictive when compared to the Qur'ān because there is a narrowing of the term's scope and application in some respects. The opinions are also noteworthy because they would imply that, under certain iterations of the law, non-virgins who, prior to their conversion to Islam, were *not* from among the People of the Book, would *not* be subject to the capital punishment. This is rather unusual insofar as what would appear to be one and the same transgression is treated differently, even among offenders who, at the time of the infraction, belong to the Muslim faith.

[92] 'Abd al-Razzāq, *al-Muṣannaf*, 7:308f, no. 13,303.
[93] 'Abd al-Razzāq, *al-Muṣannaf*, 7:309, no. 13,304; Ibn Abī Shayba, *al-Muṣannaf* (2008 ed.), 9:340, no. 29,270.
[94] Ibn Abī Shayba, *al-Muṣannaf* (2008 ed.), 9:340, no. 29,271.

Discussions about civil status, that is, freedom and slavery, further complicate the conception of *iḥṣān* in the Islamic legal tradition when compared to the Qur'ān. Recall that Q4:24 and Q24:33 affirm that chaste Muslim and non-Muslim slaves can be considered *muḥṣanāt*. The Meccan jurist 'Aṭā' (d. 115/733) holds that marriage does not result in *iḥṣān* for a female slave.[95] He also opines that a marriage between a male slave and a free woman cannot result in *iḥṣān*, presumably for either party.[96] Likewise, al-Nakha'ī (d. 96/714), al-Sha'bī (d. 104/723), and al-Ḥasan al-Baṣrī (d. 110/728) opine that a relationship between a free man and a female slave cannot lead to *iḥṣān* for either party.[97] Qatāda disagrees in part, commenting that a female slave could attain *iḥṣān* through a relationship with a free male, though it is unclear whether the reverse is true.[98] Al-Nakha'ī states that in cases involving a relationship between a male slave and a free woman, the woman cannot attain *iḥṣān*, whereas al-Ḥasan believes that she can.[99] A number of other legal opinions are recorded about the possible ways in which *iḥṣān* could come about from a relationship between a free person and a slave or between two slaves.[100] The point to emphasize here is that many Muslim jurists rule out the possibility that slaves can acquire *iḥṣān*, whereas the Qur'ān's usage of the term does not rule out the possibility and even affirms it in some instances.

Definitions about *iḥṣān* continued to be negotiated in the phase of the legal doctrinal schools (*madhāhib*, s. *madhhab*), beginning with the mid-second/eighth century. For example, the Ḥanafī jurist Muḥammad al-Shaybānī (d. 189/805) delineates the requirements of *iḥṣān* as Islam, freedom (i.e., not slaves), sound-mindedness, post-puberty, and licit sexual relations.[101] If any element from the list is missing, a person cannot be deemed a *muḥṣan/a* and, therefore, not subject to *zinā*-stoning. Al-Shāfi'ī (d. 204/820), a fierce critic of al-Shaybānī's legal thought, opines that a Muslim becomes a *muḥṣan* and

[95] 'Abd al-Razzāq, *al-Muṣannaf*, 7:306, no. 13,283 and 7:307, no. 13,289.

[96] 'Abd al-Razzāq, *al-Muṣannaf*, 7:307, no. 13,290.

[97] 'Abd al-Razzāq, *al-Muṣannaf*, 7:306, no. 13,284f; for al-Nakha'ī's position, see also Ibn Abī Shayba, *al-Muṣannaf* (2008 ed.), 9:347, no. 29,319; for al-Ḥasan's opinion, see Ibn Abī Shayba, *al-Muṣannaf* (2008 ed.), 9:347, no. 29,321; I deliberately use "relationship" because 'Abd al-Razzāq records the opinions of these jurists under the chapter heading, "Marriage to a female slave does not constitute *iḥṣān*." 'Abd al-Razzāq is presuming that such opinions are in relation to a marriage contract. He may be correct, but the reader should be aware that "relationship" could mean marriage, sexual intercourse by virtue of the master–slave relationship, or both.

[98] 'Abd al-Razzāq, *al-Muṣannaf*, 7:306, no. 13,286; al-Ṭabarī, *Jāmi'*, 8:202, no. 9,106.

[99] 'Abd al-Razzāq, *al-Muṣannaf*, 7:307, no. 13,291f; al-Ṭabarī, *Jāmi'*, 8:202, no. 9,105.

[100] E.g., see 'Abd al-Razzāq, *al-Muṣannaf*, 7:307–9, nos. 13,290–304; Ibn Abī Shayba, *al-Muṣannaf* (2008 ed.), 9:346–8, nos. 29,317–27.

[101] al-Shaybānī, *Jāmi' al-Ṣaghīr*, 279.

is subject to stoning after consummation of a lawful marriage with a free Muslim, Christian, or Jewish woman.[102] Importantly, he also remarks that Jews and Christians are capable of having *iḥṣān* and are to be stoned before or after conversion to Islam in the event they commit *zinā*.[103] With a focus on women, the Mālikī jurist Saḥnūn (d. 240/854) notes that, according to Mālik, a female Muslim who gets married without the permission of a guardian and consummates her marriage does *not* acquire *iḥṣān*.[104] Note that despite the variances in these legal opinions, marriage is a necessary condition for *iḥṣān*. And perhaps one of the more important considerations to note is that, in the Qur'ān, individuals *themselves* can become a *muḥṣan/a*.[105] Derivatives of *ḥ-ṣ-n* retain the qualities of both reflexivity and intransitivity. In the Islamic legal tradition, by contrast, derivatives of *ḥ-ṣ-n* convey the concept as transitive, that is, someone makes their sexual partner a *muḥṣan/a*. This, along with some of the other requirements, stands in contrast to the Qur'ān's conception of *iḥṣān* via the use of *al-muḥṣanāt*. The following chart provides a side-by-side comparison of the Qur'ān *muḥṣan/a* and, *iḥṣān*, the legal requirement in the Islamic legal tradition, that makes *zinā*-stoning necessary:

	The Qur'ān *muḥṣan/a*	**The Islamic Legal Tradition** *muḥṣan/a/iḥṣān*
Free persons	Yes	Yes
Slaves	Yes	No
Religious affiliation	Jews, Christians, Muslims	Muslims; Shāfi'īs: Jews, Christians, Muslims
Virgins	Yes	No
Non-virgins	Yes	Yes
Marriage	No	Yes
The requirement of consummation in a lawful marriage	No	Yes
The state of being a *muḥṣan/a*	Reflexive/intransitive	Transitive
Puberty	Silent	Yes

[102] al-Shāfi'ī, *al-Umm*, 7:391.

[103] al-Shāfi'ī, *al-Umm*, 5:709; for al-Shāfi'ī, a person cannot have *iḥṣān* at one time and lose it at another time.

[104] Saḥnūn, *al-Mudawwana*, 2:203.

[105] Motzki makes this point with regard to female slaves. See Motzki, "Wal-muhsanātu," 199–201.

	The Qur'ān *muḥṣan/a*	**The Islamic Legal Tradition** *muḥṣan/a/iḥṣān*
Mental sanity	Silent	Yes
The requirement to confirm *iḥṣān*	No	Possibly; two witnesses[106]

The distillation of the Qur'ān's expansive meanings of *al-muḥṣanāt* by Muslim jurists led to a more delimited conception. There are at least two conclusions to draw from this process. One, this distillation process is an avenue by which Muslim authorities can affirm the use of *zinā*-stoning—for them, those with *iḥṣān* are subject to lapidation in the case of adultery, a more severe form of *zinā*, in accordance with the hadith. Those without *iḥṣān* are subject to 100 lashes in the case of fornication, a less severe form of *zinā*, as per the Qur'ān. Two, *zinā*-stoning had to be absorbed into the Islamic legal tradition, that is, Muslim legal authorities were reckoning with a practice of whose scriptural legitimacy they were unsure.

That a non-Islamic mode of punishment had to be reconciled with an Islamic one can be observed in cases involving the punishment for slaves who commit *zinā*. The tension is consequential because it points to *zinā*-stoning being a post-revelatory punishment. According to Chapter 4, *al-Nisā'* (The Women):

> 25 Whosoever cannot afford to marry a believing chaste woman (pl., *al-muḥṣanāt al-mu'mināt*), then marry a believing slave girl from among your slaves (*mā malakat aymānukum min fatayātikum al-mu'mināt*). God is more knowing about your faith. You are of one another. [If you decide to marry believing slave girls], marry them with the permission of their guardians, with the appropriate bridal gift(s), and with the aim of making them *muḥṣanāt(in)*, not lewd (*musāfiḥāt(in)* that take [sexual] partners in secret. If after acquiring *iḥṣān* [i.e., *aḥṣinna/uḥṣinna*] and commit a grave sexual transgression (*fāḥisha*), they are subject to half of the punishment that [non-slave] *muḥṣanāt* receive.

Note that in the Islamic exegetical and legal tradition, there is a disagreement about the voweling of *aḥṣn*, which I translate as "after acquiring *iḥṣān*." Some read it as *uḥṣinna*, which came to mean slaves who get married. Others read

[106] E.g., see al-Sarakhsī, *al-Mabsūṭ*, 9:42f.

it as *aḥṣinna*, which came to mean slaves who convert to Islam.[107] Whatever the case may be, if, as those belonging to the classical Islamic legal tradition presume, *iḥṣān* in free women triggers death by stoning as the stipulated punishment for *zinā*, then the punishment for slave *muḥṣanāt* guilty of *zinā* renders the Qur'ān prescription nothing short of problematic.[108] Even the classical jurists themselves noted: "slaves with *iḥṣān* cannot receive half of a capital punishment."[109] As I noted above, pre-modern Muslims proscribe slavery as a condition for *iḥṣān*. This jurisprudential shift appears to be the most direct way to reconcile *zinā*-stoning with the scriptural directive for slaves.

An opinion attributed to the Companion Ibn Mas'ūd (d. 32/652) would play an important role in clarifying the applicable punishment in this regard. Ibn Mas'ūd is supposed to have ruled that slaves are to receive 50 lashes, that is, half the penalty of 100 lashes according to Q24:2.[110] The opinion as it has reached us does not clarify Ibn Mas'ūd's reasoning, particularly the shift from stoning to lashing. Even the fact that the 50-lash prescription is likely based on an attempt to harmonize Q4:25 and Q24:2, which came to be understood as stipulating 100 lashes as punishment for free, though, importantly, *unmarried*, non-*muḥṣan zinā* offenders, is not explicitly stated in Ibn Mas'ūd's report but is rather the surmise of the juristic class. This would suggest that the report may very well be an attempt to bridge the gap between *zinā* as it had been conceived in the Qur'ān and *zinā* as it developed in the Islamic legal tradition into a capital offense. At any rate, the report undoubtedly complicates the later tradition's understanding of the Qur'ānic term *muḥṣanāt*. It conveys that there exists a category of *muḥṣan* offenders that is distinct from any of the various usages attested to in the Qur'ān. A slave's *iḥṣān* has been conceived of as somehow being less equivalent—and therefore less consequential—to the *iḥṣān* of free individuals.

For many Muslims, Ibn Mas'ūd's opinion became a legal precedent. For example, Muqātil and al-Ṭabarī note that a slave is to receive fifty lashes.[111] The jurist Qatāda held the same view.[112] 'Alī b. Abī Ṭālib (d. 40/661), 'Abd

[107] See, e.g., al-Jaṣṣāṣ, *Aḥkām*, 3:93, 112, 118, 123f; on this disagreement, see Motzki, "Wal-muhsanātu," 202f.

[108] Burton, *The Sources of Islamic Law*, 145; John Burton, "The Meaning of "Ihsan,"" 62–71.

[109] See, e.g., al-Jaṣṣāṣ, *Aḥkām*, 3:124; Ibn Yūnus, *al-Jāmi'*, 22:369; Ibn Ḥazm, *al-Muḥallā*, 12:179:2,209; Ibn Qudāma, *al-Mughnī*, 12:315.

[110] al-Ṭabarī, *Jāmi'*, 8:200, no. 9,089 and 8:203, no. 9,108; al-Shaybānī, *Kitāb al-āthār*, 533, no. 615.

[111] al-Muqātil, *Tafsīr*, 1:367f; al-Ṭabarī, *Jāmi'*, 8:203.

[112] al-Ṭabarī, *Jāmi'*, 8:204, no. 9,109.

Allāh b. ʿUmar (d. 73/692), Anas b. Mālik (d. 93/712), Ḥammād b. Sulaymān (d. 120/737), and al-Zuhrī, among others, agreed that slaves are not subject to stoning.[113] By the last quarter of the second century, the dominant view was that slaves who commit *zinā* are to receive fifty lashes irrespective of their *iḥṣān* status.[114] This was the opinion of al-Shaybānī[115] and al-Shāfiʿī.[116] Yet others did not follow the majority. For example, Abū Thawr (d. 240/854) states that male and female slaves can be *muḥṣan* and be subject to *zinā*-stoning.[117] Inevitably, the challenges raised by the dependent clause of Q4:25, then, had been resolved by Muslim legal authorities by simply treating a slave's *iḥṣān* as inconsequential. Proponents of *zinā*-stoning, at least in part, turned to Ibn Masʿūd's opinion to relieve some of the tension created by Q4:25. To do otherwise would have jeopardized the veracity of lapidation as the stipulated punishment for *muḥṣan/a* offenders of illicit heterosexual intercourse.

Muslim authorities drew upon the Qur'ānic use of *ḥ-ṣ-n* to develop the legal category of *iḥṣān*. In the Islamic legal tradition, the Qur'ānic prescription of 100 lashes became applicable to virgins, unmarried individuals, persons married without consummation, or any other non-*iḥṣān*-bearing *zinā* offenders. Those with *iḥṣān* would be subject to *zinā*-stoning. Another noteworthy outcome of the differences between *ḥ-ṣ-n* as used in the Qur'ān and the Islamic legal tradition in relation to illicit sexual intercourse is that, in the Qur'ān, *ḥ-ṣ-n* in regard to sexual morality can be reflexive and/or intransitive. A person can *choose* to be a *muḥṣan/a* regardless of social status (slave or free), marital status, or sexual experience. In the Islamic legal tradition, the latter two become necessary requirements, and *ḥ-ṣ-n* becomes a transitive verb. One of the two sexual partners needs to make the other a *muḥṣan/a*. In thinking broadly about *iḥṣān*, it appears to me that moral accountability is part of the calculus in determining who is subject to stoning. Certain Muslim jurists opined that once a person is a non-virgin, a certain raised level of moral responsibility and choice devolves upon them that is

[113] ʿAbd al-Razzāq, *al-Muṣannaf*, 7:312f, nos. 13,314–7; for other authorities who prescribed fifty lashes for slaves, see Ibn Abī Shayba, *al-Muṣannaf* (2008 ed.), 9:287, nos. 27,955–7.

[114] Note that certain legal authorities opined that a female slave who commits *zinā* is not subject to a punishment. It is only the case after she is manumitted and engages in the transgression. See ʿAbd al-Razzāq, *al-Muṣannaf*, 7:392:13,595, 397–8:13,618–23.

[115] al-Shaybānī, *Kitāb al-āthār*, 534.

[116] al-Shāfiʿī, *al-Umm*, 6:551 and 7:392.

[117] Ibn Qudāma, *al-Mughnī*, 12:316.

supposedly lacking in both slaves and virgins.[118] Put differently, once a marriage is consummated, the involved parties have the benefit of regular licit sexual access (notwithstanding widows and divorcés). On the other hand, virgins and slaves do not have regular access to licit sex and, therefore, should not be held to the same moral standards as those with *iḥṣān*.[119] Accordingly, and in practical terms, under the enhanced rubric, the more severe offense of adultery would be treated with capital punishment. In contrast, the lesser transgression of fornication would be admonished with a corporeal one.

1.4. The Exegetical Tradition and *Zinā*-Stoning

It may be reasonable to deduce that some of the tensions emerging from the process of making lawful *zinā*-stoning in the Islamic legal tradition can also be found in the Islamic exegetical tradition.[120] Specifically, it could be the case that the *tafsīr* (Qur'ānic exegetical works, pl. *tafāsīr*) throws light on a time period when *zinā*-stoning may not have been deemed Islamic and then, through exegesis, became a part of the *ḥudūd* (fixed punishments). Yet in the works I surveyed, from early on, Muslim exegetes tend to adopt the same mechanisms by which Muslim jurists eventually reconcile the Qur'ānic punishment with the purported tradition of the Prophet. This reality, however, does not vindicate the claim that the Prophet had, in fact, ordered the punishment for certain types of *zinā* offenses. One reason is because of the genealogical nature of *tafsīr*. A Qur'ān commentator, in any given moment, has access to and is a part of a collective heritage of the Islamic tradition.[121] If interpreters of the Qur'ān were participants in the ingrained cultural tradition that aimed to deem *zinā*-stoning Islamic, then it is reasonable to expect that their approaches would track along the same lines as others. Yet, at the same time, there are instances that indicate a certain level of uncertainty on

118 For a more complete picture of the ethics at stake in defining *iḥṣān*, it will be necessary to explore legal discussions of its use in relation to the *ḥadd* punishment for a wrongful accusation of sexual impropriety (*qadhf*).

119 The Shīʿī jurist al-Najafī (d. 1266/1849) records opinions according to which when licit sexual access is not possible, such as when a partner is imprisoned or traveling, the commission of *zinā* results in flogging only for a *muḥṣan/a*. See al-Najafī, *al-Jawāhir*, 42:421–3.

120 For an overview on the nature, history, and historiography of Qur'ānic exegesis (*tafsīr*), see, e.g., Andrew Rippin, *The Qur'an and Its Interpretative Tradition*; Walid A. Saleh, *The Formation of the Classical Tafsīr Tradition*; Walid A. Saleh, "Preliminary Remarks on the Historiography of *tafsīr* in Arabic;" Abdullah Saeed, *Interpreting the Qur'ān*.

121 I use "genealogical" as articulated and defined by Saleh, *Formation of the Classical Tafsīr Tradition*, 14–6.

the part of an exegete. In what follows, I examine the prevailing interpretation of *zinā*-stoning in Qur'ān commentaries and then present alternative understandings of the punishment's place in the Islamic tradition.

I begin with exegetical opinions from those belonging to what I call the "pro-*zinā*-stoning camp." The famous Companion 'Abd Allāh b. 'Abbās (d. 68/687) is recorded to have stated that Q4:15, "... those of your women who [may have] committed a sexual transgression," refers to free *muḥṣanāt*, and "confine the [convicted women] to [their] houses until death overtakes them or God provides another way" is the abrogation of imprisonment with the stoning punishment.[122] Here, we observe the narrowing of the definition of *muḥṣanāt* when compared to other Qur'ānic uses of the term. We can also observe the impact of *zinā*-stoning, having already become the going punishment, as it is referenced as a punishment that can override a divine directive without the need to cite an authoritative source. As for Q24:2, "the woman and man who commit illicit sexual intercourse, flog each of them 100 times," Ibn 'Abbās opines that the verse has in mind virgins who commit *zinā*.[123] Mujāhid b. Jabr (d. *c.* 100/718) applies a more bird's eye take on both verses. Regarding Q4:15, he states that it designates *zinā* and, on Q24:2, is silent.[124] The commentary by al-Ḍaḥḥāk (d. 105/723) puts him somewhat in between Ibn 'Abbās and Mujāhid regarding Q4:15's promise that "God provides another way." He writes that this phrase means the *ḥadd* (fixed punishment) of either flogging or stoning and that these punishments abrogate the verse.[125] He does not comment on Q24:2.[126] Yaḥyā b. Sallām (d. 200/815) writes that Q24:2 is for *zinā* cases involving non-*muḥsān* transgressors. If the person is a *muḥṣan*, then the stoning punishment applies.[127] The evolving nature of the *tafsīr* tradition as a whole can be observed in the work of Ibn Sallām. After providing his explanation, he cites a report on the authority of the Companion Jābir b. 'Abd Allāh (d. 78/697) and writes:

> Regarding a virgin who gets married and commits *zinā* before consummating the marriage with his wife, [Jābir] said that he is flogged and not stoned unless he becomes a *muḥṣan*. And as for slaves, each is flogged 50 times and they are not subject to the stoning punishment.[128]

122 Ibn 'Abbās, *Tanwīr al-miqbās*, 87.
123 Ibn 'Abbās, *Tanwīr al-miqbās*, 367.
124 Mujāhid, *Tafsīr*, 269 and 489, respectively.
125 Al-Ḍaḥḥāk, *Tafsīr*, 278.
126 Al-Ḍaḥḥāk, *Tafsīr*, 607.
127 Ibn Sallām, *Tafsīr*, 1:422.
128 Ibn Sallām, *Tafsīr*, 1:422f.

Ibn Sallām continues by speaking about the legal procedures needed for conviction, for example, his mention of the testimony of four witnesses. He employs both hadith and jurisprudence in this gloss of the Qur'ān verse. Reconciliation between Q4:15, Q24:2, and *zinā*-stoning is cemented, as more exegetical commentaries emerge during and after the third/ninth century. This is the general case for both Sunnī and Twelver Shīʿī commentators.[129] What is generally observable is that the commentators surveyed reveal an environment wherein questions about the lawfulness of *zinā*-stoning are settled, and there exists a general understanding of the possible ways in which to resolve any tension that the punishment potentially creates with the Qur'ānic prescription of corporeal punishment for *zinā* offenses.

Despite the widespread acceptance of *zinā*-stoning in numerous glosses of the relevant Qur'ān verses, there are reports indicating that some did express uncertainty regarding its applicability to Muslims.[130] For example, as I noted in Section 1.2, a hadith circulated in which the Prophet adjudicates a case involving Jewish *zinā* offenders and orders stoning on the basis of the Torah. Exegetes generally employ this incident in their interpretation of Q5:41–7.[131] Some Muslims understood the Prophet's order to stone a Jewish couple as an application of a non-Qur'ān rule for non-Muslims. An entry provided by Wakīʿ (d. 306/918) reads:

> Thābit al-Thumālī said: I said to Abū Jaʿfar [Muḥammad b. ʿAlī al-Bāqir (d. 144/744)]: The Murji'a debate us about the meaning of these verses (Q5:41–7). They claim that they are for the Children of Israel.
>
> Abū Jaʿfar responded: We are the best of brothers to the Children of Israel. If the sweetness of the Qur'an is for us and the bitterness is for them, then the bitter verses came down for them and then applied to us.[132]

Abū Jaʿfar's response indicates that, despite *zinā*-stoning's applicability to Muslims, it is meant for non-Muslims.

And recall the narrative that I began with in the Introduction chapter about Ibn Abī ʿAwfā, the Companion of the Prophet.

[129] For a Sunni position, see, e.g., al-Ṭabarī (d. 310/923), *Jāmiʿ*, 8:71–85; Ibn Abī Zamanīn (d. 399/1008), *Tafsīr*, 3:217; al-Zamakhsharī (d. 538/1144), *Tafsīr*, 718f.

For a Shīʿī position, see, e.g., al-ʿAyyāshī (d. 320/932), *Tafsīr*, 1:253f:60f, al-Qummī, *Tafsīr*, 2:95f; al-Ṭūsī (d. 460/1067), *al-Tibyān*, 3:143f.

[130] Burton, *The Sources of Islamic Law*, 135.

[131] In Chapter 2, Section p. 172,I analyze exegetical commentaries on Q5:41–7.

[132] Wakīʿ, *Akhbār al-quḍāt*, 1:44.

> I asked ʿAbd Allāh b. Abī Awfā (d. *c.* 86/705, Medina and Kūfa): Did the Prophet ever order someone to be stoned?
>
> Ibn Abī Awfā said: Yes.
>
> I asked: Was it before or after *surat al-nūr* (Q24:2—100 lashes)?
>
> He said: I do not know.[133]

Again, Abū Ishāq's question makes sense if one considers that skepticism existed about *zinā*-stoning. His inquiry is also logical on the basis that it was made in Iraq, the region with a preponderant majority in support of the dual penalty, which, as I argued, likely emerged due to uncertainty about how to reconcile hadith on stoning with the Qur'ān prescription of flogging. Such countervailing narratives demonstrate that anti-*zinā*-stoning positions persisted beyond that community among the early Muslims.

Conclusion

In this chapter, I surveyed source material addressing *zinā*-stoning in the Islamic legal tradition. I presented reports involving the Prophet and his purported approval of the capital punishment for adultery. For example, according to the ʿUbāda hadith, the Prophet utters a general rule mandating *zinā*-stoning. Companions such as ʿUmar b. al-Khaṭṭāb are also reported to have proclaimed lapidation as the proper punishment for certain types of *zinā* offenders. In addition to hadith containing black-letter law statements, the Prophet and his Companions are recorded to have ordered stoning in specific *zinā* cases. For instance, the Prophet mandates it for an adulteress in the Day-Laborer narrative, for Māʿiz b. Mālik al-Aslamī, and a self-confessing woman of either Ghāmid or Juhayna. ʿAlī is noted to have ordered the stoning of a woman named Shurāḥa. These narratives, among others, are ostensibly employed to affirm *zinā*-stoning's rightful place in the Islamic legal tradition.

I also provided a brief survey of the different ways in which Muslim jurists employ *zinā*-stoning reports to justify the capital punishment and to substantiate various legal positions. For example, juristic references to the Māʿiz

[133] Ibn Abī Shayba, *al-Muṣannaf* (1989 ed.), 9:354, no. 29,353; Ibn Ḥanbal, *Musnad* (1995 ed.), 14:391, no. 19,027; al-Bukhārī, *Ṣaḥīḥ* (1976 ed.), 2498, no. 6,428 and 2509, no. 6,449; Muslim, *Ṣaḥīḥ*, 1328, no. 1,702.

report support a four-fold confession, the need to confirm mental sanity, and the standard by which witness testimony suffices to uphold a conviction. Disputes about the use of a single (stoning only) versus a dual penalty (flogging and stoning) were also settled with hadith and jurisprudential methods. The diverse array of discussions and debates provides a window into the process through which the stoning punishment was incorporated into Islamic law.

As an additional way to reconcile the Qur'ān's order to flog and the Prophetic order to stone certain types of Muslim *zinā* offenders, I reviewed the different ways in which Muslim legal authorities enumerated and established legal elements including non-virginity and/or *iḥṣān*. The latter criterion helped to clarify the type of *zinā* offender subject to the capital punishment. We observed that legal opinions of what constitutes *iḥṣān* and, thus, what makes a *muḥṣan/a*, did not mirror how the Qur'ān formulates chastity and sexual mores through the use of *ḥ-ṣ-n*. The incongruity came into sharper focus when considering *zinā* punishments for slaves. Such debates about non-virginity and/or *iḥṣān* raise important considerations about the origins and evolution of the stoning punishment in the Islamic legal tradition.

The nexus of the Prophet's authority and *zinā*-stoning is of significance because it must be asked: how did it come about? In the next chapter, I investigate in detail the incident in which the Prophet adjudicates a case involving Jewish *zinā* offenders. I analyze the numerous transmission chains associated with different versions of the report and argue for its initial circulation by the second half of the first/seventh century. I compare and contrast the corresponding textual content and the ways in which the hadith intersect with exegetical commentaries. This narrative is one of the first accounts that helped to forge a nexus between the Prophet's authority and the stoning punishment for certain forms of *zinā*. This association contributed to the beginnings of the process by which *zinā*-stoning was legitimized in the Islamic legal tradition.

2
What Does the Torah Say? The Stoning of Jewish *Zinā* Offenders

Introduction

According to the Companion Abū Hurayra (d. *c.* 58/677), "The first person the Messenger of God ordered to be stoned was from among the Jews."[1] This statement is based on a hadith according to which the Prophet's Jewish contemporaries are accused of not adhering to the Torah's directive of death by stoning as the appropriate punishment for certain kinds of sexual transgressions. The account portrays the rabbis as willfully denying the existence of a stoning verse. However, when recourse is made to the Torah, the rabbis admit their deception and reverse their position by affirming the divine instruction. On the basis of the Torah, the Prophet orders the capital punishment upon the Jewish *zinā* offenders, and they are stoned to death (henceforth 'PJZO hadith').

Muslim authorities use the narrative to support the Qur'ānic accusation (Q5:41–4) that the rabbis do not adhere faithfully to their own scriptures. I contend that, in their construction of the other, the transmitter(s) of the hadith ignore rabbinic law on the stoning punishment and whether the rabbis believed their interpretive and jurisprudential methods to be valid based on their ethical, juristic, and socio-historical considerations. I also assert that the hadith serves a broader critique of the Prophet's Jewish contemporaries in that if they can distort or conceal the truth about the stoning punishment, then they can distort or conceal the truth about the Torah's alleged pronouncement of a new prophet.

The PJZO hadith is especially important because it serves as an instructive response to the rejection by the early Muslim communities of *zinā*-stoning. Specifically, the report displays the disconcerting attitudes of early Muslims toward the justifiability of the punishment on the basis of the Qur'ān and/or

[1] al-Ṭabarī, *Jāmiʿ*, 10:305f, no. 11,924.

Stoning as Punishment in Early Islam. Syed Atif Rizwan, Oxford University Press. © Oxford University Press 2026.
DOI: 10.1093/9780197823774.003.0003

the practice of the Prophet. The PJZO mirrors the locus of authority in Islam, that is, the Qur'ān as scripture and the practice of the Prophet, by drawing on the Torah as scripture, and the respective authorities of the Prophet and the rabbis. I bring this point of mirroring into sharper focus in Chapter 4, wherein I discuss a purported sermon delivered by 'Umar b. al-Khaṭṭāb in which he claims that *zinā*-stoning is mandated by the Qur'ān and the practice of the Prophet (also see pp. 62 and p. 62 for two versions of the report). The way(s) in which Jewish communities are portrayed as either maintaining or curtailing fidelity to the Torah based on the applicability of stoning reflects a historical moment in which Muslims are debating whether the possible applicability of stoning is either maintaining or curtailing fidelity to God's Law as revealed in the Qur'ān.

I argue in this chapter that the incident as described in the PJZO hadith circulates first on the authority of the Companion Abū Hurayra (d. *c.* 58/681) and then to other Companions, who, in turn, narrate different pieces of the report to their students, and so forth. During this process, the textual contents experience modifications based on the different ways in which Muslims try to remember and make sense of the account, that is, the stabilization of memory. The PJZO hadith is not without consequence because the purported ruling establishes the nexus between the Prophet's authority and *zinā*-stoning—a nexus that is critical for understanding the beginnings of the process by which Muslim authorities justify the capital punishment in the Islamic legal tradition.

I have organized this chapter into eight sections. Five sections are dedicated to examining a version of the report on the authority of a particular Companion. These individuals are:

Abū Hurayra (d. *c.* 58/677);
al-Barā' b. 'Āzib (d. *c.* 72/691);
'Abd Allāh b. 'Umar (d. 74/693);
Jābir b. Samura (d. 74/693);
Jābir b. 'Abd Allāh (d. 78/697).

I dedicate another section to exegetical commentaries that incorporate the PJZO hadith with verses 41–44 of Chapter Five of the Qur'ān. The reason for this analysis is to demonstrate the different ways in which Muslim exegetes understand the Prophet's order to have the Jewish transgressors stoned in relation to Q5:41–4.[2] I also discuss the possible nature of Jewish communities in Medina and the ways in which rabbinic law engages the transgressions tied to the stoning punishment. It is the analysis of this point to which I turn in the next section.

2.1. The Qur'ān, Jewish Communities in Medina, and the Rabbinic Legal Tradition

The PJZO hadith serves as the dominant gloss for Qur'ānic verses 41–44 in Chapter Five, *al-Mā'ida* (The Table).[3] They read:

> 41 Messenger [of Mine], [I know] it hurts you to see those who profess faith out loud yet vie with one another to be ingrates, thereby revealing that they never intended to surrender their hearts to faith. Among them are the 'rightly-guided' ones (i.e., the Jewish communities), who listen eagerly to the lies of others without even seeing the need to give you a fair hearing. They only intend to interpret the word of God according to their whims to the point they say [to one other], 'If [he] gives a judgment [in your favor], then accept it. But if not, then be on guard!' [Messenger of Mine], there is nothing you can do to help someone for whom God intends trials and tests. Such is the case for people whose hearts God [justly] has no intention of cleansing. [This is the] disgrace for them in this world, and a heavy punishment [awaits them] in the next life,
>
> 42 they listen eagerly to lies and consume abominable things. Nevertheless, should they come to you, either offer judgment or decline to do so. If you choose to decline, [know that] they will not [be able to] harm you in any way. But if you decide to make a judgment, then judge for them in a just manner. Indeed, God loves those who are just—

[2] Burton makes a distinction between exegetical and historical material. The implication is that exegetical material is entirely falsified. On this premise, he argues that the incident involving the Prophet and the Jewish *zinā* offenders is exegetical, meaning that it is ahistorical. See Burton, "The Origin of the Islamic Penalty for Adultery," 19; Burton, *The Sources of Islamic Law*, 129; Burton, "Law and Exegesis," 271.

[3] I thank Beth Berkowitz, David Freidenreich, Admiel Kosman, Issac W. Oliver, and Jason Mokhtarian for their invaluable help with rabbinic criminal law, broadly, and rabbinic law on the stoning punishment, specifically. Any shortcomings of my analysis and conclusions on the subject matter are mine and mine alone.

43 but why do they appoint you for judgment when they have the Torah? [Surely] it contains God's judgment. What makes them turn away from it now? Folks like these are not faithful.

44 We sent down the Torah, containing in it guidance and light. Prophets [of the past], those who gave themselves over to God, judged according to it for these 'rightly-guided' ones (i.e., the Jewish communities), as did the rabbis and the sages, insofar as they were entrusted to preserve the word of God and to serve as its witnesses. [People], do not fear others out of reverence for them. Rather, revere Me! Do not barter away My words for a cheap price. Those who do not give a judgment according to the word of God are ingrates!

Given that the Qur'ān references Jewish communities of first/seventh century Arabia and their rabbis in particular, it is necessary to say a few more words about the nature of such communities.

To begin with, the term "Judaism" cannot be conformed to one specific meaning. Michael Satlow writes that scholars have noted the term may have initially been understood to "intermingle [with] characteristics that we might call 'religious' with those that we would call 'ethnic.'"[4] It is over time and in various socio-historical contexts that the term expresses its meaning(s) in the ways in which it is understood today.[5] For the purposes of this chapter and to a certain degree anachronistic, Judaism represents a collection of beliefs and practices commonly held among a group of individuals who self-identify as Jewish.[6]

By the advent of Islam, Jewish communities existed in and around the Arabian Peninsula. Both Talmudic and Islamic sources affirm the presence of a Jewish population inhabiting the southeastern parts of Palestine with an extensive common border with the Bedouin tribes.[7] This border represents an area between the Shām and the Ḥijāz that allows the reach of Jewish tribes into Medina through Wādī al-Qurā.[8] There is evidence to indicate

[4] Michael Satlow, "Account for 'Religious' in the Study of Religion," 839f. I thank Lena Salaymeh for directing me to Satlow's work.

[5] Satlow, "Account for 'Religious' in the Study of Religion," 841–7.

[6] Ilkka Lindstedt, *Muḥammad and His Followers in Context*, 54, n. 1. See same footnote for an informative discussion on the term "Jew" and the possible ways in which it, along with "Judaism," can be deemed anachronistic in their use within the context of first/seventh century Arabia.

[7] Moshe Gil, "Origin of the Jews of Yathrib," 203; from an economic standpoint, some were involved in long-distance trade, while others controlled palm-growing oases in Arabia. For a description about the professions, see Steven M. Wasserstrom, *Between Muslim and Jew*, 18–20.

[8] Gil, "Origin of the Jews of Yathrib," 203; *Encyclopaedia Judaica*, 2nd ed., s.v. "Arabia."

that Jewish communities also existed in Yemen with the Jewish kingdom of Ḥimyar as one of the main political forces of the time.[9]

There are legends that purportedly attest to the presence of Jewish communities in Arabia since the time of Moses' expeditions against the Amalekites.[10] Other reports place the migration of Jewish communities into Arabia at the time of the destruction of the Second Temple by the Romans (70 CE), which would make these refugees representative of the first Jewish tribes of the Ḥijāz.[11] All of this is to say that, though it is difficult to pinpoint exactly when Jewish communities began to inhabit Arabia, their presence there is rather ancient.

While the presence of Jewish communities in Arabia is undeniable, there are debates about the extent of this populace's adherence to rabbinic Judaism.[12] One reason I raise the matter of rabbinic Judaism is that both the Qur'ān and the PJZO hadith critique rabbis. Haggai Mazuz writes that no Jewish sources, such as the Mishna or the Palestinian or Babylonian Talmuds, provide sufficient evidence to form a comprehensive understanding of the religious customs of Arabian Jews contemporaneous with the Prophet.[13] Lena Salaymeh suggests that the Jews of Arabia may not have been uniformly rabbinic, even though some historical evidence points to communication with Babylonian rabbinic academies.[14] Other scholars, nevertheless, have proposed that at least some Jewish communities residing in Arabia likely practiced rabbinic Judaism. Moshe Gil argues that Medinan Jews had connections to Babylonia.[15] Such connections are supported by Newby, who writes that Arabian Jews attracted the attention of the Babylonian rabbis because the former were concerned with issues such as kosher food and dress.[16] This would mean, as Mazuz asserts, that the Jews of Medina likely

[9] Lindstedt, *Muḥammad and His Followers in Context*, 57 and 64–76.

[10] *Encyclopaedia Judaica*, 2nd ed., s.v. "Arabia."

[11] Gil, "Origin of the Jews of Yathrib," 206f.

[12] On the emergence of rabbinic Judaism, see, e.g., Christine Hayes, *The Emergence of Judaism*, 89–122.

[13] Haggai Mazuz, *The Religious and Spiritual Life of the Jews of Medina*, 1–7.

[14] Lena Salaymeh, *The Beginnings of Islamic Law*, 95; also see Gordon D. Newby, *A History of Jews of Arabia*, 49–75.

[15] Gil, "Origin of the Jews of Yathrib," 205; Gil also writes that there may not have been a significant difference between Arab and non-Arab Jewish communities. See Gil, "Origin of the Jews of Yathrib," 205. This framework presumes a clear line of demarcation between Arabs and non-Arabs in general, and Arab Jews and non-Arab Jews in particular. On the problem of this/these categorization(s), see Salaymeh, *The Beginnings of Islamic Law*, 95f; Wasserstrom notes that the Persian and eastern geographic sphere "was a notorious arena of Jewish pluralism." See Wasserstrom, *Between Muslim and Jew*, 41.

[16] Newby, *A History of Jews of Arabia*, 54f; the attention to such issues reflects some of the same considerations by the broader Jewish communities in late antiquity. The areas of focus also include

acknowledged the authority of the Talmud and thus shared characteristics with and perhaps even identified as rabbinic Jews.[17] Zellentin remarks that it remains unclear exactly which type of Torah, after its revelation to Moses at Mt. Sinai and through the rabbinic tradition, would have reached the Jewish communities in Medina.[18] However, he notes that while the Qur'ān does not directly refer to the tractate Sanhedrin of the (rabbinic) Mishna, a close comparison of the two texts "points to areas of overlap that are too broad to be coincidental."[19] Accordingly, "the Jews appearing in the Qur'ān as rabbinic seems relatively certain."[20] That the Jewish communities shared contours of rabbinic Judaism during the first/seventh century in Medina is material in light of the accusations made against them in the hadith that I examine in this chapter. Accordingly, I turn to a discussion on the treatment of illicit sexual intercourse in the Hebrew Bible and, subsequently, in the rabbinic legal tradition.

The Hebrew Bible delineates both general and specific definitions of sexual transgressions and, in some cases, provides guidance on how to punish them. The following two verses generally prohibit illicit sexual intercourse and deem it a capital offense:

> If a man commits adultery with the wife of his neighbor, both the adulterer and the adulteress shall be put to death (Leviticus 20:10).[21]
>
> If a man is caught lying with the wife of another man, both of them shall die, the man who lay with the woman as well as the woman (Deut. 22:22).[22]

In other instances, death by lapidation is prescribed specifically:

> If, however, this charge [of non-virginity due to illicit sexual intercourse] is true, that evidence of the young woman's virginity is not found, then they

monotheism, male circumcision, and the Sabbath. See Lindstedt, *Muḥammad and His Followers in Context*, 56f.

[17] Mazuz, *Religious and Spiritual Life of the Jews of Medina*, 7; also see Newby, *A History of Jews of Arabia*, 57.
[18] Holger M. Zellentin, "What Falls Within Judaism," 285 and 287. I thank Holger Zellentin for referring me to this article and for the electronic correspondence about the PJZO hadith.
[19] Zellentin, "What Falls Within Judaism," 285.
[20] Holger M. Zellentin, "Aḥbār and Ruhbān," 265; Zellentin, "What Falls Within Judaism," 282–4.
[21] Wayne A. Meeks, *Study Bible*, 191.
[22] Meeks, *Study Bible*, 289.

> shall bring the young woman out to the entrance of her father's house and the men of her town shall stone her to death. . . . (Deut. 22:20–21).[23]
>
> If there is [a betrothed virgin girl], and a man meets her in the towns and lies with her, you shall bring both of them to the gate of that town and stone them to death[24] (Deut. 22:23f).

The Hebrew Bible makes a distinction regarding the form of illicit sexual intercourse when noting the stoning punishment, that is, cases involving a betrothed. Because the Torah's stoning verse is mentioned in the hadith, we have to operate under the presumption that the reference is restricted to Deut. 22:20f or Deut. 22:23f.

The rabbinic period begins around the first century CE and closes around 600 CE in Babylonia. According to the Mishna—the earliest work of rabbinic literature compiled between the late second century CE and the early third century CE—the rabbis uphold their commitment to capital punishments. The tractate Sanhedrin includes a section titled, "Violations with a Penalty of Stoning." One transgression specified involves the "one who has sexual intercourse with a betrothed girl," which is in line with Deuteronomy 22:22–24.[25] Later in the same tractate, the rabbis define a betrothed by stating:

> One who has sexual intercourse with a betrothed girl—he is not liable unless the girl is a betrothed virgin and she is in her father's house.[26]

This specificity is important because, in all other cases involving illicit sexual intercourse, the transgressor may or may *not* be subject to the stoning punishment even though the offense itself is capital in nature. It is important to recognize that the specificity—a virgin residing in her father's household—conveys that the rabbis employ a distinct state of existence to delineate legal liability. These stipulations harken to the multivalent ways the Qur'ān employs the flogging directive vis-à-vis *al-muḥṣanāt*, which would include virgins as well as married individuals. Such similarities and dissimilarities are relevant because they reveal how Muslim transmitters could have misunderstood how rabbinic law employs the stoning punishment in illicit sexual intercourse cases.

[23] Meeks, *Study Bible*, 289.
[24] Meeks, *Study Bible*, 289.
[25] Shaye J.D. Cohen et al., *The Oxford Annotated Mishnah*, vol. 2, Sanhedrin 7:9, 527.
[26] Cohen et al., *The Oxford Annotated Mishnah*, vol. 2, Sanhedrin 6:4, 531.

The rabbis chart several other unlawful acts subject to the stoning punishment, including where the Hebrew Bible does not provide a specific punishment. These include adultery (as noted above in Lev. 20:10 and Deut. 22:22), incest, intercourse with a stepmother, daughter-in-law, or non-humans.[27] The rabbis also incorporate other forms of capital punishments: death by the sword, burning, or strangulation.[28] That the tractate Sanhedrin in the Mishna brings forth the capital punishment of stoning and, in some cases, applies it to other forms of sexual infractions signals that, during the Mishnaic period, rabbinic law maintains fidelity to the punishment prescribed in the Hebrew Bible.

The commitment to the stoning punishment for specific sexual transgressions is clearly evident in the post-Mishanic Palestinian and Babylonian Talmuds, both of which are compilations of rabbinic discussions on the Mishna. The Palestinian Talmud was likely completed around the fourth-fifth centuries CE, reflecting the social and political realities of late Roman Palestine. The Babylonian Talmud, finalized several centuries later (around the sixth–seventh centuries CE), is a more extensive and dialectically complex work that became the dominant foundation of later rabbinic Judaism.[29] These two authoritative texts are significant for the present study because they would be the reference points for the rabbis in Medina. As I noted above, the tractate Sanhedrin includes a section titled, "Violations with a Penalty of Stoning." In this category, one portion reads:

> One who has sexual intercourse with his mother: he is liable for her under the category of 'his mother' and under the category of "the wife of his father."[30]

In the Babylonian Talmud, one rabbinic exegetical statement on the Mishnaic passage reads:

> From the phrase 'both of them shall be put to death [Deut. 22:22]' it is derived that they are executed by stoning.[31]

[27] Cohen et al., *The Oxford Annotated Mishnah*, vol. 2, Sanhedrin 7:4–5, 526–8.
[28] Louis Epstein, *Sex Laws and Customs in Judaism*, 199; Michael Satlow, *Tasting the Dish*, 129f; Cohen et al., *The Oxford Annotated Mishnah*, vol. 2, Sanhedrin 11:1, 552.
[29] Hayes, *The Emergence of Judaism*, 93f.
[30] Cohen et al., *The Oxford Annotated Mishnah*, vol. 2, Sanhedrin 6:4, 527f.
[31] Adin Steinsaltz et al., *Koren Talmud Bavli*, 30:35.

Here, not only is death by lapidation acknowledged but it is also cited as the appropriate form of punishment for when the Hebrew Bible is silent. The applicable Babylonian Talmudic section includes several other rabbinic discussions on the Mishna text. It is noteworthy that there are no discussions on cases involving a betrothed. In other words, the stoning punishment for violations of licit sexual intercourse involving a betrothed is taken for granted. On the same Mishnaic passage cited above, the Palestinian Talmud records a lively debate among the rabbis regarding the consequence of deeming sexual intercourse with one's mother a double transgression. One rabbi is recorded to have asked:

> But in the context of the Sanhedrin, do you have the option of stating the one is stoned and goes and is stoned yet a second time?![32]

The rabbi correctly raises a practical point regarding the incoherency of subjecting a person to a capital punishment more than once. Another rabbi is recorded to have responded by stating:

> "It is for the purpose of effecting a warning that the matter is taught."[33]

The double capital punishment, therefore, is symbolic. Its purpose is to convey the severity of the transgression. But as in the case of the Babylonian Talmud, there is no explicit disregard for the stoning punishment in the Palestinian Talmud.

As for cases involving illicit sexual intercourse with a betrothed for which the Torah specifies death by lapidation, Talmudic exegetical discussions continue to demonstrate fidelity to the capital punishment. For example, on the proper punishment for a priest's daughter one passage reads:

> whosoever is subject to the death penalty as a *betrothed* daughter of an Israelite or a priest is subject to stoning.[34]

The opinion indicates that the stoning punishment is the standard by which to consider an appropriate remedy for any transgression involving

[32] Jacob Neusner (trans.), *The Talmud of the Land of Israel*, 31:219.
[33] Neusner (trans.), *The Talmud of the Land of Israel*, 31:219.
[34] Neusner (trans.), *The Talmud of the Land of Israel*, 31:196.

a betrothed. In fact, the commentaries revolve around what constitutes a maiden, not the capital punishment itself.[35] In essence, the rabbinic opinions recorded in both the Palestinian and Babylonian Talmuds explicitly and implicitly endorse the practice of death by lapidation, as stipulated in the Torah.

Despite the clear commitments to the stoning punishment in the rabbinic literature, its actual implementation was unlikely to be a reality, especially during the Second Temple period (516 BCE–70 CE).[36] The disparity between theory and practice can be attributed to at least two factors. One is that, according to the tractate Makkot in the Mishna, rabbis generally display an aversion to implementing capital punishments. Some are quoted as stating, "A Sanhedrin that executes [a perpetrator] once every seven years [. . . or . . .] once every seventy years is called destructive."[37] Another two rabbis are recorded to have claimed that, were they to be a part of a committee of judges, they would never allow anyone to be executed.[38] The phenomenon of aversion is exemplified by the mechanisms employed within rabbinic law, which establishes stringent evidentiary standards. These thresholds render the attainment of conviction in capital cases exceedingly rare. To be sure, there is another opinion in the same tractate that counters the general reluctance to implement capital punishments. Rabban Simeon b. Gamaliel is recorded to have said that those judges who would attempt to vacate a capital punishment "would have also multiplied the number of murderers in Israel."[39] Even in light of this minority opinion, Louis Epstein writes that Jewish courts did not pass a judgment in which the verdict demanded the use of a capital punishment.[40] Indeed, we cannot be certain if, in fact, rabbinic authorities adjudicated capital cases, including those involving illicit sexual intercourse. But it would appear that on ethical grounds, rabbis prioritized restraint when it came to convictions and punishments for capital transgressions.

The second reason for the difference between theory and practice is twofold. The first concerns the lack of execution power by Jewish communities since, by the time of the destruction of the Second Temple, the Roman government had taken away the Jewish court's right to decide capital cases.[41]

[35] Neusner (trans.), *The Talmud of the Land of Israel*, 31:252–4.
[36] Rachel Biale, *Women and Jewish Law*, 189.
[37] Cohen et al., *The Oxford Annotated Mishnah*, vol. 2, Makkot 1:10, 566.
[38] Cohen et al., *The Oxford Annotated Mishnah*, vol. 2, Makkot 1:10, 566.
[39] Cohen et al., *The Oxford Annotated Mishnah*, vol. 2, Makkot 1:10, 576.
[40] Epstein, *Sex Laws and Customs in Judaism*, 211.
[41] Hyman E. Goldin, *Hebrew Criminal Law and Procedure*, 26; Satlow, *Tasting the Dish*, 322.

This situation meant that the Jewish diaspora did not generally have the power to execute violators of divine law even if they passed such judgments.[42] It is precisely the Roman context that leads Christine Hayes to write that rabbinic opinions in the Palestinian Talmud demonstrate significantly more interpretative elasticity in regard to Biblical Law when compared to rabbinic opinions in the Babylonian Talmud.[43] The hermeneutical flexibility in the Palestinian Talmud indicates that rabbinic rulings did at times contradict Torah Law.[44] But as Hayes notes, this phenomenon is observable only during the first and second centuries of the Common Era, whereas starting in the third century CE, there is an increasing resistance by the rabbis to contradict Torah directives.[45] From the fourth century CE onward and, as demonstrated in the Babylonian Talmud, there is noticeable apprehension to employ interpretative jurisprudence maximally because of the risk of stepping outside the bounds of the Hebrew Bible.[46] The point is that even if during the early rabbinic period there are cases that employ maximum interpretative authority to the point of deriving a ruling that could be in direct opposition to the Torah, the practice was received with anxiety, it was largely in Roman Palestine as compared to Babylonia, and it eventually fell out of practice.[47] In my view, the narrowing of rabbinic interpretative authority is worthy of note. By the time we get to first/seventh century Arabia, it would be irregular for the rabbis to reject Torah law outright in the manner depicted in the hadith I analyze in this chapter.

The other part of the reason for a difference between theory and practice, as Rachel Biale remarks, is due to the private nature of adultery. This made convictions based on eyewitness testimonies typically difficult.[48] In fact, accusations of sexual improprieties were of equal or greater concern. Suspicion posed a threat to marital life "and a source of potential violence and danger for the suspected wife."[49] The Bible delineates procedures for resolving accusations of sexual infidelity in cases involving married couples. Numbers 5:11–15 state that the accused wife is subject to the *soṭah* ordeal.

[42] Note that Berkowitz writes, "[t]he question is far from settled whether Jews had the ability to execute Jewish criminals in the tannaitic period, even if the Roman governor and Roman emperor could." See Beth Berkowitz, *Execution and Invention*, 15–9.
[43] Christine Hayes, "Rabbinic Contestations," 124f and 138f.
[44] Hayes, "Rabbinic Contestations," 125f.
[45] Hayes, "Rabbinic Contestations," 126.
[46] Hayes, "Rabbinic Contestations," 138.
[47] Hayes, "Rabbinic Contestations," 138–41.
[48] Biale, *Women and Jewish Law*, 184.
[49] Biale, *Women and Jewish Law*, 184 and 187.

The suspected wife must drink a liquid that purportedly tests her innocence or guilt, with the latter being revealed by her death.[50] Her fate is ostensibly left to divine judgment. The *soṭah* procedure carries forward into the rabbinic period and is discussed in the Mishna under the tractate *Soṭah*.[51] While the *soṭah* ordeal helped to resolve the difficulties of conviction based on eyewitness testimonies, it too eventually lost its efficacy because it could not be equally applied to adulterous husbands. Consequently, the practice fell out of favor during the rabbinic period.[52] In sum, first, Jewish courts were generally unlikely to carry out capital punishments due to the minority status of Jewish communities, which in turn prevented them from having the legal authority to impose such kinds of penalties. Second, rabbinic law sets very high evidentiary standards, making it nearly impossible to implement a capital punishment. That the internal and external socio-legal structures made the implementation of the stoning punishment as prescribed in the Torah nearly impossible does not mean that they were being deceptive—the charge that is lobbied against the Jewish rabbis as per the hadith.

Indeed, for the rabbis, matters involving illicit sexual intercourse remained an ongoing concern. Rabbinic opinions capture and carry forward one of the underlying principles of capital punishments and the *soṭah* ordeal: public humiliation.[53] For instance, one option invokes Numbers 5, wherein an adulteress is prohibited to both her husband and lover.[54] The rabbis make divorce permanent and prevent the ex-wife from (re)joining her paramour.[55] According to Epstein, the Jewish courts were also willing to implement forms of punishment derived from non-Jewish sources.[56] These include flagellation, exile, and shaving of the head combined with parading around town.[57] The offender being flogged and having their face blackened as a form of humiliation reflects Near Eastern-Mediterranean practices of publicly punishing sexual offenders. For example, in the New Kingdom period in ancient Egypt (1520 BCE–1075 BCE), adulterers are publicly

[50] Biale, *Women and Jewish Law*, 185–7; Satlow, *Tasting the Dish*, 126.
[51] Cohen et al., *The Oxford Annotated Mishnah*, vol. 2, Sotah 1–6, 223–39.
[52] Biale, *Women and Jewish Law*, 187f; Satlow, *Tasting the Dish*, 179f.
[53] Satlow, *Tasting the Dish*, 173–9.
[54] Biale, *Women and Jewish Law*, 189.
[55] Epstein, *Sex Laws and Customs in Judaism*, 212; Biale, *Women and Jewish Law*, 189; Satlow, *Tasting the Dish*, 170f.
[56] Epstein, *Sex Laws and Customs in Judaism*, 212; for a list of the kinds of illicit sexual intercourse subject to corporal punishment, see Cohen et al., *The Oxford Annotated Mishnah*, vol. 2, Keritot 1:1, 274f and vol. 2, Makkot 3:1, 573f.
[57] Epstein, *Sex Laws and Customs in Judaism*, 212; also see Mazuz, *Religious and Spiritual Life of the Jews of Medina*, 49–51.

shamed.[58] In a later period, the male adulterer receives 1000 lashes and the female adulterer has her nose cut off.[59] In the ancient Greek city of Locri Epizephirii (founded *c.* 680 BCE), the male adulterer is blinded whereas in Lepreum (founded sometime during the Neolithic period) and Cumae (founded *c.* 750 BCE), he is tied to ropes, made to walk enchained along the streets for three days, and deprived of his civil rights.[60] In Cumae, a woman convicted of adultery has to stand on a particular stone in the marketplace for all to see.[61] She is subsequently mounted on a donkey, led around the city, made to stand on the stone for a second time, and forced to live her life bearing the name "donkey-rider."[62] As I demonstrate in the following sections, some of the aforementioned forms of alternative punishments (except divorce) are precisely the ones that the Jews of Medina are accused of implementing in the different versions of the hadith. To be sure, due to the paucity of Medinan Jewish records it is difficult to ascertain the nature of the punishments Jewish communities in Medina were implementing. But extant evidence, such as the developments in rabbinic law and jurisprudence, indicates that death by stoning was not practiced. As I discuss above, rabbinic law does not indicate that the moratorium is understood as a deliberate violation of biblical precepts. This means that the transmitter(s) of the PJZO hadith draw upon various aspects of rabbinic law's treatment of illicit sexual intercourse to construct an allegation of willful infidelity on the part of the rabbis, a characterization that I contend is inaccurate. Yet the significance of the report is that it becomes an instructive mechanism by which to explain certain verses of the Qur'ān, to uphold certain polemics against the Prophet's Jewish contemporaries, and to establish the lawfulness of *zinā*-stoning based on divine authority. This authority is then affirmed by the Prophet on the basis of his instruction, which in turn is used to help legitimize the stoning punishment's lawfulness in the Islamic legal tradition. In the sections that follow, I examine the different versions of the report to demonstrate that the PJZO hadith was in circulation by the second half of the first/seventh Islamic century. I also illustrate the different ways in which the textual content of the numerous recensions serves the multivalent purposes of the hadith.

58 Pnina Galpaz-Feller, "Private Lives and Public Censure," 154.
59 C.J. Eyre, "Crime and Adultery," 96f.
60 Eva Cantarella, "Gender, Sexuality, and Law," 244.
61 Cantarella, "Gender, Sexuality, and Law," 3, n.1.
62 Cantarella, "Gender, Sexuality, and Law," 3, n.1.

2.2. Hadith by the Companion Jābir b. Samura (d. 74/693, Kūfa and Medina)

One version of the PJZO hadith is reportedly narrated by the Companion Jābir b. Samura b. Junāda al-Suwāʾī. The extant sources indicate that the successor Simāk b. Ḥarb (d. 123/741, Kūfa) is the only person to have been taught this narrative after receiving it from Jābir b. Samura. In turn, Sharīk b. ʿAbd Allāh (d. *c.* 177/793, Baghdād, Bukhāra, Khurāsān, Kūfa, Mecca, and Wāsiṭ) and Ḥammād b. Salama b. Dīnār (d. 167, Baṣra and Wāsiṭ) learn the report from Simāk b. Ḥarb. The transmission chains and corresponding textual content of recensions on Sharīk b. ʿAbd Allāh's authority will be examined first, followed by those on Ḥammād b. Salama's authority.

The *Muṣannaf* of Ibn Abī Shayba (d. 235/849) is one of the earliest extant collections in which the narrative appears by Sharīk, the student of Simāk b. Ḥarb, who in turn is the student of the Companion Jābir b. Samura. The transmission chain and textual content read:

> Ibn Abī Shayba - Sharīk [b. ʿAbd Allāh b. al-Ḥārith al-Nakhaʿī] - Simāk b. Ḥarb - Jābir b. Samura:
>
> The Prophet had a Jewish man and a Jewish woman stoned.[63]

In addition to Ibn Abī Shayba and on the authority of several of Sharīk's students, Ibn Ḥanbal's *Musnad* (d. 241/855) includes several variants with the same textual content.[64] For example, one transmission chain in Ibn Ḥanbal's *Musnad* runs as follows:

> Ibn Ḥanbal - Aswad b. ʿĀmir [b. Shādhān] (d. 208/823, Baghdād and Syria) - Sharīk - Simāk b. Ḥarb - Jābir b. Samura.

According to the sources, Sharīk sojourned to Baghdād numerous times to teach hadith.[65] Transmissions between Ibn Shādhān and Sharīk likely took place in ʿIrāq because Ibn Shādhān is not documented as having traveled to any other cities that Sharīk is recorded to have visited.[66] Another report

[63] Ibn Abī Shayba, *al-Muṣannaf* (2008 ed.), 9:405, no. 29,614.
[64] Ibn Ḥanbal, *Musnad* (1995 ed.), 15:343, no. 20,748 and 15:350, no. 20,888.
[65] al-Khaṭīb al-Baghdādī, *Tārīkh*, 10:384.
[66] On Ibn Shādhān, see Ibn Ḥibbān, *al-Thiqāt*, 8:130; al-Khaṭīb al-Baghdādī, *Tārīkh*, 4:495 and 498; al-Dhahabī, *Siyar aʿlām*, 10:112–4.

in Ibn Ḥanbal's *Musnad* is on the authority of Abū Kāmil (al-)Muẓaffar b. Mudrik al-Khurāsānī (d. 207/822, Baghdād and Khurāsān), who received the narrative from Sharīk.[67] Biographical entries indicate that many people, including Ibn Ḥanbal, held Abū Kāmil in high regard.[68] Ibn Ḥanbal states that he spent considerable time listening to hadith from Abū Kāmil.[69] As to the teacher–student relationship between Abū Kāmil and Sharīk, it is recorded that when Sharīk came to the city in which Abū Kāmil was staying, no one was permitted to ask Sharīk questions except Abū Kāmil.[70] Regardless of the accuracy of this claim, the opinion reflects perceptions about a close relationship between Abū Kāmil and Sharīk.

Ibn Ḥanbal provides two additional versions on the authority of his informant, Khalaf b. Hishām al-Bazzār (d. 229/843, Baghdād and Kūfa). One transmission chain reads:

> (1) Ibn Ḥanbal - Khalaf [b. Hishām] - Sulaymān b. Muḥammad [b. Dāwūd] al-Mubārakī (d. 231/845, Baghdād, Mubārak, and Wāsiṭ) - Sharīk - Simāk b. Ḥarb - Jābir b. Samura.[71]

The second transmission chain and its corresponding textual content read:

> (2) Ibn Ḥanbal - Khalaf b. Hishām - Sharīk - Jābir b. Samura:

The Prophet had a Jewish man and a Jewish woman stoned.

Ibn Ḥanbal notes a certain inconsistency in the transmission lines as reported by his informant Khalaf: "This report and the one by Khalaf from Sharīk do not contain Simāk in the transmission chain." Ibn Ḥanbal's sense is that Khalaf had dropped his immediate informant in one of the transmission lines: "Khalaf heard it, and God knows best, from Sulaymān b. Muḥammad al-Mubārakī from Sharīk, because Simāk is not recorded in Khalaf's written narrative."[72]

Ibn Ḥanbal's son, ʿAbd Allāh (d. 290/903), corroborates this point, as he comments that Khalaf's direct report (2) from Sharīk is *maqṭūʿ* (a broken

[67] Ibn Ḥanbal, *Musnad* (1995 ed.), 15:377, no. 20,892.
[68] For example, see al-Khaṭīb al-Baghdādī, *Tārīkh*, 15:157f and al-Mizzī, *Tahdhīb al-kamāl*, 28:99.
[69] al-Dhahabī, *Siyar aʿlām*, 10:126.
[70] al-Khaṭīb al-Baghdādī, *Tārīkh*, 15:157; al-Mizzī, *Tahdhīb al-kamāl*, 28:100; al-Dhahabī, *Siyar aʿlām*, 10:125.
[71] Ibn Ḥanbal, *Musnad* (1995 ed.), 15:358, no. 20,812.
[72] Ibn Ḥanbal, *Musnad* (1995 ed.), 15:358, no. 20,811.

chain of transmission), whereas his report from Sulaymān al-Mubārakī (1) is *mawṣūl* (unbroken chain of transmission).[73] It is recorded that Khalaf learned hadith from Sulaymān through oral/aural sessions.[74] Also considering the regional overlap between the two individuals, Ibn Ḥanbal's two recorded transmissions indicate Sharīk's participation in disseminating the PJZO hadith.

Ibn Mājah (d. 273/887) also preserves a version of the PJZO hadith with Sharīk in the transmission chain. The textual content again simply refers to the Prophet's order to stone a Jewish man and woman. The chain of transmission reads:

> Ibn Mājah - Ismāʿīl b. Mūsā [al-Fazārī] (d. 245/859, Kūfa) - Sharīk (d. *c.* 177/793) - Simāk b. Ḥarb (d. 123/741, Kūfa) - Jābir b. Samura (d. 74/693).[75]

Most biographical dictionaries list Ibn Mūsā as one of Sharīk's students and generally consider him to be a trustworthy transmitter.[76] It is also mentioned that Ibn Mūsā supposedly narrated *mursal* hadith, in which the Companion goes unmentioned from whom a Successor ostensibly received a Prophetic report.[77] The accusation may have paved the way for a more explicit allegation by means of some raising doubts about his integrity on the basis of his purported Shīʿī sympathies.[78] Accusing transmitters of having unorthodox tendencies—Shīʿī or otherwise—was often a tactic employed to discredit transmitters who transmitted reports a hadith critic did not approve of.[79] Even assuming the veracity of the accusations does not eliminate his learning of the narrative from Sharīk. Accordingly and without countervailing evidence, Ibn Mājah's report vouches for Sharīk's participation in the dissemination of the PJZO hadith.

[73] al-Khaṭīb al-Baghdādī, *Tārīkh*, 9:270.
[74] al-Dhahabī, *Siyar aʿlām*, 10:577.
[75] Ibn Mājah, *Sunan*, 854, no. 2,557.
[76] al-Mizzī, *Tahdhīb al-kamāl*, 3:211f; al-Dhahabī, *Mīzān*, 1:251f; Ibn Ḥajar, *Tahdhīb al-tahdīb*, 1:315.
[77] Ibn Abī Ḥātim, *al-Jarḥ wa al-taʿdīl*, 2:196, al-Mizzī, *Tahdhīb al-kamāl*, 3:210; al-Dhahabī, *Mīzān*, 1:252.
[78] Ibn Abī Ḥātim, *al-Jarḥ wa al-taʿdīl*, 2:196, al-Mizzī, *Tahdhīb al-kamāl*, 3:210; al-Dhahabī, *Mīzān*, 1:252.
[79] Scott C. Lucas, *Constructive Critics*, 57, 200f, and 320–5; in Shīʿī biographical dictionaries, some notes point to a debate about his being an extremist Shīʿī (however defined). However, this charge is cited on the authority of Sunnī hadith critics. Positive attributes are made by virtue of mentioning that many narrated from him and that he had a trustworthy reputation. See ʿAbbās al-Qummī, *al-Kunā wa al-alqāb*, 3:30f.

Sharīk's involvement can also be supported by another version mentioned by his student, Hannād b. al-Sārī al-Tamīmī b. Muṣ'ab (d. 243/857, Kūfa). The *isnād* provided by al-Tirmidhī (d. 279/829) reads:

> Hannād b. al-Sārī - Sharīk - Simāk b. Ḥarb - Jābir b. Samura.[80]

Not much is written about Hannād but, according to biographical dictionaries, he was one of the more respected transmitters in Kūfa.[81] Al-Tirmidhī notes that the report on Hannād's authority "meets acceptable standards of reliability, but is unattested to (*ḥasan gharīb*)."[82] Al-Tirmidhī's evaluation accounts for the fact that in the extant sources, Sharīk's informant Simāk b. Ḥarb is the only individual to have reported the narrative from Jābir b. Samura. Al-Tirmidhī notes that his assessment of the hadith as being *ḥasan* is based, in part, on the fact that the textual content of the report is accepted by "many people of knowledge."[83] The aforementioned points of consideration, combined with Hannād's reported birth year of 150/767, Sharīk's death year of *c.* 177/793 (thus allowing for ample time for Hannād to have heard the *hadith* from Sharīk), and the regional overlap of the two transmitters makes Hannād's transmission as further corroboration of Sharīk's circulation of this report.

The *Musnad* of al-Mawṣilī (d. 307/919) is the other source among the ones I investigated that contains the PJZO hadith transmitted via Sharīk - Ibn Ḥarb - Jābir b. Samura. The respective *isnād* and *matn* reads:

> al-Mawṣilī - Isḥāq [b. Ibrāhīm] b. Abī Isrā'īl (d. 245/859, Baghdād, Baṣra, and Marw) - Sharīk - Simāk b. Ḥarb - Jābir b. Samura:
>
> The Prophet had a Jewish man and a Jewish woman stoned.[84]

Biographical dictionaries indicate that al-Mawṣilī did narrate from Isḥāq b. Abī Isrā'īl and the latter receives considerable praise from his contemporaries.[85] Given Isḥāq b. Abī Isrā'īl's birth year of 150/767, Sharīk's

[80] al-Tirmidhī, *al-Jāmi'*, 3:107, no. 1,437.
[81] Ibn Abī Ḥātim, *al-Jarḥ wa al-ta'dīl*, 9:119; al-Mizzī, *Tahdhīb al-kamāl*, 30:312; al-Dhahabī, *Siyar a'lām*, 11:465f.
[82] al-Tirmidhī, *al-Jāmi'*, 3:107, no. 1,437; On the definitions of *hasan* and *gharib*, see Mohammad H. Kamali, *Textbook of Ḥadith Studies*, 228.
[83] al-Tirmidhī, *al-Jāmi'*, 3:107, no. 1,437.
[84] al-Mawṣilī, *Musnad*, 13:460, no. 7,471.
[85] al-Khaṭīb al-Baghdādī, *Tārīkh*, 7:380–2; al-Mizzī, *Tahdhīb al-kamāl*, 2:403; al-Dhahabī, *Tadhkirat al-ḥuffāẓ*, 2:485.

death year of *c.* 177/793, and their respective travel patterns, Isḥāq b. Abī Isrāʾīl's version is additional corroboration of Sharīk's responsibility for the report.

In sum, seven of Sharīk's pupils are noted to have transmitted the PJZO hadith on his authority. The transmission chain and corresponding textual content analysis establish Sharīk's involvement in the circulation of the report. Sharīk was a respected scholar and transmitter, who served as a judge in Wāsiṭ in 150/767 and thereafter in Kūfa, where he died.[86] Reportedly, he became forgetful in later age, a fact which, according to the biographers, may have led to some errors in his later transmissions.[87] He is recorded to have said that, because of his confusion due to memory loss, he felt uncomfortable teaching hadith.[88] Perhaps this partly motivated him to eventually start writing things down.[89] His reputation for having a faulty memory led some to reject the narratives he taught.[90] The actual effects of his cognitive shortcomings are difficult to ascertain with certainty. But an important point to note is that the material from his lectures in Wāsiṭ were accepted and it is here that Isḥāq b. Ibrāhīm b. Abī Isrāʾīl receives the PJZO hadith from him.[91] Lastly, Sharīk was born in 95/713 and Simāk b. Ḥarb died sometime in 123/740. This means that, as a pupil in Ibn Ḥarb's circle, Sharīk was young and his memory then was not in question. Therefore, Sharīk knew of the report and correctly transmitted it, especially given that the textual content itself is rather brief.

The *Musnad* of al-Ṭayālisī (d. *c.* 203/818) contains the report with the same textual content as others examined thus far from Ḥammād b. Salama [b. Dīnār] (d. 167/784, Baṣra and Wāsiṭ), also a pupil of Simāk b. Ḥarb.[92] Allegedly, Ibn Salama transmitted oddities (*munkar* hadith) and attributed sayings of Companions, particularly Ibn ʿAbbās (d. 68/687), to the Prophet himself (*rafʿ*).[93] Once Ibn Salama was informed that Shuʿba b. al-Ḥajjāj (d. 160/776) was questioning reports that Ibn Salama was teaching.[94] Ibn Salama strongly objected, so much so that he ordered the person who

[86] Ibn Ḥibbān, *al-Thiqāt*, 6:444.
[87] Ibn Abī Ḥātim, *al-Jarḥ wa al-taʿdīl*, 4:366; Ibn Ḥibbān, *al-Thiqāt*, 6:444; al-Khaṭīb al-Baghdādī, *Tārīkh*, 10:391.
[88] al-Khaṭīb al-Baghdādī, *Tārīkh*, 10:385 and 392.
[89] al-Khaṭīb al-Baghdādī, *Tārīkh*, 10:385 and 392.
[90] Ibn Ḥajar, *Tahdhīb al-tahdīb*, 3:161f.
[91] Ibn Ḥibbān, *al-Thiqāt*, 6:444; Ibn Ḥajar, *Tahdhīb al-tahdīb*, 3:162.
[92] al-Ṭayālisī, *Musnad*, 2:131, no. 812.
[93] Ibn ʿAdī, *Kāmil fī ḍuʿafāʾ*, 3:36.
[94] Ibn ʿAdī, *Kāmil fī ḍuʿafāʾ*, 3:36f.

told him about Shuʿba's comment to be hit with a shoe![95] Be that as it may, Ḥammād b. Salama had a reputation for being a prolific and respected transmitter.[96] Relative to Sharīk, who also attended Simāk's circle, most biographical entries portray Ḥammād b. Salama in an overwhelmingly positive light. Accordingly, Ibn Salama did likely hear the report from Simāk.

Given the aforementioned data culled from the transmission chains as well as from the biographical sources, it can safely be concluded that Simāk b. Ḥarb (d. 123/741) was involved in the circulation of the PJZO hadith. Yes, Simāk is recorded to have sometimes made errors when he shared reports,[97] which compelled some to deem him a weak transmitter.[98] But there is little reason to believe a mistake occurs in the transmission chain or textual content in this particular case. It is also worth noting that Jābir b. Samura (d. 74/693) did, in fact, travel to Kūfa from Medina and took up residence there, where he eventually died.[99] In short, the hadith reflects a memory of Jābir that is shared in Kūfa, where Simāk spends time. The economy of the words in the report nevertheless bears weight because the narrative unquestionably interlinks the Prophet's authority and the stoning punishment.

2.3. Hadith by the Companion al-Barāʾ b. ʿĀzib b. al-Ḥārith (d. *c.* 72/691, Kūfa and Medina)

The version of the PJZO hadith by the Companion al-Barāʾ b. ʿĀzib includes the same central motif as the one on Jābir b. Samura's authority: the Prophet ordered the stoning punishment for a Jewish *zinā* offender. However, the al-Barāʾ b. ʿĀzib variants contain more details. These include things like the mention of the actual punishments implemented upon Jewish *zinā* offenders by the Prophet's Jewish contemporaries, as well as the formulation of the hadith as an exegetical commentary on the Qurʾānic charge against the Medinan Jews for not maintaining fidelity to divine prescriptions.[100]

95 Ibn ʿAdī, *Kāmil fī ḍuʿafāʾ*, 3:36f.

96 Ibn Saʿd, *al-Ṭabaqāt*, 9:282; Ibn Maʿīn, *Tārīkh*, 4:312, no. 4,547; al-Bukhārī, *Tārīkh*, 3:23; al-Mizzī, *Tahdhīb al-kamāl*, 7:259ff.

97 al-Khaṭīb al-Baghdādī, *Tārīkh*, 10:298; al-Mizzī, *Tahdhīb al-kamāl*, 12:119.

98 al-Khaṭīb al-Baghdādī, *Tārīkh*, 10:299; al-Mizzī, *Tahdhīb al-kamāl*, 12:120; al-Dhahabī, *Mīzān*, 2:232.

99 Ibn Saʿd, *al-Ṭabaqāt*, 6:206 and 8:146; al-Mizzī, *Tahdhīb al-kamāl*, 4:439.

100 On the polemical function of the hadith and in relation to Q5:41ff, see John Burton, *The Sources of Islamic Law*, 134; John Burton, "Law and Exegesis," 274–7, 280f, and 283.

The *Muṣannaf* of Ibn Abī Shayba includes the PJZO hadith on the authority of al-Barāʾ b. ʿĀzib. The transmission chain and *matn* read:

> Ibn Abī Shayba - Abū Muʿāwiya [Muḥammad b. Khāzim al-Ḍarīr] (d. 195/810, Baghdād, Baṣra, and Kūfa) *and* Wakīʿ [al-Jarrāḥ] (d. 197/812, Baghdād, Fayd, and Kūfa) - [Sulaymān b. Mihrān] al-Aʿmash (d. *c.* 147/764) - ʿAbd Allāh b. Murra (d. *c.* 99/717) - al-Barāʾ b. ʿĀzib b. al-Ḥārith:
>
> The Prophet had a Jewish man stoned.[101]

Because of Ibn Abī Shayba's use of two informants, it is unclear whether both Abū Muʿāwiya and Wakīʿ provide the same transmission chains and textual content. Additional versions help to shed light on the matter. One transmission chain and its corresponding textual content provided by Ibn Ḥanbal read:

> Ibn Ḥanbal - Wakīʿ [al-Jarrāḥ] - al-Aʿmash - ʿAbd Allāh b. Murra - al-Barāʾ b. ʿĀzib b. al-Ḥārith:
>
> The Prophet had a Jewish man stoned and said: God, I bear witness to you that I am the first one to revive Your law which they have abandoned.[102]

Both Ibn Abī Shayba and Ibn Ḥanbal have Wakīʿ in their transmission chains. This is unsurprising because many transmitters in ʿIrāq narrate from Wakīʿ.[103] This biographical note about Wakīʿ and the shared element, in effect, point to his being a legitimate source. In other words, Ibn Abī Shayba's combined transmission is accurate.

The provenance of the Prophet's comment in Ibn Ḥanbal's recension—"God, I bear witness to you that I am the first one to revive Your law which they have abandoned"—is absent from Ibn Abī Shayba's version, though both transmit the report on Wakīʿ's authority. This difference raises at least two questions. Did Wakīʿ remember to include the Prophet's statement in his narrative to Ibn Ḥanbal but not to Ibn Abī Shayba? Or, did Wakīʿ narrate the same report but Ibn Abī Shayba did not record it? Other versions are helpful in resolving the discrepancy.

[101] Ibn Abī Shayba, *al-Muṣannaf* (2008 ed.), 9:406, no. 29,617.
[102] Ibn Ḥanbal, *Musnad* (1992 ed.), 30:610, no. 18,663.
[103] Ibn Abī Ḥātim, *al-Jarḥ wa al-taʿdīl*, 1:219–22; Ibn Ḥibbān, *al-Thiqāt*, 7:562; al-Khaṭīb al-Baghdādī, *Tārīkh*, 15:648.

Abū Muʿāwiya Muḥammad b. Ḥazm (d. *c.* 194/809, Baghdād and Kūfa) narrates the PJZO hadith with more details than those given on the authority of Wakīʿ. His report is important because he is Ibn Abī Shayba's informant, a contemporary of Wakīʿ, and a student of al-Aʿmash. A version on Abū Muʿāwiya's authority reads:

> Ibn Ḥanbal - Abū Muʿāwiya - al-Aʿmash - ʿAbd Allāh b. Murra - al-Barāʾ b. ʿĀzib b. al-Ḥārith:
>
> A Jewish man, whose face had been blackened and, who had been flogged, passed by the Messenger of God.[104] The Prophet summoned the man's people and asked: Is this the fixed punishment (*ḥadd*) for *zinā* in your Book?
>
> They responded: Yes.
>
> [al-Barāʾ] said: The Prophet then called for a man from among their learned and said: I implore you by God, the One who revealed the Torah to Moses, is this the fixed punishment (*ḥadd*) for *zinā* in your Book?
>
> The man responded: I swear that had you not invoked God I would have not told you that stoning is the fixed punishment (*ḥadd*) for *zinā* in our Book. The offense was common among our nobles but, when we would catch one of them, we would let them go. But when it came to the poor, we would implement the fixed punishment (*ḥadd*). We eventually said to one another: Let us agree upon something. We will apply the same punishment to a noble person as to a poor person. So we agreed to blacken the face and flog.
>
> The Messenger of God responded: By God! I bear witness to you that I am the first one to revive Your law which they have abandoned!
>
> [al-Barāʾ] said that the Prophet gave the order and the offender was stoned. Then God revealed the verse (Q5:41): "Messenger [of Mine], [I know] it hurts you to see those who profess faith out loud yet vie with one another to be ingrates" [to the verse] "they say [to one another], 'If [he] gives a judgment [in your favor], then accept it.'"
>
> [This is an allusion to when certain members of] the Jewish communities said: Go to Muḥammad. If he gives the ruling to blacken the face and to flog, then accept it. But if he says to stone, then be wary. In response to this,

[104] The Arabic used for blackening of the face is *muḥammam*. The practice involves the use of charcoal to blacken the face. See E.W. Lane, *Arabic-English Lexicon*, 2:635, under *ḥammamahu*.

> God said (Q5:44): "Those who do not give a judgment according to the word of God are ingrates!"
>
> [Regarding the Jewish communities al-Barā'] also made note of (Q5:45): "Those who do not judge according to that which God sent down are truly iniquitous," and (Q5:47): "Those who do not judge according to that which God sent down are truly unjust."
>
> [al-Barā'] said: These verses apply [beyond the present scope] to all those who cover up the truth.[105]

This version is pregnant with details that demand considerable attention and are examined in further detail below. The immediate focus, however, is on reconciling Ibn Abī Shayba's report with other versions. In his gloss of Q5:41, al-Ṭabarī provides two exegetical reports, each a composite transmission chain but both including al-A'mash - 'Abd Allāh b. Murra - al-Barā' b. 'Āzib.[106] The *isnād* includes al-A'mash's student, Abū Mu'āwiya. Furthermore, the textual content provided in one recension by al-Ṭabarī contains a high degree of similarity to the version provided by Ibn Ḥanbal on the authority of Abū Mu'āwiya. Al-Ṭabarī's second version also includes Abū Mu'āwiya, albeit with a truncated *matn* compared to the version cited by Ibn Ḥanbal.[107] Nevertheless, the overlap between the reports provided by Ibn Ḥanbal and al-Ṭabarī points to Abū Mu'āwiya as someone who helped to circulate the PJZO hadith.

In his gloss of Q5:44, al-Ṭabarī again provides the PJZO hadith on the authority of al-Barā' b. 'Āzib. The transmission chain reads (al)-Qāsim [b. al-Ḥasan b. Yazīd al-Hamdānī] (d. 272/885, Hamdān) - al-Ḥusayn [Sunayd b. Dāwūd al-Miṣṣīṣī] (d. 226/840, Baghdād and Miṣṣīṣa)[108] - Abū Mu'āwiya - al-A'mash - 'Abd Allāh b. Murra - al-Barā' b. 'Āzib.[109] In the biographical sources, Abū Mu'āwiya's student, Sunayd, generally receives positive remarks that are peppered with some negative ones. Ibn Abī Ḥātim and al-Nasā'ī did

[105] Ibn Ḥanbal, *Musnad* (1995 ed.), 14:199f, no. 18,434.

[106] al-Ṭabarī, *Jāmi'*, 10:304, no. 11,922; al-Ṭabarī also includes 'Ubayda b. Ḥumayd [al-Laythī] (d. 190, Baghdād and Kūfa) as Hannād's informant. 'Ubayda receives the *hadith* from al-A'mash.

[107] al-Ṭabarī, *Jāmi'*, 10:316, no. 11,939.

[108] Miṣṣīṣa is a village in the district of Yüreğir, Adana Province, Turkey. After the 1960s, its name changed to Yakapınar. It was supposedly founded before the rise of Christianity and named Mopsuestia, i.e., attributed to Mopsus, one of the two seers in Greek mythology. See *The Princeton Encyclopedia of Classical Sites*, s.v. "Mopsuestia," 593f.

[109] al-Ṭabarī, *Jāmi'*, 10:351, no. 12,034; al-Ṭabarī provides another report with Abū Mu'āwiya in the transmission chain. It is a shortened version and contains a reference to the Jewish group's discussion about employing the same punishment for both nobles and commoners. See al-Ṭabarī, *Jāmi'*, 10:352, no. 12,036.

not consider him to be a strong transmitter.[110] Yet most thought that he was a solid repository for hadith.[111] In fact, it appears that he was also known to have regularly spent time with individuals with far greater reputations than himself.[112] That al-Ṭabarī was willing to use Sunayd's report, particularly given the relatively more stringent standards for authenticity set by the hadith critics in al-Ṭabarī's day, suggests that al-Ṭabarī's informant acquired the PJZO hadith from Sunayd. In turn, because the textual content provided by al-Ṭabarī shares a high degree of similarity with the version he provides for Q5:41 and the one entry by Ibn Ḥanbal, Sunayd transmitted the report on Abū Muʿāwiya's authority.

Abū Muʿāwiya's role is also corroborated by a report in the *Ṣaḥīḥ* of Muslim (d. 261/875), whose two sources are Ibn Abī Shayba and Yaḥyā b. Yaḥyā b. Bukayr (d. 226/840, Egypt, Ḥijāz, ʿIrāq, and Syria).[113] Both of these individuals name Abū Muʿāwiya as their teacher. The textual content is virtually identical to Ibn Ḥanbal's version, which means that Muslim's version is on the authority of Yaḥyā b. Yaḥyā b. Bukayr and not of Ibn Abī Shayba, whose version of the report lacks details. In comparing the respective versions of Ibn Ḥanbal, al-Ṭabarī, and Muslim, it is obvious that Ibn Abī Shayba received a variant from Wakīʿ. What remains unclear is whether responsibility for leaving out the additional information rests with Ibn Abī Shayba or Wakīʿ. Regardless, Abū Muʿāwiya's role can be treated as established in this respect.

The hadith collectors Ibn Mājah (d. 273/887),[114] Abū Dāwūd (d. 275/888),[115] al-Nasāʾī (d. 303/915),[116] and al-Bayhaqī (d. 458/1066)[117] all provide the PJZO hadith with transmission chains that include Abū Muʿāwiya. The textual content of each report shares a high degree of similarity with one another and with the versions recorded by Ibn Ḥanbal and Muslim. Not only

110 al-Mizzī, *Tahdhīb al-kamāl*, 12:164; al-Dhahabī, *Siyar aʿlām*, 10:627f; Ibn Ḥajar, *Tahdhīb al-tahdhīb*, 3:78.

111 al-Mizzī, *Tahdhīb al-kamāl*, 12:164f; al-Dhahabī, *Siyar aʿlām*, 10:627f; Ibn Ḥajar, *Tahdhīb al-tahdhīb*, 3:77f.

112 al-Mizzī, *Tahdhīb al-kamāl*, 12:164f; al-Dhahabī, *Siyar aʿlām*, 10:627f; Ibn Ḥajar, *Tahdhīb al-tahdhīb*, 3:77f.

113 Muslim, *Ṣaḥīḥ*, 1,327, no. 1,700 (28).

114 Ibn Mājah, *Sunan*, 855, no. 2,558; he also provides a summarized *matn* on Abū Muʿāwiyā's authority. See Ibn Mājah, *Sunan*, 780, no. 2,327.

115 Abū Dāwūd, *Sunan*, 6:497, no. 4,448; Abū Dawūd also provides a second version going back to al-Aʿmash while bypassing Abū Muʿāwiya. This recension is a summary of the longer version. See Abū Dāwūd, *Sunan*, 6:496, no. 4,447.

116 al-Nasāʾī, *al-Sunan al-kubrā*, 6:443, no. 7,180 and 10:82, no. 11,079.

117 al-Bayhaqī, *al-Sunan al-kubrā*, 8:373, no. 16,930 and 8:430, no. 17,118.

do the striking parallels indicate the involvement of Abū Muʿāwiya, but also that the report was transmitted in written form. Therefore, without contrary evidence, Abū Muʿāwiya must be accepted as having played a role in the dissemination of the narrative.

Information drawn from the biographical sources on Abū Muʿāwiya makes his relationship with his teacher, al-Aʿmash, historically attestable. Abū Muʿāwiya was a respected transmitter and considered to be an authoritative source for reports narrated by al-Aʿmash.[118] In fact, Abū Muʿāwiya claimed to have spent 20 years with al-Aʿmash, during which time he memorized 1,600 hadith, although he claims to have forgotten about 400 after falling ill.[119] Regardless of the exact number of reports he ultimately retained, this information functions to emphasize his close relationship with his teacher.

As for al-Aʿmash's other student, Wakīʿ, he is recorded to have been in Kūfa in 129/746 and the former to have held hadith circles in Kūfa until his death *c.* 148/765, thereby making it entirely plausible for the two to have spent time together. Indeed, Wakīʿ claims to have attended al-Aʿmash's auditions (*samāʿ*) for two years that started in 145/762.[120] The Wakīʿ-al-Aʿmash link is corroborated by al-Ṭabarī, who includes the PJZO hadith with the Wakīʿ-al-Aʿmash - al-Barāʾ b. ʿĀzib transmission line.[121] Thus, as reflected in the sources, al-Aʿmash is responsible for circulating the report.

Al-Aʿmash was a popular figure by all measures. He was widely recognized for his knowledge regarding the Qurʾān, religious obligations (*farāʾiḍ*), and hadith.[122] Supposedly, he recited 1,300 hadith.[123] However, he is accused of improper citation of authorities (*tadlīs*).[124] Despite receiving such criticism, al-Aʿmash exerted a substantial influence on two generations of hadith scholars.[125] His role in the transmission is also acceptable partly because

[118] Ibn Abī Ḥatim, *al-Jarḥ wa al-taʿdīl*, 7:247f; al-Khaṭīb al-Baghdādī, *Tārīkh*, 3:137–9 and 145; Ibn Ḥajar, *Tahdhīb al-tahdīb*, 5:558.

[119] Ibn Maʿīn, *Tārīkh*, 3:376, no. 1,827; al-Khaṭīb al-Baghdādī, *Tārīkh*, 3:138 and 140.

[120] Cohen et al., *The Oxford Annotated Mishnah*, vol. 2, Sanhedrin 6:4, 521.

[121] al-Ṭabarī, *Jāmiʿ*, 10:304, no. 11,922.

[122] Ibn Saʿd, *al-Ṭabaqāt*, 8:461; al-Khaṭīb al-Baghdādī, *Tārīkh*, 10:5, 9–11, 13–15; al-Mizzī, *Tahdhīb al-kamāl*, 12:85f.

[123] al-Dhahabī, *Tadhkira*, 153.

[124] al-Dhahabī, *Mīzān*, 2:224; Azami explains *tadlīs* to refer to a situation in which "a transmitter narrated a hadith from an authority whom he met but from whom he did not learn that particular hadith but had learned it from someone else going through that authority. Thus he did not mention the immediate authority and transmitted it from a higher authority using a term which can be used for both direct and indirect learning, or used a scholar's name which was not commonly known instead of using the name for which he was famous." See Mustafa M. Azami, *Studies in Hadith Methodology*, 65.

[125] Lucas, *Constructive Critics*, 346.

of the consistency in the reports on his authority and, as I demonstrate in subsequent sections, with other versions that do not include him. In sum, al-Aʿmash's biographical information attests to his involvement in the circulation of the PJZO hadith.

Did al-Aʿmash receive the report from his recorded teacher, ʿAbd Allāh b. Murra? To the best of my knowledge, no person save al-Aʿmash narrates the PJZO hadith from Ibn Murra, which means we do not have any other reports to help corroborate al-Aʿmash's attribution to Ibn Murra. Not much can be found in the sources about Ibn Murra except that he was a respected transmitter and that many ʿIrāqīs, including al-Aʿmash, narrated from him.[126] This information indicates that a person by the name of Ibn Murra existed and that he was a transmitter of reports, which makes al-Aʿmash's acquisition of the hadith from Ibn Murra entirely plausible. Importantly, the inability to corroborate al-Aʿmash's transmission from Ibn Murra may be a function of the nature of the sources available to us. In other words, to dismiss Ibn Murra's role would be to do so solely on *ex silentio* grounds. It is also worth considering that, given al-Aʿmash's reputation and influence, it would be difficult for him to name someone who would raise alarm bells for those studying or familiar with al-Aʿmash.[127] Finally, as I demonstrate above and again below, the report about the Prophet's involvement in the stoning of a Jewish person was well in circulation by al-Aʿmash's (d. *c.* 147/764) time. All of this is to say that an analysis of the transmission chains is indicative of their historical veracity. This confirmation means that there is more evidence to date the circulation of the hadith to the first/seventh century of Islam.

2.3.1. Textual content analysis

Al-Barāʾ b. ʿĀzib's detailed narrative serves as an explication of the Qur'ān's critique of Muḥammad's Jewish contemporaries. It sheds light on why the Prophet is remembered to have been involved in the stoning of a Jewish *zinā* offender. The account begins by indicating that a Jewish man, whose face had been blackened and had been flogged, came within the vicinity of the Prophet. In the grand scheme of the report, the offense is not immediately identified. However, the textual content reveals that the culprit had

[126] Ibn Saʿd, *al-Ṭabaqāt*, 8:408; Ibn Ḥibbān, *al-Thiqāt*, 5:18; al-Mizzī, *Tahdhīb al-kamāl*, 16:114.
[127] *cf* Gautier H.A. Juynboll, "The Role of *Muʿammarūn*," 163f.

committed a sexual transgression. The reference to the Qur'ānic verses at the end of al-Barā' b. 'Āzib's version indicates that it is based on another variant that was in circulation.

For instance, on the face of it there appears to be a tension between the reason that precipitates an interaction between the Prophet and his Jewish contemporaries and the revelation of specific verses. Near the end of the report, al-Barā' b. 'Āzib states that after the Prophet gave the order, Q5:41 was revealed. Part of the verse states, "... they say [to one another], 'If [he] gives a judgment [in your favor], then accept it.'" As we learn from al-Barā' b. 'Āzib's recension, the Prophet engages members of the Jewish community on the basis of an offender passing by him, not their coming to him for a ruling. Now, the textual content continues with al-Barā' b. 'Āzib implying that Q5:41 is an allusion to the Jewish community agreeing that they will go to the Prophet and ask him for a ruling. They supposedly decide that they will accept his judgment if he orders the blacking of the face and flogging. Yet as the hadith indicates, the Jewish offender already had his face blackened and had been flogged, thereby making the allusion a moot point. The potential tension can be resolved if al-Barā' b. 'Āzib had access to another version of the story which he then retells. As I demonstrate below, this is exactly the case at hand. It is a matter of knowing that two refrigerators exist in two different locations and inadvertently blurring which one has what things in it.

The use of the term *ḥadd* should be interpreted as a subsequent interpolation. It also has implications for establishing the provenance of the hadith. Its use in the report is premised on the idea that both Jews and Muslims share the same understanding of the term during the time of the Prophet, which means that the two communities understand *ḥadd* to signify a fixed punishment. To the best of my knowledge, there is no evidence to support such a common understanding. Also note that *ḥadd*'s plural form, *ḥudūd*, appears fourteen times in the Qur'ān and never signifies fixed punishments. Rather, it means limits.[128] The Qur'ān's use of *ḥudūd* to connote limits indicates that the definition underwent changes in the post-revelatory Islamic legal tradition to mean a set of offenses and punishments.[129] Recall that the Hebrew Bible is silent about the form of the capital punishment to be implemented for certain kinds of sexual violations. The rabbis utilize various modes,

[128] E.g., Q2:187 states, "*tilka ḥudūd Allāh fa lā taqrabūhā*—these are the limits of God, so do not go near them."

[129] On the variations in meaning of *ḥudūd* in the Qur'ān as opposed to the Islamic legal tradition, see Fazlur Rahman, "The Concept of *Ḥadd* in Islamic Law," 237–51.

including death by lapidation. Only the sexual violations with a betrothed virgin are specifically treated with the stoning punishment. That the stoning punishment from the Book—presumably the Torah—is invoked means that the reference is to a specific type of sexual transgression that is *not* treated in the Islamic tradition with *zinā*-stoning, that is, a contradiction to the eventual Islamic *ḥadd*. Therefore, when the Prophet is portrayed as asking about the *ḥadd*, what we really have is a socio-historical context in which death by lapidation is being formulated and communicated as an Islamic *ḥadd* punishment for specific types of sexual transgressions for Muslims. The textual content retains a specific transgression-*cum*-punishment conceptually through the term *ḥadd*, a conception that is unique only in the time after the Prophet.

Appeals to a learned authority, as well as the Prophet's use of an oath, imbue the conversation with a strong sense of solemnity, reflect legal procedures delineated in rabbinic laws, and represent particular values important to Muslims. In the tractate Sanhedrin of the Mishna, it is necessary that a witness must be qualified or an expert.[130] There is also a discussion about the use of oath to determine the outcomes of cases.[131] In both Jewish and Islamic law, breaking an oath necessitates an act of expiation (*kaffāra*).[132] An expiatory act indicates the gravity of violating an oath and conveys that a commitment is made to God, which in turn imposes certain obligations on the believer of the agreed-upon covenant.[133] Oaths can also be invoked to compel the oath-taker to follow through on an obligation in cases they deny the agreement.[134] The severity of the matter in regard to oaths is expressed in the report when the sage admits that, had it not been for the oath, he would have denied the existence of a stoning prescription in the Torah. The expertise of the authority, combined with the oath, serves to reinforce the accuracy of the punishment and conveys a familiarity with rabbinic court procedures and both Jewish and Islamic values regarding oaths.[135] Importantly, both scriptural and Jewish authorities, respectively, are invoked to affirm the lawfulness of stoning as the correct punishment. In other words, these elements

[130] Cohen et al., *The Oxford Annotated Mishnah*, vol. 2, Sanhedrin 3:2, 504. For differences in legal procedures between monetary and capital cases, see chap. 4 of the Sanhedrin, 509–14.

[131] Cohen et al., *The Oxford Annotated Mishnah*, vol. 2, Sanhedrin 3:2, 504.

[132] *Encyclopaedia of Islam*, 3rd ed., s.v. "Expiation."

[133] Roy Mottahedeh, "Oaths and Public Vows in the Middle East," 118.

[134] *Encyclopaedia of Islam*, 2nd ed., s.v. "Bayyina;" the Qur'ān does not employ *bayyina*, proof, in a judicial context. But it does reference witness. E.g., see Q2:282, Q4:7, Q5:106–8, and Q65:2.

[135] As Burton notes, the sages represent the Qur'ānic charge against rabbis "of concealing from people what God had revealed to them." See Burton, "Law and Exegesis," 272.

convey to Muslims that the capital punishment is divinely mandated and affirmed by those who know the revelations *correctly*.

The rebuke in the report, in my view, reflects Muslim opinions about a particular type of community, be it Jewish or Muslim, that is perceived as not implementing God's law.[136] This is why the Prophet is portrayed as saying, "By God! I bear witness to you that I am the first one to revive Your law which they have abandoned!" Recall that the rabbis have always been concerned with sexual infractions. The change was to the type of punishments prescribed, that is, from capital to corporal. In other words, the rabbis were not about abandoning the divine censures for sexual infidelity, but rather altering the methods while upholding the spirit of the law. The rebuke conveys three important points. It demonstrates that the Prophet's Jewish contemporaries are failing to maintain fidelity to Scripture. The implication is that they also deny its announcement of the coming of a new prophet. Secondly, it serves as a reminder for Muslims that they should not deny and/or change the punishment God has prescribed for Muslims, namely *zinā*-stoning. And thirdly, it forges the authority of the Prophet and the Scripture as related to the stoning punishment.

The element of concealing the true punishment also serves as an example of the Qur'ānic verses that accuse the Prophet's Jewish contemporaries of misrepresenting God as conveyed in the Torah.[137] The specific charge is *taḥrīf*, the verbal noun of *ḥarrafa*, meaning to change or alter, or to tamper with a thing.[138] The accusation of allegedly modifying the punishment in the *zinā* case reemphasizes the same implications as I noted above in regard to the Prophet's statement about reviving a punishment that had been disregarded. The accusation in the hadith is important for verifying the legitimacy of Muḥammad's prophethood. According to certain Muslim exegetical literature, the Jews of Medina possessed scripture that tells the coming of Muḥammad.[139] If the Jewish group can deny the stoning punishment, then

[136] Burton makes a distinction between exegetical and historical material. The implication is that exegetical material is entirely falsified. On this premise, he argues that the incident involving the Prophet and the Jewish *zinā* offenders is exegetical, meaning that it is ahistorical. See Burton, "The Origin of the Islamic Penalty for Adultery," 19; Burton, *The Sources of Islamic Law*, 129; Burton, "Law and Exegesis," 271.

[137] E.g., see Q2:75–9, Q5:13, and Q5:41; Burton, "Law and Exegesis," 274–8; Burton, *The Sources of Islamic Law*, 132f.

[138] For an overview of *taḥrīf*, see *Encyclopaedia of Islam*, 2nd ed., s.v. "Taḥrīf;" *Encyclopaedia of the Qur'ān*, s.v. "Revision and Alteration;" Camilla Adang, *Muslims Writers of Judaism*, 223–48; Nickel provides an analysis of the different ways in which *taḥrīf*, i.e., tampering with meaning vs. tampering with text, is understood by Muslim scholars. On this point and his discussion on *taḥrīf*, see Gordon Nickel, *Narratives of Tampering*, 15–36, 57–9, 87, 109f, 129–36, and 190f.

[139] Nickel, *Narratives of Tampering*, 178f.

they can deny Muḥammad being sent as a legitimate prophet of God. And again, the presence of the Prophet communicates to Muslims about the legitimacy of *zinā*-stoning. In the PJZO hadith, Muhammad's case is made to stand on the firmest of grounds: his point is conceded rather explicitly by his opponents, though only after much resistance, whence a Jewish authority on the Law, bound to a solemn oath, forces him to admit that stoning is, in fact, in the Hebrew Bible. That the Jewish group must admit the correctness of the stoning punishment necessitates that they must admit the correctness of a purported reference to the coming of Muḥammad in the Torah. Their admission in turn serves to put pressure on Muslims to concede that death by lapidation is Islamic.

In this section, I analyzed the PJZO hadith on the authority of the Companion al-Barāʾ b. ʿĀzib (d. *c.* 72/691). As noted above, limited biographical information on ʿAbd Allāh b. Murra (d. *c.* 99/717), the only student of al-Barāʾ who, in the sources, circulates the report on the authority of al-Barāʾ, makes it difficult to establish his involvement. This does not detract from his being a participant nor that the hadith was already in circulation by the end of the first/seventh century. As for the textual content, we found that the primary focus is to emphasize the framework of scriptural distortion (*taḥrīf*), to establish such a charge against the Jewish community, and to affirm that the implementation of the stoning punishment is an organic outgrowth of the Prophet's exercise of religio-legal authority. Given that the Qur'ān elsewhere does not permit the Prophet simply to go along with the false legislations of past communities, the Prophet's order, then, becomes something itself divinely legislated. This is instructive for Muslims and their disagreements about the legitimacy for *zinā*-stoning because the story establishes a relationship between the Prophet's authority and death by lapidation for *zinā* .

2.4. Hadith by the Companion Jābir b. ʿAbd Allāh (d. 78/697, Baghdād, Egypt, Medina, and Syria)

The Companion Jābir b. ʿAbd Allāh is also recorded among those to have transmitted the PJZO hadith. According to the sources, two of his students circulated the report on his authority. They are Abū Zubayr Muḥammad b. Muslim (d. 128/746, Mecca and Medina) and ʿĀmir b. Sharāḥīl al-Shaʿbī (d. *c.* 105/723, Hamdān, Kūfa, and Syria). In the first section, I analyze versions on the authority of Abū Zubayr. In the second section, I focus on those circulated on the authority of al-Shaʿbī. Not only do these variants help to further establish the circulation of the hadith by the end of the first/seventh century of Islam, they also help to shift the time period to at least two decades earlier. Many of the elements found in al-Barāʾ b. ʿĀzib's version are also found in Jābir b. ʿAbd Allāh's recension.

2.4.1. Reports on the authority of Abū Zubayr (d. 128/746, Mecca and Medina)

ʿAbd al-Malik b. ʿAbd al-ʿAzīz b. Jurayj (d. 150/767, Baghdād, Mecca, Yemen) is one of the students of Abū Zubayr who circulates the PJZO hadith on the latter's authority. One version is in ʿAbd al-Razzāq's (d. 211/829) *al-Muṣannaf* and reads:

> ʿAbd al-Razzāq - Ibn Jurayj - Abū Zubayr - Jābir b. ʿAbd Allāh:
>
> The Prophet stoned a man from Aslam, a Jewish man, and a woman.[140]

Ibn Jurayj's role in the report's circulation is corroborated by two entries reported in Muslim and another in Abū Dāwūd. In one of Muslims' versions, uncertainty exists about the woman's background.[141] This uncertainty about the woman appears to be rectified in the other report by Muslim, which reads:

> Hārūn b. ʿAbd Allāh [b. Marwān] (d. 243/857, Baghdād) - Ḥajjāj b. Muḥammad (d. 206/821, Baghdād, Miṣṣīṣī, and Tirmidh) - Ibn Jurayj - Abū Zubayr - Jābir b. ʿAbd Allāh:
>
> The Prophet stoned a man from Aslam and a man from the Jews and his female companion (*imraʾatahu*).[142]

The pronoun *hu* added to 'the woman (*imraʾa*)' indicates that she is associated in some way with the Jewish man. This is different from ʿAbd al-Razzāq's

[140] ʿAbd al-Razzāq, *al-Muṣannaf*, 7:319, no. 13,333; Ibn Ḥanbal provides the same report on the authority of ʿAbd al-Razzāq. See Ibn Ḥanbal, *Musnad* (1992. ed.), 22:342, no. 14,447.

[141] The *isnād* is Isḥāq b. Ibrāhīm (d. 238/852, Ḥijāz, ʿIrāq, Marw, Nīshāpūr, and Syria) - Rawḥ b. ʿUbāda (d. *c.* 205/820, Baghdād and Baṣra) - Ibn Jurayj - Abū Zuybayr - Jābir b. ʿAbd Allāh, see Muslim, *Ṣaḥīḥ*, 1,328, no. 28 (1,701); al-Bayhaqī, *al-Sunan al-kubrā*, 8:374, no. 16,931; Abū Dāwūd also uses the same *isnād* and *matn*. See Abū Dāwūd, *Sunan*, 6:503, no. 4,455.

[142] Muslim, *Ṣaḥīḥ*, 1,328, no. 28 (1,701); al-Bayhaqī, *al-Sunan al-kubrā*, 8:374, no. 16,931.

variant above, which simply states 'a woman (*imra'a*).' The clarification is significant because it conveys the religious background of the female offender. Otherwise, the report could be taken to mean that a Muslim woman was stoned on the authority of the Prophet. The absence of a religious affiliation is consequential for two reasons. First, I discuss in Chapter 3 a hadith according to which a woman is stoned on the Prophet's order. In several versions of this story, she is explicitly cast as a Muslim. Second, it was observed in al-Barā' b. 'Āzib's account that only a Jewish man is stoned. Yet in Jābir b. Samura's recension, the Prophet is remembered to have ordered the stoning of both a Jewish man *and* a Jewish woman. As is made evident in subsequent sections, most variants of the PJZO hadith include both a Jewish man and a Jewish woman. Hence, the clarifying remark about the woman's (religious) affiliation in Muslim's record suggests that the version found there circulated within the purview of those PJZO hadith versions in which the Prophet orders the stoning of a Jewish couple. The important upshot of Muslim's and 'Abd al-Razzāq's entries is that they indicate Ibn Jurayj's participation in the circulation of the report, and, therefore, of the historicity of the Ibn Jurayj - Abū Zubayr transmission line.[143]

Ibn Ḥanbal relates a version on the authority of 'Abd Allāh b. Lahī'a (d. 174/790, Egypt, Medina, and Ḥaḍramawt), who is also a student of Abū Zubayr. The *isnād* and *matn* read:

> Ibn Ḥanbal - Ḥasan [b. Mūsā] (d. *c.* 209/824, Baghdād, Ḥimṣ, Khurasān, Kūfa, and Rayy) - ['Abd Allāh] b. Lahī'a - Abū Zubayr - Jābir b. 'Abd Allāh:
>
> I (Abū Zubayr) asked Jābir: Did the Messenger of God ever order the stoning punishment?
>
> Jābir replied: Yes. A man from Aslam, a man from the Jews, and a woman [were ordered to be stoned]. The Prophet said, "We will give a ruling for you today."[144]

This version is unusual in that Jābir's locution emerges as a response to a question by Abū Zubayr. It is possible that someone believed the locution originated in Abū Zubayr's asking Jābir b. 'Abd Allāh about the Prophet's involvement in the ordering of the stoning punishment. The mindset is

[143] Motzki demonstrates the strong likelihood of historical transmissions between Abū Zubayr and Ibn Jurayj and between Ibn Jurayj and 'Abd al-Razzāq. See Motzki, *Origins of Islamic Jurisprudence*, 204–11.

[144] Ibn Ḥanbal, *Musnad* (1992 ed.) v. 23, 347, no. 15,151.

reflected in the textual content by way of the question. Alternatively, it may be that the report began as an inquiry from Abū Zubayr. But the transmitters in the versions recorded by ʿAbd al-Razzāq and Muslim did not deem it necessary to include Abū Zubayr's question. One important takeaway from this report is that, in my view, the question echoes a socio-historical context in which uncertainty existed about the punishment's legitimacy for Muslims. Otherwise, why ask if the Prophet ever ordered the capital punishment?

The transmission chain furnished by Ibn Ḥanbal requires attention. Some critics reportedly did not value anything narrated by Ibn Lahīʿa.[145] Ibn Ḥanbal himself said that he would only transmit reports from Ibn Lahīʿa if they could be corroborated by other, presumably more reliable, narrators.[146] Contrary to such critical opinions, others respected Ibn Lahīʿa and accepted his transmissions without qualifications.[147] Ibn Lahīʿa served as a judge in Egypt, which testifies to his expertise in legal matters.[148] That he was in Egypt narrating from an ʿIrāqī authority confirms Abū Zubayr's role. Ibn Ḥanbal's informant was also active in ʿIrāq. If Ḥasan was simply inventing *isnād*s, he could have picked someone with an impeachable reputation as compared to one of Ibn Lahīʿa. That Ibn Lahīʿa is involved in the circulation of the PJZO hadith, among other considerations, affirms the historical veracity of the transmission chain.

There is a high probability, then, that both Ibn Jurayj and Ibn Lahīʿa narrated the PJZO hadith and that they did so on the authority of Abū Zubayr (d. 128/746). As for Abū Zubayr, biographers remark that he was known to have regularly studied with Jābir b. ʿAbd Allāh and, accordingly, consider him to be a trustworthy narrator of Jābir's reports.[149] Yet there are some critics who convey that they did not respect him as a narrator and reportedly burned books that were written on his authority.[150] But none of these disputed Abū Zubayr's being a student of Jābir. Besides, Abū Zubayr was generally considered to be a reliable narrator. Such being the case, I contend that Abū Zubayr helped to circulate the PJZO hadith on the authority of Jābir b. ʿAbd Allāh. This Companion's teaching of the report can be settled based on the report's circulation by his other student, al-Shaʿbī (*c.* d. 102/723). It is to this version that I turn to next.

[145] al-Mizzī, *Tahdhīb al-kamāl*, 15:490f.
[146] al-Mizzī, *Tahdhīb al-kamāl*, 15:491 and 494; al-Dhahabī, *Siyar aʿlām*, 8:15f.
[147] al-Mizzī, *Tahdhīb al-kamāl*, 15:495; al-Dhahabī, *Siyar aʿlām*, 8:13.
[148] al-Mizzī, *Tahdhīb al-kamāl*, 15:488; al-Dhahabī, *Siyar aʿlām*, 8:11.
[149] Ibn Saʿd, *al-Ṭabaqāt*, 8:42; Ibn Abī Ḥātim, *al-Jarḥ wa al-taʿdīl*, 8:76; Ibn Ḥibbān, *al-Thiqāt*, 5:352.
[150] Ibn Abī Ḥātim, *al-Jarḥ wa al-taʿdīl*, 8:75; al-Mizzī, *Tahdhīb al-kamāl*, 26:407.

2.4.2. Reports on the authority of al-Shaʿbī (d. *c.* 105/723, Hamdān, Kūfa, and Syria)

The version taught by al-Shaʿbī has more details than the version(s) by Abū Zubayr. Moreover, some motifs in al-Shaʿbī's recension are also in the report on the authority of al-Barāʾ b. ʿĀzib, whose version was reviewed in the previous section. In this subsection, I examine the reports on the authority of al-Shaʿbī from Jābir b. ʿAbd Allāh and compare them to those on the authority of al-Barāʾ b. ʿĀzib. One aim is to shed light on some of the additional ways in which transmitters stabilize the memory of the Prophet's order to stone *zinā* offenders. Another goal is to help substantiate the provenance of the hadith in the first/seventh century and connect it to a common source belonging to that time period. As I argue in this chapter, this common source is Abū Hurayra.

Three individuals are recorded to have acquired the PJZO hadith from al-Shaʿbī. One such person is Mujālid b. Saʿīd al-Hamdānī (d. 144/761, Hamdān, Kūfa, and Syria). Al-Ḥumaydī (d. 219/834) includes the recension in his *Musnad*:

> al-Ḥumaydī - Sufyān [b. ʿUyayna] (d. 198/813, Kūfa, Medina, and Syria) - Mujālid b. Saʿīd al-Hamdānī - al-Shaʿbī - Jābir b. ʿAbd Allāh:
>
> A man from Fadak committed *zinā*. His people wrote to the Jews of Medina advising them to ask Muḥammad about how to deal with the matter. Those from Fadak instructed that if the Prophet commands them to flog, then they should accept his judgment. But if he commands them to stone him, then they should not. Thereafter the Jews of Medina approached the Prophet about the case.
>
> [The Prophet] said: Bring me the two most learned [in scripture] from among you.
>
> The Jews of Medina came with a man blinded in one eye named Ibn Ṣūriyā and someone else.
>
> The Prophet asked the two men: Are you two the most learned [in scripture]?
>
> They responded: Our community certainly believes so.
>
> Then the Prophet asked them: Is there not a ruling by God in your Torah?
>
> They responded: Of course there is!
>
> The Prophet replied: I implore you by the One Who parted the sea for the People of Israel, Who shaded you with clouds, Who rescued you from the

Pharaoh, Who sent favors and consolation onto the People of Israel, what do you find in the Torah regarding the matter of stoning?

Upon hearing [the Prophet speak] one of the two learned men said to the other: No one has ever implored us in this way.

Then they both said to the Prophet: We find that constant looking is *zinā*, embracing is *zinā*, and kissing is *zinā*. And if four witnesses testify that they saw the male member appear and disappear into the female just like a needle is inserted into a kohl bottle, then stoning is obligatory.

The Prophet responded: That is it!

Thereafter the Prophet gave the command and the offender was stoned. This incident occasioned verse (Q5:42): "they listen eagerly to lies and consume abominable things. Nevertheless, should they come to you, either offer judgment or decline to do so. If you choose to decline, [know that] they will not [be able to] harm you in any way. But if you decide to make a judgment, then judge for them in a just manner. Indeed, God loves those who are just."[151]

Note the following side-by-side comparison of the Jābir b. ʿAbd Allāh and al-Barāʾ b. ʿĀzib respective versions:

	Jābir b. ʿAbd Allāh (d. 78/697)	**al-Barāʾ b. ʿĀzib (d. *c.* 72/691)**
How the matter comes to the Prophet's attention:	Jews of Fadak advise the Jews of Medina to ask the Prophet to adjudicate a *zinā* matter.	Prophet sees the offender who had been flogged and whose face had been blackened. He makes an inquiry about the *zinā* punishment.
Indication of the way in which the Jewish group moves away from using the stoning punishment:	Jews of Fadak instruct that if the Prophet orders flogging, then accept it. If he orders stoning, then reject it.	Nobles are let go. Commoners are stoned. Agree to treat all the same by flogging and blackening the face.
Use of Jewish legal authorities:	Prophet summons *two* of the most knowledgeable men. They bring a man with one eye named Ibn Ṣūriyā and a second learned person.	Prophet summons *one* of the learned men. He remains unidentified.

[151] al-Ḥumaydī, *Musnad*, 2:352f, no. 1,331.

	Jābir b. ʿAbd Allāh (d. 78/697)	**al-Barāʾ b. ʿĀzib (d. *c.* 72/691)**
The Prophet's strategy of using an oath to force the Jewish authorities to admit to the proper stoning punishment:	Prophet implores the two learned men on the basis of an oath to tell him what they find in the Torah about the *stoning* punishment for *zinā*.	Prophet implores one learned man on the basis of an oath to tell him what he finds in the Book (Torah) regarding the *ḥadd* for *zinā*.
Jewish authorities admit that stoning is the proper punishment:	The knowledgeable men respond by defining the legal elements necessary for conviction and confirm stoning.	The knowledgeable man confirms stoning as the proper punishment.
The Prophet's response:	Prophet (re)confirms the punishment.	Prophet claims to (re) implement the stoning punishment.
Exegetical relevance:	Connection to Q5:42.	Connection to Q5:41, 44, 45, and 47.

In Jābir's recension, the consultation between the Jews of Fadak and Medina establishes the occasion for the Prophet's involvement in the adjudication of a *zinā* case of a Jewish offender. This is in contrast to al-Barāʾ b. ʿĀzib's variant from the previous section in which the offender passes by the Prophet.

Recall from earlier in this chapter that, on the eve of Islam, rabbinic law had *already* established flogging—a corporal punishment in place of death by stoning—a capital punishment. Given that the Jewish authorities of Medina were likely aware of the change, it stands to reason that they would not have had a compelling motivation to solicit a judgment on the matter from the Prophet. The purported discussion between the Jewish communities of Fadak and Medina serves as a literary device to explain how the Jewish community's inquiry to the Prophet came to be.

The construction of the Mujālid-al-Shaʿbī-Jābir account shows that the transmitters possessed familiarity with an alternative version of the report. Recall that in the al-Barāʾ b. ʿĀzib recension, the Jewish members are portrayed as deliberately lying to the Prophet:

> The Prophet summoned the man's people and asked: Is [flogging, blackening of the face, and parading around town] the fixed punishment (*ḥadd*) for *zinā* in your Book?
>
> They [viz. Jewish group] responded: Yes.

In the Mujālid-al-Sha'bī-Jābir version, the Prophet automatically asks the learned authorities about the stoning punishment in the Torah, to which they respond in the affirmative. In other words, they do not lie about the stoning punishment. Because the Prophet is recorded to have invoked an oath, the presumption is that had he not done so, they would have hid the truth. This presumption indicates that the transmitters of Jābir's account were working under an already-established understanding that the Jewish community was not maintaining fidelity to the stoning punishment. The Prophet being portrayed as immediately asking about the stoning punishment in the Torah is indicative of a familiarity with the story.

The use of two individuals in place of one (as in Ibn 'Āzib's case) is designed to cement the probative value of affirming the stoning punishment. Moreover, the specific mention of Ibn Ṣūriyā is not coincidental.[152] It is also recorded that Ibn Ṣūriyā was one of the leaders of Banū Tha'laba and considered one of the most learned men of the Torah in the Ḥijāz.[153] Ibn Ṣūriyā appears in several reports in which the Prophet interacts with the Jewish community. Early Muslim reports appear to be ambivalent about him. In some accounts, Ibn Ṣūriyā appears in a positive light and in others in a negative one. For example, note the following narrative:

> The Messenger of God went to [their] *bayt al-midrās* (place dedicated for the study of the Torah) and said: Tell me who among you is your most learned [in scripture].
>
> They answered said: 'Abd Allāh b. Ṣūriyā.
>
> The Messenger of God went away with him and made him swear by his religion and by the favors God bestowed upon them, such as food, comfort, and shade from grief.
>
> The Prophet asked Ibn Ṣūriyā: Do you know that I am a messenger of God?
>
> Ibn Ṣūriyā responded: By God, yes. Indeed, the community knows what I know because your description and qualifications are stated clearly in the Torah. But they envy you.
>
> The Prophet asked: And what stops you from accepting Islam?

152 On the significance of Ṣūr for the early Muslim communities, see Yāqūt, *Mu'ajam al-Buldān*, 3:433f.

153 Mazuz, *Religious and Spiritual Life of the Jews of Medina*, 15.

He responded: I would hate to go against my community but it remains possible that they may give allegiance to you and convert.

After that Ibn Ṣūriyā converted.[154]

According to another version of the narrative, Ibn Ṣūriyā converts and then reverts to his original religion.[155] Yet other reports indicate that Ibn Ṣūriyā had a less favorable attitude toward the Prophet.[156] Irrespective of Ibn Ṣūriyā's conversion to Islam or opinion about the Prophet, the account is relevant for the study of the PJZO hadith. The parallels between these reports and Jābir b. ʿAbd Allāh's narrative involving Ibn Ṣūriyā are undeniable. Ibn Ṣūriyā, as a Jewish scholar, directly confirms Muḥammad's prophethood in one interaction and indirectly in another by affirming the punishment of stoning for *zinā*. The use of Jewish scholars such as Ibn Ṣūriyā functions to demonstrate acknowledgment on the part of the Jewish community's own learned sages that the community is guilty of the practice of *taḥrīf*, particularly in relation to the *zinā* punishment, just as his acknowledgment conveys their deliberately veiled belief of Muḥammad's status as a prophet. His role as a learned individual also communicates to Muslims that, in the case of Islam, if someone of analogous authority is asked about the lawfulness of *zinā*-stoning, they would answer in the affirmative.

The reference to Ibn Ṣūriyā as having one eye serves to underscore the characteristics of those who deceive, that is, practice *taḥrīf*. In verse 55 of Chapter Three of the Qur'ān, God is portrayed as saying to Jesus, "I will take you back and raise you up to Me." To gloss the potential meaning of this verse, al-Ṭabarī provides a hadith on the authority of none other than the Jewish convert to Islam, Kaʿb al-Aḥbār (d. *c*. 33/653), who states that God will send Jesus to kill the "one-eyed liar (*al-aʿwar al-dajjāl*).[157] The motif of liars being one-eyed—who betray divine revelations—is incorporated to describe the Prophet's Jewish interlocutors. Whatever positive or negative historical dynamics existed between the Prophet and his Jewish contemporaries, the relationship is preserved as concepts and, in the case of the PJZO hadith, transmitted by the post-Prophetic Muslim communities in the negative.

Al-Shaʿbī's student Mujālid (d. 144/761) cited above quotes Q5:42, but other versions mention a different verse or none whatsoever. The discrepancies raise questions about al-Shaʿbī's participation in the circulation of the

[154] Ibn Saʿd, *al-Ṭabaqāt*, 1:38; Ibn ʿAsākir, *Tārīkh*, 3:417f.
[155] al-Ṭabarī, *Jāmiʿ*, 10:304.
[156] Mazuz, *Religious and Spiritual Life of the Jews of Medina*, 15.
[157] al-Ṭabarī, *Jāmiʿ*, 6:456f, no. 7,137.

Qur'ānic references. Additional variants on his authority can help to resolve the discrepancies. The following report in the *Musnad* of al-Mawṣilī reads:

> al-Mawṣilī - Isḥāq [b. (Ibrāhīm) b. Abī Isrā'īl] (d. 245/859, Baghdād, Marw, Rayy) - Sufyān [b. 'Uyayna] (d. 198/813) - Mujālid (d. 144/761) - al-Sha'bī (d. *c.* 105/723) - Jābir b. 'Abd Allāh (d. 78/697):
>
> [As to Q5:41, which reads:] "'If [he] gives a judgment [in your favor], then accept it. But if not, then be on guard!'" Ibn Ṣūriyā and another are referred. The Prophet came to them and said to the two of them: By the One Who sent the Torah to Moses, and the One Who parted the sea, and the One Who sent favors and consolation, are you the most learned [in scripture]?
>
> The two of them responded: Our community certainly believes it to be the case.
>
> Then one of them said: I cannot believe he has implored us in this way!
>
> [The Prophet] asked: Do you find that constant looking is *zinā*, embracing is *zinā*, and kissing is *zinā*? And if four witnesses testify that they saw the male member appear and disappear into the female, just as a needle is inserted into a kohl bottle, that stoning is then obligatory?[158]

The textual content of al-Mawṣilī's account is a summary of the version found in the *Musnad* of al-Ḥumaydī even though both reports include Ibn 'Uyayna-Mujālid in the transmission chain. The exegetical clause in al-Mawṣilī's entry cites Q5:41 and al-Ḥumaydī's version notes Q5:42.

Al-Ḥumaydī provides another recension that is on the authority of another of al-Sha'bī's students, Zakariyyā [b. Abī Zā'ida] (d. *c.* 147/764). It reads:

> al-Ḥumaydī - Sufyān [b. 'Uyayna] (d. 198/813) - Zakariyyā [b. Abī Zā'ida] (d. *c.* 147/764, Ḥamdān and Kūfa) - al-Sha'bī (d. *c.* 105/723) - Jābir b. 'Abd Allāh (d. 78/697):
>
> Jābir said that God's words (Q5:41), "those 'rightly-guided' ones (i.e. the Jews) listen eagerly to the lies of others," is a reference to the Jews of Medina.
>
> (Q5:41 cont.) "of others" is a reference to the Jews of Fadak.
>
> (Q5:41 cont.) "without even seeing the need to give you a fair hearing. They only intend to interpret the word of God according to their whims," is a reference to the Jews of Fadak who instructed [their interlocutors]: If the

[158] al-Mawṣilī, *Musnad*, 4:103, no. 2,136.

> Prophet commands you to flog, then accept it. But if he does not, then be wary of the command to stone.[159]

Here, only Q5:41 is mentioned. This is different than the version above by al-Ḥumaydī with the Ibn ʿUyayna-Mujālid transmission line, which references Q5:42. Al-Ḥumaydī's two entries and al-Mawṣilī's one entry indicate that Ibn ʿUyayna did likely receive the report from Mujālid and Zakariyyā (a student of al-Shaʿbī). How, then, are the references to different Qur'ānic verses to be explained? The most reasonable explanation is that during the transmission process, different individuals associated the hadith with different verses from the Qur'ān. They remembered the concept of *taḥrīf* and connected it to different parts of the Qur'ān. In light of this scenario and the similarities among the reports, al-Shaʿbī helped to circulate the exegetical clauses.

Note that Abū Dāwūd provides a report that includes Mujālid in the transmission chain without Ibn ʿUyayna. This narrative does not have *any* references to the Qur'ān. The entry reads:

> Abū Dāwūd - Yaḥyā b. Mūsa al-Balkhī (d. 240/854, Balkh and Kūfa) - Abū Usāma [Ḥammād b. Usāma] (d. 201/816, Kūfa) - Mujālid - ʿĀmir [al-Shaʿbī] - Jābir b. ʿAbd Allāh:
>
> A Jewish group came with a man and a woman who committed *zinā*. [The Prophet] commanded: Bring me the two most knowledgeable men from among you.
>
> They brought Ibn Ṣūriyā and another. The Prophet implored the two of them by saying: "What is the command that the two of you find in the Torah about the punishment for these two?"
>
> They responded: We find in the Torah that if four witnesses testify that they saw his member go into her just as a needle is inserted into a kohl bottle, then they are to be stoned.
>
> He[160] asked: Then what prevents you from stoning them?
>
> They responded: Once our kingdom fell, we were reluctant to kill one of our own *(dhahaba sulṭānunā fa karahnā al-qatl)*.
>
> The Messenger of God called for the Jews [to produce witnesses] and four witnesses came. They testified that they witnessed the man's member go

159 al-Ḥumaydī, *Musnad*, 2:353, no. 1,332.

160 Unidentifiable. Presumably the Prophet, based on other versions.

into the woman just as a needle goes into a kohl bottle. Upon hearing the evidence the Messenger of God gave the command for them to be stoned.[161]

At a minimum, the overlap between this report and the other recensions examined above serves as additional evidence of al-Shaʿbī as a common source. In fact, two reports in the *Muṣannaf* of Ibn Abī Shayba corroborate both Mujālid's and al-Shaʿbī's involvement in the circulation of the PJZO hadith. The *matn* of one narrative reads:

The Prophet stoned a Jewish man and a Jewish woman.

The first *isnād* reads:

Ibn Abī Shayba - ʿAbd al-Raḥīm b. Sulaymān (d. 187/802, Kūfa, Marw, and Rayy) - Mujālid (d. 144/761)) - [al-Shaʿbī] (d. *c.* 105/723) - Jābir b. ʿAbd Allāh (d. 78/697).[162]

The second *isnād* reads:

Ibn Abī Shayba - Jarīr [b. ʿAbd al-Ḥamīd] (d. 188/803, Kūfa and Rayy) - Mujālid - [al-Shaʿbī].[163]

But in Abū Dāwūd's record translated above, there is no reference to a Qur'ānic verse. Abū Usāma is noted to only transmit reports he acquires and writes down from his sessions with his teachers.[164] According to biographical opinions, Mujālid's transmissions from al-Shaʿbī-Jābir are approved as reliable.[165] Thus, the absence of references to the Qur'ān may be explained by way of omissions. To support this assertion, I draw attention to its legal significance.

The metaphorical description of sexual relations in Jābir b. ʿAbd Allāh's version indicates a familiarity with both the Hebrew Bible and the rabbinic tradition. In the biblical narrative found in Genesis 9:20–27, it is stated that Ham observes his father Noah's nakedness when he enters Noah's tent and

[161] Abū Dāwūd, *Sunan*, 6:501f, no. 4,452; al-Bayhaqī, *al-Sunan al-kubrā*, 8:402, no. 16,013. The respective versions of al-Bayhaqī and Abū Dāwūd share a high degree of similarity.
[162] Ibn Abī Shayba, *al-Muṣannaf* (2010 ed.), 9:406, no. 29,616.
[163] Ibn Abī Shayba, *al-Muṣannaf* (2010 ed.), 9:406, no. 29,618.
[164] al-Mizzī, *Tahdhīb al-kamāl*, 27:223; al-Dhahabī, *Siyar aʿlām*, 9:278.
[165] al-Mizzī, *Tahdhīb al-kamāl*, 27:223f.

discovers him in a state of unconsciousness resulting from intoxication.[166] The phrase that describes Ham's *seeing* "the nakedness of his father" is, in fact, an idiom for sexual intercourse.[167] In other words, Ham's seeing of his father naked constituted illicit sexual intercourse (*zinā*). There is also a connection between this incident involving Noah and Hamm and Leviticus 18 and 20 on the basis of the phrase "to see nakedness."[168] Leviticus 18 deals with prohibiting consanguineal sexual relationships and Leviticus 20 with adultery—all transgressions deemed capital in nature for which death by lapidation may be applicable. As for embracing and kissing, commentary in the Babylonian Talmud indicates that any physical touch outside of licit relationships is strictly prohibited.[169] In Jābir b. ʿAbd Allāh's account, there also appears to be a conflation of actual illicit sexual intercourse with figurative illicit sexual intercourse. In the Hebrew Bible, adultery serves as a metaphor for idolatry (e.g., Exod.34:16 and Num. 15:39f). According to the rabbinic texts, idolatry is a transgression subject to the stoning punishment.[170] In defining an idolator, a carve out is made for the "one embraces, kisses . . . ."[171] In my view, the transmitter(s) of the hadith underscore the relationship between various acts of transgressions and their relationship to the stoning punishment.

The metaphorical delineation of what constitutes *zinā* reflects (early?) Muslim efforts to shape the definition of illicit sexual intercourse subject to *zinā*-stoning. Recall from Chapter 1 a hadith about a man named Māʿiz who self-confesses to illicit sexual intercourse in the presence of the Prophet. In one version, the Prophet attempts to give Māʿiz exculpatory strategies to avoid the consequence of confession. According to one version of the report, the Prophet is recorded to have stated:

[166] This episode has been the subject of various interpretations within scholarly discourse, particularly concerning its implications on familial relationships and societal norms in ancient texts. See generally, John Sietze Bergsma and Scott Walker Hahn et al., "Noah's Nakedness."

[167] Bergsma and Hahn et al., "Noah's Nakedness," 29.

[168] Bergsma and Hahn et al., "Noah's Nakedness," 31.

[169] For example, the tractate Bava Batra records an incident according to which Rabbi Bena'a wanted to enter the cave of Abraham. The servant of Abraham advised Bena'a that Abraham was "lying in the arms of Sarah, and she examining his head," to which Bena'a asked the servant to advise Abraham to "assume an appropriate position to receive a visitor." See Steinsaltz et al., *Koren Talmud Bavli*, 27:267. The rabbinic opinion indicates that the non-sexual yet physical interaction between Abraham and Sarah is the kind that is private and only permissible within a lawful relationship.

[170] Cohen et al., *The Oxford Annotated Mishnah*, vol. 2, Sanhedrin 7:4, 527; Steinsaltz et al., *Koren Talmud Bavli*, 30:75ff.

[171] Cohen et al., *The Oxford Annotated Mishnah*, vol. 2, Sanhedrin 7:6, 529; Steinsaltz et al., *Koren Talmud Bavli*, 30:75ff.

> Perhaps you kissed her, or groped her (*ghamazta*), or maybe just stared at her with the intention [of having sex with her] (*naẓarta*)?

These stipulations to avoid conviction contrast those purportedly articulated by the rabbis in the narrative on the authority of Jābir b. Abd Allāh. The textual content of the hadith functions as a negotiation mechanism by which to distinguish and articulate differences between rabbinic law and the Islamic definition of *zinā*.

The four-witness clause in Jābir b. ʿAbd Allāh's version also functions to articulate the Islamic legal conditions for conviction and punishment, and thus must be taken as an interpolation on the part of Muslim transmitters. When it comes to rabbinic law, there is no mention of a four-witness evidentiary standard for conviction in the Torah. According to the *Sifre Bemidbar* and the Babylonian Talmud, two or three witnesses are needed for a conviction involving adultery.[172] Moreover, the metaphor of a needle being inserted into a kohl bottle is legally consequential for Islamic *zinā* laws because it serves as one way of establishing the occurrence of sexual intercourse.[173] Ibn Abī Shayba provides a version that focuses on the four-witness element as well as the minimal standards of testimony needed to confirm the occurrence of the sexual act. The transmission chain and textual content read:

> Ibn Abī Shayba - Hushaym [b. Bashīr] (d. 183/799, Baghdād, Baṣra, and Wāsiṭ) - al-Mughīra [b. Miqsam] (d. 136/753, Kūfa) - al-Shaʿbī:
>
> The Jewish group asked the Prophet: What necessitates the imposition of the stoning punishment?
>
> The Prophet responded: When four witnesses testify that they saw the male member enter the female just like a needle is inserted into a kohl bottle. Then stoning is necessary.[174]

Here, the roles are flipped. The Prophet is asked about the elements needed to convict someone of *zinā*, and he provides the four-witness requirement. This may be due to a transmission error or as a way to establish the eventual Islamic legal precedent on the Prophet's authority. In any case, al-Mughīra,

[172] Shamma Friedman, "Sorting Out the Wages of Adultery: Execution, Ordeal or Divorce," 77–99; on the function of witnesses in cases of adultery in rabbinic law, see Mazuz, *Religious and Spiritual Life of the Jews of Medina*, 47f.

[173] E.g., see al-Shāfiʿī, *al-Umm*, 7:391; (Mālikī) Saḥnūn, *al-Mudawwana*, 4:486; (Ḥanafī) al-Jaṣṣāṣ, *Ahkām al-Qur'ān*, 5:129; (Ḥanbalī) Ibn Qudāma, *al-Mughnī*, 12:364.

[174] Ibn Abī Shayba, *al-Muṣannaf* (2010 ed.), 9:367, no. 29,406.

the student of al-Shaʿbī, was a jurist in his own right, famous for his judicial and legal acumen.[175] It makes sense, then, to find that his narrative—clearly legal in character—is cited by the Ḥanafī jurist Abū Yūsuf (d. 181/797) to explain the nature of the testimony required from witnesses to confirm *zinā*.[176] Accordingly, the varied or absence of references to the Qur'ān in Abū Dawūd's variant may be best explained by the report's legal relevance and not its exegetical applicability. By the time we get to the middle of the second/eighth century, the PJZO hadith is being extricated from its initial variant and is being used for the purpose of legal argumentation. The shift explains why there is no longer a connection to Qur'ānic verses that purportedly occasioned the incident.[177]

By analyzing reports on al-Shaʿbī's authority and comparing their textual content with that on the authority of al-Barā b. ʿĀzib (by way of Ibn Murra), there is good evidence to accept the participation of al-Mughīra (d. 136/753), Mujālid (d. 144/761), and Zakariyyā (d. *c.* 147/764) in the circulation of the PJZO hadith. This, in turn, means that al-Shaʿbī (d. *c.* 105/723) helped to circulate the report. He is a well-known transmitter and legal authority and garners considerable respect. He is known for practicing *tadlīs*, but hadith critics nevertheless consider him an authority to be relied upon. They assert that al-Shaʿbī's transmissions based on *tadlīs* are acceptable because they are done so with reliable authorities.[178] The Syrian jurist Ibn Shihāb al-Zuhrī (d. 124/742) believes there are four outstanding legal authorities and al-Shaʿbī is the best in Kūfa.[179] Al-Shaʿbī's reputation as a legal authority probably informed ʿUmar b. ʿAbd al-ʿAzīz's (r. 99/717–101/720) decision to appoint him as judge in Kūfa.[180] It thus stands to reason that al-Shaʿbī would have been involved in the circulation of a narrative in which the Prophet orders the stoning of a Jewish couple.

The disparity between Abū Zubayr's and al-Shaʿbī's respective versions cannot dismiss the possibility of Jābir b. ʿAbd Allāh's involvement in the

[175] Ibn Abī Ḥātim, *al-Jarḥ wa al-taʿdīl*, 1:153; al-Mizzī, *Tahdhīb al-kamāl*, 28:399.

[176] Abū Yūsuf, *al-Kharāj*, 162; al-Bayhaqī records the jurist Ibrāhīm al-Nakhaʿī (d. 96/714, Kūfa and Yemen) as an intermediary between al-Mughīra and al-Shaʿbī. See al-Bayhaqī, *al-Sunan al-kubrā*, 8:402, no. 16,014; however, no correction is made to al-Mughīra's transmission chain in the *ʿilal* collections I investigated.

[177] By using al-Shāfiʿī's (d. 204/820) jurisprudence as an example, Burton argues that the PJZO hadith took on legal significance to justify *zinā*-stoning. See Burton, *The Sources of Islamic Law*, 153–8; Burton, "Law and Exegesis," 278f.

[178] Ibn ʿAsākir, *Tārīkh*, 25:346; Ibn Ḥajar, *Tahdhīb al-tahdhīb*, 3:341; al-ʿUqaylī, *al-Ḍuʿafāʾ*, 2:35f, no. 450.

[179] al-Khaṭīb al-Baghdādī, *Tārīkh*, 14:144.

[180] Ibn Saʿd, *al-Ṭabaqāt*, 8:370f.

circulation of the PJZO hadith. Abū Zubayr's recension can be best seen as a concise statement designed to capture the essence of the legal ruling establishing that the Prophet mandated the stoning punishment for *zinā* and that, among those who were subject to this ruling was a Jewish man and (possibly) a Jewish woman. Transmission chain and comparative textual content analysis of reports on al-Shaʿbī's authority results in a high degree of confidence that he did transmit the narrative. Jābir's detailed report contains many of the same motifs found in versions recorded by the Companion al-Barāʾ b. ʿĀzib. The fact that their accounts are similar in themes but not in exact wording suggests that the Jābir and al-Barāʾ recensions come from a common source in the first/seventh century.

2.5. Hadith by the Companion ʿAbd Allāh b. ʿUmar (d. 74/693, Medina)

The PJZO hadith is widely reported on the authority of the Companion ʿAbd Allāh, the son of ʿUmar b. al-Khaṭṭāb. Ibn ʿUmar's two *mawlā*s, Nāfiʿ (d. *c.* 117/735, Egypt and Medina) and ʿAbd Allāh b. Dīnār (d. 127/745, Medina), are recorded to have transmitted the narrative from Ibn ʿUmar. Additionally, Zayd b. Aslam (d. *c.* 140/757, Medina), *mawlā* of ʿUmar b. al-Khaṭṭāb, is also noted to have received the hadith from Ibn ʿUmar. In this section, I initially focus on variants on Nāfiʿ's authority and, thereafter, on versions circulated by Ibn Dīnār and Ibn Aslam, respectively.

2.5.1. Reports on the authority of Nāfiʿ (d. *c.* 117/735, Egypt and Medina) *Mawlā* Ibn ʿUmar

2.5.1.1. Mālik b. Anas (d. 179/795, Medina)

In his *Muwaṭṭaʾ*, Mālik b. Anas records the PJZO hadith on the authority of one of his teachers, Nāfiʿ. The *isnād* and *matn* read:

> Mālik - Nāfiʿ - ʿAbd Allāh b. ʿUmar:
>
> A Jewish group came to the Messenger of God and told him about a case involving a man and a woman from among them who committed *zinā*. The Messenger of God asked: What do you find in the Torah about the matter of stoning?

They responded: We shame (*nafḍaḥuhum*) and flog them.

ʿAbd Allāh b. Salām interjected: You lie! Stoning is in the Torah!

So they brought the Torah and turned to the relevant passage. One of the Jewish individuals put his hand on the stoning verse and read what was before and after it. "Lift up your hand!" ʿAbd Allāh b. Salām demanded.

The man did as he was told and everyone saw the stoning verse. The Jewish group admitted: He was right, Muḥammad. It does contain the stoning verse.

The Messenger of God gave the command and the two who committed *zinā* were stoned. ʿAbd Allāh b. ʿUmar said: I saw the man lean over to protect the woman from the stones.

Yaḥyā [b. Yaḥyā] said: I heard Mālik say: The man leaned over to protect the woman from the stones.[181]

The arc of the hadith is teleological. This report conveys that a group of Jews sought out the Prophet's judgment for their *zinā* case. Though this is not explicitly stated, there is a palpable aura of hope on their part of receiving a ruling other than stoning. In any case, the Prophet asks them about the matter of stoning in the Torah. Their response is to deflect by mentioning the current practice. Once again, the Qur'ān's charge of *taḥrīf* plays a central role in how the narrative plays out.

Along similar lines, a Qur'ānic verse can be tied to this version of the hadith. Q6:91 states, "...Say, 'Who was it that sent down the Scripture, which Moses brought as a light and a guide to people, which you made into separate sheets, showing some but hiding many?"[182] The motif of the hand being used to cover the stoning verse and then being moved away to reveal the divine command tracks with "showing some but hiding many." Here, a parallel can be established with the hadith I examine in Chapter 4, in which the caliph ʿUmar b. al-Khaṭṭāb claims that at one time a stoning verse existed in the Book of God (read: the Qur'ān) but its inclusion was rejected. Just as the Prophet's Jewish interlocutors cover up the stoning directive by hiding many sheets, so do Muslims when they deny the existence of a stoning verse.

Reference to ʿAbd Allāh b. Salām is not without significance.[183] According to Muslim biographical sources, he was a prominent Jewish scholar and

[181] Mālik, *Muwaṭṭa'* (narrated by Yaḥyā b. Yaḥyā), 1195, no. 623/3,035.
[182] M.A.S. Abdel Haleem, *The Qur'an*, 86.
[183] For an insightful work on Ibn Salām, see generally Samuel A. Stafford, "Constructing Muḥammad's Legitimacy."

leader in Medina, and his Jewish tribesmen considered him to be the most knowledgeable about the Torah.[184] Ibn Salām claims that after his conversion to Islam, the Prophet asked him to read the Qur'ān and the Torah on alternating nights.[185] Ibn Salām's reputation as an important scholarly figure endured after his conversion to Islam. Biographical entries indicate that some considered him to be as knowledgeable as the well-known Companion 'Abd Allāh b. Mas'ūd (d. 32/652).[186] The Jewish convert garners such significance that some exegetes go as far as to claim that the Qur'ān speaks about him specifically. For example, the exegete Mujāhid b. Jabr (d. *c.* 100/718) writes that reference to 'Abd Allāh b. Salām can be found in Q46:10, where the Qur'ān chastises Muhammad's clansmen for rejecting its divine origins while "one of the Children of Israel testifies to its veracity and believes in it, and yet you are too proud to [do the same]?"[187] Recall that in al-Barā' b. 'Āzib's version, there is one learned scholar and, in Jābir b. 'Abd Allāh's version, there are two (one being Ibn Ṣūriyā), who all attest to the stoning punishment being in the Torah. Also, recall that Ibn Ṣūriyā functions in the sources as an eminent Jewish scholar who converts to Islam and authenticates Muḥammad's status as a prophet. The same is reflected in Ibn Salām.[188] Thus, in Ibn 'Umar's recension, Ibn Salām stands in as the learned Jewish convert who helps to substantiate the correct punishment on the basis of the Torah.[189]

As for the transmission chain, Mālik records what he heard from his teacher, Nāfi'. Mālik's version cited above is based on a redaction by Yaḥyā b. Yaḥyā (d. 234/848). The report is also in the recension of the *Muwaṭṭa'* on the authority of the Ḥanafī jurist Muḥammad al-Shaybānī (d. 182/805).[190] Textual variations exist between the two versions. Though negligible in terms of meaning, they are substantial enough to indicate that two separate acts of transmission occurred. For example, in Yaḥyā's version, it states that

[184] Ibn Sa'd, *al-Ṭabaqāt*, 5:380; Ibn 'Asākir, *Tārīkh*, 29:99–104 and 115; W. Montgomery Watt, *Muhammad in Medina*, 197; Mazuz, *Religious and Spiritual Life of the Jews of Medina*, 13f.

[185] Ibn Sa'd, *al-Ṭabaqāt*, 5:383; Ibn 'Asākir, *Tārīkh*, 29:132.

[186] Ibn Sa'd, *al-Ṭabaqāt*, 2:304.

[187] Ibn Sa'd, *al-Ṭabaqāt*, 2:305; others also tie Ibn Salām to this verse. For example, see Ibn 'Asākir, *Tārīkh*, 29:118, 130f; but some rejected the claim that the verse is referencing Ibn Salām. See al-Mizzī, *Tahdhīb al-kamāl*, 15:74; Stafford, "Constructing Muḥammad's Legacy," 157–60.

[188] Ibn Sa'd, *al-Ṭabaqāt*, 5:378f; Ibn 'Asākir, *Tārīkh*, 29:108; Stafford, "Constructing Muḥammad's Legacy," 152–6.

[189] The change to the textual content may be possible in light of the polemical ways in which the figure of Ibn Salām is utilized; on additional biographical information and the polemical function of Ibn Salām, see Hartwig Hirschfeld, "Controversies Between Mohammed and Rabbis," 110–6; Wasserstrom, *Between Muslim and Jew*, 175–8; *Encyclopedia of Jews in the Islamic World*, s.v. "'Abd Allāh ibn Salām."

[190] Mālik, *Muwaṭṭa'* (narrated by al-Shaybānī), 221.

"one of them placed (*fa-waḍaʿa aḥaduhum*) his hand over the stoning verse (*yadahu ʿalā āyat al-rajm*)." In al-Shaybānī's version, it specifies the reciter of the Torah and states that he "made his hand (*fa jaʿala yadahu*) [to cover] the stoning verse *ʿalā āyat al-rajm*." But from a motif standpoint, there exists a high degree of similarity between the two narratives. This points to Yaḥyā and al-Shaybānī sharing a common source: Mālik.[191]

Al-Bukhārī (d. 256/870) twice records the PJZO hadith with Mālik in the transmission chain. One *isnād* is: ʿAbd Allāh b. Yūsuf (d. 218/833, Damascus and Tūnis) - Mālik b. Anas - Nāfiʿ - Ibn ʿUmar.[192] Supposedly al-Bukhārī relies heavily on Ibn Yūsuf's confirmation of hadiths in the *Muwaṭṭaʾ*.[193] This makes sense given that Ibn Yūsuf is considered to be one of the best narrators of Mālik's *Muwaṭṭaʾ*.[194] He is also recorded to have said that Mālik supervised his reception of the *Muwaṭṭaʾ* by means of audition (*samāʿ* or *ʿarḍ*, listening and monitoring).[195] The entry on Ibn Yūsuf's authority is virtually identical to the recension by Yaḥyā b. Yaḥyā. Accordingly, al-Bukhārī's report on the authority of Ibn Yūsuf reaffirms Mālik's participation in the circulation of the report.

The second entry by al-Bukhārī is on the authority of Ismāʿīl b. ʿAbd Allāh [b. Uways al-Iṣfahānī (d. c. 216/831, Damascus and ʿIrāq)]. The transmission chain reads: Ismāʿīl b. ʿAbd Allāh - Mālik - Nāfiʿ - Ibn ʿUmar.[196] The textual content is identical to the version al-Bukhārī provides on the authority of Ibn Yūsuf. According to biographical sources, Ismāʿīl b. ʿAbd Allāh did not have the most favorable reputation as a transmitter. For example, some thought that he was unintelligent, untruthful, and absent-minded.[197] With such a reputation, one has to wonder why al-Bukhārī references the version on Ismāʿīl b. ʿAbd Allāh's authority. As it turns out, al-Bukhārī himself states that Ismāʿīl b. ʿAbd Allāh is associated with other reliable

[191] Motzki convincingly argues that Yaḥyā's and al-Shaybānī's respective versions of the *Muwaṭṭaʾ* result from a common source that can be identified as Mālik. See Harald Motzki, "Der Fiqh des Zuhrī: die Quellenproblematik," 1–44; Schoeler also provides a brief explanation on why different versions of the *Muwaṭṭaʾ* exist, with the primary reason being that it is Mālik's students who give the work its final form, though at times Mālik "did read or recite the text himself in the presence of his students." See Gregor Schoeler, *The Genesis of Literature in Islam*, 73.

[192] al-Bukhārī, *Ṣaḥīḥ* (1976 ed.), 1330, no. 3,436.

[193] al-Mizzī, *Tahdhīb al-kamāl*, 16:336.

[194] al-Mizzī, *Tahdhīb al-kamāl*, 16:335; al-Dhahabī, *Siyar aʿlām*, 10:358.

[195] al-Mizzī, *Tahdhīb al-kamāl*, 16:336; Ibn Ḥajar, *Tahdhīb al-tahdhīb*, 3:714f; *ʿarḍ* (similar to *samāʿ*) is when a student reads texts and the teacher listens and monitors the recitation. See Schoeler, *Genesis of Literature in Islam*, 73.

[196] al-Bukhārī, *Ṣaḥīḥ* (1976 ed.), 2,510, no. 6,450.

[197] al-Mizzī, *Tahdhīb al-kamāl*, 3:127–9; Ibn Ḥajar, *Tahdhīb al-tahdhīb*, 1:292.

transmitters.[198] It would appear that for al-Bukhārī such an association gives him more confidence about Ismāʿīl b. ʿAbd Allāh's transmissions. In the case of the PJZO hadith, al-Bukhārī could also corroborate the report with the version he possessed on Ibn Yūsuf's authority. It is also worth mentioning that Mālik is Ismāʿīl b. ʿAbd Allāh's maternal uncle.[199] Cumulatively, the extant evidence only serves to bolster Mālik's role, as well as that of his two students, in the circulation of the PJZO hadith.

Mālik's dissemination of the PJZO hadith can also be substantiated by entries recorded in other collections. Abū Dāwūd (d. 275/888) provides the report from ʿAbd Allāh b. Maslama al-Qaʿnabī (d. 221/835, Baṣra and Medina), who in turn narrates it from Mālik.[200] ʿAbd Allāh b. Maslama was a well-known transmitter in general and, of Mālik's *Muwaṭṭaʾ* in particular.[201] Al-Nasāʾī (d. 303/915) records a recension on the authority of Qutayba b. Saʿīd (d. 240/854, Balkh, Baghlān, and Baghdād),[202] which is popular among other collectors such as Ibn Abī Shayba and Ibn Ḥanbal.[203] Qutayba is recorded to have been born in the year 150, which would give him a fair amount of time to meet Mālik. In fact, it is written that he participated in audited sessions (*samāʿ*) with Mālik.[204] As for the textual contents, all share markedly high degrees of similarity with one another and with those found in the two recensions of the *Muwaṭṭaʾ* and the *Ṣaḥīḥ* of al-Bukhārī. Therefore, Abū Dāwūd's and al-Nasāʾī's respective entries again point to Mālik as someone who helped to circulate the PJZO hadith.

Mālik's recension contains key motifs found in versions by al-Barāʾ b. ʿĀzib and Jābir b. ʿAbd Allāh. These include the testimony of a Jewish sage, an allusion to the charge of *taḥrīf*, and a confirmation of stoning as the proper punishment for Jewish *zinā* offenders. The substantiation of Mālik's involvement in the report, moreover, points to Nāfiʿ's participation in the transmission, particularly since it is corroborated by other transmitters.

198 Ibn Ḥajar, *Tahdhīb al-tahdhīb*, 1:293.
199 al-Mizzī, *Tahdhīb al-kamāl*, 3:124.
200 Abū Dāwūd, *Sunan*, 6:494f, no. 4,446; al-Bayhaqī's transmission chain goes back to al-Qaʿnabī as well. See al-Bayhaqī, *al-Sunan al-kubrā*, 8:373, no. 16,929.
201 Ibn Abī Ḥātim, *al-Jarḥ wa al-taʿdīl*, 5:181; al-Mizzī, *Tahdhīb al-kamāl*, 16:139–41; al-Dhahabī, *Siyar aʿlām*, 10:259–64.
202 al-Nasāʾī, *al-Sunan al-kubrā*, 6:483f, no. 7,294.
203 Ibn Abī Ḥātim, *al-Jarḥ wa al-taʿdīl*, 7:150; Ibn Ḥibbān, *al-Thiqāt*, 9:20.
204 al-Khaṭīb al-Baghdādī, *Tārīkh*, 14:481.

2.5.1.2. Ayyūb b. Kaysān al-Sakhtiyānī (d. 131/749, Baṣra and Medina)

Ayyūb b. Kaysān al-Sakhtiyānī is another individual in the sources to have circulated the PJZO hadith on the authority of Nāfiʿ. In the sources I investigated, three individuals are recorded to have transmitted the report from al-Sakhtiyānī. Analysis of al-Sakhtiyānī's recension helps to confirm the respective roles of Mālik, Nāfiʿ, and himself in the circulation of the report.

Ibn Ḥanbal provides a version of the PJZO hadith on al-Sakhtiyānī's authority. The transmission chain and textual content read:

> Ibn Ḥanbal - Ismāʿīl b. Ibrāhīm [b. ʿUlayya][205] (d. 193/809, Baghdād, Baṣra, and Kūfa) - Ayyūb [al-Sakhtiyānī] - Nāfiʿ - ʿAbd Allāh b. ʿUmar:
>
> A Jewish group came to the Prophet with a man and a woman from among them who had committed *zinā*. The Prophet asked: What do you find in your Book?
>
> They responded: We blacken their faces and humiliate them (*ukhyazayān*).
>
> The Prophet responded: You lie! Indeed stoning is in the Book. Bring the Torah and read it out loud if you are telling the truth.
>
> So the Jewish group brought the Torah along with a reciter with one eye named Ibn Ṣūriyā. He read the Torah up to a certain point and then put his hand on the page to cover up something. He was instructed, "Lift up your hand."
>
> When he moved his hand away, the stoning verse came into view. Either Ibn Ṣūriyā or the Jewish group together said: Muḥammad, indeed it says stoning but we have not been using it.
>
> The Messenger of God ordered the couple to be stoned and they were stoned. Ibn ʿUmar said: Indeed, I saw him bend over and cover her with his hands when the stones began to hit her.[206]

Note the following transmission chains leading back to Ibn ʿUlayya, a student of al-Sakhtiyānī:

> al-Bukhārī - Musaddad b. Musarhad (d. 228/843, Baṣra) - Ibn ʿUlayya[207];

[205] *Mawlā* Banī Asad b. Khuzayma.
[206] Ibn Ḥanbal, *Musnad* (1995 ed.), 4:284, no. 4,498.
[207] al-Bukhārī, *Ṣaḥīḥ* (2002 ed.), 1864, no. 7,543.

al-Nasāʾī - Ziyād b. Ayyūb Dalluwayh (d. 252/866, Baghdād) - Ibn ʿUlayya;[208]

The following table compares and contrasts the respective entries of Ibn Ḥanbal, al-Bukhārī and, al-Nasāʾī with the Ibn ʿUlayya-al-Sakhtiyānī line:

al-Sakhtiyānī	**al-Sakhtiyānī**	**al-Sakhtiyānī**
Ibn Ḥanbal - Ibn ʿUlayya	al-Nasāʾī - Ziyād b. Ayyūb - Ibn ʿUlayya	al-Bukhārī - Musaddad - Ibn ʿUlayya
What do you find in your Book?	What do you find in your Book?	What do you do with them?
Blacken faces and humiliate (*ukhyazayān*).	Blacken faces and humiliate (*ukhyazayān*).	Blacken faces and humiliate (*nukhzayuhumā*).
Interjection by an unidentifiable person who states the Jewish group is lying.	Interjection by an unidentifiable person who states the Jewish group is lying.	
Bring the Torah if you are honest.	Bring the Torah if you are honest.	Bring the Torah if you are honest.
One-eyed man named *Ibn Ṣūriyā* reads the Torah.	One-eyed man reads the Torah.	One-eyed man reads the Torah.
The Jewish group confirms stoning as the proper punishment but admits it is not being used.	The Jewish group confirms stoning as the proper punishment but admits it is not being used.	The Jewish group confirms stoning as the proper punishment but admits it is not being used.
Unidentified person claims to have witnessed the stoning of the Jewish couple.	No reference to someone being present, but *kadhā* may be intended to signify the witness clause.[209]	Unidentified person claims to have witnessed the stoning of the Jewish couple.

One difference among the three versions is that in the recension recorded by al-Bukhārī, there is no interjection clause that accuses the Jewish group of lying. Here, the Prophet already knows that they are not telling the truth. Another variation is that Ibn Ḥanbal's version includes Ibn Ṣūriyā by name. Recall that his name is included in the recension on the authority of Jābir b. ʿAbd Allāh (Section 2.3.2). The absence or addition can be best explained as changes during the

[208] al-Nasāʾī, *al-Sunan al-kubrā*, 6:441, no. 7,175.
[209] The editor of the text states that he could not read the manuscript and therefore wrote *kadhā*. See al-Nasāʾī, *al-Sunan al-kubrā*, 6:441, no. 7,175, fn. 1.

course of the transmission, though not without purpose. Beyond the aforementioned distinctions, however, all three versions are highly similar, which points to Ibn 'Ulayya's involvement. This, by extension, indicates al-Sakhtiyānī to have been Ibn 'Ulayya's teacher as reflected in the transmission chains.

In the biographical sources, Ibn 'Ulayya is listed as one of the preferred Baṣran transmitters of reports.[210] Reportedly he and Ibn Ḥanbal had such a favorable rapport that the latter said he went only as far as Ibn 'Ulayya to confirm the strength of narratives circulating in Baṣra.[211] This makes Ibn 'Ulayya's being Ibn Ḥabal's informant entirely unsurprising. Biographical dictionaries also point to a student–teacher connection between Ibn 'Ulayya and al-Sakhtiyānī.[212] Moreover, Ibn 'Ulayya's birth year of 728 indicates that he was in his twenties when al-Sakhtiyānī died, which makes it reasonable to believe him to have met and studied with al-Sakhtiyānī. In sum, transmission chain and comparative textual content analysis indicate that Ibn 'Ulayya acquired the report from al-Sakhtiyānī.

Shu'ba b. al-Ḥajjāj (d. 160/776, Baṣra and Wāsiṭ) is also noted to have learned the PJZO hadith from al-Sakhtiyānī. The variant is recorded by al-Nasā'ī with the following transmission chain and textual content:

> al-Nasā'ī - from the book of Yaḥyā b. Ḥabīb b. 'Arabī (d. 248/862, Baṣra) - Yazīd b. Zuray' (d. 182/798, Baṣra) - Shu'ba b. al-Ḥajjāj (d. 160/776) - al-Sakhtiyānī (d. 131/749) - Nāfi' (d. *c.* 117/735) - Ibn 'Umar (d. 74/693):
>
> When they were brought to the Prophet, he asked: What do you find in your book?
>
> They responded: We do not find stoning.
>
> 'Abd Allāh b. Salām interjected: They are lying! Stoning is in their Book!
>
> It was said: Bring the Torah and open it up if you are truthful.
>
> So they brought the Torah along with their readers and he put his hand over the stoning verse and read what was before and after it.
>
> 'Abd Allāh b. Salām ordered him forcefully: "Move your hand away!"
>
> When he did, the stoning verse came into view. So the Messenger of God gave the order and the two offenders were stoned.[213]

[210] Ibn Abī Ḥātim, *al-Jarḥ wa al-ta'dīl*, 2:153f; al-Mizzī, *Tahdhīb al-kamāl*, 3:28; he is not liked by all. See al-Dhahabī, *Siyar a'lām*, 9:112.

[211] Ibn Abī Ḥātim, *al-Jarḥ wa al-ta'dīl*, 2:154; al-Mizzī, *Tahdhīb al-kamāl*, 3:29.

[212] Ibn Abī Ḥātim, *al-Jarḥ wa al-ta'dīl*, 2:153; al-Mizzī, *Tahdhīb al-kamāl*, 3:23f; al-Dhahabī, *Siyar a'lām*, 6:16.

[213] al-Nasā'ī, *al-Sunan al-kubrā*, 6:441f, no. 7,176.

This version does not contain some of the clauses found in the recensions of either Mālik or Ibn-ʿUlayya from al-Sakhtiyānī. The differences can be explained in a number of ways. First, al-Sakhtiyānī may never have transmitted the missing clauses, meaning they were added in Ibn ʿUlayya's account on the basis of Mālik's version. Second, it is possible that al-Sakhtiyānī did not communicate the same elements to all his students. Third, it is plausible that information was left out during the transmission after al-Sakhtiyānī in al-Nasāʾī's transmission chain. Lastly, it may be that the transmission chain was forged. Scenario three emerges as the most probable because al-Nasāʾī's entry retains all of the core motifs. Furthermore, by Shuʿba's time, the report had sufficient circulation in ʿIrāq, which has been demonstrated in my previous analysis of the narratives circulated on the respective authorities of al-Barāʾ b. ʿĀzib and Jābir b. ʿAbd Allāh. Shuʿba or someone below him could have amended the text by adding the missing details. Because no such modifications occur, it means that, during the transmission process after al-Sakhtiyānī, certain textual material was deemed irrelevant for preserving the important aspects of the conceptual understanding of the Prophet's involvement in the stoning of Jewish *zinā* offenders.

Transmission chain analysis indicates that Shuʿba obtained the report from his recorded teacher, al-Sakhtiyānī. To begin with, very little is written on al-Nasāʾī's informant, Yaḥyā b. Ḥabīb (d. 248/862). Only later biographical dictionaries point to his reliability as a transmitter.[214] Al-Nasāʾī writes that he received the narrative from Ibn Ḥabīb's written notes, that is, "from the book of...." To the best of my knowledge, there is nothing in the sources indicating that Ibn Ḥabīb did write a book or that someone had access to it. That no information exists about Yaḥyā b. Ḥabīb's notebooks cannot be assumed to mean that they did not exist. Hence, barring the emergence of any evidence that may indicate otherwise, al-Nasāʾī's claim that he acquired the report "from a book of Yaḥyā b. Ḥabīb" stands.

As for Ibn Ḥabīb's teacher Yazīd b. Zurayʿ, it is recorded that he was a reliable transmitter who circulated several reports that were useful for legal proofs.[215] It is also noted that some transmitters preferred Yazīd b. Zurayʿ's narratives over Ibn ʿUlayya's.[216] Yazīd b. Zurayʿ's teacher, Shuʿba b. al-Ḥajjāj

[214] al-Mizzī, *Tahdhīb al-kamāl*, 31:265; al-Dhahabī, *Siyar aʿlām*, 31:156f; Ibn Ḥajar, *Tahdhīb al-tahdhīb*, 7:24.
[215] Ibn Saʿd, *al-Ṭabaqāt*, 9:290.
[216] Ibn Abī Ḥātim, *al-Jarḥ wa al-taʿdīl*, 9:264; al-Mizzī, *Tahdhīb al-kamāl*, 32:127–9.

(d. 160/776), is more respected and better known.[217] It appears that moving earlier in the transmission chain corresponds to improving reputations of the transmitters. The increasing favorability of each narrator could lead to the conclusion that the increasingly polished character of the emerging transmission chains transpired out of a desire to establish the authenticity of the report by attributing it to reputable transmitters. But the evidence invoked thus far from the sources refutes this conclusion. Rather, particularly given the flawed character of many of the transmission chains that turn up even in later sources, it is more probable that a historical transmission occurred.

Al-Sakhtiyānī's recension contains the main themes found in Mālik's version, differing only in terms of literary style and expressions of various motifs, for example, forms of punishments being used instead of stoning or identity of the authority who confirms the punishment of stoning. The following side-by-side comparison of al-Sakhtiyānī's and Mālik's versions can help to shed light on the significance of particular motifs:

Ibn Ḥanbal - Ibn 'Ulayya - al-Sakhtiyānī	**Mālik**
A Jewish group brings a man and a woman who have committed *zinā* and asks the Prophet to adjudicate the case.	A Jewish group brings a man and a woman who have committed *zinā* and asks the Prophet to adjudicate the case.
Prophet asks what do they find in their Book.	Prophet asks what do they find *in the Torah about stoning.*
Humiliate (*ukhyazayān* or *nukhzayuhumā*) and blacken the face.	Shame (*nafḍaḥuhum*) and *flog.*
Interjection by an unidentifiable person who states the Jewish group is lying.	Interjection by *'Abd Allāh b. Salām* who states the Jewish group is lying.
The Torah is brought forth and read to determine the existence of a stoning verse and attempts to cover it up; in one version by a reciter with one eye named Ibn Ṣūriyā, in the other?	The Torah is brought forth and read to determine the existence of a stoning verse and attempts to cover it up by *an unidentified person.*
On the basis of an anonymous person's comment, the Jewish group confirms stoning as the proper punishment *but admits it has not been using it.*	On the basis of *Ibn Salām's* comment, the Jewish group confirms stoning as the proper punishment.

Flogging is not in al-Sakhtiyānī's version but both his and Mālik's recensions include humiliation. Note that the Arabic term used for

[217] For a detailed biographical commentary on Shu'ba, see *Encyclopaedia of Islam* 2nd ed., s.v. "S͟hu'ba b. al-Ḥad͟jd͟jād͟j."

humiliation is different in al-Sakhtiyān's and Mālik's respective accounts. In the former, the verb is *khaziya* whereas in the latter it is *faḍaḥa*. The difference indicates transmission from memory than from a written copy. The concept is the same, but the specific words are different. Importantly, a variance in the term with the same underlying meaning suggests that both individuals were drawing upon the report from a common source through unique transmissions. Furthermore, the purpose of recalling the punishment used by the Jewish group affirms a critical point, namely, their reluctant admission of practicing *taḥrīf* by neglecting the divinely ordained punishment of stoning. It also signals two relevant verses from the Qur'ān. Q4:16 instructs that the two transgressors of illicit sexual intercourse should suffer in an unspecified manner (*fa-ādhūhumā*) and Q24:2 instructs 100 lashes. Humiliation, shaming, and flogging all reflect potential Qur'ānic injunctions that rejectors of *zinā*-stoning are appealing to. The PJZO hadith serves to counter such objections. Also noteworthy is that in the version by Shu'ba and in two of the three versions reported by Ibn 'Ulayya—all on the authority of al-Sakhtiyānī—there is no specific reference to Ibn Ṣūriyā. This name is also absent from Mālik's recension. But Ibn Ṣūriyā is identified in one of al-Sakhtiyānī's versions transmitted by Ibn 'Ulayya, which finds corroboration in the reports on the authorities of the Companions al-Barā' b. 'Āzib and Jābir b. 'Abd Allāh that were examined in the previous sections.

Biographical data raise the degree of confidence about al-Sakhtiyānī's acquisition of the report from Nāfi'. Al-Sakhtiyānī is considered to be one of the most authoritative sources for reports by Nāfi'.[218] Many biographers praise al-Sakhtiyānī's transmission and legal acumen.[219] In fact, during his lifetime, he was considered to be the most authoritative legal mind in Baṣra.[220] Born *c.* 66/685,[221] his life overlaps with Nāfi''s for at least 30 years. This information, taken together with the conclusions drawn from our comparative textual analysis, indicates a strong connection to Nāfi' as the common source for both al-Sakhtiyānī and Mālik's recensions.

[218] Ibn Abī Ḥatim, *al-Jarḥ wa al-ta'dīl*, 2:256; al-Mizzī, *Tahdhīb al-kamāl*, 3:461; Ibn Ḥajar, *Tahdhīb al-tahdhīb*, 1:375.
[219] Ibn Sa'd, *al-Ṭabaqāt*, 9:246; al-Mizzī, *Tahdhīb al-kamāl*, 3:461f.
[220] al-Mizzī, *Tahdhīb al-kamāl*, 3:461; al-Dhahabī, *Siyar a'lām*, 6:17ff.
[221] al-Mizzī, *Tahdhīb al-kamāl*, 3:463; al-Dhahabī, *Siyar a'lām*, 6:20 and 24.

2.5.1.3. Mūsā b. ʿUqba (d. *c.* 141/748, Medina)

Mūsā b. ʿUqba is also reported to have transmitted the PJZO hadith on Nāfiʿ's authority. His recension further corroborates the involvement of both Mālik, al-Sakhtiyānī, and Nāfiʿ. ʿAbd al-Razzāq records a version of the PJZO hadith on Ibn ʿUqba's authority which reads:

> ʿAbd al-Razzāq - Ibn Jurayj (d. 150/767) - Mūsā b. ʿUqba - Nāfiʿ - Ibn ʿUmar:
>
> A Jewish group came to the Prophet with a man and a woman from among them who committed *zinā*. The Prophet asked them: In what manner do you treat someone who commits *zinā*?
>
> They responded: We subject them to a corporal punishment.
>
> The Prophet then asked: And what do you find in the Torah?
>
> They responded: We do not find anything.
>
> ʿAbd Allāh b. Salām interjected: You lie! Stoning is in the Torah. Bring it forth and read it if you are truthful!
>
> They brought the Torah and one of their learned scholars, who studies the Torah, put his hand over the stoning verse and began to read what was before and after it, skipping the verse itself. ʿAbd Allāh b. Salām pulled the reader's hand away from the verse and exclaimed: What is this?!
>
> When they saw it, they acknowledged that it was the stoning verse. The Messenger of God ordered that the offenders be stoned and they were stoned in the area where funeral prayers are held.
>
> ʿAbd Allāh said: I saw her lover shield her from the stones as they were stoning her.[222]

Note the side-by-side comparison of Ibn ʿUqba's version with the textual content of variants on the respective authorities of Mālik and al-Sakhtiyānī:

Mūsā b. ʿUqba (d. *c.*142/ 748)	**Ibn ʿUlayya (d. 193/809) - al-Sakhtiyānī (d. 131/749)**	**Mālik (d. 179/795)**
A Jewish group brings a man and a woman who have committed *zinā* and asks the Prophet to adjudicate the case.	A Jewish group brings a man and a woman who have committed *zinā* and asks the Prophet to adjudicate the case.	A Jewish group brings a man and a woman who have committed *zinā* and asks the Prophet to adjudicate the case.

[222] ʿAbd al-Razzāq, *al-Muṣannaf*, 7:318f, no. 13,332.

Mūsā b. ʿUqba (d. *c.*142/748)	**Ibn ʿUlayya (d. 193/809) - al-Sakhtiyānī (d. 131/749)**	**Mālik (d. 179/795)**
The Prophet asks in what manner do they punish someone who commits *zinā. Then he asks what they find in the Torah.*	The Prophet asks what they find in their Book.	The Prophet asks what they find *in the Torah about stoning.*
Hit them/Do not find stoning.	Humiliate and blacken the face.	Shame and *flog*.
Interjection by *ʿAbd Allāh b. Salām* who states the Jewish group is lying.	Interjection by an unidentifiable person who states the Jewish group is lying.	Interjection by *ʿAbd Allāh b. Salām* who states the Jewish group is lying.
The Torah is brought out and read to determine the existence of a stoning verse and *a learned scholar* attempts to cover it up.	The Torah is brought out and read to determine the existence of a stoning verse and *a man with one eye named Ibn Ṣūriyā* attempts to cover it up.	The Torah is brought out and read to determine the existence of a stoning verse and *an unidentified person* attempts to cover it up.
On the basis of *Ibn Salām's* comment, the Jewish group confirms stoning as the proper punishment.	On the basis of a comment,[223] the Jewish group confirms stoning as the proper punishment *but admits they have not been using it.*	On the basis of *Ibn Salām's* comment, the Jewish group confirms stoning as the proper punishment.

The manner in which the Prophet asks the first question is similar in Ibn ʿUqba's and al-Sakhtiyānī's versions. Specifically, he does *not* initially question them about stoning. But in Mālik's recension, the Prophet immediately attempts to solicit a response about the stoning punishment. In my view, the transmitters already had the stoning punishment in mind and thus began the report with an early reference to it. This would mean that the transmitter(s)'s focus on stoning is a way to convey the *taḥrīf* issue and that Muslims should not do the same thing by avoiding death by lapidation.

In Ibn ʿUqba's version the response to the Prophet's question is "we subject them to a corporal punishment," not "blacken faces and flog" (al-Sakhtiyānī) or "shame and flog" (Mālik). The differences noted here notwithstanding, they each serve to substantiate the charge of *taḥrīf* and identify a Qur'ānic punishment. Again, it is a deliberate attempt to respond to elements within the Muslim community who held that the imposition of flogging in Q24:2 by

[223] Recall that Shuʿba's account on the authority of al-Sakhtiyānī references Ibn Salām.

having the Prophet consciously sidestepping the implementation of flogging in favor of stoning.

'Abd Allāh b. Salām is specified in the respective versions of Ibn 'Uqba and Mālik, but not in al-Sakhtiyānī's report on the authority of Ibn 'Ulayya, in which the identity of the individual responsible for exposing his co-religionists' playing light with their scriptural ordinances is left anonymous. The omission is likely due to transmitter uncertainty, or perhaps a transmitter felt the identity of the said individual was irrelevant.

The presence of a learned sage is characteristic of Ibn 'Uqba's variant. Initially, it is unknown who this learned person is, but eventually, Ibn Salām's name comes to light. The recensions circulating in 'Irāq describe the expert as a man with a blind eye named Ibn Ṣūriyā. That the identification of this sage with Ibn Ṣūrīyā is an 'Irāqī regional peculiarity can now be conclusively negated based on Ibn 'Uqba's version, as the latter is not recorded to have traveled to 'Irāq and the different versions of his account variously specify the authoritative person as being a blind man, name him as Ibn Ṣūriyā, while in some versions both details are provided.

In Ibn 'Uqba's version, a specific reference is made about the location of where the punishment is meted out. This is not mentioned in the other accounts, which suggests either that Ibn 'Uqba or someone below him in the *isnād* helped to circulate this element or that Ibn 'Uqba preserved a detail of the original incident that other transmitters either neglected to mention or were unaware of. At this point, the answer is indeterminable.

Al-Bukhārī,[224] al-Nasā'ī,[225] and al-Bayhaqī[226] provide recensions with the Ibn 'Uqba - Nāfi' link in their respective transmission chains. The reports share high degrees of similarities with the version recorded by 'Abd al-Razzāq. Al-Bukhārī's report, in particular, does not mention Ibn 'Umar by name as part of the witness motif. But aside from this difference, the commonality among the different versions points to Ibn 'Uqba as the common source.

Given Ibn 'Uqba's birth year of 55/674, Ibn 'Umar's death year of circa 73/692, and regional overlap, one has to wonder why Ibn 'Uqba is not recorded to have received the PJZO hadith directly from Ibn 'Umar. This is further

[224] al-Bukhārī, *Ṣaḥīḥ* (2002 ed.), 1118, no. 4,556. Al-Bukhārī also provides a truncated version on Ibn 'Uqba's authority, which states the Prophet stoned a Jewish man and a Jewish woman at the site where funeral services take place. See al-Bukhārī, *Ṣaḥīḥ* (2002 ed.), 320, no. 1,329 and 1810, no. 7,332.

[225] al-Nasā'ī, *al-Sunan al-kubrā*, 6:442, no. 7,177.

[226] al-Bayhaqī, *al-Sunan al-kubrā*, 8:429, no. 17,117.

complicated by the fact that some sources testify to the fact that Ibn ʿUqba did, in fact, relate hadith on Ibn ʿUmar's authority.[227] Assuming the information in these sources proves to be accurate, the fact that Ibn ʿUqba resisted the temptation to attribute the report directly to an authority he had heard from on previous occasions is evidence for the accuracy of the transmission line provided by him and that Nāfiʿ was indeed circulating the report.

The biographical information on Ibn ʿUqba does not raise sufficient doubts about his transmission. Yes, Ibn Saʿd writes—without an explanation—that Ibn ʿUqba is reliable for only a small number of reports.[228] This may be because at times he did not clarify his source(s).[229] There is also a remark that certain hadith authorities distrusted his transmissions from Nāfiʿ.[230] Indeed, Ibn ʿUqba admits to having hadith on the authority of Nāfiʿ that he did not hear directly from him, but the biographical report conveys that he confirms such hadith with authoritative sources of Nāfiʿ.[231] The upshot of these views on Ibn ʿUqba is that the transmission chain cannot be dismissed. Importantly, the overwhelming majority of biographical comments serve to swing the pendulum in favor of Ibn ʿUqba's reception of the narrative from Nāfiʿ. This is especially the case when it comes to *maghāzī* reports (narratives about the Prophet's military campaigns) because Ibn ʿUqba is considered to be a reliable source.[232] In fact, Mālik actively encouraged people to record *maghāzī* accounts from him.[233] Certain individuals such as Ibn Ḥanbal considered Ibn ʿUqba to be a reliable transmitter without any qualifications.[234] Lastly, Ibn ʿUqba was born in 70/689 and by the time of Nāfiʿ's death, he was around forty-six years old. This means that he had ample time to study with his teacher. In sum, the multiple attestations of the Ibn ʿUqba - Nāfiʿ link,[235] the totality of Ibn ʿUqba's biographical information, and the comparative textual analysis indicate that he did receive the PJZO hadith from Nāfiʿ.

Thus far, we have examined the transmission chains and corresponding textual content of variants on the authority of al-Sakhtiyānī, Ibn ʿUqba, and

[227] Ibn Saʿd, *al-Ṭabaqāt*, 4:149.
[228] Ibn Saʿd, *al-Ṭabaqāt*, 7:519.
[229] Ibn ʿAsākir, *Tārīkh*, 60:466.
[230] al-Mizzī, *Tahdhīb al-kamāl*, 29:120f; al-Dhahabī, *Siyar aʿlām*, 6:117.
[231] Ibn ʿAsākir, *Tārīkh*, 60:466.
[232] Ibn ʿAsākir, *Tārīkh*, 60:464f; al-Dhahabī, *Siyar aʿlām*, 6:114.
[233] al-Mizzī, *Tahdhīb al-kamāl*, 29:118f; al-Dhahabī, *Siyar aʿlām*, 6:115.
[234] Ibn Abī Ḥātim, *al-Jarḥ wa al-taʿdīl*, 8:154.
[235] In addition to the al-Bukhārī, al-Nasāʾī, and al-Bayhaqī versions, the *Sunan* of al-Dārimī (d. 255/869) includes a report with Ibn ʿUqba - Nāfiʿ in the transmission chain. See al-Dārimī, *Sunan*, 2:233, no. 2,321.

Mālik, all of whom cite Nāfiʿ as their source for the report. The versions circulated by Nāfiʿ's three students contain many of the same elements also found in other recensions of the PJZO hadith that do not involve these individuals. For example, their respective accounts include the use of a learned sage to confirm the stoning punishment and to establish the charge of *taḥrīf* against Medina's Jewish community. Accordingly, the versions of the PJZO hadith reviewed in this section affirm Nāfiʿ's involvement.

2.5.1.4. Other students of Nāfiʿ

This section focuses on recensions by students of Nāfiʿ that were not investigated in previous sections. The variants are aggregated here because they are rare in the sources, yet they retain their importance because they add further evidence to Nāfiʿ being a source involved in the circulation of the PJZO hadith.

Juwayriya b. Asmāʾ b. ʿUbayd (d. 173/789, Baṣra) is recorded to have acquired the report from Nāfiʿ.[236] His recension is provided by al-Ṭayālisī (d. 204/819):

> al-Ṭayālisī - Juwayriya - Nāfiʿ - Ibn ʿUmar:
>
> The Messenger of God was brought a Jewish man and a Jewish woman who had committed *zinā*. The Messenger of God asked: What do you find in your Book?
>
> The Jewish group replied: We do not find the punishment of stoning.
>
> Ibn Salām interjected: They are lying. Stoning is in their Book.
>
> The two of them summoned Ibn Ṣūriyā and he began to read the Book up until the stoning verse. He tried to cover it up by putting his hand over it, but Ibn Salām interjected: Lift up your hand!
>
> He did and the stoning verse could be seen. He said: Muḥammad, stoning is in our Book.
>
> The Messenger of God had them stoned at *al-Balāṭ*.[237] He[238] said: The man tried to shield his lover with his body.[239]

[236] On Juwariya see, e.g., Ibn Abī Ḥātim, *al-Jarḥ wa al-taʿdīl*, 2:531 and Ibn Ḥajar, *Tahdhīb al-tahdhīb*, 1:594f. He was a peer of Mālik b. Anas.

[237] *Al-Balāṭ* was located in Medina, and it was filled with stones. It was supposedly between the Prophet's mosque and Medina's market. See Yāqūt, *Muʿjam*, 1:477f.

[238] It is unclear to whom *qāla* (he said) is referring.

[239] al-Ṭayālisī, *Musnad*, 3:384f, no. 1,967; al-Ṭayālisī also includes a truncated version that goes back to the Companion Jābir b. Samura. See al-Ṭayālisī, *Musnad*, 2:131, no. 812. I analyze this short recension below.

Comparing Juwayriya's version with that of the aforementioned three reveals that the former is composed of various elements derived from the latter three. For example, in Mālik's and Ibn 'Uqba's reports, Ibn Salām is explicitly named whereas Ibn Ṣūriyā is not. In al-Sakhtiyānī's version, Ibn Ṣūriyā is named whereas Ibn Salām is not. However, in Juwayriya's account, both Ibn Ṣūriyā and Ibn Salām are named. This indicates the stabilization of a memory involving the concept of the Prophet's interaction with his Jewish co-Medinans on the basis of the stoning of Jewish *zinā* offenders with the presence of an authoritative figure who confirms the stoning punishment.

Another difference has to do with the initial conversation the Prophet has with the Jewish group. Recall from Mālik's recension that the Prophet immediately asks about the stoning punishment. In Juwayriya's report, the Prophet first inquires, "What do you find in your Book?" The report indicates a familiarity with the story as it appears in other variants. In this sense, the question can easily be read as: What do you find in your Book *with respect to a punishment for zinā*? Otherwise, left as is and without reading the issue of the proper punishment for *zinā* into the question, exactly what the Prophet intends to resolve is left rather open. Yet the Jewish group responds to the Prophet's question by awkwardly bringing up the punishment of stoning when, strictly speaking, the Prophet never explicitly asks them about it. It is clear, then, that the transmitter(s) convey(s) familiarity with the story. This explains why no mention is made of the Medinan Jews' practice of blackening the face and/or flogging for *zinā* offenders, which is instead replaced with an immediate denial of the stoning punishment. Once again, these elements indicate an intermingling of multiple versions of the report with a first/seventh century provenance.

Standing alone, Juwayriya's recension constitutes evidence of a transmission line to Nāfi' and, having been corroborated by the three others, it provides support. Based on the analysis of the textual content, Juwayriya's transmission is demonstrated to be independent of the other three. Indeed, Juwayriya is considered a highly learned person whose transmissions on the authority of Nāfi' are as valued as those of Mālik.[240] In short, Juwayriya's recension reaffirms the involvement of Nāfi'.

Ma'mar b. Rāshid (d. 153/770, Baṣra, Medina, and Yemen) is also recorded to have acquired the report from Nāfi'. This recension is in the *Muṣannaf* of 'Abd al-Razzāq and reads:

[240] Ibn Sa'd, *al-Ṭabaqāt*, 9:281; Ibn Abī Ḥātim, *al-Jarḥ wa al-ta'dīl*, 2:531.

ʿAbd al-Razzāq - Maʿmar b. Rāshid - Nāfiʿ - Ibn ʿUmar:

I was witness to the incident when two Jews who committed *zinā* were brought before the Messenger of God. He sent for their readers and they came with the Torah. He asked: Do you not find stoning in your Book?

The Jewish group responded: No. We blacken their faces, mount them on a donkey with their backs to one another, and parade them around town (*yujabbahān wa yuḥammamān*).[241]

So he said to him: Read!

He began reading, placing his hand over the stoning verse while proceeding to read the verse before and the verse after it. ʿAbd Allāh b. Salām commanded: Move your hand away!

The reader moved his hand, and there was the stoning verse. Thereafter the Messenger of God rendered judgment on the two offenders and they were stoned. Ibn ʿUmar said: Indeed I saw them being stoned. The man tried to protect her from the stones.[242]

Maʿmar's variant contains many of the same motifs found in versions circulated by other students of Nāfiʿ, such as the Jewish group's claims about *taḥmīm*. As demonstrated earlier, the Ḥijāzi recensions characteristically name ʿAbd Allāh b. Salām as an authority on the Torah and his name appears in Maʿmar's account. Certain details found in Maʿmar's textual content, moreover, point to Maʿmar as an independent source. Specifically, there is a reference to the way in which the offenders are humiliated: they are mounted on a donkey and paraded around town. This is, to be sure, another way of expressing the humiliation motif, and it conveys the supposed *taḥrīf* on the part of the Median Jews. It is best to say that Maʿmar can be treated as independently attesting to Nāfiʿ's role in the report, even though there is evidence that he had access to other versions.

ʿUbayd Allāh b. ʿUmar is also recorded to have transmitted the PJZO hadith from Nāfiʿ. His recension is in the *Ṣaḥīḥ* of Muslim and the transmission chain and textual content read:

Muslim - al-Ḥakam b. Mūsā Abū Ṣāliḥ (d. 232/847, Baghdād and al-Qanṭara) - Shuʿayb b. Isḥāq (d. 189/804, Baṣra and Syria) - ʿUbayd Allāh [b. ʿUmar b. Ḥafṣ] (d. *c.* 147/764, Baghdād and Medina) - Nāfiʿ - Ibn ʿUmar:

241 See Lane, *Arabic-English Lexicon*, 2:13, under *jabaha*.
242 ʿAbd al-Razzāq, *al-Muṣannaf*, 7:318, no. 13,331.

> A Jewish man and a Jewish woman who committed *zinā* were brought before The Messenger of God. The Messenger of God took leave to see a Jewish person.
>
> The Prophet asked: What do you find in the Torah for someone who commits *zinā*?
>
> They responded: We blacken their faces and parade them around town with their faces opposite to one another.
>
> He said: Bring the Torah if you are being truthful.
>
> So they brought it and read it up to the point of the stoning verse. A young man who was reading the text put his hand over the stoning verse and read what was before and after it. 'Abd Allāh b. Salām, who was with the Messenger of God, said to the reader: Lift up your hand!
>
> The reader did as he was told and the stoning verse came into view. The Messenger of God gave the ruling and the couple was stoned. 'Abd Allāh b. 'Umar said: I was one of those who stoned them and indeed I saw the man trying to protect the woman from the stones with his body.[243]

Ibn Abī Shayba[244] and Ibn Mājah[245] also provide a shortened version with 'Ubayd Allāh in the transmission chain. Both collectors reference Ibn Numayr as their respective source. The reports read:

> ['Abd Allāh] b. Numayr (d. 199/814, Hamdān and Kūfa) - 'Ubayd Allāh b. 'Umar [b. Ḥafṣ] (d. *c.* 147/764, Baghdād and Medina) - Nāfi' - Ibn 'Umar:
>
> The Messenger of God stoned two Jews and I was one of those who stoned them.

'Ubayd Allāh is the great grandson of 'Umar b. al-Khaṭṭāb, which makes it unsurprising to find his circulation of a report involving a family member. 'Ubayd Allāh was born some time after 70/689, thirty years before Nāfi''s death date, which leaves quite some time for 'Ubayd Allāh to have acquired material from Nāfi'. The recension by Muslim preserves several elements found in other versions on Nāfi''s authority, and their presence serves to reinforce Nāfi''s involvement in the dissemination of the PJZO hadith.

243 Muslim, *Ṣaḥīḥ*, 1326, no. 1,699, 1326f, no. 27.
244 Ibn Abī Shayba, *al-Muṣannaf* (2008 ed.), 9:405f, no. 29,615 and Ibn Abī Shayba, *al-Muṣannaf* (2008 ed.), 7:380, no. 22,198.
245 Ibn Mājah, *Sunan*, 854, no. 2,556.

Several versions of the PJZO hadith on the authority of Nāfiʿ have been furnished in this section. The transmission chains and textual contents by six of Nāfiʿ's students have been reviewed. The individuals are Ayyūb b. Kaysān al-Sakhtiyānī (d. 131/749, Baṣra and Medina), ʿUbayd Allāh (d. *c.* 147/764, Baghdād and Medina), Mūsā b. ʿUqba (d. 141/748, Medina), Maʿmar b. Rāshid (d. 153/770, Baṣra, Medina, and Yemen), Juwayriya (d. 173/789, Baṣra), and Mālik (d. 179/795, Medina). Cumulatively, the evidence results in a high degree of confidence about a transmission on the part of Nāfiʿ. That Nāfiʿ taught the report means it had to have been in circulation by the end of the first/seventh century, which is about the same time that the respective versions on the authority of al-Barāʾ b. ʿĀzib (the teacher of ʿAbd Allāh b. Murra [d. *c.* 99/717]) and Jābir b. ʿAbd Allāh (the teacher of al-Shaʿbī [d. *c.* 105/723]) entered into circulation. In Section 2.2, I noted that it was difficult to establish Ibn Murra's involvement in the circulation of the report because of the paucity of both biographical information and corroborating versions on his authority. Having examined the textual contents of three different Companions, I believe al-Aʿmash received the report from someone living in the early part of the second century, and this person is his reported teacher, Ibn Murra. In the next section, I review biographical information on Nāfiʿ and compare and contrast his recension with the detailed versions reported on the authorities of al-Barāʾ and Jābir, respectively. I conduct the analysis to demonstrate additional ways in which transmitters are attempting to stabilize a memory about the Prophet's involvement in the stoning of Jewish *zinā* offenders. In my view, the similarities and differences shed light on how groups of individuals understand the past and make sense of it in their own socio-historical context(s). Finally, comparing and contrasting the various iterations of the textual content helps to affirm the dating of the hadith to the first/seventh century and to a common source, namely, Abū Hurayra.

2.5.1.5. Nāfiʿ *mawlā* Ibn ʿUmar (d. *c.* 117/735, Egypt and Medina)

The following chart provides salient motifs from the various recensions transmitted by Nāfiʿ's six students. The chart thereafter presents key details from versions circulated on the authorities of the Companions al-Barāʾ b. ʿĀzib and Jābir b. ʿAbd Allāh, respectively. For the most part, the same motifs are expressed across all transmitted versions of the PJZO hadith.

al-Sakhtiyānī (d. 131/749)	**'Ubayd Allāh (d. *c.* 147/764)**	**Mūsā b. 'Uqba (d. 141/748)**	**Ma'mar b. Rāshid (d. 153/770)**	**Juwayriya (d. 173/789)**	**Mālik (d. 179/795)**
A Jewish group brings a man and a woman who have committed *zinā* and asks the Prophet to adjudicate the case.	A Jewish man and a Jewish woman who committed *zinā* are brought to the Prophet.	A Jewish group brings a man and a woman who have committed *zinā* and asks the Prophet to adjudicate the case.	A Jewish man and a Jewish woman who committed *zinā* are brought to the Prophet.	A Jewish man and a Jewish woman who committed *zinā* are brought to the Prophet.	A Jewish group brings a man and a woman who have committed *zinā* and asks the Prophet to adjudicate the case.
The Prophet asks what do they find in their book.	The Prophet asks what do they find in the Torah for someone who commits *zinā*.	The Prophet asks in what manner do they treat someone who commits *zinā*.	The Prophet sends for two readers and asks them if they find stoning in the Torah and they say no.	The Prophet asks what do they find in their book.	The Prophet asks what do they find *in the Torah about stoning*.
Humiliate and blacken the face.	Blacken the face and parade them around town.	The offenders are hit (presumably flogged), but they do not find stoning.	Blacken face with charcoal, mount the offender on a donkey, and parade them around town.	Do not find stoning.	Shame and *flog*.
Interjection by an unidentifiable person who accuses the Jewish group of lying.	Interjection by an unidentifiable person who calls for the Torah.	Interjection by *'Abd Allāh b. Salām* who accuses the Jewish group of lying.	Interjection by an unidentifiable person who instructs the reciter of the Torah.	Interjection by *'Abd Allāh b. Salām* who accuses the Jewish group of lying.	Interjection by *'Abd Allāh b. Salām* who accuses the Jewish group of lying.
The Torah is brought forth and read to determine the existence of a stoning verse, with attempts to cover it up by a reciter with one eye named Ibn Ṣūriyā.	The Torah is brought forth and read to determine the existence of a stoning verse, with attempts to cover it up by *an unidentified person.*	The Torah is brought forth and read to determine the existence of a stoning verse, with attempts to cover it up by *a learned scholar.*	The Torah is brought forth and read to determine the existence of a stoning verse, with attempts to cover it up by *an unidentified person.*	The Torah is brought forth and read to determine the existence of a stoning verse, with attempts to cover it up by Ibn Ṣūriyā.	The Torah is brought forth and read to determine the existence of a stoning verse, with attempts to cover it up by *an unidentified person.*

al-Sakhtiyānī (d. 131/749)	'Ubayd Allāh (d. *c.* 147/764)	Mūsā b. 'Uqba (d. 141/748)	Ma'mar b. Rāshid (d. 153/770)	Juwayriya (d. 173/789)	Mālik (d. 179/795)
On the basis of the reading, the Jewish group confirms stoning as the proper punishment *but admit they have not been enforcing it.*	On the basis of *Ibn Salām's* instruction, the reciter removes his hand and the stoning verse is revealed.	*Ibn Salām* demands that the reader remove his hand; the Jewish group confirms stoning as the proper punishment.	*Ibn Salām* demands that the reader remove his hand and the stoning verse is revealed.	*Ibn Salām* demands that the reader remove his hand; the Jewish group confirms stoning as the proper punishment.	*Ibn Salām* demands that the reader remove his hand; the Jewish group confirms stoning as the proper punishment.
Unidentified person claims to have witnessed the stoning of the Jewish couple.	*Ibn 'Umar* claims to have witnessed the stoning of the Jewish couple.	*'Abd Allāh* claims to have witnessed the stoning of the Jewish couple.	*Ibn 'Umar* claims to have witnessed the stoning of the Jewish couple.	Unidentified person claims to have witnessed the stoning of the Jewish couple.	*Ibn 'Umar* claims to have witnessed the stoning of the Jewish couple.

Jābir b. 'Abd Allāh (d. 78/697)	al-Barā' b. 'Āzib (d. *c.* 72/691)
Jews of Fadak advise the Jews of Medina to ask the Prophet to adjudicate a *zinā* matter.	Prophet sees the offender who was flogged and whose face was blackened. He makes an inquiry about the punishment.
Jews of Fadak instruct that if the Prophet orders flogging, then accept it. But if he orders stoning, then they should not.	Nobles are let go. Commoners are stoned. Agree to treat all the same by flogging and blackening the face.
Prophet asks the Jews to call their two most knowledgeable men.	Prophet calls for one learned person.
Prophet implores them on the basis of an extensive oath to tell him what they find in the Torah regarding the punishment for *zinā*.	Prophet implores *one* learned person on the basis of a short oath to tell him what he finds in the Book (Torah) regarding the punishment for *zinā*.
On the basis of an oath, 'Abd Allāh b. Ṣūriyā responds by defining what constitutes *zinā* and confirm stoning as the proper punishment.	On the basis of an oath, the learned person confirms stoning is the proper punishment.
Prophet (re)confirms the punishment.	Prophet claims to reimplement the stoning punishment.
Exegetical connection to Q5:41f.	Exegetical connection to Q5:41, 44, 45, and 47.

Jābir b. ʿAbd Allāh (d. 78/697)	al-Barāʾ b. ʿĀzib (d. *c.* 72/691)
	In connection with Q5:41, the accusation against the Jewish group, who gave instructions to go to the Prophet and to accept his ruling if he says blacken face and flog, and to be wary if he says to stone.

Note that some elements found in the al-Barāʾ b. ʿĀzib and Jābir b. ʿAbd Allāh recensions are not in Ibn ʿUmar's account. For example, there is no background story that explains why the Jewish group asks the Prophet to adjudicate their *zinā* case, nor is there any reference to the Qurʾānic verses. Nevertheless, the core elements do remain intact, with the implicit Qurʾānic charge of *taḥrīf* functioning as the backbone of Ibn ʿUmar's report and the basis for the Prophet's ordering of the stoning punishment.

The following is a comparative summary:

1) Conveyance of *taḥrīf*:
   a. In Nāfiʿ's recension, a Jewish man and a Jewish woman who commit *zinā* are brought to the Prophet. He asks the Jewish group whether they find stoning for *zinā* in the Torah, to which they respond in the negative. The Jewish group instead claims a different punishment or, as in the case in some versions, denies the use of stoning altogether;
   b. In Jābir's version, the Jews of Fadak instruct the Jews of Medina to ask the Prophet about adjudicating a *zinā* matter and to accept his decision only if he orders the punishment of flogging;
   c. In the variant by al-Barāʾ, an offender who has been flogged and whose face has been blackened passes by the Prophet;

   The background story is important because it ostensibly provides the reason(s) for the Prophet's involvement. In other words, it helps to answer the question about why the Jewish group is asking the Prophet to adjudicate their *zinā* case. Note that Ibn ʿUmar's version of the report does not provide the background story. As I demonstrate in the next two sections, the background story was in circulation during the first/seventh century. Ibn ʿUmar's recension is based on the narrative circulating on Abū Hurayra's authority. The wide attestation of the report impacted the background story's relevance or lack thereof and was eventually dropped from certain versions. Nevertheless, the concept of *taḥrīf* remains intact as well as the legitimating function of the Prophet's *zinā*-stoning instruction.

2) Style and content of initial question:
    a. In the al-Sakhtiyānī, 'Ubayd Allāh, Ibn 'Uqba, and Juwayriya's versions, the Prophet asks the Jewish group about what the Torah prescribes as punishment for someone who commits *zinā*. In the Ma'mar and Mālik recensions, the Prophet specifically asks about stoning. The Prophet's unsolicited yet specific inquiry about the capital punishment must have been added after the report's initial circulation. It emerged as part of the textual content(s) by the time several versions were in circulation about the Prophet's order to stone Jewish *zinā* offenders. *Zinā*, *taḥrīf*, and stoning were fused together as concepts for those who were transmitting the report, thereby inducing them to recall the story with a seemingly spontaneous question about stoning for the *zinā* offense;
    b. In Jābir's and Ibn al-'Āzib's respective narratives, the Prophet asks about what is found in the Torah. Once it is confirmed that the divine directive is stoning, the Prophet affirms it. As noted earlier, the sources include accounts according to which Muḥammad is questioned by various interlocutors to prove his prophethood. That the Torah confirms the correct prescribed punishment operates in the background as a mechanism by which to show that the Torah also confirms Muḥammad as a prophet of God;
3) Imploring a truthful response:
    a. In the respective versions of al-Sakhtiyānī, Ibn 'Uqba, and 'Ubayd Allāh, after the Jewish group reportedly makes a false representation about the *zinā* punishment, they are ordered to "Bring the Torah if [they] are truthful." The wording echoes verses from the Qur'ān. Q3:93f reads:

    > Except for what Israel made unlawful for himself, all food was lawful to the Children of Israel before the Torah was revealed. Say, 'Bring the Torah and read out [loud the relevant passage] if you are telling the truth.'[246]

    The appearance of the command clause serves to (re)emphasize the Qur'ān instruction to challenge the fidelity of the Prophet's

[246] Haleem, *The Qur'an*, 41.

Jewish contemporaries to their scripture. Indeed, the same motif flows through Mālik's version. While there is no specific order to bring the Torah, it is nevertheless brought and read to confirm their act of deception, which is then exposed by 'Abd Allāh b. Salām;

b. In the recensions of al-Barā' b. 'Āzib and Jābir b. 'Abd Allāh, the Prophet uses an oath to secure a truthful response. The oath is a substitute for the Torah;

4) Expert testimony:

a. In the al-Sakhtiyānī, 'Ubayd Allāh, and Ma'mar versions, stoning is confirmed on the basis of an unidentified expert, who accuses the Jewish group of lying. To corroborate the accusation and affirm the correct punishment, the Torah is used;

b. In 'Ubayd Allāh's recension, an eventual reference is made to 'Abd Allāh b. Salām, the Jewish learned sage who converts to Islam. He is the same person who appears in the textual contents of the report by Ibn 'Uqba, Juwayriya, and Mālik;

c. In the variants of al-Sakhtiyānī, Juwayriya, and the Companion Jābir b. 'Abd Allāh, Ibn Ṣūriyā is named instead. His name appears predominantly in versions of the report transmitted by 'Irāqīs.[247] Non-'Irāqi versions instead name Ibn Salām.

Nevertheless, all versions encompass the theme of a sage who is proficient in the Torah. This expert (two, in some variants) plays an important part in the narrative, as he invariably ends up establishing the Qur'ānic charge of *taḥrīf* against his own community;

5) Denouement:

a. All versions of the report on Ibn 'Umar's authority conclude with someone claiming to have witnessed the stoning of the couple. The motif functions to convey a sense of legitimacy of the incident's occurrence. Per the chart above with Nāfi', Ibn 'Umar is specified in recensions narrated by Ma'mar, 'Ubayd Allāh b. 'Umar, Mālik, al-Ḥumaydī, and Muslim. But in other accounts, Ibn 'Umar's name is absent. It is also worth noting that the clause is entirely missing from the respective versions of al-Barā' b. 'Āzib and Jābir. What can explain this difference? In the next section, I present evidence to

[247] The exception being al-Barā' b. 'Āzib's version.

demonstrate that it must have been Ibn ʿUmar's son, Sālim (d. *c.* 106/724), who helped to circulate the witness clause;

b. In place of the witness clause, the al-Barāʾ b. ʿĀzib and Jābir b. ʿAbd Allāh versions end by directly tying the incident with certain Qurʾānic verses that charge the Jewish community of practicing *taḥrīf*. Because the transmitters of these recensions are from ʿIrāq, one is left with the initial impression that it was there that the PJZO hadith came to be viewed as an exegetical story. However, I demonstrate below that the exegetical connection emerges in the Ḥijāz.

Biographical information about Nāfiʿ, the client (*mawlā*) of Ibn ʿUmar, contains much that substantiates Nāfiʿ's role in the circulation of the PJZO hadith. Some present-day scholars, however, have raised questions regarding the historicity of some of the attributions to Nāfiʿ in the transmission of reports. For example, Joseph Schacht (d. 1969) argues that because Islamic law proper only emerges in the third century, "traditions pretending to express the doctrines of the Successors, in the second half of the first/seventh century, are to a great extent fictitious."[248] For this reason, he doubts "whether the historical Nāfiʿ is responsible for everything that is ascribed to him. . . ."[249] Others have taken Schacht's skepticism further, at times even outright dismissing his very existence as a historical figure. Juynboll remarks that in Ibn Saʿd's biographical collection, "Nāfiʿ, although mentioned often, is talked about in such a manner that a reader may be left with the impression a historical person is not being described.[250] In Juynboll's view, the story of Nāfiʿ is more intimately tied to the story of Mālik, which for him implies that Mālik is the real source of reports attributed to Nāfiʿ.[251] Transmission chain analysis led Juynboll to conclude that the Mālik-Nāfiʿ-Ibn ʿUmar link "cannot be maintained as a historically feasible chain of transmission."[252]

Motzki has refuted many of Juynboll's arguments and, by extension, Schacht's.[253] Motzki takes issue with the judgment Juynboll passes on Nāfiʿ based on Ibn Saʿd's entries. Motzki states that Juynboll makes poor use of the *ex silentio* argument; simply because there are no extensive details on Nāfiʿ in

[248] Schacht, *Origins*, 176.
[249] Schacht, *Origins*, 177.
[250] Gautier H.A. Juynboll, "Nāfiʿ, the *malwā* of Ibn ʿUmar," 218.
[251] Juynboll, "Nāfiʿ, the *malwā* of Ibn ʿUmar," 238f.
[252] Juynboll, "Nāfiʿ, the *malwā* of Ibn ʿUmar," 241.
[253] Harald Motzki, *Analysing Muslim Traditions*, 61–89.

one biographical source should not, and cannot, logically lead to the conclusion that he did not exist.[254] Furthermore, Motzki notes that when compared to biographical entries on other *mawalī*, concise biographical entries on Nāfiʿ are hardly a divergent phenomenon.[255] As for a historical relationship between Mālik and Nāfiʿ, Motzki asserts that it is highly plausible because Mālik was born in 93 and was in his twenties by the time of Nāfiʿ's death. This overlap based on birth and death dates makes transmissions between the two conceivable, especially by audition.[256] Based on an analysis of transmissions between Mālik and his two teachers, Nāfiʿ and Ibn Shihāb al-Zuhrī, Motzki opines that unique language patterns within the textual contents of each student–teacher dialectic demonstrate that communication between Mālik and his teachers did take place and is historical.[257] Lastly, by examining and comparing transmission chains and textual contents from pre-canonical collections such as those found in the second-/eighth century Yemeni ʿAbd al-Razzāq's famous compendium *al-Muṣannaf*, Motzki demonstrates that Juynboll's claims about Nāfiʿ are improbable at best. In the next section, I furnish additional evidence to support Nāfiʿ's involvement in the transmission of the PJZO hadith.

2.5.2. ʿAbd Allāh b. Dīnār (d. 127/745, Medina) - Ibn ʿUmar

ʿAbd Allāh b. Dīnār is another *mawlā* of Ibn ʿUmar to have transmitted the PJZO hadith. In the sources I investigated, al-Bukhārī is the only one to include the report on Ibn Dīnār's authority. The entry reads:

> al-Bukhārī - Muḥammad b. ʿUthmān [b. Karāma] (d. after *c.* 254/868, Baghdād, Kūfa, or Rayy) - Khālid b. Makhlad (d. 213/828, Kūfa and Medina) - Sulaymān [b. Bilāl] (d. 177/793, Medina) - ʿAbd Allāh b. Dīnār - Ibn ʿUmar:
>
> The Messenger of God was brought a Jewish man and a Jewish woman.
>
> The Prophet said to the Jewish group: What do you find in your book?

[254] Motzki, *Analysing Muslim Traditions*, 66.
[255] Motzki, *Analysing Muslim Traditions*, 66.
[256] Motzki, *Analysing Muslim Traditions*, 68f.
[257] Motzki, "Jurisprudence of Ibn Shihāb," 22–5.

> They responded: Our learned scholars have instructed us to blacken their faces and make them bow down in shame (*al-tajbiya*).
>
> ʿAbd Allāh b. Salām said: Messenger of God, tell them to bring the Torah.
>
> They did and someone from the Jewish group put his hand over the stoning verse and read what was before and after it. Ibn Salām instructed to him: Lift up your hand!
>
> He did and the stoning verse came into view. The Messenger of God gave his ruling and the Jewish couple was stoned. Ibn ʿUmar also said: They were stoned at *al-Balāṭ*. I saw the man trying to shield the woman.[258]

The textual content has several motifs found in other versions on the authority of Ibn ʿUmar. First, in all accounts the Prophet asks his Jewish interlocutors about what their Book prescribes as a punishment for *zinā*. Second, some form of punishment aside from stoning is furnished as a response. Third, there is the interjection by Ibn Salām, the attempt to cover up the stoning verse, and the witness clause. Therefore, the overlap between Nāfiʿ's and Ibn Dīnār's respective versions suggests that Ibn ʿUmar was their common source.

An examination of the biographical and transmission data reveals no reason to discredit the chain of transmission recorded by al-Bukhārī. Khālid b. Makhlad (d. 213/828, Kūfa) reportedly possessed numerous reports from Medinan informants.[259] Supposedly, he narrated *munkar* hadith (uncorroborated reports), which led some to use his reports out of necessity and not preference.[260] But attempts to discredit him may be on the basis of his conversion to Shīʿī Islam.[261] Moreover, the hadith critic Ibn ʿAdī (d. 365/967) is noted to have said that he did not find the reports from Ibn Makhlad that he investigated to be uncorroborated.[262] Yet others were willing to accept *munkar* reports if they could be corroborated with narratives by reliable transmitters.[263] In this particular case, the status of Ibn Makhlad's narratives

258 al-Bukhārī, *Ṣaḥīḥ* (1976 ed.), 2,499f, no. 6,433.

259 Ibn Saʿd, *al-Ṭabaqāt*, 8:530; al-Dhahabī, *Siyar aʿlām*, 10:217.

260 Ibn Saʿd, *al-Ṭabaqāt*, 8:530; al-Mizzī, *Tahdhīb al-kamāl*, 8:165; al-Dhahabī, *Siyar aʿlām*, 10:218; Ibn Ḥajar, *Tahdhīb al-tahdhīb*, 3:293; Ibn al-Ṣalāḥ writes that there are two types of unfamiliar, i.e., uncorroborated reports: (1) an isolated report that is not narrated by reliable transmitters or (2) an isolated report whose narrator is not reliable nor proficient (*itqān*) to transmit it on his own. See Ibn Ṣalāḥ, *ʿUlūm al-ḥadīth*, 81f; on *munkar* reports also see Kamali, *Hadith Studies*, 148.

261 Ibn Saʿd, *al-Ṭabaqāt*, 8:530; al-Mizzī, *Tahdhīb al-kamāl*, 8:165.

262 Ibn Ḥajar, *Tahdhīb al-tahdhīb*, 3:293.

263 Brown, *Hadith*, 94.

is not consequential since we have several other attestations. In short, we can set aside the charge of transmitting *munkar* reports, leaving us no reasons to deny that Ibn Makhlad acquired the narrative from his teacher, Sulaymān b. Bilāl. The latter was a Berber and served as a tax collector in Medina.[264] Several biographical entries record that he was known to be a shrewd individual,[265] and Mālik thought highly of him.[266] All in all, we have no grounds to dismiss Sulaymān b. Bilāl, thus leaving his place in the transmission chain intact.

Ibn Dīnār receives considerable praise in biographical sources. Any criticism is met with correctives. For instance, Ibn Dīnār is accused of at times for circulating reports deemed to be *muḍṭarib* (disrupted).[267] Hadith critics, however, discredit this claim, noting that if any errors do occur in transmissions related to his authority, then they are on the part of those who come after him.[268] Ibn Dīnār is also known to have learned hadith from Nāfiʿ,[269] the latter considered to be older and, importantly, stronger in transmissions than the former.[270] This comparison strengthens the transmission event as recorded by al-Bukhārī. Why would someone forge a transmission chain utilizing someone with a weaker reputation when a stronger individual is available and is connected to the same report? Given the general overlap between the Nāfiʿ-Ibn ʿUmar and Ibn Dīnār-Ibn ʿUmar recensions, one is left either with claiming that Ibn Makhlād or Ibn Bilāl procured the narrative from Mālik and supplied a false but counterintuitively *less* sound chain of transmission to their students that Ibn Dīnār obtained the report from Nāfiʿ or that Ibn Dīnār acquired the entirety of the report from Ibn ʿUmar per the transmission chain. Recall that it is only in the Juwayriya - Nāfiʿ recension that the stoning occurs at *al-Balāṭ*. This specificity is in the Ibn Dinār - Ibn ʿUmar recension, which suggests that Ibn Dinār likely picked up this element from his study session with Nāfiʿ. At any rate, we can reasonably take Ibn ʿUmar to be the common source of the two *mawlā*s.

264 Ibn Saʿd, *al-Ṭabaqāt*, 7:598.
265 Ibn Ḥibbān, *al-Thiqāt*, 6:388; al-Mizzī, *Tahdhīb al-kamāl*, 11:375; al-Dhahabī, *Siyar aʿlām*, 7:426.
266 Ibn Ḥajar, *Tahdhīb al-tahdhīb*, 3:14f.
267 al-Dhahabī, *Siyar aʿlām*, 5:254f; Ibn Ḥajar, *Tahdhīb al-tahdhīb*, 3:463f. On *muḍṭarib*, see Ibn Ṣalāḥ, *al-ʿUlūm al-ḥadīth*, 41f and under subsection (Category 19) "*Maʿrifa al-muḍṭarib min al-ḥadīth*," 93–5.
268 al-Dhahabī emphasizes that the accusation was never taken seriously. See al-Dhahabī, *Mīzān*, 2:417.
269 al-Mizzī, *Tahdhīb al-kamāl*, 14:472; Ibn Ḥajar, *Tahdhīb al-tahdhīb*, 3:463.
270 Ibn Ḥajar, *Tahdhīb al-tahdhīb*, 3:463.

2.5.3. Zayd b. Aslam (d. 140/757, Medina) - Ibn ʿUmar

In addition to Ibn ʿUmar's two *mawlās*, Zayd b. Aslam is recorded to have narrated the PJZO hadith on Ibn ʿUmar's authority. The report can be found in Abū Dāwūd's *Sunan* and the transmission chain and textual content read:

> Abū Dāwūd - Aḥmad b. Saʿīd al-Hamdānī (d. 253/867, Hamdan and Egypt) - ʿAbd Allāh b. Wahb (d. 197/813, Egypt and Medina) - Hishām b. Saʿd (d. 160/776, Medina) - Zayd b. Aslam - Ibn ʿUmar:
>
> A Jewish group came and called for the Messenger of God to [meet them on] a hill. Then they went to a *bayt al-midrash* and said: Abū al-Qāsim, a man from among us committed *zinā* with a woman, so make a judgement.
>
> They put down a cushion for the Messenger of God and he sat on it. Then the Prophet said: Bring me the Torah.
>
> They did that. Then the Prophet took the cushion out from under him and placed the Torah on it and said: I believe in you and in the Messenger who was sent to you. [He then turned to the men and said:] Bring me your most learned.
>
> So they brought him a young man. Then the story about stoning was mentioned in accordance with Mālik's report from Nāfiʿ.[271]

Both the Torah, a learned person, and presumably the charge of *taḥrīf* remain key elements in this variant. But some material is not in any other versions on Nāfiʿ's authority. For example, Ibn Aslam's narrative includes the Prophet's remark about trusting the messenger, that is, Moses. The mentioning of his name underscores an appeal to the most fundamentally authoritative source of the Jewish community, whose authority is above all, including that of the learned sages. Note that the Prophet's being called to a hill parallels the story of how Moses himself is said to have been called by God to the mountain top to receive the promulgations of the Torah.[272] How are the variations to be explained? Efforts to stabilize a memory using concepts related to Jewish authoritative sources such as Moses and the Torah, as well as the relevance of the legal precedent being established by report, contributed to some changes after its teaching by Ibn ʿUmar. Importantly, the metanarrative remains

[271] Abū Dāwūd, *Sunan*, 6:498, no. 4,449.
[272] Exod. 19:1–25.

intact. A scholar is at the center of Ibn Aslam's recension, with modifications to the story explaining that the Prophet's involvement is designed, ostensibly, to further buttress the legitimacy of his prophethood. Zayd b. Aslam was a client (*mawlā*) of 'Umar b. al-Khaṭṭāb and noted to have attended study sessions with Ibn 'Umar.[273] He is considered a reputable legal authority as well as someone highly knowledgeable in Qur'ānic exegesis.[274] Given the PJZO hadith's exegetical and eventual legal relevance, Zayd b. Aslam would be among those familiar with the narrative.

The above analysis demonstrates that Nāfi', Ibn Dīnār, and Zayd b. Aslam helped to circulate the PJZO hadith. That they were involved in the report's transmission signifies Ibn 'Umar as their earlier shared source, whose involvement can also be substantiated based on the transmission chain and comparative textual content examination with recensions on the respective authorities of the Companions al-Barā' b. 'Āzib and Jābir b. 'Abd Allāh. While changes emerge in Ibn 'Umar's report as it circulates in different regions of the Islamic polity, key motifs remain intact. Importantly, the report serves to establish the Prophet as having ordered the stoning punishment on the basis of a divine directive.

2.6. Hadith by the Companion Abū Hurayra (d. *c.* 58/677, Mecca, Medina, and Yemen)

The Companion Abū Hurayra is recorded to have circulated the PJZO hadith, and his recension is critical for establishing the provenance of a report in which the Prophet orders the stoning of Jewish *zinā* offenders. In the collections that I examined for this project, the *Muṣannaf* of 'Abd al-Razzāq, the *Sunan* of Abū Dāwūd,[275] the exegetical work of al-Ṭabarī,[276] and the *Sunan al-kubrā* of al-Bayhaqī contain the report.[277] Abū Hurayra's version does not have wide circulation in the sources and is not in the *Ṣaḥīḥ*s of al-Bukhārī or Muslim, respectively. The likely reason is that Abū Hurayra's recension has an unnamed transmitter in the transmission chain. As I illustrate, this type of anomaly can be advantageous for shedding light on the

[273] Ibn Sa'd, *al-Ṭabaqāt*, 7:507; al-Bukhārī, *al-Tārīkh*, 3:387.
[274] al-Mizzī, *Tahdhīb al-kamāl*, 10:17; Ibn Ḥajar, *Tahdhīb al-tahdhīb*, 3:536.
[275] Abū Dāwūd, *Sunan*, 5:471f, no. 3,624f and 6:498–501, no. 4,450 and 6:501, no. 4,451.
[276] al-Ṭabarī, *Jāmi'*, 10:303f, no. 11,921.
[277] al-Bayhaqī, *al-Sunan al-kubrā*, 8:374f, no. 16,933.

transmission history of a report when it is part of a hadith complex. The entry in ʿAbd al-Razzāq's *Muṣannaf* reads:

> ʿAbd al-Razzāq - Maʿmar b. Rāshid (d. 153/770) - Ibn Shihāb al-Zuhrī (d. 124/742) - a man from the tribe of Muzayna - and we were with Saʿīd b. al-Musayyab (d. *c.* 93/711, Medina) - Abū Hurayra:
>
> The first person to have been stoned on the order of the Messenger of God was from among the Jews. A man from among them committed *zinā* with a woman. Their learned scholars consulted one another before bringing the matter to the Messenger of God. Some said to others: This prophet was sent with a more lenient Law (*bi-takhfīf*), and we know that stoning is a religious obligation (*farḍ*) in the Torah.
>
> Then others among them said: Let us go and ask the Prophet about the matter involving our people who committed *zinā* after having *iḥṣān*. Let us agree that if the Prophet gives us a non-stoning judgment, then we will accept the less severe punishment. We will then plead our case to God about forgoing the stoning punishment when we meet Him. We will say: 'We accepted the ruling of a Prophet from among your prophets'. But if the Prophet commands us to stone the offenders, then we will reject the ruling, since we have already disobeyed that which God has written for us about stoning in the Torah.[278]
>
> So they went to the Messenger of God while he was sitting with his companions in the mosque. The Jewish group said: Abū Qāsim, how would you deal with a man and a woman who commit *zinā* after they have *iḥṣān*?
>
> The Prophet and some of the Muslims sitting with him got up without responding and left for the Beit Hamidrash. The Messenger of God arrived at the door and said: People, I implore you by God, Who sent the Torah to Moses, what do you find in the Torah regarding the matter involving someone who commits *zinā* after having *iḥṣān*?
>
> The Jewish group replied: We blacken their faces and parade them around town by putting them on a donkey with their backs to one another.
>
> Their learned person, who happened to be a young man, remained quiet. When the Prophet saw him, he remained in place. Then the learned

[278] This section harkens back to Q5:41, which reads: "'If you are given this ruling, accept it, but if you are not, then beware!'"

scholars remarked: Had you made us swear to God, then we would have admitted to the stoning punishment as found in the Torah.

The Messenger of God then said: When was the first time that you turned away from the punishment God decreed upon you?

The Jewish group responded: A man, who had familial ties to our King, committed *zinā*. So the King imprisoned him and excused him from getting stoned. Thereafter, a commoner committed *zinā* and the King wanted to stone him. The offender's people intervened and protested by saying: 'By God, we will not be stoned until you stone those from among yourselves!' So we reformed the punishment for everyone.

The Prophet said: I will rule in accordance with the Torah.

With that comment, the Prophet rendered judgment on the matter and the offenders were stoned.

Al-Zuhrī commented: I was informed by Sālim (d. *c.* 106/724, Medina, and son of Ibn 'Umar) that Ibn 'Umar said: 'Indeed I saw the offenders whom the Messenger of God ordered to be stoned. When the stoning took place, I saw the man trying to protect her with his hands.'

Al-Zuhrī said: It has reached us that this incident occasioned the verse [Q5:44]: "We sent down the Torah, containing in it guidance and light. Prophets [of the past], those who gave themselves over to God, judged according to it for these 'rightly-guided' ones (i.e., the Jews)."

The Prophet is from among such prophets.[279]

The arc of this story is an explication of the theme of *taḥrīf* – of denying God's command. This is the same type of criticism that 'Umar b. al-Khaṭṭāb is recorded to have made against Muslims that reject *zinā*-stoning (see Chapter 4). The notion of actively disregarding a directive is sharply observable in the supposed comment of the Jewish group, "... then we will reject the ruling since we have already disobeyed that which God has written for us about stoning in the Torah." The element of *taḥrīf* on the part of members of the Jewish community is expressed through the stoning punishment and at the same time conveys its justification on divine authority. These two

279 'Abd al-Razzāq, *al-Muṣannaf*, 7:316–8, no. 13,330; al-Ṭabarī, *Jāmi'*, 10:305f, no. 11,924. In al-Ṭabarī's transmission chain, the man from Muzayna receives it from Ibn al-Musayyab; in his gloss of Q5:41 on the portion, "... they listen to one another ...," al-Ṭabarī notes the same account on the authority of al-Suddī (d. 127/745, Ḥijāz and Kūfa). See al-Ṭabarī, *Jāmi'*, 10:310f, no. 11,929.

elements—stoning and scriptural legitimacy—are thereby brought into the Prophet's jurisdiction by virtue of his involvement in the adjudication of the case.

Let us compare Abū Hurayra's recension with variants reviewed in previous sections. The first chart compares al-Barā' b. 'Āzib's and Jābir b. 'Abd Allāh's respective versions followed by variants on the authority of 'Abd Allāh b. 'Umar.

	Jābir b. 'Abd Allāh	**al-Barā' b. 'Āzib**
How the matter comes to the Prophet's attention:	1J) Jews of Fadak advise the Jews of Medina to ask the Prophet to adjudicate a *zinā* matter.	1B) Prophet sees the offender who had been flogged and whose face had been blackened. He makes an inquiry about the *zinā* punishment.
Indication of the way in which the Jewish group moves away from using the stoning punishment:	2J) Jews of Fadak instruct that if the Prophet orders flogging, then accept it. And if he orders stoning, then reject it.	2B) Nobles are let go. Commoners are stoned. Agree to treat all the same by flogging and blackening the face.
Use of Jewish legal authorities:	3J) The Prophet summons two of the most knowledgeable men. They bring a man with one eye named Ibn Ṣūriyā and a second learned person.	3B) Prophet summons *one* of the learned men. He remains unidentified.
The Prophet's strategy of using an oath to force the Jewish authorities to admit to the proper stoning punishment:	4J) Prophet implores the two learned men on the basis of an oath to tell him what they find in the Torah about the *stoning* punishment for *zinā*.	4B) Prophet implores one learned man on the basis of an oath to tell him what he finds in the Book (Torah) regarding the *ḥadd* for *zinā*.
Jewish authorities admit that stoning is the proper punishment:	5J) The knowledgeable men respond by defining the legal elements necessary for conviction and confirm stoning.	5B) The knowledgeable man confirms stoning as the proper punishment.
The Prophet's response:	6J) Prophet (re)confirms the punishment.	6B) Prophet claims to (re) implement the stoning punishment.
Exegetical relevance:	7J) Connection to Q5:42.	7B) Connection to Q5:41, 44, 45, and 47.

ʿAbd Allāh b. ʿUmar's (d. 74/693) comparative chart:

al-Sakhtiyānī (d. 131/749)	**ʿUbayd Allāh (d. *c.* 147/764)**	**Mūsā b. ʿUqba (d. 141/748)**	**Maʿmar b. Rāshid (d. 153/770)**	**Juwayriya (d. 173/789)**	**Mālik (d. 179/795)**
A Jewish group brings a man and a woman who have committed *zinā* and asks the Prophet to adjudicate the case.	A Jewish man and a Jewish woman who committed *zinā* are brought to the Prophet.	A Jewish group brings a man and a woman who have committed *zinā* and asks the Prophet to adjudicate the case.	A Jewish man and a Jewish woman who committed *zinā* are brought to the Prophet.	A Jewish man and a Jewish woman who committed *zinā* are brought to the Prophet.	A Jewish group brings a man and a woman who have committed *zinā* and asks the Prophet to adjudicate the case.
The Prophet asks what do they find in their book.	The Prophet asks what do they find in the Torah for someone who commits *zinā*.	The Prophet asks in what manner do they treat someone who commits *zinā*.	The Prophet sends for two readers and asks them if they find stoning in the Torah and they say no.	The Prophet asks what do they find in their book.	The Prophet asks what do they find *in the Torah about stoning.*
Humiliate and blacken the face.	Blacken the face and parade them around town.	The offenders are hit (presumably flogged), but they do not find stoning.	Blacken face with charcoal, mount the offender on a donkey, and parade them around town.	Do not find stoning.	Shame and *flog.*
Interjection by an unidentifiable person who accuses the Jewish group of lying.	Interjection by an unidentifiable person who calls for the Torah.	Interjection by *ʿAbd Allāh b. Salām* who accuses the Jewish group of lying.	Interjection by an unidentifiable person who instructs the reciter of the Torah.	Interjection by *ʿAbd Allāh b. Salām* who accuses the Jewish group of lying.	Interjection by *ʿAbd Allāh b. Salām* who accuses the Jewish group of lying.
The Torah is brought forth and read to determine the existence of a stoning verse, with attempts to cover it up by a reciter with one eye named Ibn Ṣūriyā.	The Torah is brought forth and read to determine the existence of a stoning verse, with attempts to cover it up by *an unidentified person.*	The Torah is brought forth and read to determine the existence of a stoning verse, with attempts to cover it up by *a learned scholar.*	The Torah is brought forth and read to determine the existence of a stoning verse, with attempts to cover it up by *an unidentified person.*	The Torah is brought forth and read to determine the existence of a stoning verse, with attempts to cover it up by Ibn Ṣūriyā.	The Torah is brought forth and read to determine the existence of a stoning verse, with attempts to cover it up by *an unidentified person.*

al-Sakhtiyānī (d. 131/749)	**'Ubayd Allāh (d. *c.* 147/764)**	**Mūsā b. 'Uqba (d. 141/748)**	**Ma'mar b. Rāshid (d. 153/770)**	**Juwayriya (d. 173/789)**	**Mālik (d. 179/795)**
On the basis of the reading, the Jewish group confirms stoning as the proper punishment *but admit they have not been enforcing it.*	On the basis of *Ibn Salām's* instruction, the reciter removes his hand and the stoning verse is revealed.	*Ibn Salām* demands that the reader remove his hand; the Jewish group confirms stoning as the proper punishment.	*Ibn Salām* demands that the reader remove his hand and the stoning verse is revealed.	*Ibn Salām* demands that the reader remove his hand; the Jewish group confirms stoning as the proper punishment.	*Ibn Salām* demands that the reader remove his hand; the Jewish group confirms stoning as the proper punishment.
Unidentified person claims to have witnessed the stoning of the Jewish couple.	*Ibn 'Umar* claims to have witnessed the stoning of the Jewish couple.	*'Abd Allāh* claims to have witnessed the stoning of the Jewish couple.	*Ibn 'Umar* claims to have witnessed the stoning of the Jewish couple.	Unidentified person claims to have witnessed the stoning of the Jewish couple.	*Ibn 'Umar* claims to have witnessed the stoning of the Jewish couple.

The versions on the respective authorities of al-Barā' b. 'Āzib, Jābir b. 'Abd Allāh, and Ibn 'Umar contain some aspects of the variant on Abū Hurayra's authority. The overlaps point to Abū Hurayra's as the "predecessor text form"—to use Epp's concept.

In what follows, I compare and contrast textual elements found in Abū Hurayra's version with the recensions previously examined.

1) According to Abū Hurayra's version, the Medinan Jews discuss the hope of receiving permission to apply a non-*zinā*-stoning punishment if the Prophet is asked to adjudicate the case. This motif is principally expressed in Jābir b. 'Abd Allāh's version (1J and 2J);
2) The Jewish group's response about why they reduced the *zinā* punishment in Abū Hurayra's report parallels that which is in Ibn 'Āzib's recension (1B). And while the specific reason is omitted from Ibn 'Umar's transmissions, the provenance of the motif involving a Jewish man and a Jewish woman is now clear;
3) In Abū Hurayra's version, the Jewish group asks the Prophet about how he would treat (punish) someone who commits *zinā*. In Jābir b. 'Abd Allāh's recension, the question is implied with the comment, "the Jews of Medina approached the Prophet about the case." In Ibn 'Āzib and Ibn 'Umar, the Prophet asks the Jewish group about the mandated punishment for *zinā* offenders. Recall that in Zayd b. Aslam's version,

the Prophet is referred to with his eponym Abū al-Qāsim, just as in Abū Hurayra's report;

4) The specific reason for substituting a corporal punishment—to mitigate the uneven application of penalties based on social class—is found both in Abū Hurayra's and Ibn ʿĀzib's (2B) respective reports;[280]
5) In Abū Hurayra's version, the Jewish scholars advise the Prophet that they blacken the faces of the condemned and parade them around town on a donkey with their backs to one another. Ibn ʿĀzib narrates that the punishment is blackening of the face and flogging. Ibn ʿUmar mentions blackening the condemned's face and parading them around;
6) Maʿmar's recensions on the authorities of Ibn ʿUmar and al-Zuhrī have high degrees of similarities but also key differences: in the Maʿmar-Ibn ʿUmar version, there is the attempt to conceal the stoning verse, the witness clause, and the presence of ʿAbd Allāh b. Salām, none of which are in the Maʿmar-al-Zuhrī recension. These variations indicate that he was transmitting what he acquired from two different teachers. If Maʿmar had simply been inventing details—for the purpose of justifying one legal position over another, for instance—and attributing them falsely to prior authorities, he could have easily made both recensions identical;
7) The oath motif appears in Ibn ʿĀzib and some versions of Jābir.[281] The oath is also in Ibn ʿUmar's report as related by Zayd b. Aslam, which generally contains the elements found in Abū Hurayra's recension;
8) In Abū Hurayra's version, after the Prophet implores the Jewish scholars with a solemn oath, they tell him about the use of a non-stoning punishment. But why, without any explicit motivation, do they disclose the stoning punishment when doing so would be detrimental to their standing? In all likelihood, the transmitter(s) had the charge of *taḥrīf* in mind, so what appears to be self-indicting to a later reader/listener may not have been so for the earlier narrator(s);
9) According to Abū Hurayra, it is the Jewish scholars who affirm *zinā*-stoning as the correct punishment. The authority motif is observable in all other versions, represented variously by ʿAbd Allāh b. Salām, Ibn Ṣūriyā, unidentified learned men, or, in Ibn ʿUmar, the Torah itself;

[280] The motif of differentiated social classes informing the applicable punishment may reflect the stratified leadership within the Jewish communities of Khaybar. See Newby, *A History of the Jews of Arabia*, 74f.

[281] This can be further substantiated by a version Abū Dāwūd provides on the authority of ʿIkrima (d. 160/776, Baṣra and Yamāma). ʿIkrima does not provide his source. The textual content focuses on

10) Abū Hurayra's recension includes the Jewish group's discussion about their reason for seeking out the Prophet. Their rationale, though given in passing, is rather noteworthy and has weighty implications. Some among the Jewish group assert that Muḥammad is sent with "a more lenient Law," juxtaposing Muhammad's law against stoning as mandated in the Torah. This implies that, at the time the narrative took place, Q24:2, which stipulates flogging for *zinā* offenders, had already been put into effect, and that the Jews in question were hoping to benefit from this more lenient approach to penalizing the same type of *zinā*;
11) The inclusion of the term *iḥṣān* must be viewed as an emendation to the textual content. Indeed, certain pre-modern Muslim scholars believed this to be the case.[282] The aim would be to harmonize the *zinā* offense in the report with the requirements for stoning in the later Islamic legal tradition. As discussed in Chapter 1, *iḥṣān* is a legal element that connotes the types of Muslim *zinā* offenders subject to the stoning punishment. In Abū Hurayra's report, both the Jewish group and the Prophet talk about the punishment for someone who commits *zinā* after having *iḥṣān*. Considering that Muslim legal authorities continued to debate the term's meaning centuries later, not to mention in ways completely incongruous with its usage in the Qur'ān, such a scenario is highly improbable, at least until evidence emerges that the Medinan Jews developed rabbinical law on this point in ways unheard of elsewhere. Had *iḥṣān* been understood in the manner proposed by later Muslim tradition, and the Prophet and his community were implementing *zinā*-stoning on the basis of *iḥṣān*, then it would have been quite unreasonable for the Jews to have assumed a likelihood that the Prophet would judge their case more leniently under his own law. Now, suppose the case may be that the Prophet and the Jewish interlocutors are employing *iḥṣān* based on the use of *muḥṣanāt* by the Qur'ān. Here, *iḥṣān* represents a shared *concept* about the type of *zinā* offender that should be subject to

the manner by which the Prophet made Ibn Ṣūriyā take the oath. It parallels the forms found in the Ibn 'Āzib and Jābir recensions. See Abū Dāwūd, *Sunan*, 5:472, no. 3,626.

[282] For example, the Ḥanafī jurist al-Sarakhsī writes that *iḥṣān* was added to some of the [PJZO] narratives. See al-Sarakhsī, *al-Mabsūṭ*, 9:39; *cf* the Shāfi'ī al-Māwardī, who accepts the hadith with *iḥṣān* in the textual content. See al-Māwardī, *al-Ḥāwī*, 9:386.

the stoning punishment. This makes sense in light of Hebrew Bible stipulations wherein unlawful sexual intercourse with a betrothed virgin girl/maiden, that is, a *muḥṣana*, results in the stoning punishment. The upshot of this scenario is that the Jewish group (1) would seek out Muḥammad for a more lenient ruling via the Q24:2 flogging mandate, and this would indicate that (2) the type of *zinā* the Jewish group had in mind and for which stoning was the prescribed punishment in their law reflects pre-classical understandings of the term that is attested to in the Qur'ān, for which the latter text prescribes flogging instead of stoning. In sum, *iḥṣān* in the report is an interpolation intended to ground later practice in Prophetic legal precedent. The natural consistency and clarity of the narrative can remain only if *iḥṣān* is removed or it is interpreted as a concept rather than a technical legal term[283];

12) Note that in Abū Hurayra's version, there is no mention of a stoning verse in the Torah. Rather, the Prophet is recorded to only make a passing reference to it. The Hebrew Bible delineates specific instances in which stoning is mandated as a form of punishment, while in other cases, it merely asserts that the capital punishment is warranted. For the scenarios in which the Hebrew Bible is silent, rabbinic law utilizes various forms of capital punishment, including death by lapidation. In Abū Hurayra's narrative, the implicit reference to the Torah's stoning verse, coupled with the explicit mention of public humiliation—as an alternative punitive measure for illicit sexual relations within the rabbinic tradition—suggests both a familiarity with rabbinic jurisprudence and an apparent indifference toward the specific circumstances that require the application of the stoning penalty. For the transmitter(s), if the rabbinic tradition can misrepresent one Torah directive, that is, the stoning punishment, then it can misrepresent another, which is, its mention of the coming of a new prophet.

As for the transmission chain of the report, we can conclude that Maʿmar (d. 153/770) learned the report from two sources, one of them being Ibn

[283] Donner astutely observes that there was an *ecumenical* relationship between early Muslims (during the lifetime of the Prophet) and Christians and Jews, that is, they were collectively a community of believers on the basis of monotheism and the practice of righteous behavior. See Fred M. Donner, *Muhammad and the Believers*, 68–74. Accordingly, the Prophet and his Muslim contemporaries could have overlapping conceptions of sexual morality with their Jewish counterparts. On this latter point, see Chapter 2, "Sex as Crime," in Zellentin, *Law Beyond Israel*.

Shihāb al-Zuhrī (d. 124/742). Maʿmar was born in *c.* 95/713, which means he had time to meet and study with his recorded teacher. In fact, Maʿmar explicitly confirms that he spent time with al-Zuhrī when he visited Medina.[284] For a host of reasons, Maʿmar eventually comes to be acknowledged as the best transmitter of al-Zuhrī's transmissions.[285] Comparing the versions of the PJZO hadith that Maʿmar teaches on the respective authorities of Ibn ʿUmar and al-Zuhrī—whose version of the report differs from Abū Hurayra's version—indicates that the transmissions by Maʿmar are historical. Specifically, in his version on Ibn ʿUmar's authority, the textual content includes ʿAbd Allāh b. Salām and the covering up of the Torah. These two elements are absent from Maʿmar's transmission on the authority of al-Zuhrī. This means that Maʿmar was not inventing details and then attributing them to respected authorities of the previous generation. Otherwise, we would expect Maʿmar to have harmonized the two accounts to support his inventions. Accordingly, Maʿmar's biographical information and a comparative analysis of the reports he transmits on behalf of his two teachers indicate that he acquired the hadith from his noted teacher, al-Zuhrī.

Ibn Shihāb al-Zuhrī receives extensive accolades in biographical sources, and his reputation as an early legal authority is well-documented.[286] Mālik had nothing but the highest praise for him.[287] In Damascus, al-Zuhrī made such a favorable impression on the Umayyad caliph ʿAbd al-Malik b. Marwān (r. 65–86/685–705) that he hired al-Zuhrī to tutor his children.[288] After ʿAbd al-Malik's death, al-Zuhrī remained in the service of subsequent Umayyad caliphs and, at one time, was appointed as a judge in the Umayyad courts.[289] Nevertheless, there are some evaluations of his conduct as a teacher that warrant attention. According to Maʿmar, an Umayyad prince once sought al-Zuhrī's approval for a notebook containing the latter's legal opinions and hadith. When al-Zuhrī was presented the notebook, he commented, "Who else but me could have said them (i.e., the words in the notebook)?"[290] According

[284] al-Dhahabī, *Siyar aʿlām*, 7:6f.

[285] Ibn Abī Ḥātim, *al-Jarḥ wa al-taʿdīl*, 8:256; al-Mizzī, *Tahdhīb al-kamāl*, 28:306f and 308.

[286] Ibn Saʿd, *al-Ṭabaqāt*, 7:434 and 439; al-Mizzī, *Tahdhīb al-kamāl*, 26:431; *EI*^{2}, s.v. al-Zuhrī (Michael Lecker).

[287] al-Mizzī, *Tahdhīb al-kamāl*, 26:436; Ibn Ḥajar, *Tahdhīb al-tahdhīb*, 6:50; Ibn Abī Ḥātim records other opinions, which, like Mālik's, praise al-Zuhrī's legal acumen. See Ibn Abī Ḥātim, *al-Jarḥ wa al-taʿdīl*, 8:73f.

[288] Ibn Saʿd, *al-Ṭabaqāt*, 7:432; Ibn ʿAsākir, *Tārīkh*, 55:297f; al-Mizzī, *Tahdhīb al-kamāl*, 26:438.

[289] Ibn ʿAsākir, *Tārīkh*, 55:324f; al-Mizzī, *Tahdhīb al-kamāl*, 26:438 and al-Dhahabī, *Siyar aʿlām*, 5:330–2 and 339.

[290] Ibn Saʿd, *al-Ṭabaqāt*, 7:435; Michael Lecker, "Biographical Notes on Ibn Shihāb al-Zuhrī," 28ff.

to al-Mizzī (d. 742/1342), when al-Zuhrī was asked if a book could be ascribed to him, he responded in the affirmative, presumably without reviewing it.[291] But why did a motif concerning transmission practices circulate about such a famous transmitter? Al-Zuhrī's method for authenticating notebooks that were compiled on his authority is beyond the scope of the present work and certainly merits further study. After all, he is one of the most frequently cited authorities for hadith and, in the present case, an important source. For now, I offer three likely explanations for this phenomenon: (1) these claims do not challenge al-Zuhrī's own reliability as a transmitter but merely question some of the attributions put to him on the part of some of his students. In fact, they attest to the fact that there was sufficient interest in attributing material of questionable provenance to an otherwise reliable transmitter; (2) these claims may be a result of al-Zuhrī's practice of lending notebooks for copying (*munāwala*),[292] a practice that was excessively attacked by some but affirmed by others as a reliable means of transmitting legal and non-legal material. In other words, these reports reflect the preferences of a certain class of scholars rather than an actual criticism of al-Zuhrī's learning or conduct; (3) we do not know the circumstances under which al-Zuhrī made his alleged remark (i.e., "Who else but me . . . "). Was he irked? This is a legitimate question, as al-Zuhrī is noted for being one to scorn the act of reducing knowledge to written form and complained that he and others were being forced to do so.[293] He may have been contemptuous of the process because he never respected the reduction of knowledge into written form in the first place. The critiques lodged against al-Zuhrī in the sources regarding some of his transmission habits, then, do not dismiss his being a source for the PJZO hadith.

Two entries by Abū Dāwūd also point to al-Zuhrī's involvement in the circulation of the narrative. The hadith collector records Muḥammad b. Yaḥyā b. Fāris (d. 258/871, Baghdād, Baṣra, Iṣfahān, Khurasān, and Nīshāpūr) as his informant, who in turn transmits the report from ʿAbd al-Razzāq - Maʿmar - al-Zuhrī. It states:

[291] al-Mizzī, *Tahdhīb al-kamāl*, 26:439f; see also Ibn ʿAsākir, *Tārīkh*, 55:364f, esp. 365; for an informative biographical study on al-Zuhrī, see generally, Lecker, "Biographical Notes on Ibn Shihāb al-Zuhrī," esp. pp. 22–40.

[292] See Schoeler, *Genesis of Literature in Islam*, 48.

[293] ʿAbd al-Razzāq, *al-Muṣannaf*, 11:258, no. 20,486; but cf. Pavel Pavlovitch, "*Kunnā nakrahu al-kitāb*: Scripture, Transmission of Knowledge, and Politics in the Second Century AH (719–816 CE)," 9–26.

> The Messenger of God said to the Jewish group: I implore you by God, the One who sent the Torah to Moses, what punishment do you find in the Torah for someone who commits *zinā*?
>
> Abū Dāwūd states: And the report continues about the stoning incident.[294]

Abū Dāwūd provides a lengthier narration on the basis of two transmission chains.[295] One chain of transmission is the same as above, suggesting that the truncated form of the report as presented there is of Abū Dāwūd's own editorial doing. The second reads:

> Aḥmad b. Ṣāliḥ (d. 248/862, Egypt and Syria) - 'Anbasa [b. Khālid b. Yazīd] (d. 198/813, Ayla) - Yūnus [b. Yazīd al-Aylī] (d. 152/796, Ayla and Egypt) - al-Zuhrī.[296]

Because Abū Dāwūd provides two transmission chains, it becomes more difficult to resolve who may have narrated particular information. However, the textual content does share a high degree of similarity with the version in 'Abd al-Razzāq's *Muṣannaf*. The commonality suggests Abū Dāwūd had access to the version by Muḥammad b. Yaḥyā b. Fāris on the authority of 'Abd al-Razzāq. The differences between Abū Dāwūd's and 'Abd al-Razzāq's respective variants are non-consequential and, in fact, indicate a common source. A historical transmission is further corroborated by the fact that Muḥammad b. Yaḥyā b. Fāris collected and wrote down al-Zuhrī's transmissions in a *muṣannaf*.[297] In light of the teacher–student relationship between 'Abd al-Razzāq and Muḥammad b. Yaḥyā b. Fāris, this indicates that the latter recorded the PJZO hadith during a study session with 'Abd al-Razzāq.

A few points are to be noted about Yūnus b. Yazīd al-Aylī. Though at times he is accused of making errors when narrating reports that he receives from al-Zuhrī,[298] he is also considered to be one of al-Zuhrī's best students, on par with Mālik and Ma'mar.[299] His relationship with al-Zuhrī is exemplified

[294] Abū Dāwūd, *Sunan*, 5:471, no. 3,624.
[295] Abū Dāwūd, *Sunan*, 6:498–501, no. 4,450.
[296] Abū Dāwūd, *Sunan*, 6:498–501, no. 4,450. He also adds the comment, "It was mentioned to me that a man from Muzayna, who was from among those that seek knowledge and retain it, narrated to Sa'īd b. al-Musayyab."
[297] al-Khaṭīb al-Baghdādī, *Tārīkh*, 4:656.
[298] al-Mizzī, *Tahdhīb al-kamāl*, 32:555; al-Dhahabī, *Siyar a'lām*, 6:298.
[299] Ibn Abī Ḥātim, *al-Jarḥ wa al-ta'dīl*, 9:248; al-Mizzī, *Tahdhīb al-kamāl*, 32:555f.

by a report which states that when al-Zuhrī visited Ayla,[300] he stayed with Yūnus al-Aylī and, when al-Zuhrī traveled to Medina, he was accompanied by Yūnus al-Aylī.[301] With this information and taking into consideration the high degree of overlap between the versions examined above, al-Zuhrī is Yūnus al-Aylī's source. Broadly, al-Zuhrī's biographical information and the three collective attestations produced by 'Abd al-Razzāq and Abū Dāwūd serve to establish al-Zuhrī's circulation of the report.

In my view, the defective transmission chain prevents the wide circulation of this report involving someone as famous as al-Zuhrī. The issue stems from the unidentified individual belonging to the Muzayna tribe. Who are the Muzanīs? According to Watt, the Muzayna[302] were supposedly of little influence in the pre-Islamic period.[303] They trace their lineage back to Abraham,[304] and are one of the first nomadic tribes west of Medina to establish a covenant with the Prophet upon his arrival to the city.[305] Muzayna quickly gained importance in the nascent Muslim community. As part of the treaties the Prophet establishes with various tribes, the Muzayna are designated as Emigrants despite the fact that they did not leave their home district, as was expected of other Emigrants.[306] A famous Muzanī is al-Nu'mān b. 'Amr b. Muqarrin al-Muzanī (d. 21/641, Baṣra, Kūfa, Mecca, and Medina). He carried the flag of the tribe during the conquest of Mecca in the eighth year of the hijra.[307] He also served as the leader of the armies involved in the conquest of 'Irāq during the caliphate of 'Umar.[308] In fact, the Caliph held al-Nu'mān in such high regard that he supposedly wept when publicly announcing al-Nu'mān's death.[309] Another famous Muzanī, Iyās b. Mu'āwiya (d. 122/739, Baṣra, Medina[?],[310] and Wāsiṭ), held the judgeship in the city of Baṣra.[311] Additionally, several other Muzanīs held leadership posts,

[300] Ayla is now known as al-'Aqaba; see also Yāqūt, *Mu'jam al-buldān*, 1:292f.

[301] Ibn Abī Ḥātim, *al-Jarḥ wa al-ta'dīl*, 9:249; al-Mizzī, *Tahdhīb al-kamāl*, 32:556; al-Dhahabī, *Siyar a'lām*, 6:300.

[302] In biographical dictionaries, Muzayna and Muzani connote the same tribe.

[303] Watt, *Muhammad in Medina*, 86.

[304] *Encyclopaedia Islamica*, s.v. "Bilāl b. Ḥārith."

[305] Ibn Sa'd, *al-Ṭabaqāt*, 1:252; al-Sam'ānī, *al-Ansāb*, 12:227; *Encyclopaedia of Islam*, 2nd ed., s.v. "Muzayna."

[306] Watt, *Muhammad in Medina*, 86; Ibn Sa'd, *al-Ṭabaqāt*, 1:252.

[307] al-Dhahabī, *Siyar a'lām*, 1:404; Ibn Ḥajar, *al-Iṣāba*, 6:357.

[308] Ibn Sa'd, *al-Ṭabaqāt*, 5:146; Ibn Ḥajar, *al-Iṣāba*, 6:357.

[309] al-Mizzī, *Tahdhīb al-kamāl*, v. 29, 461.

[310] According to al-Mizzī, Iyās b. Mu'āwiya narrated reports from Nāfi'. See al-Mizzī, *Tahdhīb al-kamāl*, 3:407f. To the best of my knowledge, Nāfi' did not travel to Baṣra or Wāsiṭ. Therefore, either Iyās b. Mu'āwiya practiced *tadlīs* or traveled to Medina and met Nāfi' there. A third possibility is that they met during the *ḥajj*.

[311] al-Sam'ānī, *al-Ansāb*, 12:230.

including governorships, in a number of ʾIrāqī cities.[312] Thus, while the Muzanīs may have led an uneventful existence before the Prophet's arrival to Medina, after their conversion to Islam they became a tribe of considerable importance.

The unidentified Muzanī in the transmission chain may be ʿAbd Allāh b. Mughaffal al-Muzanī (d. *c.* 60/679, Baṣra and Medina). The ʾIrāqī jurist al-Ḥasan al-Baṣrī (d. 110/728) is recorded to have said that Ibn Mughaffal was one of ten men ʿUmar sent to Baṣra for the purpose of teaching *fiqh*.[313] The reports could be used as an instructive tool for the legality of *zinā*-stoning as well as for providing an example of *taḥrīf* in regions with Jewish residents and new Muslim converts. The unidentified Muzanī could also be ʿAbd Allāh b. Mughaffal's son Bakr (d. *c.* 107, Baṣra), who could have received the report from his father. Bakr b. ʿAbd Allāh was a known transmitter and jurist, which makes it plausible that he would be interested in a report about the Prophet's order to stone a *zinā* offender.[314] Thus, the appearance of a Muzanī in the transmission chain is unlikely to be incidental.

That the exact person is indeterminable would become problematic within the developing standards of hadith transmission. This complication explains why we find Saʿīd b. al-Musayyab (d. *c.* 93/711, Medina), the recorded teacher of al-Zuhrī, in the transmission chain. Ibn al-Musayyab is deemed to be one of the earliest and most respected legal authorities of the post-Companion generation in Medina.[315] This emigrant's legal acumen was so well regarded that the caliph ʿUmar b. ʿAbd al-ʿAzīz (r. 99–101/717–20) would allegedly not give judgments without consulting Ibn al-Musayyab.[316] As for the relationship between al-Zuhrī and Ibn al-Musayyab, it is thought to have begun when al-Zuhrī asked about a legal matter and was directed to Ibn al-Musayyab.[317] Al-Zuhrī was so impressed with the Medinan jurist that he ended up spending seven (or ten) years with him.[318] That the two were close can be inferred from the fact that biographical entries about Ibn al-Musayyab often cite al-Zuhrī as the source of their information.[319]

[312] al-Samʿānī, *al-Ansāb*, 12:228f.
[313] al-Dhahabī, *Siyar aʿlām*, 2:484; Ibn Ḥajar, *al-Iṣāba*, 4:207.
[314] For biographical information on Bakr b. ʿAbd Allāh, see, e.g., al-Mizzī, *Tahdhīb al-kamāl*, 4:218 and al-Dhahabī, *Siyar aʿlām*, 4:536.
[315] Ibn Saʿd, *al-Ṭabaqāt*, 2:325–7, and 7:121f; Ibn Abī Ḥatim, *al-Jarḥ wa al-taʿdīl*, 4:61; Ibn Ḥibbān, *al-Thiqāt*, 4:274; Ibn Ḥajar, *Tahdhīb al-tahdhīb*, 3:690.
[316] Ibn Saʿd, *al-Ṭabaqāt*, 7:122.
[317] al-Mizzī, *Tahdhīb al-kamāl*, 11:70; Ibn Ḥajar, *Tahdhīb al-tahdhīb*, 3:690.
[318] Ibn Abī Ḥatim, *al-Jarḥ wa al-taʿdīl*, 4:60; al-Mizzī, *Tahdhīb al-kamāl*, 11:70.
[319] See, e.g., Ibn Saʿd, *al-Ṭabaqāt*, 7:121 and 131.

Of relevance to the present analysis is the fact that a large portion of Ibn al-Musayyab's reports are related on the authority of Abū Hurayra. In fact, he is considered to be Abū Hurayra's most reliable transmitter.[320] The historical connection between Ibn al-Musayyab and Abū Hurayra is cemented by virtue of Ibn al-Musayyab being Abū Hurayra's son-in-law.[321] In short, there is little to dispute concerning the historical relationships between al-Zuhrī, Ibn al-Musayyab, and Abū Hurayra. These relationships and, specifically, the citation of Ibn al-Musayyab, are precisely what is required to prevent the unidentified individual from impugning the quality of the transmission chain. Maintaining the unknown person is an echo of an earlier version of the transmission chain and the practice of *isnād* preservation.

Abū Hurayra's (d. *c.* 58/677) involvement in the circulation of the PJZO hadith is anything but coincidental. To begin with, he is considered to be one of the most popular Companions of the Prophet, with some 3,500 reports recorded on his authority.[322] But even during Abū Hurayra's lifetime, skepticism existed about the large number of narratives he circulated. He is even recorded as having made comments justifying the legitimacy of his reports. For example, Abū Hurayra states that he went to the Prophet and lamented that he had difficulty remembering what the Prophet would say. Reportedly the Prophet cupped his hands as if they were filled with water and placed them inside Abū Hurayra's open robe and then took them out. Then the Prophet instructed Abū Hurayra to close his robe, following which, Abū Hurayra remarked, he never again forgot a report.[323] After Abū Hurayra's death, controversy persisted about his trustworthiness. It is recorded that in the court of the caliph Hārūn al-Rashīd (r. 170–93/786–809), a rather vehement dispute took place about the reliability of Abū Hurayra's transmissions.[324] It is also worth mentioning that Ka'b b. al-Aḥbār (d. 32/652), a Yemeni Jewish convert to Islam, is recorded to have said, "When it comes to the Torah, I have never met anyone more knowledgeable than Abū Hurayra."[325] In fact, many of Abū Hurayra's reports correlate with Jewish folklore and mythology.[326] In previous sections, I presented reports on the authority of Abū Hurayra in which

[320] Ibn Sa'd, *al-Ṭabaqāt*, 2:327 and 7:121; al-Mizzī, *Tahdhīb al-kamāl*, 11:74.
[321] Ibn Sa'd, *al-Ṭabaqāt*, 2:327.
[322] Ibn Sa'd, *al-Ṭabaqāt*, 5:232; *Encyclopaedia of Islam*, 2nd ed., s.v. "Abū Hurayra."
[323] Ibn Sa'd, *al-Ṭabaqāt*, 5:234; al-Mizzī, *Tahdhīb al-kamāl*, 34:378.
[324] al-Khaṭīb al-Baghdādī, *Tārīkh*, 13:28.
[325] al-Dhahabī, *Siyar a'lām*, 2:600; on Ka'b b. al-Aḥbār, see *Encyclopaedia of Jews in the Islamic World*, s.v. "Ka'b b. al-Aḥbār."
[326] Abou El Fadl, *Speaking in God's Name*, 216.

Jewish scholarly authorities convert to Islam and affirm the prophethood of Muḥammad. In other words, the very same person circulating reports about Jewish-Muslim polemics concerning the Prophet's legitimacy is identifiable in the dissemination of a story about Jewish community members, *zinā*, and the punishment of stoning.

The aim of this section has been to determine the significance of the PJZO hadith circulated on the authority of Abū Hurayra (d. *c.* 58/677). When this variant is compared to those on the respective authorities of Ibn ʿUmar, al-Barāʾ b. ʿĀzib, Jābir b. ʿAbd Allāh, and Jābir b. Samūra, significant overlaps are detectable. The common elements point to Abū Hurayra's report being the "predecessor text form" of the PJZO hadith. Certain questions that I raised when examining other versions, for example, why is the Prophet intervening in the case of Jewish *zinā* offenders, can be answered by Abu Hurayra's hadith. Aspects from his recension are remembered as concepts and expressed differently through the subjective transmission process. For example, the unnamed learned person in Abū Hurayra's report is expressed as ʿAbd Allah b. Salām in Ibn ʿUmar's version and Ibn Ṣūriyā in other accounts. In short, it is also not a matter of happenstance that Abū Hurayra is recorded to have been involved in the incident referred to in the PJZO hadith.

2.7. A Brief Excursus

In this section, I would like to revisit the version on Ibn ʿUmar's authority that I examined in Section 2.4 of this chapter. I reproduce the earlier part of the transmission chain here: Nāfiʿ (d. *c.* 117/735) - ʿAbd Allāh b. ʿUmar (d. 74/693). Indeed, the evidence points to Ibn ʿUmar's circulation of the report. First, his involvement can be corroborated if the Muzanīs are called back into the conversation. During the caliphate of ʿUmar, al-Nuʿmān al-Muzanī (d. 21/641) oversaw much of the conquest of ʿIrāq.[327] Not only is Ibn ʿUmar recorded to have fought in ʿIrāq, but he is also noted to have served in al-Nuʿmān's battalion during the conquest of Isfahān.[328] The PJZO hadith could have been circulating within the tribe and shared with individuals such as Ibn ʿUmar. This would support Ibn ʿUmar's independent role in transmitting the report. Second, Abū Hurayra and Ibn ʿUmar are recorded

[327] Ibn Saʿd, *al-Ṭabaqāt*, 5:146; Ibn Ḥajar, *al-Iṣāba*, 6:357.
[328] Ibn Saʿd, *al-Ṭabaqāt*, 4:158; al-Mizzī, *Tahdhīb al-kamāl*, 29:460.

to have narrated hadith from one another. Given that Abū Hurayra is one of the earliest authorities to have circulated the PJZO hadith, two avenues are established for Ibn 'Umar to have circulated the report.

But the plain explanation presents itself in Abū Hurayra's version. In it, al-Zuhrī names Sālim (d. *c.* 106/724, Medina), the son of Ibn 'Umar, as the person to have specifically communicated the witness clause about Ibn 'Umar. Two observations can be made from the reference to Sālim. First, over time, the witness clause begins to circulate without Sālim's name. The absence of his or Ibn 'Umar's name can be substantiated by a report that circulates on the authority of the Companion 'Abd Allāh b. 'Abbās (d. 68/687, Baṣra, Mecca, Medina, Syria, and Ṭā'if). The transmission chain and textual content read:

> Ibn Ḥanbal - Ya'qūb b. Ibrāhīm (d. 208/823, Baghdād and Medina) and Sa'īd b. Ibrāhīm (d. 201/816, Baghdād, Khurāsān, and Wāsiṭ) - Sa'īd's Father - [Muḥammad] b. Isḥāq (d. *c.* 155/771, Baghdād, Mecca, Medina, Kūfa) - Muḥammad b. Ṭalḥa b. Yazīd b. Rukāna (d. 110/728, Jazīra and Mecca) - Ismā'īl b. Ibrāhīm al-Shaybānī (d. unknown, Jazīra and Mecca) - ['Abd Allāh] b. 'Abbās (d. 68/687, Baṣra, Mecca, Medina, Syria, and Tā'if):
>
> The Messenger of God gave an order to stone a Jewish man and a Jewish woman at the door of his mosque. When the Jewish man began to get stoned, he tried to protect his lover until they both perished. This is what God has ordained for his messenger for their offense of *zinā*.[329]

No mention is made of Sālim or his father, Ibn 'Umar. Different transmitters shared the hadith and preserved the witness clause to underscore that a stoning incident did in fact occur. Another version of the PJZO hadith in the *Sunan* of al-Bayhaqī affirms this process. The variant is transmitted on the authority of the Companion 'Abd Allāh b. al-Ḥarith b. Jaza' al-Zubaydī (d. 86/705, Egypt and Zubayd), who is recorded to have claimed that *he* witnessed the stoning of the Jewish couple.[330]

It is likely that Nāfi', the student of Ibn 'Umar, circulated some portions of the report that he learned from Ibn 'Umar and other parts that he acquired from Sālim. First, Sālim is recorded to have acquired narratives from

[329] Ibn Ḥanbal, *Musnad* (2009 ed.), 4:196, no. 2,368; al-Bayhaqī, *al-Sunan al-kubrā* 8:374, no. 16,932.
[330] al-Bayhaqī, *al-Sunan al-kubrā*, 8:374, no. 16,932.

Abū Hurayra[331] and, as demonstrated, Abū Hurayra is a key party to the dissemination of the PJZO hadith. Second, certain biographical entries indicate Nāfiʿ did not begin teaching reports until after Sālim's death, which would mean that Nāfiʿ did not narrate his recension during Ibn ʿUmar's lifetime.[332] If Nāfiʿ received the report from Sālim and did not commence his transmissions until both Ibn ʿUmar and Sālim died, then Nāfiʿ narrated the report—or some portion of it—without acknowledging Sālim's intervention. To reiterate the point I made above, recall that al-Zuhrī remarks that it was Sālim who claimed his father was a witness to the stoning. In sum, there are several pieces of evidence that point to Sālim as the source for naming his father, Ibn ʿUmar, as a witness to the stoning incident and now Ibn ʿUmar himself.

2.8. The PJZO Hadith in *Tafsīr*s

Recall that in Q5:41–4, the Prophet's Jewish contemporaries are criticized for altering prescriptions in the Torah, and instructions are provided on how the Prophet is to adjudicate their cases in the event that they seek his judgment on a matter. The incident referred to in the PJZO hadith aims to add color to these verses by making it the occasion for the particular revelations. In this section, I illustrate the different ways in which the PJZO hadith is directly incorporated into Qur'ān exegetical commentaries on these verses and how certain exegetes, in turn, understood the Prophet's order to stone the Jewish couple. Here again are the relevant verses:

> 41 Messenger [of Mine], [I know] it hurts you to see those who profess faith out loud yet vie with one another to be ingrates, thereby revealing that they never intended to surrender their hearts to faith. Among them are the 'rightly-guided' ones (i.e. the Jewish communities), who listen eagerly to the lies of others without even seeing the need to give you a fair hearing. They only intend to interpret the word of God according to their whims to the point they say [to one other], 'If [he] gives a judgment [in your favor], then accept it. But if not, then be on guard!' [Messenger of Mine], there is nothing you can do to help someone for whom God intends trials and tests.

[331] Ibn Saʿd, *al-Ṭabaqāt*, 7:199; Ibn Abī Ḥātim, *al-Jarḥ wa al-taʿdīl*, 4:184; Ibn ʿAsākir, *Tārīkh*, 20:48.
[332] Ibn ʿAsākir, *Tārīkh*, 20:56; al-Dhahabī, *Siyar aʿlām*, 4:464.

> Such is the case for people whose hearts God [justly] has no intention of cleansing. [This is the] disgrace for them in this world, and a heavy punishment [awaits them] in the next life,
>
> 42 they listen eagerly to lies and consume abominable things. Nevertheless, should they come to you, either offer judgment or decline to do so. If you choose to decline, [know that] they will not [be able to] harm you in any way. But if you decide to make a judgment, then judge for them in a just manner. Indeed, God loves those who are just -
>
> 43 but why do they appoint you for judgment when they have the Torah? [Surely] it contains God's judgment. What makes them turn away from it now? Folks like these are not faithful.
>
> 44 We sent down the Torah, containing in it guidance and light. Prophets [of the past], those who gave themselves over to God, judged according to it for these 'rightly-guided' ones (i.e., the Jewish communities), as did the rabbis and the sages, insofar as they were entrusted to preserve the word of God and to serve as its witnesses. [People], do not fear others out of reverence for them. Rather, revere Me! Do not barter away My words for a cheap price. Those who do not give a judgment according to the word of God are ingrates!

Again, one message from these verses is that individuals are categorized as believers or unbelievers based on their adherence or willful deviation (*taḥrīf*) from divine commandments.

One of the earliest extant exegetical works is that of Mujāhid b. Jabr (d. *c.* 100/718, Mecca), an exegete and a scholar of both law and hadith.[333] There are some concerns about the methodology he uses for his exegesis, in that he reportedly incorporated Jewish and Christian material in his work.[334] This criticism reflects later attitudes, as earlier Muslims earlier were indifferent to the use of materials sourced in Jewish, Christian, and other literary sources.[335] Part of the reason is that such information would be helpful for the listeners and their understanding of certain Qur'ānic verses. At any rate, the early date of Mujāhid's work makes it relevant to the present study.

[333] Ibn Sa'd, *al-Ṭabaqāt*, 8:28; al-Dhahabī, *Siyar a'lām*, 4:453.
[334] Ibn Sa'd, *al-Ṭabaqāt*, 8:28; al-Dhahabī, *Mīzān*, 3:439.
[335] For a brief but informative background on the use of such sources in Qur'ānic commentaries, see Mustafa Shah, *Tafsīr: Interpreting the Qur'ān*, 31–5.

Mujāhid taught his commentary to several students, but some biographers report that it is only one pupil, al-Qāsim b. Abī Bazza (d. *c.* 114/732, Mecca), who acquired the work through audition.[336] It is also recorded that Mujāhid's pupil 'Abd Allāh b. Abī Najīḥ (d. 131/748, Mecca) heard some parts of the work directly from his teacher.[337] The extant recension available for analysis is Ibn Abī Najīḥ's, not al-Qāsim's. To the best of my knowledge, there is no reason to doubt the reliability of Ibn Abī Najīḥ's recension.

Mujāhid comments that Q5:41–2 is a reference to the punishment of stoning for *zinā* in accordance with the Torah and the Jewish group's refusal to implement it. Mujāhid opines:

> Regarding: "... they only intend to interpret the word of God according to their whims...," it means stoning. Stoning is in the Torah. If someone from a lower social class committed *zinā*, they would stone him. If a noble person did the same, they would blacken his face and parade him around town. Then they sought the legal counsel of the Prophet and he judged for them the stoning punishment. He asked the Jewish people about what they find in their Book and they tried to conceal it, save for one lazy-eyed sage. He said: They lie to you, Messenger of God. Stoning is in the Torah.[338]

Mujāhid does not provide his source(s), but it is recorded that he learned reports from the Companions Ibn 'Abbās, Ibn 'Umar, and Abū Hurayra.[339] Recall that the PJZO hadith circulated on the authority of each of these individuals. As for the Mujāhid-Abū Hurayra relationship, it is noted that Mujāhid's sister employed Abū Hurayra for a short period of time.[340] All of the elements found in Mujāhid's gloss are also in Abū Hurayra's recension. The overlaps mean that Mujāhid's commentary represents an early connection to Abū Hurayra's report and, to particular Qur'ān verses that create a nexus between the Prophet's authority, stoning, and the charge of *taḥrīf* against those who disobey God's commands.

[336] Ibn Abī Ḥātim, *al-Thiqāt*, 7:331; Schoeler, *Genesis of Literature in Islam*, 45f.

[337] Arif Kemil Abdullah, *The Qur'an and Normative Religious Pluralism*, 210f; Warqā' is recorded to have said that he read half of Mujāhid's *tafsīr* to Ibn Abī Najīḥ, and Ibn Abī Najīḥ read the other half back to him. Ibn Abī Najīḥ then comments that the *tafsīr* in his possession is one that he heard from Muḥammad b. 'Abd al-Wāḥid. See al-Khaṭīb al-Baghdādī, *Tārīkh*, 15:673.

[338] Mujāhid, *Tafsīr*, 308; al-Ṭabarī employs Mujāhid's gloss for the same verse. See al-Ṭabarī, *Jāmi'*, 10:325, no. 11,970.

[339] al-Bukhārī, *Tārīkh al-kabīr*, 7:411f; Ibn Abī Ḥātim, *al-Jarḥ wa al-ta'dīl*, 8:319; al-Mizzī, *Tahdhīb al-kamāl*, 27:230.

[340] Ibn Ḥajar, *al-Iṣāba*, 6:218.

The gloss of another exegete, Muqātil (d. 150/767), also has significant overlap with Abū Hurayra's variant. Because Muqātil's exegetical remarks are extensive, I will only note the relevant portions. The most consequential piece of information is related to the Jewish group's motivation for seeking out the Prophet's judgment. In reference to a portion of Q5:41, "Among them are the 'rightly-guided' ones (i.e., the Jewish communities), who listen eagerly to the lies of others without even seeing the need to give you a fair hearing. They only intend to interpret the word of God according to their whims...," Muqātil writes:

> The reference is to a Jewish man named Yahūdhā and a woman named Busra from Khaybar, both from among the Jewish nobles. They committed *zinā* and they had *iḥṣān*. The Jews were loath to stone them on the account of their nobility and social position, so the Jews of Khaybar said: We will go with these two to Muḥammad *because in his religion, the punishment is striking, not stoning* (*fa inna fī dīnihī al-ḍarb wa laysa fī dīnihī al-rajm*), so we will follow his judgment. If he orders you to strike them, then accept it.[341]

I noted in Jābir b. ʿAbd Allāh's recension that the Jews of Fadak advised the Jews of Medina to accept the Prophet's ruling if he orders flogging. In light of Muqātil's commentary, different transmitters are attempting to stabilize the memory of purported *taḥrīf* on the part of a Jewish communities by specifying locales: Khaybar or Fadak.

In Muqātil's gloss, the purported desire for a more lenient outcome functions (1) to substantiate the Jewish community's *taḥrīf* on the basis of the Qur'ānic verses and (2) to counter the argument by Muslims that flogging is in the Qur'ān [i.e., "their religion"], not *zinā*-stoning. In Muqātil's gloss, the phrase by the Jewish group stating that "the punishment is striking, not stoning" should therefore be read as an objection by Muslims of *zinā*-stoning for their own communities.

Approximately one and a half centuries after Muqātil, al-Ṭabarī (d. 310/923) provides a number of exegetical reports to gloss Q5:41–4. In some cases, his commentary overlaps with Mujāhid's and Muqātil's respective remarks, but, in other instances, not so much. For example, as for Q5:41, "Messenger

[341] Muqātil, *Tafsīr*, 1:475. My emphasis; for an analysis of Muqātil's gloss on Q5:41, see Nickel, *Narratives of Tampering in the Earliest Commentaries of the Qur'ān*, 82–9.

[of Mine], [I know] it hurts you to see those who profess faith out loud yet vie with one another to be ingrates, thereby revealing that they never intended to surrender their hearts to faith," al-Ṭabarī writes that this verse is about the "liar Ibn Ṣūriyā."[342] In the case of Q5:42, "Nevertheless, should they come to you, either offer judgment or decline to do so. If you choose to decline, [know that] they will not [be able to] harm you in any way. But if you decide to make a judgment, then judge for them in a just manner," al-Ṭabarī provides two sets of reports covering two different explanations. One set indicates that the verse applies to the Jewish stoning incident.[343] Importantly, another set conveys that the verse is about the adjudication of a homicide case among the Jewish tribes.[344] According to one hadith, the Companion Ibn ʿAbbās (d. 68/687) narrates that a dispute about proper compensation for an unlawful homicide emerged between the Jewish tribes of Qurayẓa and Naḍīr, and they brought the matter to the Prophet.[345] While al-Ṭabarī provides this alternative material, he does not make clear which account he deems correct. For the purpose of the present study, of consequence is that the sources preserve historical material indicating that among the early Muslim communities, there was no consensus about the events occasioning Q5:42. That Q5:42 could have been purportedly revealed by an incident other than PJZO hadith raises another important consideration about the veracity of the story involving the Prophet, his Jewish contemporaries, a *zinā* case, and the connection to the applicable verse(s).

With regard to Q5:43, " . . . but why do they appoint you for judgment when they have the Torah? [Surely] it contains God's judgment," al-Ṭabarī states that this portion of the verse is about the stoning punishment for those who have *iḥṣān* and commit *zinā*.[346] He reaffirms his understanding based on Q5:44, which states " . . . as did the rabbis and the sages, insofar as they were entrusted to preserve the word of God and to serve as its witnesses. [People], do not fear others out of reverence for them. Rather, revere Me! Do not barter away My words for a cheap price. Those who do not give a judgment according to the word of God are ingrates!" Al-Ṭabarī asserts that it is a

[342] al-Ṭabarī, *Jāmiʿ*, 10:308; for a summary of al-Ṭabarī's gloss of Q5:41, see Nickel, *Narratives of Tampering in the Earliest Commentaries of the Qur'ān*, 129–36.
[343] al-Ṭabarī, *Jāmiʿ*, 10:325f.
[344] al-Ṭabarī, *Jāmiʿ*, 10:326–8.
[345] al-Ṭabarī, *Jāmiʿ*, 10:326f, no. 11,974.
[346] al-Ṭabarī, *Jāmiʿ*, 10:336. He also cites a comment from the exegete al-Suddī (d. 127/744, Medina and Kūfa), who states that this portion of the verse is referring to the stoning incident. See al-Ṭabarī, *Jāmiʿ*, 10:337, no. 12,005.

reference to stoning for the *muḥṣan* and *muḥṣana* who commit *zinā*. In sum, al-Ṭabarī's exegesis of Q5:41–4 reflects a general position that the verses are about the Prophet's adjudication of a *zinā* case involving Jewish offenders and that the Prophet's order to stone them *is based on the Hebrew Bible*.[347]

Muslims understood the Prophet to have the authority to implement the laws of the People of the Book on their behalf. This is evidenced by the above analysis of Q5:41–4. The exegete Ibn Wahb (d. 197/812) also believes this to be the case when he comments that Q5:42, "... Nevertheless, should they come to you, either offer judgment . . . ," is a reference to the issue of stoning.[348] And without a reference to the punishment of stoning, al-Ḍaḥḥāk (d. 105/723) remarks that Q5:44 is about the People of the Book, meaning they should be judged according to their own laws.[349] In his gloss of Q5:48, "... We have assigned a law and a path (*sharīʿa*) to each of you . . . ," Muqātil writes that the *sharīʿa* for the Jewish communities signifies stoning for the *muḥṣan* and *muḥṣana* who commit *zinā*, and the *sharīʿa* for the Christians means flogging without stoning for the same transgression.[350] Such remarks illustrate that the Prophet is understood to have been authorized to implement divine laws for a particular community based on their *own* respective rules and regulations.

The adjudication of cases on the basis of a specific community's own laws in the days after the Prophet's death can be observed in commentaries in Wakīʿ's (d. 306/918) *Akbār al-quḍāt*. He provides a report from the judge Ismāʿīl b. Isḥāq (d. 282/895, ʿIrāq), who remarks:

> Regarding the *tafsīr* of Zayd b. Aslam (d. *c.* 140/757) [on Q5:47], "And let the People of the Gospel judge by what God has sent to them. And those who do not judge by what God has sent, they are the disobedient." He said: With this provision in the Qur'ān, the Prophet made a judgment in

[347] al-Ṭabarī, *Jāmiʿ*, 10:344f; he again notes that Q5:45 is a reference to stoning. See al-Ṭabarī, *Jāmiʿ*, 10:359; throughout his exegesis, al-Ṭabarī provides alternative reports for specific portions of verses Q5:41–8. However, he generally makes a connection with the PJZO hadith. See al-Ṭabarī, *Jāmiʿ*, 10:302, no. 11,918; but al-Ṭabarī cites an alternative exegesis on the authority of al-Suddī (d. 127/744, Medina and Kūfa) which states that Q5:41 is a reference to the war against the Banū Qurayẓa, and another on the authority of al-Shaʿbī which states that it is a reference to a homicide committed by one Jewish person against another. See al-Ṭabarī, *Jāmiʿ*, 10:302, no. 11,919; Burton provides a summary of the various alternative glosses provided by al-Ṭabarī on Q5:42ff. See Burton, *Sources of Islamic Law*, 129–36.

[348] Ibn Wahb, *Tafsīr*, 1:15, no. 28.

[349] al-Ḍaḥḥāk, *Tafsīr*, 329, no. 716.

[350] Muqātil, *Tafsīr*, 1:482.

> accordance with God's book. And whosoever disregards the rulings in God's Book, he certainly becomes an unbeliever.[351]

Earlier in the chapter, I provided a version of the PJZO hadith on the authority of Zayd b. Aslam, who, as noted, narrates the variant from Ibn 'Umar. According to Wakī', Zayd b. Aslam's opinion corroborates that the Prophet's order to stone is based on the Torah and, ostensibly, not applicable to Muslims. In other words, Zayd b. Aslam's remarks connote a specific attitude about the Prophet: he could and did make rulings in accordance with the previous scriptures for their respective communities, with the order to stone being one example.

Another report by Wakī' reveals how some Muslims came to perceive the application of the Hebrew Biblical prescription upon Muslims. He notes:

> Thābit al-Thamālī said: I said to Abū Ja'far [Muḥammad b. 'Alī al-Bāqir (d. 144/744)]: The *Murji'a* debate us about the meaning of these verses (Q5:41–7). They claim that they are for the Children of Israel.
>
> Abū Ja'far responded: We are the best of brothers to the Children of Israel. If the sweetness of the Qur'an is for us and the bitterness is for them, then the bitter verses came down for them and then applied to us.[352]

Thābit al-Thamālī's comment and Abū Ja'far's response indicate that some Muslims understood that non-Qur'ānic prescriptions were meant for non-Muslims but inevitably applied to Muslims. The PJZO hadith tracks with the exegetical dialectic noted in Wakī''s report.

In summary, the exegetical commentaries reviewed in this section convey that the Prophet's involvement in the adjudication of a case for Jewish *zinā* offenders was understood to be a result of attempts by his Jewish contemporaries to avoid the implementation of the penalty of death by stoning as prescribed in the Torah. For the most part, it seems that Muslims from earlier periods understood the Prophet's order to stone as applying

[351] Wakī', *Akhbār al-quḍāt*, 1:44; Zayd b. Aslam is one of Mālik's main informants. His sons, including 'Abd al-Raḥmān, who narrates his father's comments, do not have favorable reputations as transmitters. Pavlovitch argues that criticisms against Zayd's sons may have been attempts to disparage Zayd's own reputation, albeit not entirely with success. See Pavlovitch, *Formation of the Islamic Understanding of Kalāla*, 258–60.

[352] Wakī', *Akhbār al-quḍāt*, 1:44.

a non-Qur'ānic punishment to non-Muslims.[353] But as per Abū Ja'far's opinion, that which applied to the Jewish community was inevitably applied to Muslims.

Conclusion

In this chapter, I examined transmission chains, corresponding textual content, and exegetical commentaries associated with numerous versions of the PJZO hadith. Through my analysis, I have argued that the recension transmitted on the authority of Abū Hurayra (d. c. 58/677) represents the primary form. His version formed the foundation upon which other recensions developed and circulated. Abū Hurayra's variant did not experience wide popularity in the authoritative hadith sources due to the presence of the unidentified Muzanī in the transmission chain. That it was Abū Hurayra who first helped to circulate the hadith means it was in circulation by the second half of the first/seventh century. This early provenance is of significance because of the multi-layered discourse in the hadith. By discourse, I mean what Michel Foucault describes as a system of representation based on language that helps to talk about a particular topic in a specific context to generate knowledge.[354]

One layer of the discourse in the hadith is about the representation of the alleged conversations among Jewish groups, their rabbinic identity, and their supposed *intentional* betrayal of divine scripture. As I discussed earlier, rabbinic law and jurisprudence had resolved the stoning punishment issue before the advent of Islam, and the rabbis did not believe themselves to be violating God's command. This being the case, it is difficult to surmise why they would seek the Prophet's judgment. This disconnect, between what is alleged in the hadith and what is in rabbinic law, is one indication of the didactic aspects of the report.

The issue of death by lapidation for illicit sexual intercourse is about conveying an imagined view of Jewish communities as disobeying the command delineated in the Torah. By portraying them as concealing or altering

[353] For a summary of how some Muslim authorities came to view the Prophet's order to stone as part of the Islamic *sharī'a*, see Faisal Z. Abdullah, "Pre-Muḥammadan Law," 59–62.

[354] Stuart Hall (ed.), *Representations*, 44.

the stoning prescription, the hadith narrative functions as an example of *taḥrīf*, with an important implication that if the Jewish communities of Medina could obscure the truth about stoning, they could similarly obscure the Torah's revelation concerning Muḥammad. The Prophet's unwavering fidelity to the Scriptures serves as a testament to his prophetic legitimacy.

The purported event as described in the PJZO hadith becomes a teachable moment for Muslims living in the liminal space before which *zinā*-stoning is not part of Islam. By interlinking scriptural authority and the Prophet's authority to the stoning of Jewish *zinā* offenders, the hadith instructs Muslims to maintain fidelity to God's command and the practice of the Prophet by not practicing *taḥrīf*, namely, by implementing the stoning punishment. This lesson is precisely what becomes clear in a Muslim version of the report—the sermon of 'Umar b. al-Khaṭṭāb—which I examine in Chapter 4. As Abū Hurayra reportedly states, "The first person the Messenger of God ordered to be stoned was from among the Jews." This anchoring of the practice of stoning within the purview of the Prophet and divine legislation contributes to the beginnings of the process by which the justification of *zinā*-stoning eventually emerges in Islam.

3

The Islamization of the Stoning Punishment (Part 1): The Self-Confessing Woman

Introduction

Recall from Chapter 2 that in some versions of the hadith in which the Prophet is portrayed as ordering the stoning punishment upon Jewish offenders, an effort is made by the transmitters to affirm that the woman is indeed the paramour of the man (see pp. 95, 96, 98, and 111). According to the Companion Abū Bakra (d. *c.* 55/674), "The Prophet had a woman stoned but, before [he did so], he had a hole dug up for her up to her chest."[1] Could this statement by Abū Bakra be connected to the Jewish *zinā* offender? It is possible but, to the best of my knowledge, there is no extant evidence that can make a strong case for the connection. Nevertheless, the Companion's assertion is important because it represents a hadith complex that is central in the process of making *zinā*-stoning lawful. Accordingly, in this chapter I analyze several versions of a hadith, according to which the Prophet orders the stoning of a woman who, in all but one case, confesses to committing illicit sexual intercourse. Whereas one aspect of the Prophet's order to stone the Jewish *zinā* offenders is an indirect instruction to Muslims to maintain fidelity to *zinā*-stoning, his order to stone a self-confessing woman is representative of a clear Islamic practice. The definitive position is conveyed by elements in the report that identify the female offender as a Muslim. In line with these observations, I shed light on the different ways in which the narrative helps to shape early discourse around the legality and enforcement of death by lapidation upon Muslim transgressors of illicit sexual intercourse. And through an examination of the report's transmission history, I argue that its provenance is in the first/seventh century of Islam.

[1] Ibn Abī Shayba, *al-Muṣannaf* (2008 ed.), 9:360f, no. 29,374.

Stoning as Punishment in Early Islam. Syed Atif Rizwan, Oxford University Press. © Oxford University Press 2026.
DOI: 10.1093/9780197823774.003.0004

The chapter is organized in relation to the Companions cited as the sources of the different versions of the report. Section 3.1 examines variants transmitted on the authority of ʿImrān b. Ḥuṣayn (d. c. 52/672). In his account, the self-confessing woman is either unnamed or identified as a member belonging to the tribe of Juhayna. Section 3.2 focuses on reports attributed to Burayda b. al-Ḥuṣayb (d. 63/682). According to the sources, this version is transmitted by his two sons, ʿAbd Allāh (d. *c.* 110/728) and Sulaymān (d. 105/723). In Burayda b. al-Ḥuṣayb's account, the woman is identified as belonging to the tribe of Ghāmid. Section 3.3 reviews versions of the hadith on the authority of Abū Bakra Nufayʿ b. al-Ḥārith al-Thaqafī (d. *c.* 55/674). Finally, Section 3.4 provides biographical information on the three Companions and discusses why these individuals are cited as sources for the hadith.

Notably, Abū Bakra's version is less commonly found in later sources because it fails to meet the standards of authenticating the transmission history of hadith as established by traditional and modern hadith criticism (e.g., ICMA). The reason is that it has an unnamed transmitter in the transmission chain. However, as in Chapter 2, my methodological approach—which incorporates reports with "defective transmission chains"—allows me to demonstrate the historical value of Abū Bakra's variant. I argue that his report's significance lies in its early contribution to understanding the emergence of the self-confessing woman hadith specifically, and to establishing the legitimacy of using death by lapidation for Muslim *zinā* offenders, generally.

3.1. Reports by the Companion ʿImrān b. Ḥuṣayn (d. *c.* 53/672, Baṣra, Kūfa, Medina, and Syria)

3.1.1. The unidentified self-confessing woman

This section is dedicated to a report in which an *unidentified* woman self-confesses to illicit sexual intercourse in the presence of the Prophet. Based on her confession, the Prophet orders the punishment of lapidation, and she is stoned to death. One group of variants is based on the authority of the Companion ʿImrān b. Ḥuṣayn. In the transmission chains at our disposal, he is supposed to have passed on his narrative to a certain Abū al-Muhājir, who then passed it on to Abū Qilāba (d. *c.* 105/723, Baṣra and Ḥimṣ). Abū Qilāba, in turn, relates the hadith to his student, Yaḥyā b. Abī Kathīr (d. *c.* 130/747,

Baṣra, Medina, Yemen). Note that an analysis of Abū Qilāba's biography is deferred to subsection 3.1.2, which focuses on variants in which the woman is specified as belonging to the tribe of Juhayna, as Abū Qilāba is also part of the transmission chains of that report.

The renowned Syrian jurist and hadith narrator 'Abd al-Raḥmān b. 'Amr al-Awzā'ī (d. 157/774, Syria) is recorded to have transmitted the report on the authority of Yaḥyā b. Abī Kathīr. Ibn Mājah, Abū Dāwūd, and al-Nasā'ī record the narrative on al-Awzā'ī's authority. Their respective entries read:

> Ibn Mājah - (al)-'Abbās b. 'Uthmān [b. Muḥammad] al-Dimashqī (d. 239/853, Syria) - (al)-Walīd b. Muslim (d. *c.* 194/809, Syria) - al-Awzā'ī (d. 157/774) - Yaḥyā b. Abī Kathīr (d. *c.* 130/747) - Abū Qilāba (d. *c.* 105/723) - Abū al-Muhājir (d. unknown, Baṣra) - 'Imrān [b. Ḥuṣayn]:
>
> A woman came to the Prophet and confessed to *zinā*. The Prophet sentenced her [to death by lapidation]. She was bound up with her clothing and stoned. Then he led the congregation in reciting a funeral prayer for her.[2]
>
> Abū Dāwūd - Muḥammad b. al-Wazīr al-Dimashqī (d. 250/864, Syria) - (al)-Walīd b. Muslim - al-Awzā'ī:
>
> She was bound up with her clothes, meaning tightly.[3]
>
> Al-Nasā'ī - Muḥammad b. Khālid al-Dimashqī (d. *c.* 248/862, Syria) - (al)-Walīd b. Muslim (d. *c.* 194/809, Syria) - al-Awzā'ī (d. 157/774, Syria) - Yaḥyā b. Abī Kathīr - Abū Qilāba - Abū al-Muhājir - 'Imrān [b. Ḥuṣayn]:
>
> A woman came to the Prophet and confessed to *zinā*. The Messenger of God sentenced her [to death by lapidation]. She was bound up with her clothing, meaning tightly, and stoned. Then he led the congregation in reciting a funeral prayer for her. Ayyūb[4] narrated the same thing.[5]

These variants contain the following elements:

1) a woman confesses to *zinā* in the presence of the Prophet;
2) the Prophet sentences her to death by lapidation;

[2] Ibn Mājah, *Sunan*, 854, no. 2,555; I interpret *thumma ṣallā 'alayhā* as indicative of the ritual prayer conducted for a deceased Muslim (*jināza*).
[3] Abū Dāwūd, *Sunan*, 6:488, no. 4,441.
[4] Ayyūb al-Sakhtiyānī (d. 131/749, Baṣra and Medina).
[5] al-Nasā'ī, *al-Sunan al-kubrā*, 6:430, no. 7,157.

3) the woman is bound up by her clothes;
4) she is stoned on the order of the Prophet;
5) the Prophet leads the congregation in reciting a funeral prayer for her.

The commonality among the respective versions of Ibn Mājah and al-Nasā'ī (and to a limited extent Abū Dāwūd) points to al-Walīd b. Muslim as their common source, responsible in part for the circulation of the report on al-Awzā'ī's authority. Al-Walīd b. Muslim (d. *c.* 194/809) was a manumitted slave.[6] He was respected among his peers and, according to one report, was thought to be the most knowledgeable about al-Awzā'ī's transmissions.[7] Al-Nasā'ī especially thought highly of him, which is likely one reason why he furnishes the report on al-Walīd b. Muslim's authority.[8] But al-Walīd is criticized for taking narratives transmitted by an accused forger of hadith, Ibn Abī al-Safar, and attributing them directly to al-Awzā'ī, all the while concealing that he received the report from Ibn Abī al-Safar.[9] Al-Walīd apparently made a habit of not properly naming known weak transmitters in transmission chains that included al-Awzā'ī.[10] I view these critiques as those focused on the accuracy of the transmission chains he cites, not the textual contents themselves. Accordingly, al-Walīd's biographical information does not preclude his *own* participation in the circulation of the report, even if doubts may exist about the exact source(s) for his information.

Al-Nasā'ī provides a version that does not include al-Walīd b. Muslim in the transmission chain but points to his teaching of it on the authority of al-Awzā'ī. The transmission chain furnished by al-Nasā'ī includes Muḥammad al-Faryābī (d. *c.* 211/826, Kūfa, Mecca, and Syria), who transmits the report on the authority of al-Awzā'ī. The entry reads:

> Isḥāq b. Manṣūr al-Marwazī (d. 251/865, Marw and Nīshāpūr) - Muḥammad b. Yūsuf [b. Wāqid b. 'Uthmān al-Faryābī] (d. *c.* 211/826, Kūfa, Mecca, and Syria) - al-Awzā'ī (d. 157/774) - Yaḥyā b. Abī Kathīr (d. *c.* 130/747) - Abū Qilāba (d. *c.* 105/723) - Abū al-Muhājir (d. unknown, Baṣra) - 'Imrān [b. Ḥuṣayn]:

[6] Ibn Sa'd, *al-Ṭabaqāt*, 9:475; Ibn 'Asākir, *Tārīkh*, 63:281.
[7] Ibn Sa'd, *al-Ṭabaqāt*, 9:475; Ibn Abī Ḥātim, *al-Jarḥ wa al-ta'dīl*, 9:17 and 1:290; Ibn 'Asākir, *Tārīkh*, 63:282 and 297.
[8] al-Mizzī, *Tahdhīb al-kamāl*, 31:84.
[9] Ibn 'Asākir, *Tārīkh*, 63:291f; al-Mizzī, *Tahdhīb al-kamāl*, 31:96f; al-Dhahabī, *Siyar a'lām*, 9:216f.
[10] Ibn 'Asākir, *Tārīkh*, 63:291f; al-Mizzī, *Tahdhīb al-kamāl*, 31:96f; al-Dhahabī, *Mīzān*, 4:347.

A woman came to the Messenger of God and said: Messenger of God, I have committed a *ḥadd* [i.e., *zinā*] so apply the *ḥadd* [punishment] to me.

The Prophet called for her guardian and said to him: Go take care of this woman and bring her back after she has given birth.

After she gave birth, she was brought back and the Messenger of God sentenced her [to death]. The Prophet gave the order for her to be stoned. She was bound up with her clothes and stoned. The Prophet led the congregation in reciting a funeral prayer for her. ʿUmar [b. al-Khaṭṭāb] said: Messenger of God, how could you pray for her despite the fact that she committed *zinā*?

The Prophet explained: Her [manner of] repentance [produced spiritual effects so powerful] that, were they spread over 70 people, it would be sufficient for all of them [to be forgiven for their sins]. Do you not see how [noble] it is that she was willing to sacrifice her life in order to earn God's forgiveness?[11]

The following chart offers a comparison between the respective recensions of (al)-Walīd b. Muslim and al-Faryābī:

Yaḥyā b. Abī Kathīr (d. *c.* 130/747, Baṣra, Medina, Yemen):	
al-Awzāʿī (d. 157/774, Syria and Yemen) - (al)-Walīd b. Muslim (d. *c.* 194/809, Syria)	al-Awzāʿī - al-Faryābī (d. *c.* 211/826, Kūfa, Mecca, and Syria)
A woman confesses to *zinā* in the presence of the Prophet.	A woman confesses to a *ḥadd* (i.e., *zinā*) in the presence of the Prophet and asks that the *ḥadd* be applied to her.
	Prophet calls for her guardian and tells him to take care of her until she gives birth and then bring her back.
She was bound up with her clothing and stoned.	She was bound up with her clothing and stoned.
Prophet prays for her.	Prophet prays for her.
	Conversation between the Prophet and ʿUmar.
	Repentance equal to that of 70 people of Medina.

11 al-Nasāʾī, *al-Sunan al-kubrā*, 6:426f, no. 7,150.

Both al-Walīd b. Muslim's and al-Faryābī's versions share the following elements:

1) A woman confesses to *zinā* in the presence of the Prophet;
2) The Prophet sentences her to death by lapidation;
3) The woman is bound up by her clothes;
4) She is stoned on the order of the Prophet;
5) The Prophet led the congregation in reciting a funeral prayer for her.

Al-Faryābī's variant further includes:

1) *Ḥadd* represents both an offense and a punishment;
2) The self-confessor is pregnant;
3) The Prophet stays the punishment and releases the offender into the care of her guardian, who is to produce her once she gives birth;
4) The conversation between the Prophet and ʿUmar b. al-Khaṭṭāb.

The differences raise questions. Were modifications made to al-Awzāʿī's recension by al-Faryābī or his student? Were errors made in al-Awzāʿī's recension by al-Walīd b. Muslim or his students? Or, did al-Awzāʿī communicate different elements to different students? From a transmission chain standpoint, al-Nasāʾī's informant, Isḥāq b. Manṣūr al-Marwazī, is a known legal authority and transmitter.[12] As for al-Faryābī, it is recorded that his collections of hadith, especially from the well-known legal authority Sufyān al-Thawrī (d. 161/778),[13] are the more respected among scholarly circles.[14] Lastly, al-Awzāʿī himself is among the most sought legal authorities and is the eponym of the later defunct Awzāʿī school.[15] On the basis of the aforementioned biographical information, at the very least the report was shared among the individuals named in the transmission chains with al-Awzāʿī (d. 157/774) as a common source, the differences among them notwithstanding.

Another version of the report in which the self-confessor remains unidentified is provided by al-Bayhaqī. This version involves Hishām b. Abī ʿAbd

[12] al-Mizzī, *Tahdhīb al-kamāl*, 2:476f; al-Dhahabī, *Siyar aʿlām*, 12:259f.
[13] al-Mizzī, *Tahdhīb al-kamāl*, 27:56f and 59; al-Dhahabī, *Siyar aʿlām*, 10:117.
[14] al-Mizzī, *Tahdhīb al-kamāl*, 27:56–9; al-Dhahabī, *Siyar aʿlām*, 10:114–6; Ibn Ḥajar, *Tahdhīb al-tahdhīb*, 6:130.
[15] Ibn Saʿd, *al-Ṭabaqāt*, 9:494; Ibn Abī Ḥātim, *al-Jarḥ wa al-taʿdīl*, 1:203–8 and 5:266f; Lucas, *Constructive Critics*, 132.

Allāh al-Dastuwāʾī (d. *c*. 153/770, Baṣra).[16] He, like al-Awzāʿī, is a student of Yaḥyā b. Abī Kathīr. The entry reads:

> ʿAlī b. Aḥmad b. ʿAbdān [al-Shīrāzī] (d. 415/1024, Baghdād and Nishapur) - Aḥmad b. ʿUbayd [b. Ismāʿīl] al-Ṣaffār (d. after 341/952, Baghdād and Baṣra) - Ibrāhīm b. ʿAbd Allāh [b. Muslim] (d. 292/904, Baghdād, Baṣra, and Syria) - Muslim b. Ibrāhīm (d. 222/837, Baṣra) - Hishām b. Abī ʿAbd Allāh al-Dastuwāʾī - Yaḥyā b. Abī Kathīr - Abū Qilāba - Abū al-Muhallab (d. first/seventh c.) - ʿImrān b. Ḥuṣayn:
>
> A pregnant woman came to the Prophet and said she committed *zinā*.
>
> The Prophet called for her guardian and said to him: Go take care of this woman and bring her back after she has given birth.
>
> After she gave birth she was brought back to the Prophet. He ordered that she be bound up tightly with her clothes and stoned, and she was stoned. Then he commanded the people to perform the funeral prayer for her and to bury her. ʿUmar b. al-Khaṭṭāb said: Messenger of God, [how could] you [have] prayed for her despite the fact that she committed *zinā*?
>
> The Prophet responded: I swear by the One [God], in whose hand is my soul, her [manner of] repentance [produced spiritual effects so powerful] that, were they spread over 70 people, it would be sufficient for all of them [to be forgiven their sins]. Do you not see how [noble] it is that she was willing to sacrifice her life in order to earn God's forgiveness?[17]

This version contains the following elements:

1) A woman confesses to *zinā* in the presence of the Prophet;
2) The Prophet sentences her;
3) She is pregnant;
4) The Prophet stays the punishment and releases the offender into the care of her guardian, who is to produce her once she gives birth;
5) When she is brought back, she is bound by her clothes;
6) She is stoned on the Prophet's authority;

[16] Also known as Hishām b. Sanbar.

[17] al-Bayhaqī, *Sunan*, 8:392, no. 16,989; Abū ʿAwāna also provides a version with al-Dastuwāʾī in the transmission chain. The textual content shares a number of features that are recorded in al-Bayhaqī's version, which increases the likelihood of al-Dastuwāʾī's involvement. See Abū ʿAwāna, *Musnad*, 4:133, no. 6,288.

7) The Prophet participates in the *janāza* prayer for her (in al-Dastuwāʾī's version, there is only a reference to the Prophet's command to bury her);
8) The conversation between the Prophet and ʿUmar b. al-Khaṭṭāb.

The following chart compares al-Dastuwāʾī's version with those on the respective authorities of al-Awzāʿī's two students, (al)-Walīd b. Muslim and al-Faryābī:

	Yaḥyā b. Abī Kathīr (d. *c.* 130/747, Baṣra, Medina, Yemen):	
al-Awzāʿī (d. 157/774, Syria and Yemen) - (al)-Walīd b. Muslim (d. *c.* 194/809, Syria)	al-Awzāʿī - al-Faryābī (d. *c.* 211/826, Kūfa, Mecca, and Syria)	Hishām al-Dastuwāʾī (d. *c.* 153/770, Baṣra)
A woman confesses to *zinā* in the presence of the Prophet.	A woman confesses to a *ḥadd* (i.e., *zinā*) in the presence of the Prophet.	A woman confesses to *zinā* in the presence of the Prophet.
	Prophet calls for her guardian and tells him to take care of her until she gives birth and then bring her back.	Prophet calls for her guardian and tells him to take care of her until she gives birth and then bring her back.
She was bound up with her clothing and stoned.	She was bound up with her clothing and stoned.	She was bound up with her clothing and stoned.
Prophet prays for her.	Prophet prays for her.	Prophet prays for her.
	Conversation between the Prophet and ʿUmar.	Conversation between the Prophet and ʿUmar.
	Repentance equal to that of 70 people of Medina.	Repentance equal to that of 70 people of Medina.

At this point, the absence of certain elements in two of al-Awzāʿī's transmissions remains unexplainable. But the overlap in the textual content of the reports by al-Awzāʿī's students points to him as their common source and also helps to positively situate the role of al-Dastuwāʾī. These versions combined point to Ibn Abī Kathīr as the earlier teacher.

As for al-Bayhaqī's transmission chain, biographical information is helpful in establishing the place of al-Dastuwāʾī. Alī b. Aḥmad b. ʿAbdān al-Shīrāzī (d. 415/1024),[18] Aḥmad b. ʿUbayd b. Ismāʿīl al-Ṣaffār (d. after 341/

[18] al-Khaṭīb al-Baghdādī, *Tārīkh*, 13:232, no. 6,108.

952),[19] and Ibrāhīm b. ʿAbd Allāh (d. 292/904)[20] are hardly discussed in the sources. However, the paucity of material cannot *a priori* lead to the conclusion of their irrelevance. Their place in the transmission chain, accordingly, must be accepted unless outside evidence can establish otherwise. As for al-Dastuwāʾī, he is recorded to have been a respected transmitter whose reports are employed for legal rulings.[21] Some went as far as to claim that once they heard a report from al-Dastuwāʾī, they never looked anywhere else.[22] In fact, al-Dastuwāʾī receives preference over al-Awzāʿī for narratives from their mutual teacher, Ibn Abī Kathīr. Al-Dastuwāʾī was known to transmit the latter's material from memory, whereas al-Awzāʿī did so from written notes.[23] It is also reported that al-Dastuwāʾī was Ibn Abī Kathīr's best student.[24] All things equal, then, al-Dastuwāʾī played a role in the circulation of the report during the first half of the second/eighth century. To be sure, several hadith collections include versions on al-Dastuwāʾī's authority that include a tribal affiliation, among other differences. I examine these recensions in the next section, which again support al-Dastuwāʾī's involvement. The combination of reports on the respective authorities of al-Dastuwāʾī and al-Awzāʿī points to Ibn Abī Kathīr (d. *c.* 130/747) as their teacher.

A version in ʿAbd al-Razzāq's *Muṣannaf* raises important considerations about the participation of certain transmitters involved in the circulation of the report in which the woman remains unidentified. The entry reads:

> Maʿmar [b. Rāshid] (d. 153/770, Baṣra, Medina, and Yemen) **and** [Sufyān] al-Thawrī (d. 161/778, Baṣra, Kūfa, and Ḥijāz) - Ayyūb [al-Sakhtiyānī] (d. 131/749, Baṣra and Medina) - Abū Qilāba (d. *c.* 105/723) - ʿImrān [b. Ḥuṣayn] (d. *c.* 53/672):
>
> A woman confessed to *zinā* in the presence of the Prophet and he adjudicated her case. She was bound up with her clothes and stoned. Then he participated in the *jināza* prayer for her. ʿUmar asked the Prophet: Messenger of God, you prayed for her despite the fact you gave the order for her to be stoned?

[19] al-Khaṭīb al-Baghdādī, *Tārīkh*, 5:433, no. 2,271.
[20] al-Khaṭīb al-Baghdādī, *Tārīkh*, 7:36, no. 3,104.
[21] Ibn Saʿd, *al-Ṭabaqāt*, 9:279.
[22] Ibn Abī Ḥātim, *al-Jarḥ wa al-taʿdīl*, 9:59f; al-Mizzī, *Tahdhīb al-kamāl*, 30:218f.
[23] Ibn Abī Ḥātim, *al-Jarḥ wa al-taʿdīl*, 9:61; al-Mizzī, *Tahdhīb al-kamāl*, 30:221.
[24] Ibn Abī Ḥātim, *al-Jarḥ wa al-taʿdīl*, 9:60f; al-Mizzī, *Tahdhīb al-kamāl*, 30:220f.

> The Prophet responded: Her repentance is such that if it is spread over 70 people of Medina, it would be sufficient for all of them. Could you find anything better than her generosity with her soul to God?[25]

Here, al-Sakhtiyānī, a student of Abū Qilāba, is in place of Ibn Abī Kathīr, also a student of Abū Qilāba, as noted above. Several of the features previously identified are also in 'Abd al-Razzāq's recension. Note the following chart:

Abū Qilāba (d. *c.* 105/723) - 'Imrān [b. Ḥuṣayn] (d. *c.* 53/672)			
	Yaḥyā b. Abī Kathīr (d. *c.* 130/747, Baṣra, Medina, Yemen):		Ayyūb [al-Sakhtiyānī] (d. 131/749, Baṣra and Medina)
al-Awzā'ī (d. 157/774, Syria and Yemen) - (al)-Walīd b. Muslim (d. *c.* 194/809, Syria)	al-Awzā'ī - al-Faryābī (d. *c.* 211/826, Kūfa, Mecca, and Syria)	Hishām al-Dastuwā'ī (d. *c.* 153/770, Baṣra)	Ma'mar [b. Rāshid] (d. 153/770, Baṣra, Medina, and Yemen) **and** [Sufyān] al-Thawrī (d. 161/778, Baṣra, Kūfa, and Ḥijāz)
A woman confesses to *zinā* in the presence of the Prophet.	A woman confesses to a *ḥadd* (i.e., *zinā*) in the presence of the Prophet.	A woman confesses to *zinā* in the presence of the Prophet.	A woman confesses to *zinā* in the presence of the Prophet.
	Prophet calls for her guardian and tells him to take care of her until she gives birth and then bring her back.	Prophet calls for her guardian and tells him to take care of her until she gives birth and then bring her back.	
She was bound up with her clothing and stoned.	She was bound up with her clothing and stoned.	She was bound up with her clothing and stoned.	She was bound up with her clothing and stoned.
Prophet prays for her.	Prophet prays for her.	Prophet prays for her.	Prophet prays for her.
	Conversation between the Prophet and 'Umar.	Conversation between the Prophet and 'Umar.	Conversation between the Prophet and 'Umar.
	Repentance equal to that of 70 people of Medina.	Repentance equal to that of 70 people of Medina.	Repentance equal to that of 70 people of Medina.

25 'Abd al-Razzāq, *al-Muṣannaf*, 7:325, no. 13,347.

Note that the pregnancy clause is missing from al-Sakhtiyānī's recension. Given that two of al-Awzāʿī's students narrate the report without this element, and now we have two additional informants of ʿAbd al-Razzāq transmitting similarly, the pregnancy clause is an interpolation after the initial report's emergence. This later appearance of the clause is reaffirmed by my analysis of additional versions in the next subsection.

ʿAbd al-Razzāq provides a collective transmission chain, which may complicate the determinacy of what Maʿmar (d. 153/770) communicates versus al-Thawrī (d. 161/778). The most practical explanation is that both were transmitting the same information, and this is why ʿAbd al-Razzāq cites them together. Importantly, al-Sakhtiyānī's version shares numerous elements with other versions transmitted by Ibn Abī Kathīr. Presently and with corroborating information, we have to consider that al-Sakhtiyānī (d. 131/749) and Ibn Abī Kathīr (d. *c.* 130/747) are teaching the report on the authority of Abū Qilāba (d. 105/723).

In this section, comparative textual content and transmission chain analysis yielded fruitful results that are helpful in establishing the provenance and involvement of certain narrators of the hadith. Difficulties, however, do remain about the inception of some elements in particular variants. There remains uncertainty pertaining to the pregnancy clause's provenance. This element is not in al-Sakhtiyānī's version on Maʿmar's authority, nor in al-Walīd b. Muslim's two versions on al-Awzāʿī's authority. In order to resolve such disparities, to add evidence about the report's provenance, and to understand the significance of the ways in which the incident is conceptually understood, I turn now to versions in which the self-confessing woman is identified as being from the tribe of Juhayna.

3.1.2. The self-confessing woman from the tribe of Juhayna

The recensions in which the woman is identified as being from the tribe of Juhayna are exclusively on the authority of Ibn Abī Kathīr. This difference leads to three immediate possibilities: (1) a transmitter deliberately amends the textual content to include Juhayna, (2) a transmitter includes the tribe in some teaching sessions but not in others, or (3) transmitters included or excluded the tribal affiliation for no special reasons. The upshot of these reports is that they reaffirm the involvement of Ibn Abī Kathīr and, importantly, indicate that the hadith was at the latest in circulation by the end of the first/seventh century.

One set of Juhayna reports is on the authority of Hishām al-Dastuwāʾī (d. *c.* 153/770, Baṣra), a student of Ibn Abī Kathīr, who is the student of Abū Qilāba. Recall that from the previous section, we learned al-Dastuwāʾī helped to circulate a variant in which a self-confessing woman remains unidentified. In his *Musnad*, al-Ṭayālisī (d. 204/819) provides one version on al-Dastuwāʾī's authority. The entry reads:

> Hishām [b. Abī ʿAbd Allāh al-Dastuwāʾī] - Yaḥyā b. Abī Kathīr (d. *c.* 130/747, Baṣra, Medina, Yemen) - Abū Qilāba (d. *c.* 105/723, Baṣra and Ḥimṣ) - Abū al-Muhallab [ʿAbd al-Raḥmān b. Muʿāwiya] (d. first/seventh c.) - ʿImrān [b. Ḥuṣayn]:
>
> A woman from Juhayna, who became pregnant after committing *zinā*, came to the Prophet. The Messenger of God ordered her guardian to take care of her and once she gave birth, to bring her to [him]. [Upon her return,] the Prophet ordered that she be bound up with her clothes and stoned, and then she was stoned. Thereafter, the Prophet led the congregation in reciting a funeral prayer for her, after which ʿUmar said to the Prophet: Messenger of God, [how could] you [have] prayed for her despite the fact that she committed *zinā*?
>
> The Prophet responded: Her [manner of] repentance [produced spiritual effects so powerful] that, were they spread over the people of Medina, it would be sufficient for all of them [to be forgiven their sins]. Do you not see how [noble] it is that she was willing to sacrifice her life in order to earn God's forgiveness?[26]

As to the two versions by al-Dastuwāʾī, that is, one mentioning the woman's tribal affiliation and the other not, note the following overlap:

1) A woman confesses to *zinā* in the presence of the Prophet;
2) The Prophet sentences her to death;
3) She is pregnant after having committed *zinā*;
4) The Prophet stays the punishment and releases her into her guardian's care until she gives birth, after which he is to produce her to the Prophet;

[26] al-Ṭayālisī, *Musnad*, 2:182f, no. 888.

5) When she is brought back, she is bound by her clothes;
6) She is stoned on the Prophet's authority;
7) The Prophet leads the congregation in reciting a funeral prayer for her;
8) The conversation between the Prophet and 'Umar b. al-Khaṭṭāb.

The overlap in most elements and the language differences indicate a transmission from a common source: al-Dastuwā'ī.

The hadith collectors Abū 'Awāna (d. 316/928) and al-Bayhaqī provide the Juhayna versions that include al-Ṭayālisī in the transmission chain.[27] Abū 'Awāna's differs from, whereas al-Bayhaqī's is virtually identical to, al-Ṭayālisī's recension. The following is Abū 'Awāna's entry:

> Yūnus b. Ḥabīb al-Iṣbahānī (d. 267/880) and 'Ammār b. Rajā' (d. 267/880) - Abū Dāwūd [al-Ṭayālisī] - Hishām al-Dastuwā'ī - Ibn Abī Kathīr - Abū Qilāba - Abū al-Muhallab - 'Imrān b. Ḥuṣayn:
>
> A woman belonging to the tribe of Juhayna came to the Prophet. She had committed *zinā*. She said: I have committed *zinā* and she was pregnant.
>
> [The Prophet] called for her guardian and said: Go take care of her. After she gives birth, bring her back to me.
>
> The guardian acted accordingly and came back with her. She was bound up with her clothes. The Prophet then gave the order for her to be stoned, and she was stoned. Thereafter, the Prophet prayed over her.
>
> 'Umar asked: You [have] prayed for her despite the fact that you ordered her to be stoned?
>
> [The Prophet responded]: Her [manner of] repentance [produced spiritual effects so powerful] that, were they spread over 70 people of Medina, it would be sufficient for all of them [to be forgiven their sins]. Do you not see how [noble] it is that she was willing to sacrifice her life in order to earn God's forgiveness?

As noted in the transmission chain, Abū 'Awāna uses two informants. The same transmitter used by al-Bayhaqī (Yūnus b. Ḥabīb al-Iṣbahānī) and an additional one, 'Ammār b. Rajā'. In addition to having an impeccable reputation, Yūnus b. Ḥabīb's citation in the transmission chain reflects the fact that he was known as an authority for the *Musnad* of al-Ṭayālisī.[28] 'Ammār

[27] Abū 'Awāna, *Musnad*, 4:133, no. 6,287; al-Bayhaqī, *Sunan*, 8:379, no. 16,951.
[28] al-Dhahabī, *Siyar a'lām*, 12:596f.

b. Rajā' is recorded to have produced his own *muṣannaf* and, like Yūnus b. Ḥabīb, had a strong public standing.[29] Given that each transmitter can stand on his own merit, in my view, it would be odd for Abū 'Awāna to amend the transmission chain by including another person, thereby leaving him susceptible to attacks for manipulating transmission chains. As for the differences in the textual contents, they can also be explained by virtue of being produced via oral/aural study sessions. These considerations, plus the version wherein the woman's tribal affiliation is absent but has several overlapping elements and is on the authority of al-Dastuwā'ī (previous subsection), attest to the circulation of the report by al-Dastuwā'ī and, in turn, Ibn Abī Kathīr.

Turning to al-Dastuwā'ī, his involvement in the circulation of the Juhayna version can be further substantiated by additional recensions. Ibn Ḥanbal's *Musnad* has two, each related by different students of al-Dastuwā'ī: (1) Yaḥyā b. Sa'īd al-Qaṭṭān (d. 198/813, Baṣra and Baghdād), a *mawlā* of Banū Tamīm,[30] and (2) Abū 'Āmir ['Abd al-Malik b. 'Amr] (d. *c.* 204/819, Baṣra), a *mawlā* of Banū Qays b. Tha'laba.[31] According to biographical dictionaries, Ibn Sa'īd al-Qaṭṭān is a narrator whose transmissions are especially valued for their legal quality.[32] He had such high regard for al-Dastuwā'ī that he claims to have never verified the reports he received from him.[33] Similar to Ibn Sa'īd al-Qaṭṭān, Abū 'Āmir is also recorded to have been a sought-after transmitter.[34] In fact, it is documented that Ibn Ḥanbal eagerly searched for Abū 'Āmir's reports from among the Baṣrans.[35] This information adds cumulative weight to the evidence for Ibn Sa'īd al-Qaṭṭān and Abū 'Āmir receiving the Juhayna version of the report from al-Dastuwā'ī.

As for the textual contents of Ibn Ḥanbal's two recensions on al-Dastuwā'ī's authority, overall, there is significant overlap among the various recensions.[36]

[29] al-Dhahabī, *Siyar a'lām*, 13:35.
[30] Ibn Ḥanbal, *Musnad* (1995 ed.), 15:72f no. 19,789.
[31] Ibn Ḥanbal, *Musnad* (1995 ed.), 15:57f, no. 19,811.
[32] Ibn Sa'd, *al-Ṭabaqāt*, 9:294; Ibn Abī Ḥātim, *al-Jarḥ wa al-ta'dīl*, 1:232–4 and 9:151; Ibn Ḥibbān, *al-Thiqāt*, 7:611; al-Khaṭīb al-Baghdādī, *Tārīkh*, 16:206–10.
[33] Ibn Ma'īn, *Tarīkh*, 4:209, no. 3,992f.
[34] al-Mizzī, *Tahdhīb al-kamāl*, 18:367f; al-Dhahabī, *Siyar a'lām*, 9:471f; Ibn Ḥajar, *Tahdhīb al-tahdhīb*, 4:255f.
[35] Ibn Ḥajar, *Tahdhīb al-tahdhīb*, 4:255.
[36] One difference is that in Ibn Ḥanbal's versions, the woman says that she has committed a *ḥadd* and that the *ḥadd* should be applied to her. I consider this a natural change during the transmission process because the concept of the transgression remains the same, which is associated with the punishment of lapidation.

In combination with his biographical information previously noted and the parallels in the textual content recorded by three of al-Dastuwāʾī's students, including al-Ṭayālisī, means that al-Dastuwāʾī was involved in the transmission of the hadith. It remains to be determined whether al-Dastuwāʾī himself or his teacher, Ibn Abī Kathīr, is responsible for the inclusion/exclusion of reference to the woman's tribal affiliation.

Muslim, Abū Dāwūd, and al-Nasāʾī also provide Juhayna versions with al-Dastuwāʾī in the transmission chain. In Muslim's *Ṣaḥīḥ*, al-Dastuwāʾī shares the report with his son, Muʿādh (d. 200/815, Baṣra and Yemen).[37] In Abū Dāwūd's *Sunan*, al-Dastuwāʾī transmits it to Muslim b. Ibrāhīm (d. 222/837, Baṣra).[38] And in al-Nasāʾī's *Sunan*, al-Dastuwāʾī passes it on to Khālid b. al-Ḥārith (d. 186/802, Baṣra),[39] who, according to biographical dictionaries, was one of the better-known transmitters in Baṣra.[40] The textual content recorded by each of the three collectors shares high degrees of similarities via motifs with one another and with other recensions on al-Dastuwāʾī's authority. These versions, combined with the others discussed above, yield a total of seven individuals transmitting the report from al-Dastuwāʾī, which, in my view, more than corroborates al-Dastuwāʾī's involvement.

Maʿmar b. Rāshid is also recorded to have learned the report from Ibn Abī Kathīr. The following transmission chain and textual content are provided by ʿAbd al-Razzāq on Maʿmar's authority:

> Maʿmar [b. Rāshid] (d. 153/770) - Yaḥyā b. Abī Kathīr (d. *c.* 130/747) - Abū Qilāba (d. *c.* 105/723) - Abū al-Muhallab (d. first/seventh c.) - ʿImrān [b. Ḥuṣayn] (d. *c.* 53/672):
>
> A woman from Juhayna confessed to *zinā* in the presence of the Prophet. She also told him that she was pregnant. The Prophet called for her guardian and said: Go take care of her and let me know once she has given birth.
>
> The guardian did as he was told. [Upon her return,] the Prophet ordered that she be bound up with her clothes and stoned, and then she was stoned. Then he led the congregation in reciting a funeral prayer for her. ʿUmar

[37] Muslim, *Ṣaḥīḥ*, 1324, no. 24 (1,696).
[38] Abū Dāwūd, *Sunan*, 6:487, no. 4,440.
[39] al-Nasāʾī, *al-Sunan al-kubrā*, 6:427, no. 7,151.
[40] Ibn Abī Ḥātim, *al-Jarḥ wa al-taʿdīl* 3:325; al-Mizzī, *Tahdhīb al-kamāl* v. 8, 37f; al-Dhahabī, *Siyar aʿlām* v. 9, 127f.

asked: Messenger of God, [how could] you [have] prayed for her despite the fact that you had her stoned?

The Prophet explained: Her [manner of] repentance [produced spiritual effects so powerful] that, were they spread over 70 people of Medina, it would be sufficient for all of them [to be forgiven their sins]. Do you not see how [noble] it is that she was willing to sacrifice her life in order to earn God's forgiveness?[41]

In this report (see the comparison chart on p. 197,):

1) A woman from Juhayna confesses to *zinā* in the presence of the Prophet;
2) The Prophet sentences her to death;
3) She is pregnant but uncertain if pregnancy results from *zinā*;
4) The Prophet stays the punishment and releases her into the care of her guardian, who is to produce her once she gives birth;
5) When she returns, she is bound by her clothes;
6) She is stoned on the Prophet's authority;
7) The Prophet led the congregation in reciting a funeral prayer for her;
8) The conversation between the Prophet and ʿUmar b. al-Khaṭṭāb.

All of these elements are in both of al-Dastuwāʾī's recensions. The overlap in textual contents indicates that al-Dastuwāʾī and Maʿmar transmitted the narrative as taught to them by their recorded teacher, Ibn Abī Kathīr.

In addition to al-Dastuwāʾī and Maʿmar, Abān b. Yazīd al-ʿAṭṭār (d. 160/776, Baṣra) narrates a Juhayna variant on the authority of Ibn Abī Kathīr. This version is provided by Ibn Abī Shayba, and the entry reads:

ʿAffān b. Muslim [b. ʿAbd Allāh] (d. 220/835, Baghdād and Baṣra) - Abān [b. Yazīd] al-ʿAṭṭār (d. 160/776, Baṣra) - Yaḥyā b. Abī Kathīr (d. *c.* 130/747) -

[41] ʿAbd al-Razzāq, *al-Muṣannaf*, 7:325f, no. 13,348; on ʿAbd al-Razzāq's authority, see also Ibn Ḥanbal, *Musnad* (1995 ed.), 15:57f, no. 19,747; al-Tirmidhī, *Jāmiʿ*, 3:105f, no. 1,435; al-Nasāʾī, *al-Sunan al-kubrā*, 6:430, no. 7,156; the *matn*s are virtually identical with the exception of the dialogue clause. It is not in al-Nasāʾī's version. The omission is likely due to his informant, Muḥammad b. Rāfiʿ al-Nīshāpūrī (d. 245/859), because al-Nasāʾī provides another recension that has the dialogue clause. I note this version on page 184.

Abū Qilāba (d. *c.* 105/723) - Abū al-Muhallab (d. first/seventh c.) - ʿImrān [b. Ḥuṣayn] (d. 53/672):

A woman from Juhayna came to the Prophet and said: I have committed a *ḥadd*, so apply it to me.

This conversation took place while she was pregnant. The Prophet ordered that she be taken care of until she gives birth. Once she gave birth, her guardian brought her back to the Messenger of God. The Prophet ordered that she be bound up and stoned. After the stoning, the Prophet prayed for her.

ʿUmar said: Messenger of God, [how could] you [have] prayed for her despite the fact that you had her stoned?

The Prophet explained: Her [manner of] repentance [produced spiritual effects so powerful] that, were they spread over 70 people of Medina, it would be sufficient for all of them [to be forgiven their sins]. Do you not see how [noble] it is that she was willing to sacrifice her life in order to earn God's forgiveness?[42]

As noted above, Muslim provides the report with al-Dastuwāʾī in the transmission chain. Note here that he includes an additional transmission chain on the authority of Ibn Abī Shayba, who in turn narrates the hadith on the authority of Abān [b. Yazīd] al-ʿAṭṭār.[43] Ibn Ḥanbal also provides a recension on the authority of Abān b. Yazīd al-ʿAṭṭār.[44] While some had a more tempered opinion of Abān,[45] his transmissions were generally accepted.[46] In fact, Ibn Ḥanbal had a highly favorable view of Abān.[47] The respective textual content provided by Ibn Abī Shayba and Ibn Ḥanbal shares high degrees of similarity with other recensions transmitted on Ibn Abī Kathīr's authority. Accordingly, Abān's version supports Ibn Abī Kathīr's role in the circulation of the textual elements analyzed thus far. To review, the following chart compares the different versions:

42 Ibn Abī Shayba, *al-Muṣannaf* (2010 ed.), 9:362, no. 29,389,
43 Muslim, *Ṣaḥīḥ*, 1324, no. 24 (1,696).
44 Ibn Ḥanbal, *Musnad* (1995 ed.), 15:85f, no. 19,839.
45 Ibn Ḥajar, *Tahdhīb al-tahdhīb*, 1:96.
46 al-Mizzī, *Tahdhīb al-kamāl* v. 2, 25; al-Dhahabī, *Siyar aʿlām*, 7:432.
47 Ibn Abī Ḥātim, *al-Jarḥ wa al-taʿdīl*, 2:299; al-Mizzī, *Tahdhīb al-kamāl*, 2:25; al-Dhahabī, *Siyar aʿlām*, 7:432.

Al-Sakhtiyānī (d. 131/749, Baṣra and Medina)	Yaḥyā b. Abī Kathīr (d. *c.* 130/ 747, Baṣra, Medina, and Yemen)	Yaḥyā b. Abī Kathīr	Yaḥyā b. Abī Kathīr	Yaḥyā b. Abī Kathīr	Yaḥyā b. Abī Kathīr
	al-Awzāʿī (d. 157/774, Syria and Yemen) - (al)-Walīd b. Muslim (d. *c.* 194/809, Syria)	al-Awzāʿī - al-Faryābī (d. *c.* 211/826, Kūfa, Mecca, and Syria)	Maʿmar (d. 153/ 770, Baṣra, Medina, and Yemen)	Hishām al-Dastuwāʾī (d. *c.* 153/770, Baṣra)	Abān [b. Yazīd] al-ʿAṭṭār (d. 160/776, Baṣra)
Unidentified (no tribe name)	Unidentified (no tribe name)	Unidentified (no tribe name)	Juhayna	Juhayna	Juhayna
A woman confesses to *zinā* in the presence of the Prophet.	A woman confesses to *zinā* in the presence of the Prophet.	A woman confesses to *zinā* in the presence of the Prophet.	A woman from Juhayna confesses to *zinā* in the presence of the Prophet.	A woman from Juhayna confesses to *zinā* in the presence of the Prophet.	A woman from Juhayna confesses to *zinā* in the presence of the Prophet.
		Prophet calls for her guardian and tells him to take care of her until she gives birth and then bring her back.	Prophet calls for her guardian and tells him to take care of her until she gives birth and then bring her back.	Prophet calls for her guardian and tells him to take care of her until she gives birth and then bring her back.	Prophet calls for her guardian and tells him to take care of her until she gives birth and then bring her back.
She was bound up with her clothing and stoned.	She was bound up with her clothing and stoned.	She was bound up with her clothing and stoned.	She was bound up with her clothing and stoned.	She was bound up with her clothing and stoned.	She was bound up with her clothing and stoned.
Prophet prays for her.	Prophet prays for her.	Prophet prays for her.	Prophet prays for her.	Prophet prays for her.	Prophet prays for her.
Conversation between the Prophet and ʿUmar.		Conversation between the Prophet and ʿUmar.	Conversation between the Prophet and ʿUmar.	Conversation between the Prophet and ʿUmar.	Conversation between the Prophet and ʿUmar.
Repentance equal to that of 70 people of Medina.		Repentance equal to that of 70 people of Medina.	Repentance equal to that of 70 people of Medina.	Repentance equal to that of 70 people of Medina.	Repentance equal to that of 70 people of Medina.

Recall that in the previous section, one account has the al-Sakhtiyānī (d. 131/749) - Abū Qilāba (d. *c.* 105/723) link as part of the transmission chain. That is the same Abū Qilāba who is recorded as the source of Ibn Abī Kathīr in this section. Missing from the al-Sakhtiyānī-Abū Qilāba version are the elements of tribal affiliation and pregnancy. Otherwise, the elements in that version parallel those recorded on the respective authorities of Maʿmar, al-Dastuwāʾī, and Abān al-ʿAṭṭār—all students of Ibn Abī Kathīr, who in turn is a student of Abū Qilāba. Turning now to a comparison of these recensions:

1) The motifs about a woman confessing to *zinā*, being bound by her clothes, being stoned on the Prophet's authority, the Prophet's participation in her funeral prayer, and him having a conversation with ʿUmar are circulating in various intellectual centers. The versions on the respective authorities of al-Sakhtiyānī (d. 131/749), Maʿmar (d. 153/770), al-Dastuwāʾī (d. *c.* 153/770), and Abān al-ʿAṭṭār (d. 160/776) indicate that the report was in circulation with the help of Abū Qilāba (d. *c.* 105/723) by the turn of the first/seventh century;
2) Two students of al-Awzāʿī (d. 157/774) do not account for the tribal reference, pregnancy, or dialogue clauses. But as mentioned above, his student al-Faryābī (d. *c.* 211/826) does note the pregnancy and dialogue clauses. What explains these differences? It may be that al-Awzāʿī was interested in using a Prophetic report to only justify *zinā*-stoning. It is also possible that the recension via al-Faryābī underwent modifications by the time we get to al-Faryābī or his pupil Isḥāq b. Manṣūr al-Marwazī (d. 251/865). The plausibility of these scenarios can be verified on the basis of what both comparative textual analysis and biographical information yield:
    a) Ibn Manṣūr al-Marwazī's version contains the term *ḥadd* as supposedly uttered by the confessing woman. The two other versions in which *ḥadd* is used are on the authorities of Yaḥyā b. Saʿīd and Abān al-ʿAṭṭār. It is recorded that Yaḥyā b. Saʿīd is one source of reports for Ibn Manṣūr al-Marwazī;[48]
    b) There is some controversy surrounding Ibn Manṣūr al-Marwazī's reputation as a transmitter. Ibn Ḥanbal was said to have been repulsed when he discovered that Ibn Manṣūr al-Marwazī was teaching prophetic and non-prophetic reports on his authority.[49]

[48] al-Khaṭīb al-Baghdādī, *Tārīkh*, 7:385.
[49] al-Khaṭīb al-Baghdādī, *Tārīkh*, 7:386f.

> When Ibn Manṣūr al-Marwazī heard of Ibn Ḥanbal's displeasure, he went to Ibn Ḥanbal and recited to him that which he was sharing with others. After hearing Ibn Manṣūr al-Marwazī recite the reports, Ibn Ḥanbal relented and gave his approval of the transmissions.[50] This incident involving Ibn Ḥanbal appears to militate against possible concerns about Ibn Manṣūr as a narrator. Whatever issues there may have been with Manṣūr al-Marwazī's transmission acumen, given the striking disparity between the content of al-Faryābī's report and the respective reports of al-Awzāʿī's other two students, we have reason to believe it is al-Faryābī's version that underwent subsequent changes. By al-Faryābī's time (d. *c.* 211/826), the pregnancy and dialogue clauses are in wide circulation and, accordingly, are found in his version.

As demonstrated in the chart above, al-Sakhtiyānī's report on the authority of Abū Qilāba does not contain the pregnancy clause either. But another report suggests that he was aware of the pregnancy issue. A narrative he transmits on the authority of the Meccan jurist 'Aṭā' (d. 115/733) reads:

> Maʿmar [b. Rāshid] - Ayyūb [al-Sakhtiyānī] (d. 131/749, Baṣra and Medina) - 'Aṭā' b. Abī Rabāḥ (d. 115/733, Mecca):
>
> A woman came to the Prophet and confessed to *zinā* and the Prophet sent her away four times. On the fourth confession, she asked him: Messenger of God, are you sending me away like you did Māʿiz b. Mālik?
>
> The Prophet said: Take care of her until she gives birth. [Once she gave birth, she returned, and] then he said: [Go, and come back once] the child no longer needs nursing.
>
> A man said: I can arrange for the child to have a wet nurse.
>
> Then the Prophet sentenced her [to death] and she was stoned.[51]

Had al-Sakhtiyānī or any transmitters in the later portions of the transmission chain intended to falsely attribute material to earlier authorities, such as Abū Qilāba or ʿImrān b. Ḥuṣayn, they could have included the pregnancy

[50] al-Khaṭīb al-Baghdādī, *Tārīkh*, 7:387, al-Mizzī, *Tahdhīb al-kamāl*, 7:477, al-Dhahabī, *Siyar aʿlām*, 12:259f.

[51] 'Abd al-Razzāq, *al-Muṣannaf*, 7:324f, no. 13,345.

element, but they did not. The preservation of two different reports on the authority of the same transmitter(s) attests to historical transmissions.

An early provenance regarding the concept of staying a punishment for a pregnant woman is further established by another report:

> [Sufyān] al-Thawrī (d. 161/778, Baṣra, Kūfa, and Ḥijāz) - Muḥammad b. Sālim [al-Hamdānī] (d. early second/eighth c., Hamdān, Kūfa, and Mecca) - [ʿĀmir] al-Shaʿbī (d. *c.* 105/723, Baghdād, Hamdān, Kūfa, and Syria):
>
> The *ḥadd* is not applied to a pregnant woman until after she has given birth.[52]

Al-Sakhtiyānī's report on the authority of Abū Qilāba, then, illustrates that the self-confessing woman hadith was in circulation in both the Ḥijāz and ʿIrāq on the authority of ʿImrān b. Ḥuṣayn. His report also indicates that the pregnancy issue may not have been present in the textual content immediately after the report's emergence. Accordingly, we have additional evidence to explain the disparities with respect to the pregnancy matter in al-Awzāʿī's various transmissions and support the notion that al-Faryābī's report underwent changes. It is also worth mentioning that all the transmitters noted to reside in Syria only do not report the pregnancy clause. Rather, it is those transmitters who spend time in ʿIrāq that circulate the particular element. Accordingly, the pregnancy clause was not part of the hadith as circulated by al-Awzāʿī. Be as it may, the analysis, however, does not account for the absence of a reference to the woman's tribal affiliation of Juhayna. One can only speculate that the tribal reference was not sufficiently important to note for transmitters in the al-Awzāʿī-al-Faryābī transmission chain.

3) To be clear, there are variations in the ending of al-Ṭayālisī's, Ibn Abī Shayba's, and ʿAbd al-Razzāq's respective versions. In the former two, ʿUmar is recorded to have said to the Prophet: "Messenger of God, [how could] you [have] prayed for her despite the fact that she committed *zinā*?" In ʿAbd al-Razzāq's variant, ʿUmar purportedly said: "Messenger of God, you had her stoned and you [still] prayed for her!" The three versions have Ibn Abī Kathīr in common, but the students are different. ʿAbd al-Razzāq's version has Maʿmar b. Rāshid

[52] ʿAbd al-Razzāq, *al-Muṣannaf,* 7:325, no. 13,346.

(d. 153/770) as the student of Ibn Abī Kathīr. And Ibn Abī Shayba's variant has Abān b. Yazīd al-ʿAṭṭār (d. 160/776). And the third is of course al-Dastuwāʾī, that is, al-Ṭayālisī's teacher. Since we are dealing with three different transmission lines with three different students, variations are to be expected. The contrasts, in fact, point to historical oral/aural transmissions wherein the concept of *zinā*-stoning remains intact and the expression of this concept are divergent.

In sum, despite some irregularities in al-Awzāʿī's recensions, there is sufficient evidence to indicate that he, al-Sakhtiyānī (d. 131/749), Maʿmar (d. 153/770), al-Dastuwāʾī (d. *c.* 153/770), and Abān (d. 160/776) helped to circulate the hadith as received by Yaḥyā b. Abī Kathīr (d. *c.* 130/747), who in turn learned it from Abū Qilāba (d. *c.* 105/723).

There are additional reasons to accept Ibn Abī Kathīr as having taught the report. To begin with, Ibn Abī Kathīr (d. *c.* 130/747) was a *mawlā* of Ṭayyīʾ, grew up in Baṣra, and eventually moved to Yamāma, where he died.[53] He was a renowned transmitter and thought of as being on equal footing with, or even higher than, the famous Ibn Shihāb al-Zuhrī (d. 124/742).[54] Al-Dastuwāʾī reportedly opined that 'no one like Ibn Abī Kathīr has ever walked the earth'.[55] Al-Dastuwāʾī, al-Awzāʿī, and Abān—in that order—are considered to be Ibn Abī Kathīr's best pupils.[56] Al-Awzāʿī supposedly compiled a book on the basis of Ibn Abī Kathīr's written notes, possibly at the instruction of his teacher, because Ibn Abī Kathīr also made Maʿmar record his lectures.[57] Ibn Abī Kathīr is also noted to have occasionally narrated from written texts.[58] Perhaps this method of teaching can partly explain the consistency found in the recensions transmitted by Ibn Abī Kathīr's students. Based on the information from Ibn Abī Kathīr's biographical data and the overlap among the various textual contents transmitted by his students on his authority, Ibn Abī Kathīr participated in the transmission of the self-confessing woman hadith.

The similarities found in the textual content of the respective versions of al-Sakhtiyānī and Ibn Abī Kathīr indicate their having received the report

[53] Ibn Saʿd, *al-Ṭabaqāt*, 8:116; Ibn Abī Ḥātim, *al-Jarḥ wa al-taʿdīl*, 9:141.
[54] Ibn Abī Ḥātim, *al-Jarḥ wa al-taʿdīl*, 9:141; al-Mizzī, *Tahdhīb al-kamāl*, 31:508.
[55] Ibn Saʿd, *al-Ṭabaqāt*, 8:116; al-Bukhārī, *Tārīkh*, 8:301; Ibn Abī Ḥātim, *al-Jarḥ wa al-taʿdīl*, 9:141; al-Mizzī, *Tahdhīb al-kamāl*, 31:507.
[56] Ibn Maʿīn, *Tārīkh*, 4:180, no. 3,825 and 4:457, no. 5,279.
[57] al-Dhahabī, *Siyar aʿlām*, 6:29.
[58] Ibn Maʿīn, *Tārīkh*, 4:351, no. 4,732; Ibn Abī Ḥātim, *al-Jarḥ wa al-taʿdīl*, 1:184; al-Dhahabī, *Siyar aʿlām*, 6:30.

from the common source Abū Qilāba (d. *c.* 105/723). Ayyūb al-Sakhtiyānī, the student of Abū Qilāba, was a respected transmitter and considered to be the best legal mind in Baṣra during his lifetime.[59] With the exception of the pregnancy clause, the unidentified woman's recension on al-Sakhtiyānī's authority contains the same motifs found in versions on Ibn Abī Kathīr's authority, the other student of Abū Qilāba. As for Abū Qilāba 'Abd Allāh b. Zayd al-Jarmī, he was a well-known legal authority in his time, which is unsurprising given that, prior to his conversion to Islam, he held a judicial rank similar to that of a chief judge.[60] After his conversion, Abū Qilābā was asked by al-Ḥajjāj (governor in Ḥijāz r. 72–4/692–4, governor in 'Irāq r. 74–95/694–714) to serve as a judge in Baṣra. He declined the appointment and instead fled to Yamāma and then to Syria, where he died.[61] His being both a transmitter and a legal authority makes along with relatively similar transmissions by his two students, indicate that he helped to circulate the report about the self-confessing woman.

The student–teacher relationships between Abū Qilāba, Ibn Abī Kathīr, and al-Sakhtiyānī also affirm the sharing of the narrative. Ibn Abī Kathīr, like Abū Qilāba, moved from Baṣra to Yamāma, though for different reasons. The similar travel patterns created opportunities for the two men to meet and participate in study sessions. Al-Sakhtiyānī was known to have held Abū Qilāba in high regard, as can be gleaned from several favorable biographical entries about Abū Qilāba on al-Sakhtiyānī's authority.[62] In his will, Abū Qilāba bequeathed his books to al-Sakhtiyānī.[63] Hence, the regional overlap and shared travel patterns of Ibn Abī Kathīr and Abū Qilāba, along with the close relationship between al-Sakhtiyānī and Abū Qilāba, as well as the similarities in the textual content of Ibn Abī Kathīr's and al-Sakhtiyānī's recensions, attest to Abū Qilāba as their common source.

What is the likelihood that Abū Qilāba taught the report that he acquired from an earlier source(s)? Recall that the version circulated by al-Sakhtiyānī in which the woman's tribal affiliation is absent, Abū Qilāba directly references the Companion 'Imrān b. Ḥuṣayn. To the best of my knowledge, there is nothing in the biographical sources that testifies to Abū Qilāba having acquired reports directly from 'Imrān b. Ḥuṣayn. Also recall

[59] Ibn Sa'd, *al-Ṭabaqāt*, 9:246–50; Ibn Ḥibbān, *al-Thiqāt*, 6:53.
[60] Al-Mizzī, *Tahdhīb al-kamāl*, 14:545; al-Dhahabī, *Siyar a'lām*, 4:472.
[61] Ibn Sa'd, *al-Ṭabaqāt*, 9:183; Ibn Ma'īn, *Tārīkh*, 4:224, no. 4,076; Ibn 'Asākir, *Tārīkh*, 28:284 and 302f; al-Mizzī, *Tahdhīb al-kamāl*, 14:546.
[62] Ibn Sa'd, *al-Ṭabaqāt*, 9:182–4; Ibn Abī Ḥātim, *al-Jarḥ wa al-ta'dīl*, 5:58; al-Mizzī, *Tahdhīb al-kamāl*, 14:546.
[63] Ibn Sa'd, *al-Ṭabaqāt*, 9:185; Ibn 'Asākir, *Tārīkh*, 28:284; al-Dhahabī, *Siyar a'lām*, 4:475.

that in all the transmission chains with Ibn Abī Kathīr, intermediaries (i.e., either Abū al-Muhājir or Abū al-Muhallab) exist between Abū Qilāba and the Companion. It is only in al-Sakhtiyānī's transmission chain that the intermediary is absent. In my view, Abū Qilāba did teach the report but did not properly name his direct source since he was known to do that at times.[64]

Limited biographical data are available on both Abū al-Muhājir (d. unknown, Baṣra) and Abū al-Muhallab (d. first/seventh c., 'Irāq and Syria). Note that Abū al-Muhājir is recorded to have narrated only three reports, including the one about the self-confessing woman, and all passing through al-Awzā'ī in the chain of transmission.[65] One of the other two is noted to have al-Walīd b. Muslim as the student of al-Awzā'ī, the same student–teacher connection noted in the previous section, in which the woman remains unidentified.[66] It is the remaining one out of the three about which disagreements exist regarding al-Awzā'ī's involvement.[67] But that two of the three reports have the same individuals in the transmission chain—al-Walīd b. Muslim - al-Awzā'ī—indicates a historical relationship involving al-Awzā'ī. The biographer Ibn Ma'īn (d. 233/848) notes that for reports in which al-Awzā'ī mentions Abū al-Muhājir, the correct source is Abū al-Muhallab.[68] In other words, the transmission line al-Awzā'ī-Abū Qilāba-Abū al-Muhājir should in fact be al-Awzā'ī- Abū Qilāba-Abū al-Muhallab. Ibn Ma'īn does not provide a reason for the possible confusion, but it is worth consideration. Students of early Islam know that Arabic was not always written with diacritics and, importantly, letters like *bā'* and *nūn* were written sideways to appear as *rā'*. This being the case, a scribe could have come across Muhallab but observed the *bā'* written as a *rā'* and presumed that the *lām* was in fact an *alif*. Accordingly, the word would initially be read as *mahār*, which makes no sense. Therefore, the scribe guessed it to be Muhājir instead of Muhallab. The confusion may explain why al-Sakhtiyānī does not include an intermediary between Abū Qilāba and 'Imrān b. Ḥuṣayn. He had notes bequeathed to him by Abū Qilāba and may have found reference to Abū Qilāba's informant indiscernible and, accordingly, left it out. Setting aside the grapheme issue, it is especially worth noting that Abū al-Muhallab is Abū Qilāba's uncle.[69] Thus, it is likely that Abū al-Muhallab is Abū Qilāba's source.

[64] Ibn 'Asākir, *Tārīkh*, 28:285 and 298.
[65] al-Mizzī, *Tahdhīb al-kamāl*, 34:326.
[66] al-Mizzī, *Tahdhīb al-kamāl*, 34:326.
[67] al-Mizzī, *Tahdhīb al-kamāl*, 34:326.
[68] Ibn Ma'īn, *Tārīkh*, 4:467, no. 5,330.
[69] Ibn Sa'd, *al-Ṭabaqāt*, 9:124; Ibn Abī Ḥātim, *al-Jarḥ wa al-ta'dīl*, 6:260; Ibn Ḥibbān, *al-Thiqāt*, 5:110.

3.1.3. The significance of the textual elements

In this subsection, I review several elements to illustrate the ways in which they contribute to the process of naturalizing *zinā*-stoning in the Islamic legal tradition. For instance, after the woman approaches the Prophet, she addresses him as "Messenger of God." The use of this phrase conveys that the woman is Muslim. In some recensions, the woman declares that she commits a *ḥadd* and wishes for the Prophet to apply the *ḥadd* to her. As discussed in Chapter 2, the notion of *ḥadd* representing both an offense and a punishment reflects a post-Qur'ānic legal development, as the term does not connote such meanings in the Qur'ān. The appearance of *ḥadd* here represents an interpolation into the textual content after it acquires a clear legal definition. It serves to teach Muslims that *zinā*-stoning is part of the *ḥudūd*.

Binding those who are punished for sexual offenses reflects cultural practices prevalent in the area prior to the advent of Islam. In the ancient Greek cities of Lepreium and Cumae, a male offender is bound with ropes and walked around town for three days.[70] The Hammurabi Code mandates that an adulterous wife and her paramour be bound up and thrown into a river to drown.[71] That the self-confessing woman is bound prior to receiving the punishment echos a practice native to the socio-historical milieu of the nascent Muslim community.

In some versions of the report, the self-confessing woman is pregnant, and the Prophet stays the implementation of the punishment until after she gives birth. This course of action is also part of the procedures in another legal systems belonging to the Near East in late antiquity. According to the Justinian Code, "The punishment of a pregnant woman who has been condemned to death is deferred until she gives birth."[72] To be sure, I am not suggesting that Muslims could not have, on their own accord, devised a similar rule to stay the implementation of a capital punishment upon a pregnant woman. In fact, Muslim jurists discuss all manners of conditions under which a *ḥadd* punishment must be delayed or suspended. For example, in the hypothetical case that a convicted person is subject to the Qur'ānically prescribed punishment of flogging, the jurists insist that such a punishment should not be implemented if and so long as the offender suffers from a physical comorbidity that would raise the risk of death were the penalty to be applied.

[70] Cantarella, "Gender, Sexuality, and Law," 244.
[71] Driver and Miles, *The Babylonian Law*, 281; Roth, *Law Collections*, 106.
[72] Mommsen et al., *The Digest of Justinian*, 845, 19:3.

Al-Shaybānī (d. 189/805) opines that in such cases, an offender should be imprisoned until they physically recuperate.[73] Al-Shāfiʿī (d. 204/820) even suggests modifying the form and number of lashes to be given.[74] In light of the aforementioned legal considerations to delay the implementation of a punishment, the pregnancy clause helps to affirm a staying procedure in *zinā* laws, an established feature of late antique Near Eastern legal systems.

As for the tribe of Juhayna, they carry importance in Islamic history. Several Juhanīs pledged allegiance to the Prophet upon his initial arrival in Medina.[75] Juhayna's importance is deepened with Zayd b. Khālid al-Juhanī (d. 68/687 in Kūfa or 78/697 in Medina), a Companion of the Prophet, who was at Ḥudaybiyya (6/628).[76] It is also recorded that he served as a general for the tribe of Juhayna in the conquest of Mecca (8/630).[77] After expansion to the east, the Juhanīs were one of the first tribes to settle in Baghdād, then in Baṣra, and finally in Kūfa.[78] Abū Qilāba is recorded to have been a descendant of the Qaḍāʿa, a large tribe to whom the Juhayna belonged.[79] Thus, the historical significance of the tribe, its settlement in ʿIrāq, and Abū Qilāba's ties seem to have prompted the mention of the woman's tribal affiliation.

The theme of self-confession invokes important legal and theological considerations. From a legal standpoint, the report establishes a process by which a person can be convicted of an offense without the need for witnesses to testify to the unlawful conduct. This is especially relevant, given the nature of the challenges that emerge with accusations of illicit sexual intercourse. Specifically, confessions do away with the heavy burden of proof required in the case of witnesses testifying to illicit sexual conduct, even if, over time, the Islamic legal tradition came to diminish the probative value of confessions as a means of conviction for illicit sexual relations.[80]

In terms of theological considerations, a confession symbolizes the idea that a sincere believer would desire the punishment to secure absolution.[81]

[73] al-Shaybānī, *al-Aṣl*, 7:187.
[74] al-Shāfiʿī, *al-Umm*, 7:344.
[75] Ibn Saʿd, *al-Ṭabaqāt*, 1:287.
[76] Ibn Abī Ḥātim, *al-Jarḥ wa al-taʿdīl*, 3:562; Ibn al-Athīr, *Usd al-Ghāba*, 429, no. 1832; Ibn Ḥajar, *al-Iṣāba*, 2:499, no. 2,902.
[77] Ibn ʿAbd al-Barr, *al-Istīʿāb*, 2:549, no. 845; Ibn Ḥajar, *Tahdhīb al-tahdhīb*, 3:547.
[78] Al-Samʿānī, *al-Ansāb*, 3:439; Yāqūt, *Muʿjam al-buldān*, 2:194.
[79] Ibn ʿAsākir, *Tārīkh*, 28:284; al-Mizzī, *Tahdhīb al-kamāl*, 14:542.
[80] For general information on confessions, including the requisite elements for their validity, probative value, and scope, see R. Gaiser Adam, *Encyclopaedia of Islam*, 3rd ed., s.v. "Confession."
[81] Asad examines the different ways in which confessions interlink with penance, religious discipline, and reintegration in early Christian communities. As he remarks, "The marks of sin are made on the soul *and* on the body." See Talal Asad, *Genealogies of Religion*, 97–106 and 128–31; White notes that according to Greek and Roman religious practices, a "cultic or ritual sacrifice ... ensured

This would imply that surrendering to death by stoning constitutes an expiatory remedy. The concept is more readily expressed in the Prophet's comment to 'Umar about the significance of the woman's repentance. A relationship between self-confession and forgiveness is cemented by the clause, which can be taken to reflect debates in the early Muslim community about how the community ought to regard a fellow Muslim who has been convicted and punished for a major transgression such as illicit sexual intercourse.[82] An entry in the *Muṣannaf* of 'Abd al-Razzāq speaks to the differing attitudes that existed at such an early stage in the community's development:

> Ibn Jurayj (d. 150/767, Baghdād, Mecca, Yemen) - Muḥammad b. al-Munkadir (d. 130/747, Medina):
>
> The Prophet had a woman stoned. Some Muslims proclaimed in the presence of the Prophet: This woman does not have a prayer in heaven!
>
> The Prophet responded: Far from it! Indeed, this was an expiation for her offense (*ḥādhihi kaffāra li-mā 'amilat*). You, on the other hand, have yet to be held to account for your offenses.[83]

In this report, the term *kaffāra* (expiation) is used, but in other variants examined above, the term *tawba* (repentance) occurs instead. Al-Nasā'ī also provides a report with the same theme:

> al-Nasā'ī - Ya'qūb b. Sufyān al-Fārisī (d. 277/890, Egypt, Fārs, Fasā, Nishapur, and Palestine) - [Abū Isḥāq] Ibrāhīm b. al-Mundhir (d. 236/850, Medina) - al-Qāsim b. Rushdīn b. 'Umayr (d. unknown, Medina) - Makhrama b. Bukayr (d. 159/775, Medina) - Bukayr b. 'Abd Allāh (d. *c.* 122/739, Egypt and Medina) - al-Sharīd b. Suwayd (d. unknown, Ḥijāz and Ṭā'if):[84]

the correct contractual response from the deity ... [it] would grant the request of the worshipper." See Cynthia White, *The Emergence of Christianity*, 2f; I believe the two scholars' theoretical framework is helpful in understanding the function(s) of the self-confession and the punishment.

[82] For one approach to the concept of repentance and expiation vis- à-vis punishment in the Qur'ān, hadith, and legal literature, see generally Christian Lange, "Sins, Expiation and Non-Rationality."

[83] 'Abd al-Razzāq adds that Ibrāhīm b. Abī Yaḥyā (d. *c.* 184/900 or 191/806, Medina) narrates the same comment from al-Munkadir. See 'Abd al-Razzāq, *al-Muṣannaf*, 7:326, no. 13,349; the concept of expiation is conveyed in two versions provided by al-Nasā'ī. See al-Nasā'ī, *al-Sunan al-kubrā*, 6:460f, nos. 7,232f.

[84] al-Nasā'ī, *al-Sunan al-kubrā*, 6:460, no. 7,232.

> A woman was stoned during the time of the Messenger of God. Once we were finished with her, I went to the Messenger of God and said: That witch breathes no more, Messenger of God.
>
> The Messenger of God shot back: [Do not badmouth her.] She has atoned for what she did.

It is evident, then, that controversy over how the Muslim community is to relate with individual members guilty of committing cardinal transgressions spurred efforts on the part of some to generate a sense of compassion and consideration for the fallen members of the community. This was accomplished by emphasizing the existence of multiple avenues available for the transgressor to atone and expiate for their transgressions and thus earn God's forgiveness. The self-confessing woman's commitment to her faith is framed as an expiatory act and broadly helps to shape the *ḥudūd* (which includes *zinā*) as part of God's rights.

The conversation between the Prophet and ʿUmar is of significance and correlates to a similar conversation the two supposedly had in a different situation. According to a report provided by al-Bukhārī on the authority of ʿAbd Allāh b. ʿUmar:

> When ʿAbd Allāh b. Ubayy died, his son came to the Prophet and said: Messenger of God, give me your shirt so that I can bury my father in it, lead the Muslims in reciting a funeral prayer for him, and ask God for forgiveness on his behalf.
>
> The Prophet gave Ibn Ubayy's son his shirt, who then asked that the Prophet lead the Muslims in reciting a funeral prayer for his father. The Prophet granted his request.
>
> When the Prophet was getting ready to recite the funeral prayer, ʿUmar got the Prophet's attention and asked: Did God not prohibit you from praying for the hypocrites?
>
> The Prophet responded: I was offered a choice in the matter, and I am choosing one of two choices available to me.
>
> The Prophet then recited Q9:80: So [either] pray for their forgiveness or don't. Were you to pray for forgiveness on their behalf seventy times over, God will not forgive them! They have rejected God and His messenger. God does not redeem the corrupt.

> Then the Prophet recited the funeral prayer for Ibn Ubayy. Thereafter Q9:84 was revealed: Do not ever pray for any of them when they die![85]

Here, the issue that takes center stage is whether it is permissible to conduct the funeral prayer for someone who commits a serious transgression against God and the Prophet, which, ostensibly, might put the person outside the fold of Islam. This element of the textual content echoes the broader theological debates occurring in the community soon after the death of the Prophet, wherein certain groups, such as the *Shurāṭ* (i.e., *khawārij*), are claiming that the commission of a grave transgression should not result in leniency by the community.[86] The exegetical report puts ʿUmar once again at odds with the Prophet, with the latter taking a more accommodating view. The connection between the motif and the consequences of its interpretation cannot be ignored in light of the narrative about the woman who confesses to *zinā* in the presence of the Prophet and the conversation between him and ʿUmar. The clause serves to convey that, although the Prophet ordered the stoning of a Muslim wrongdoer, he nonetheless regarded her within the fold of Islam.

The number 70 is used to portray abundance and significance. In another derivative of seven, the Prophet remarks that the first 70,000 believers will automatically be granted entrance into paradise.[87] In the Hebrew Bible, Lamech, the father of Noah, is portrayed as telling his wives that he has killed a man. He then says to them, "If Cain is avenged seven times, then Lamech seventy-seven times."[88] And in the New Testament, Peter is depicted as asking Jesus, "Lord, how many times shall I forgive my brother or sister who sins against me? Up to seven times?" To this question, Jesus responds, "I tell you, not seven times, but seventy-seven times."[89] The appearance of the number 70 in the hadith follows the use of a derivative of seven for expressing importance and represents shared cultural ideas. [90]

The self-confessing woman's report engages a number of issues of central concern on the issue of *zinā*-stoning for the early Muslim community. That the religious affiliation of the self-confessing woman has to be made abundantly clear, such as the Prophet's participation in her funeral prayer,

85 al-Bukhārī, *Ṣaḥīḥ* (2002 ed.), 307, no. 1269; 330, no. 1,366; 1,152, nos. 4,670–2; 1467, no. 5,796.
86 On this, see Joseph van Ess, *Theology and Society*, vol. 2, 258–65.
87 Muslim, *Ṣaḥīḥ*, 177f, no. 316.
88 Gen. 4:23f.
89 Matt. 18:21f; also see Luke 17:3f for the use of seven in relation to forgiveness.
90 On numerology and the Christian tradition, see, for example, Mikeal C. Parson, "Exegesis 'By the Numbers,'" esp. 27–30 on the significance of the number seven.

indicates a historical period during which Muslims reject *zinā*-stoning. It needs to be also pointed out that the textual content as transmitted in the numerous versions of the report does not clarify if the self-confessing woman, in fact, meets all the legal elements for conviction as later established in the Islamic legal tradition. Specifically, there is no mention of *iḥṣān* to determine her legal status: it has to be read into the report. The report is also unclear about the type of *zinā* the woman commits, that is, the less severe or the more severe kind. Such ambiguities signal that when the self-confessing woman's reports associated with ʿImrān b. Ḥuṣayn went into circulation, the Islamic legal tradition was still developing substantive and procedural rules vis-à-vis *zinā*-stoning. Important, his recension affirms death by lapidation upon Muslim *zinā* offenders by drawing on the Prophet's authority.

3.2. Reports by the Companion Burayda b. al-Ḥuṣayb (d. 63/683, Baṣra, Khurāsān, Marw, Mecca, Medina, and Syria)

Burayda b. al-Ḥuṣayb's two sons, ʿAbd Allāh (d. *c.* 110/728) and Sulaymān (d. 105/723), are recorded to have acquired the report from their father and, in turn, shared it with others. These versions of the hadith contain several elements that are also consequential for the development of both procedural and substantive *zinā* laws. For example, the reports harmonize the number of confessions to the four-witness Qurʾān requirement for a *zinā* conviction. They also encompass components that hold theological significance by strengthening the position that *zinā*-stoning is a form of expiation. Because of such legal and theological features, in my view, the detailed Burayda versions emerge during the second/eighth century, that is, during the time of his two sons. Importantly, these variants reaffirm the justification for *zinā*-stoning on the authority of the Prophet.

3.2.1. Versions on the authority of ʿAbd Allāh b. Burayda

Bashīr b. al-Muhājir (d. second/eighth c., Kūfa) circulates the report to several individuals on the authority of ʿAbd Allāh b. Burayda. With one exception, the different versions of the report on Ibn al-Muhājir's authority are virtually identical. The prevailing congruity points to Ibn al-Muhājir as a common source, and that his version circulates on the basis of a written text.

The *Muṣannaf* of Ibn Abī Shayba is the earliest extant collection in which I located the Burayda recension on ʿAbd Allāh's authority. The transmission chain and textual content read:

> ʿAbd Allāh b. Numayr (199/814, Hamdān and Kūfa) - Bashīr b. al-Muhājir (d. second/eighth c., Kūfa) - ʿAbd Allāh b. Burayda (d. *c.* 110/728) - Burayda b. al-Ḥuṣayb (d. 63/683):
>
> A woman belonging to the tribe of Ghāmid[91] came to the Prophet and said: Messenger of God, I have committed *zinā* and I [am here] so that you may cleanse me [of this sin].
>
> The Prophet sent her away. She came back the next day and said: Prophet of God, why are you sending me away? Perhaps you are doing the same with me as you did with Māʿiz b. Mālik? [Or is it because,] by God, I am pregnant?
>
> The Prophet responded: The reason I am sending you away is because you are pregnant, so go away until you have given birth.
>
> After she gave birth, she returned to the Prophet with a swaddled (*fī kh'Irāq*) baby boy and said: Look, I have given birth.
>
> The Prophet responded: Go and nurse him until he is weaned.
>
> Once she weaned the baby, she returned to the Prophet with the boy, who had a small piece of bread in his hand. She said: Look, Prophet of God, I have weaned him and he now eats solid food.
>
> The Prophet placed the boy in the custody of the Muslims and ordered that a chest-deep hole be dug up for her. Then he gave the order to the people and they began to stone her. Khālid b. al-Walīd picked up a stone and threw it at her head and, when some of her blood hit his face, he cursed at her. The Prophet of God heard him and said: Enough, Khālid b. al-Walīd! By the One [God] in whose Hand is my soul, [the spiritual effects of] her repentance [are of such power] that even a tax collector (*ṣāḥib maks*) would be forgiven [by it]!
>
> Then the Prophet gave the order to the people [to gather behind him] and he and others conducted the funeral prayer for her, after which she was buried.[92]

[91] For information on the Ghāmid tribe, see *Encyclopaedia of Islam* 2nd ed., s.v. "Ghāmid."
[92] Ibn Abī Shayba, *al-Muṣannaf* (2008 ed.), 9:361f, no. 29,388.

Ibn Abī Shayba also provides a shorter version of the report involving the same transmitters. The entry reads:

> ʿAbd Allāh b. Numayr (d. 199/814) - Bashīr b. al-Muhājir (d. second/eighth c.) - ʿAbd Allāh b. Burayda (d. *c.* 110/728) - Burayda b. al-Ḥuṣayb al-Aslamī (d. 63/683):
>
> A woman belonging to the tribe of Ghāmid came to the Prophet and confessed to *zinā* in his presence. He ordered that a chest-deep hole be dug up for her. Then he gave the order to the people and they began to stone her. Then he gave the order to the people [to gather behind him,] and he and others recited a funeral prayer for her, after which she was buried.[93]

The differences between the two versions can be explained by the headings under which each of them appears. The longer version is provided under the heading "When someone says: If she has committed a transgression and is pregnant, wait until she gives birth and then have her stoned." The shorter version appears under the heading "How to [properly] carry out the stoning punishment and how deep to dig the hole." As for Ibn Abī Shayba's informant and Bashīr b. al-Muhājir's student, ʿAbd Allāh b. Numayr, he is reported to have been a legal authority, a reliable transmitter, and someone with whom several ʿIrāqīs, such as Ibn Abī Shayba, studied.[94] Overall, I do have any reason to dismiss the relationship between the individuals, and therefore, the report is acceptable on the authority of ʿAbd Allāh b. Numayr.

Al-Nasāʾī provides a recension that cites Abū Nuʿaym (d. *c.* 215/830, Kūfa), who is another student of Bashīr b. al-Muhājir. The entry's transmission chain reads:

> Aḥmad b. Yaḥyā [b. Zakariyyā] al-Ṣūfī [more famously known as] 'the Kūfan' (d. 264/877, Kūfa) - Abū Nuʿaym [al-Faḍl b. Dukayn] (d. *c.* 215/830, Kūfa) - Bashīr b. al-Muhājir (d. second/eighth c.) - ʿAbd Allāh b. Burayda (d. *c.* 110/728) - Burayda b. al-Ḥuṣayb (d. 63/683).[95]

Ibn Abī Shayba's and al-Nasāʾī's respective versions share many of the same elements. The following chart compares the two recensions:

[93] Ibn Abī Shayba, *al-Muṣannaf* (2008 ed.), 9:361, no. 29,386.
[94] Ibn Saʿd, *al-Ṭabaqāt*, 8:516; Ibn Ḥibbān, *al-Thiqāt*, 7:60; al-Mizzī, *Tahdhīb al-kamāl*, 16:228.
[95] al-Nasāʾī, *al-Sunan al-kubrā*, 6:431, no. 7,159.

Bashīr b. al-Muhājir (d. second/eighth c.) - ʿAbd Allāh b. Burayda (d. *c.* 110/728) - Burayda b. al-Ḥuṣayb al-Aslamī (d. 63/683)	
ʿAbd Allāh b. Numayr (199/814, Hamdān and Kūfa) -Ibn Abī Shayba	Abū Nuʿaym [al-Faḍl b. Dukayn] (d. *c.* 215/830, Kūfa) to al-Nasāʾī
A woman from Ghāmid comes to the Prophet and says that she has committed *zinā* and that she wants him to cleanse her of her sin.	Folks are sitting with the Prophet, and a woman from Ghāmid comes to the Prophet and says that she has committed *zinā* and that she wants him to cleanse her of her sin.
The Prophet sends her away, and she returns the next day.	The Prophet sends her away and she returns the next day.
She asks the Prophet if he is treating her in the same manner as Māʿiz b. Mālik or because she is pregnant.	She returns the next day with the same request and asks the Prophet if he is treating her in the same manner as Māʿiz b. Mālik or because she is pregnant.
The Prophet sends her away until she gives birth.	The Prophet sends her away until she gives birth.
The woman returns to the Prophet with a swaddled boy.	The woman returns to the Prophet with a swaddled boy.
Prophet sends her away until she weans him.	Prophet sends her away until she weans him.
The woman returns with a boy who has a small piece of bread in his hand.	The woman returns with a boy who has a small piece of bread in his hand.
The Prophet places the boy in the custody of Muslims.	The Prophet places the boy in the custody of Muslims.
The Prophet orders the digging of a chest-deep hole.	The Prophet orders the digging of a chest-deep hole.
The Prophet orders the stoning punishment.	The Prophet orders the stoning punishment.
The conversation with the Prophet and Khālid b. al-Walīd.	The conversation with the Prophet and Khālid b. al-Walīd.
Repentance's spiritual effects such that a tax collector would be forgiven.	Repentance's spiritual effects such that a tax collector would be forgiven.
The Prophet leads the funeral prayer for her and has her buried.	The Prophet leads the funeral prayer for her and has her buried.

At times, the language is different, which indicates two separate transmissions. As for biographical information, aside from a few acclamations, not much is written about al-Nasāʾī's source and Abū Nuʿaym's student, Aḥmad b. Yaḥyā, a client (*mawlā*) of the tribe of Thaqīf.[96] As for Abū Nuʿaym, biographical

[96] Ibn Ḥibbān, *al-Thiqāt*, 8:40, no. 12,152; al-Mizzī, *Tahdhīb al-kamāl*, 1:518; Ibn Ḥajar, *Tahdhīb al-tahdhīb*, 1:85.

entries predominantly indicate that he was a respected transmitter whose reports were often used for legal proofs.[97] Ibn Ḥanbal thought highly of him and, in fact, narrates a version of the report on Abū Nuʿaym's authority.[98] Ibn Ḥanbal's recension shares a high degree of similarity with the version recorded by al-Nasaʾī. One important difference, however, is that in Ibn Ḥanbal's version, the Prophet sends the woman away twice before she asks him if he is treating her in the same manner as Māʿiz. Al-Bayhaqī furnishes a version of the report that also includes Abū Nuʿaym in the transmission chain. The textual content reads:

> We were sitting with the Prophet when a woman from the tribe of Ghāmid came to him and said: I have committed *zinā* and I [am here so that] you [may] cleanse me [of my sin].
>
> [Here, al-Bayhaqī interjects that his informant narrated the report up to the point where the woman says]: By God I am pregnant.
>
> The Prophet said to her: Go away until you give birth.
>
> Once she gave birth, she returned to the Prophet with a swaddled baby boy and said: Prophet of God, I have given birth.
>
> The Prophet responded: Go away until he is weaned.
>
> Once she weaned him, she returned to the Prophet with the boy, who had a small piece of bread in his hand and said: Prophet of God, I have weaned him.
>
> The Prophet ordered the boy to be placed in the custody of a man from among the Muslims. He then ordered a chest-deep hole be dug up for her and gave the order to the people to stone her. Then the remainder of the account was told.[99]

Presuming that the beginning and the end of the report are the same as others on Abū Nuʿaym's authority, al-Bayhaqī's entry again points to Abū Nuʿaym as being a common source for the Burayda recension. Accordingly, the overlap among the textual contents provided by Ibn Ḥanbal, al-Nasāʾī, and al-Bayhaqī indicates that Abū Nuʿaym taught the report, or at least some

[97] Ibn Saʿd, *al-Ṭabaqāt*, 8:524; al-Khaṭīb al-Baghdādī, *Tārīkh*, 14:313–5; Ibn Ḥajar, *Tahdhīb al-tahdhīb*, 5:255.
[98] al-Khaṭīb al-Baghdādī, *Tārīkh*, 14:310f; al-Mizzī, *Tahdhīb al-kamāl*, 23:206ff; Ibn Ḥanbal, *Musnad* (1995 ed.), 16:476f, no. 22,845.
[99] al-Bayhaqī, *al-Sunan al-kubrā*, 8:399f, no. 17,007.

version of it, to his students.[100] This indicates that Abū Nuʿaym's and Ibn Numayr's respective variants point to Bashīr b. al-Muhājir (d. second/eighth c.) as the common source for the report.

Abū ʿAbd Allāh al-Ḥāfiẓ al-Nīsābūrī (d. 405/1014, ʿIrāq and Mecca), in his *al-Mustadrak*, provides the narrative on the authority of another of Ibn al-Muhājir's student, Khallād b. Yaḥyā (d. *c.* 215/830, Kūfa and Mecca). The transmission chain and textual content read:

> Abū al-Naḍr al-Faqīh [Muḥammad b. Muḥammad al-Ṭūsī] (d. 344/955, Ṭūs) - Muʿādh b. Najda (d. 282/895, Ḥarra) - Khallād b. Yaḥyā (d. *c.* 215/830, Kūfa and Mecca) - Bashīr b. al-Muhājir - ʿAbd Allāh b. Burayda - Burayda:
>
> A woman belonging to Ghāmid came to the Prophet and said: I have committed a transgression (*qad fajartu*).
>
> [The Prophet] responded: Go away.
>
> She went away and returned and said: Perhaps you are intending to treat me the same way as you did Māʿiz b. Mālik. [Or is it because,] by God, I am pregnant?
>
> [The Prophet] said: Go away until you have given birth.
>
> She returned [after giving birth] with the swaddled boy and said: I have given birth and now I [am here] so that you may cleanse me [of this sin].
>
> [The Prophet] responded: Go away until you have weaned him.
>
> [After having weaned him], she returned to the Prophet with the boy, who had a small piece of bread in his hand and said: Prophet of God, I have weaned him.
>
> The Prophet gave the order for her to be stoned.[101]

Here is a chart that compares the version on Khallād b. Yaḥyā's authority with the ones above by two other students of Bashīr al-Muhājir - ʿAbd Allāh b. Numayr (199/814) and Abū Nuʿaym (d. *c.* 215/830):

[100] Al-Dārimī also cites the hadith on the authority of Abū Nuʿaym. This version shares a high degree of similarity with the recensions provided by Ibn Abī Shayba and al-Nasāʾī. Thus, the additional version attests to Abū Nuʿaym's involvement. See al-Dārimī, *Sunan*, 2:234f: 2,324.

[101] Abū ʿAbd Allāh al-Ḥākim al-Nīsābūrī, *al-Mustadrak*, 4:404, no. 8,083.

Bashīr b. al-Muhājir (d. second/eighth c.) - ʿAbd Allāh b. Burayda (d. *c.* 110/728) - Burayda b. al-Ḥuṣayb al-Aslamī (d. 63/683)		
ʿAbd Allāh b. Numayr (199/814, Hamdān and Kūfa) via Ibn Abī Shayba	Abū Nuʿaym [al-Faḍl b. Dukayn] (d. *c.* 215/830, Kūfa) via al-Nasāʾī	Khallād b. Yaḥyā (d. *c.* 215/830, Kūfa and Mecca)
A woman from Ghāmid comes to the Prophet and says that she has committed *zinā* and that she wants him to cleanse her of her sin.	Folks are sitting with the Prophet and woman from Ghāmid comes to the Prophet and says that she has committed *zinā* and that she wants him to cleanse her of her sin.	A woman from Ghāmid comes to the Prophet and says that she has committed a transgression.
The Prophet sends her away and she returns the next day.	The Prophet sends her away and she returns the next day.	The Prophet sends her away and she returns the next day.
She asks the Prophet if he is treating her in the same manner as Māʿiz b. Mālik or because she is pregnant.	She returns the next day with the same request about cleansing and asks the Prophet if he is treating her in the same manner as Māʿiz b. Mālik or because she is pregnant.	She asks the Prophet if he is treating her in the same manner as Māʿiz b. Mālik or because she is pregnant.
The Prophet sends her away until she gives birth.	The Prophet sends her away until she gives birth.	The Prophet sends her away until she gives birth.
The woman returns to the Prophet with a swaddled boy.	The woman returns to the Prophet with a swaddled boy.	The woman returns to the Prophet with a swaddled boy and makes the request about cleansing her.
Prophet sends her away until she weans him.	Prophet sends her away until she weans him.	Prophet sends her away until she weans him.
The woman returns with a boy who has a small piece of bread in his hand.	The woman returns with a boy who has a small piece of bread in his hand.	The woman returns with a boy who has a small piece of bread in his hand.
The Prophet places the boy in the custody of Muslims.	The Prophet places the boy in the custody of Muslims.	
The Prophet orders the digging of a chest-deep hole.	The Prophet orders the digging of a chest-deep hole.	
The Prophet orders the stoning punishment.	The Prophet orders the stoning punishment.	The Prophet orders the stoning punishment.
The conversation with the Prophet and Khālid b. al-Walīd.	The conversation with the Prophet and Khālid b. al-Walīd.	

Repentance's spiritual effects such that a tax collector would be forgiven.	Repentance's spiritual effects such that a tax collector would be forgiven.	
The Prophet leads the funeral prayer for her and has her buried.	The Prophet leads the funeral prayer for her and has her buried.	

This version shares a number of the elements in the variants analyzed thus far. Al-Bayhaqī also provides the narrative on the authority of the above hadith compiler al-Ḥāfiẓ al-Nīsābūrī, who furnishes the report on the authority of Khallād b. Yaḥyā. The entry by al-Bayhaqī reads:

> [Abū ʿAbd Allāh al-Ḥāfiẓ] Muḥammad b. ʿAbd Allāh (d. 405/1014, ʿIrāq and Mecca) - Abū al-Naḍr al-Faqīh [Muḥammad b. Muḥammad al-Ṭūsī] (d. 344/955, Ṭūs) - Muʿādh b. Najda (d. 282/895, Ḥarra) - Khallād b. Yaḥyā (d. *c.* 215/830, Kūfa and Mecca) - Bashīr b. al-Muhājir - ʿAbd Allāh b. Burayda - Burayda:
>
> Burayda narrated the story of the woman of Ghāmid, her being stoned, and Khālid b. al-Walīd's comment about her. Burayda said: The Prophet of God heard Khālid curse her and said: Enough, Khālid b. al-Walīd! Do not curse her! By the One [God] in whose Hand is my soul, her repentance [is of such spiritual strength] such that a tax collector would be forgiven [by it!]
>
> Then the Prophet ordered the people [to gather behind him] and they conducted the funeral prayer for her, after which she was buried.[102]

This entry summarily references the story of the woman from the tribe of Ghāmid. The focus is on the conversation between the Prophet and Khālid b. al-Walīd. In addition to this truncated version, al-Bayhaqī furnishes a third version on the authority of Khallād b. Yaḥyā, whose textual content is fundamentally the same as the one provided by Ibn Abī Shayba and al-Nasāʾī.[103] Therefore, the absence of certain elements in Abū ʿAbd Allāh al-Ḥāfiẓ al-Nīsābūrī's truncated version can be best explained as a result of a focus on particular aspects of the account versus others. But this short version combined with the expanded recensions presented above point to Khallād b. Yaḥyā as a common source.

[102] al-Bayhaqī, *al-Sunan al-kubrā*, 8:379, no. 16,953.
[103] al-Bayhaqī, *al-Sunan al-kubrā*, 8:385, no. 16,966.

Not much is written about Khallād b. Yaḥyā save the fact that he was deemed trustworthy and did, at times, make mistakes with his transmissions.[104] He is attested to have predominantly transmitted from Sufyān al-Thawrī (d. 161/778), and the reports are generally acceptable. In my estimation, if someone after Khallād b. Yaḥyā desired to include in the chain of transmission an otherwise nonexistent link to Ibn al-Muhājir, then they could have done so with someone of unquestionable repute. Moreover, it is odd to me that al-Bayhaqī would furnish at least two separate reports involving the same "suspect" transmitter. These considerations in combination with comparative textual analysis affirm Khallād's involvement is historical, which in turn helps to further substantiate the involvement of Bashīr al-Muhājir, the student of 'Abd Allāh b. Burada.

Abū Dāwūd provides the hadith on the authority of another student of Ibn al-Muhājir, and this report's textual content shares a high degree of similarity with Ibn Abī Shayba's version. The chain of transmission is:

> Ibrāhīm b. Mūsā al-Rāzī (d. *c.* 223/837, Rayy) - 'Īsā b. Yūnus [b. Abī Isḥāq] (d. *c.* 189/804, Baghdād, Hamdān, Kūfa, and Syria) - Bashīr b. al-Muhājir.[105]

Abū Dāwūd's informant, Ibrāhīm b. Mūsā al-Rāzī, is noted to have only narrated from written notes.[106] In fact, he is considered to be more proficient and accurate in his transmissions than Ibn Abī Shayba.[107] Similarly, 'Īsā b. Yūnus is also noted to be a reliable transmitter.[108] To the best of my knowledge, the hadith about the self-confessing woman from Ghāmid is the only report that establishes a relationship between 'Īsā b. Yūnus and Bashīr al-Muhājir. Now, biographers could not possibly know all the transmission chains correlating to all reports. It would be equally impossible for them to be familiar with all the relationships between teachers and students. The absence of additional transmission chains that could help to verify a relationship between Īsā b. Yūnus and Bashīr al-Muhājir is due to mere ignorance. But note that much of the information available on 'Isā b. Yūnus accounts for

[104] Ibn Abī Ḥātim, *al-Jarḥ wa al-ta'dīl*, 3:368; al-Mizzī, *Tahdhīb al-kamāl*, 8:361; al-Dhahabī, *Siyar a'lām*, 10:165; Ibn Ḥajar, *Tahdhīb al-tahdhīb*, 3:343.

[105] Abū Dāwūd, *Sunan*, 6:488, no. 4,442.

[106] Ibn Abī Ḥātim, *al-Jarḥ wa al-ta'dīl*, 2:137; al-Mizzī, *Tahdhīb al-kamāl*, 2:220; al-Dhahabī, *Siyar a'lām*, 11:141.

[107] Ibn Abī Ḥātim, *al-Jarḥ wa al-ta'dīl*, 2:137; al-Mizzī, *Tahdhīb al-kamāl*, 2:220; al-Dhahabī, *Siyar a'lām*, 11:141.

[108] Ibn Sa'd, *al-Ṭabaqāt*, 9:494; Ibn Abī Ḥātim, *al-Jarḥ wa al-ta'dīl*, 6:291f; al-Khaṭīb al-Baghdādī, *Tārīkh*, 12:475–7; al-Mizzī, *Tahdhīb al-kamāl*, 23:69.

his time in Syria, that is, away from his birth city of Kūfa.[109] This means that it was during his short time in Kūfa that he acquired the report from Bashīr b. al-Muhājir, and this was not widely known. It may also be that Ibn Yūnus acquires the report from another student of Ibn al-Muhājir, and Ibn Yūnus or someone after him fails to mention the particular source. All of this is to say that while it may be difficult to establish a historical transmission between Ibn Yūnus and Bashīr al-Muhājir on the basis of extant sources, at the very least, Abū Dāwūd's entry points to Ibn al-Muhājir as a source for the report.

Up to this point, I have reviewed the Ghāmid self-confessing woman's hadith versions transmitted by four of Bashīr al-Muhājir's (d. second/eighth c., Kūfa) students. These individuals are:

> ʿĪsā b. Yūnus (d. *c.* 189/804, Baghdād, Hamdān, Kūfa, and Syria);
> ʿAbd Allāh b. Numayr (199/814, Hamdān and Kūfa);
> Abū Nuʿaym (d. *c.* 215/830, Kūfa);
> Khallād b. Yaḥyā (d. *c.* 215/830, Kūfa and Mecca).

A relationship between Ibn al-Muhājir and three out of his four students can be established with a high degree of confidence. Given the consistent pattern found across various textual contents attributed to him, it is clear that he played a direct role in transmitting the report. The biographical information on Bashīr b. al-Muhājir indicates that his reputation as a transmitter is anything but exceptional. To begin with, he is a *mawlā*, though he lacks affiliation with any known person or tribe.[110] It is possible that he converted to Islam and received the *mawlā* designation on the basis of his conversion, that is, he becomes the *mawlā* of the person(s) who accepted his conversion, or becomes a *mawlā* of a *mawlā* of a tribe.[111] Some biographers convey that he makes errors when narrating, that he only teaches *munkar* reports, or that his reports do not have any legal value.[112] Ibn al-Muhājir is also described as being a *murjiʾ* who practiced *kalām*.[113] The remark works in favor of Ibn al-Muhājir's involvement. A *murjiʾ* is someone who claims that a transgression

[109] Ibn ʿAsākir, *Tārīkh*, 48:25–45.
[110] Ibn Saʿd, *al-Ṭabaqāt*, 8:481.
[111] Ibn Ṣalāḥ, *ʿUlūm al-ḥadīth*, 400–4.
[112] Ibn Ḥibbān, *al-Thiqāt*, 6:98, no. 6,885; al-Mizzī, *Tahdhīb al-kamāl*, 4:177; Ibn Ḥajar, *Tahdhīb al-tahdhīb*, 1:439f; certain jurists employ the Ghāmidiyya hadith in their discussions on *zinā* laws. However, they do not provide the authority from whom they received the report, which makes it impossible to know such jurists' sources. E.g., see Abū Yūsuf, *al-Kharāj*, 162f and al-Jaṣṣāṣ, *Aḥkām al-Qurʾān*, 5:97.
[113] Ibn Ḥajar, *Tahdhīb al-tahdhīb*, 1:440; al-ʿUqaylī, *Kitāb al-ḍuʿafāʾ*, 1:144.

does not affect a Muslim's faith.[114] This ties directly to the textual content, according to which the Prophet prays over the self-confessing woman after she has been stoned. Be that as it may, other biographical entries praise him for being a reliable narrator.[115] Thus, textual analysis and biographical material (rea)ffirms Ibn al-Muhājir's participation in the circulation of the Burayda *zinā*-stoning report.

Bashīr b. al-Muhājir's direct acquisition of the hadith from ʿAbd Allāh b. Burayda requires a pause. Biographical dictionaries written by al-Bukhārī, Ibn Abī Ḥātim, Ibn Ḥibbān, and Ibn ʿAsākir—all belonging to the sixth/tenth century or earlier—do not mention Ibn al-Muhājir as someone who narrates from Ibn Burayda. The former's name does appear in the works of authors from the eighth/fourteenth century onward, for example, al-Mizzī, al-Dhahabī, and Ibn Ḥajar. It may be that later compilers of biographies became aware of reports with an Ibn Buryada-Ibn al-Muhājir connection and recorded the teacher–student link accordingly. Also worth noting is that the same later biographers also include several other students of Ibn Burayda who are not found in the works of the earlier compilers. I am not comfortable with reading too much into the absence of biographical comments acknowledging a relationship between Bashīr al-Muhājir and ʿAbd Allāh b. Burayda by earlier biographers when compared to later biographers. There are a number of variables that can explain this phenomenon, some of which I have discussed. Besides, the different versions are strikingly similar to one another, meaning that a written source was in play. That a forgery had taken place during his time or thereafter would suggest a conspiracy by his students or their students. In my view, efforts to falsely develop and ascribe the report would have been exposed since most of the transmitters of the hadith frequent the same areas. Accordingly, the text's stabilization occurs by the time of Ibn al-Muhājir. As such, ʿAbd Allāh b. Burayda, then, has to be considered Ibn al-Muhājir's source.

ʿAbd Allāh b. Burayda (d. *c.* 110/728) was born sometime during the third year of ʿUmar b. al-Khaṭṭāb's caliphate, that is, after 15/636.[116] It is recorded that he, along with his father, traveled to Damascus to give allegiance to Muʿāwiya (d. 60/680).[117] During the later part of his life, he served as a

[114] See generally *Encyclopaedia of Islam* 2nd ed., s.v. "Murdji'a;" van Ess, *Theology and Society*, vol. 1, 173–253.
[115] al-Mizzī, *Tahdhīb al-kamāl*, 4:177; Ibn Ḥajar, *Tahdhīb al-tahdhīb*, 1:439f.
[116] Ibn Saʿd, *al-Ṭabaqāt*, 9:220; Ibn ʿAsākir, *Tārīkh*, 27:139; al-Mizzī, *Tahdhīb al-kamāl*, 14:332.
[117] Ibn ʿAsākir, *Tārīkh*, 27:126.

judge in Marw.[118] That ʿAbd Allāh was a judge explains why, in the sources, he is associated with legally relevant hadith.[119] Generally, Ibn Burayda is considered to be a reliable transmitter. However, Ibn Ḥanbal states that he heard someone claim that Ibn Burayda did not acquire any hadith from his father, yet Ibn Ḥanbal himself, among others, affirms the sharing of reports between son and father.[120] Certainly, in Khurāsān, Ibn Burayda is known to have narrated several hadith on the authority of his father.[121] In my view, ʿAbd Allāh b. Burayda came into possession of a hadith about a woman who is subjected to the stoning punishment. He acquired this report from his father. But based on the clear legal and theological implications of his recension, I am not convinced that he received the entirety of the report from his father.

Even if it is difficult to situate the provenance of the entire hadith or parts of it with ʿAbd Allāh b. Burayda, the extant sources indicate that considerations surrounding *zinā*-stoning and pregnancy were present by Ibn Burayda's time. A report provided by Mālik corroborates this time period:

> Mālik - Yaʿqūb b. Zayd b. Ṭalḥa (d. *c.* 136/753, Mecca and Medina) - Zayd b. Ṭalḥa (d. unknown) - ʿAbd Allāh b. [ʿUbayd Allāh] b. Abī Mulayka (d. *c.* 117/735, Mecca, Medina, and Ṭāʾif):
>
> A woman came to the Messenger of God and told him that she had committed *zinā* and that she was pregnant. The Messenger of God said to her: Go away until you give birth.
>
> When she gave birth, she came back to the Prophet and he said: Go away until you are finished nursing him.
>
> After she did that, she came back and the Prophet said: Go away so you can take care of him.
>
> She did that and then came back again, at which point the Prophet gave the order and she was stoned.[122]

[118] Ibn Abī Ḥātim, *al-Jarḥ wa al-taʿdīl*, 5:13; Ibn Ḥibbān, *al-Thiqāt*, 5:16; Ibn ʿAsākir, *Tārīkh*, 27:133.

[119] E.g., see Muslim, *Ṣaḥīḥ*, 1563f, no. 37 (1,977). ʿAbd Allāh narrates from his father that the Prophet said: "I have forbidden you from visiting graves, but now you may visit them. I have forbidden you from saving the meat from your sacrifice for more than three days, but now you may keep it longer. I have forbidden you from drinking date wine except what is stored in a leather container, but now you may drink it unless it turns into an intoxicant."

[120] Ibn ʿAsākir, *Tārīkh*, 27:133–5; Ibn Ḥajar, *Tahdhīb al-tahdhīb*, 3:422f.

[121] Ibn ʿAsākir, *Tārīkh*, 27:130.

[122] Mālik, *Muwaṭṭaʾ*, 1199, no. 3039/627.

And as noted in the previous section, a report provided by ʿAbd al-Razzāq states:

> Maʿmar [b. Rāshid] (d. 153/770) - Ayyūb [al-Sakhtiyānī] (d. 131/749) - ʿAṭāʾ b. Abī Rabāḥ (d. 115/733, Mecca):
>
> A woman came to the Prophet and confessed to *zinā*. The Prophet sent her away four times. On the fourth confession, she asked him: Messenger of God, are you sending me away as you did Māʿiz b. Mālik?
> The [first time the] Prophet said: Take care of her until she gives birth.
> The [final time] he said: Nurse the child.
> A man said: I can arrange for someone to take care of that.
> Then the Prophet gave the order and she was stoned.[123]

Both reports contain elements found in Burayda's detailed version, that is, they have ostensibly been stripped down to the legal issues. What the two hadith demonstrate is that, around ʿAbd Allāh's (d. *c.* 110/728) death, certain aspects of the hadith known on his authority are circulating on the authority of other individuals. In fact, Ibn Abī Shayba provides a report on the authority of al-Ḥasan al-Baṣrī (d. 110/728) with similar elements.[124] The commonalities denote that by the early second/eighth century, the hadith is reflecting legal development in *zinā* laws. The overlap among these recensions also demonstrates that there is access to an earlier common source about a woman being stoned for *zinā* on the authority of the Prophet. ʿAbd Allāh b. Burayda and his father are two individuals to have helped circulate such a hadith.

3.2.2. The significance of particular textual content elements

In the versions examined in this section, a reference is made to a person named Māʿiz b. Mālik. As noted in Chapter 1, one set of *zinā*-stoning reports on the authority of the Prophet involves a male self-confessor named Māʿiz. A version about the stoning of Māʿiz in Ibn Abī Shayba's *Muṣannaf* reads:

123 ʿAbd al-Razzāq, *al-Muṣannaf*, 7:324f, no. 13,345.
124 Ibn Abī Shayba, *al-Muṣannaf* (2008 ed.), 9:361, no. 29,387.

ʿAbd Allāh b. Numayr (d. 199/814) - Bashīr b. al-Muhājir (d. unknown) - ʿAbd Allāh b. Burayda (d. *c.* 110/728) - Burayda b. al-Ḥuṣayb al-Aslamī (d. 63/683)

Māʿiz b. Mālik al-Aslamī came to the Messenger of God and said: I have wronged myself by committing *zinā* and I want you to cleanse me [of my sin].

The Prophet sent him away and he came back the next day and said: Messenger of God, I have committed *zinā*.

The Prophet sent him away for a second time and sent for his people. He asked them: Do you know if he is mentally competent? Is there anything amiss about him?

Māʿiz's people responded: Why, there is nothing we are more sure of than that his mental competency is better than any of ours.

Māʿiz came to the Prophet for a third time and the Prophet again went to Māʿiz's people with him to inquire about his mental competency. They again informed the Prophet that there was nothing wrong with him. After the fourth confession, a hole was dug up for Māʿiz and the Prophet gave the order for him to be stoned, and he was stoned.[125]

The following is a comparison of the Māʿiz and Ghāmid reports:

Māʿiz	**Ghāmid Woman**
Confesses to *zinā* and asks the Prophet to purify him.	Confesses to *zinā* and asks the Prophet to purify her.
Returns the next day for a second confession.	Returns the next day for a second confession.
Prophet sends him away and goes to his people to inquire about his mental sanity.	Prophet sends her away until she gives birth.
Returns for a third confession.	Returns with baby. *Implicit is third confession.*
Prophet goes with Māʿiz to his people and inquires about his competency.	Prophet sends her away until she weans the baby.
Returns for a fourth confession.	Returns after child is weaned off of nursing. *Implicit is fourth confession.*
Orders a hole to be dug up for him and then has him stoned.	Orders a chest-high hole to be dug for her and then has her stoned.

[125] Ibn Abī Shaybā, *al-Muṣannaf* (2008 ed.), 9:352f, no. 29,350.

Note that in some recensions of the Māʿiz report, such as the one furnished above, the transmission chains include ʿAbd Allāh and his father, Burayda. The parallels and the common transmitters are not coincidental and point to the two narratives emerging within the purview of one another.[126] Moreover, certain hadith compilers linked together the two incidents. For example, Muslim (d. 261/875) provides the self-confessing woman's report directly from Ibn Abī Shayba with virtually identical textual content.[127] However, unlike Ibn Abī Shayba, Muslim first records a report about Māʿiz on the authority of ʿAbd Allāh b. Burayda (who, in turn, relates the report on the authority of his father, Buryada). Muslim's ordering of the reports makes sense in light of the fact that the Ghāmid self-confessing woman asks the Prophet if he is sending her away as he did Māʿiz. Muslim, is therefore, affirming the temporal aspects of the textual content by the order in which he lists the hadith about a self-confessing man and a self-confessing woman.

Situating the Māʿiz and Ghāmid incidents chronologically is also conveyed by a comment from al-Bayhaqī. He first notes Ibn Abī Shayba's version of the Māʿiz narrative on the authority of Muslim and then writes:

> And we narrate the report of ʿAbd Allāh b. Burayda, who narrates from his father, who spoke about the Prophet and the story of the Ghāmid woman. The Prophet ordered that she be stoned. Then he prayed for her, after which she was buried. The story of the Ghāmid [woman] is *after* the story of Māʿiz in accordance with her comment: Messenger of God, do not send me away. Perhaps you wish to send me away as you did Māʿiz, [or is it] by God, that I am pregnant?[128]

In my view, there are two possible reasons for the chronological remark in the text. The first is that while the self-confessing woman hadith emerges before the self-confessing man report, the need to account for the unique aspects

[126] In some versions of the Māʿiz report, it is recorded that Māʿiz attempts to flee once the stones start to hit him. E.g., see ʿAbd al-Razzāq, *al-Muṣannaf*, 13:322f, no. 13,341; in one particular case, the textual content specifies that no hole was dug up for him, nor was he tied down. See Ibn Abī Shayba, *al-Muṣannaf* (2008 ed.), 9:353, no. 29,251; I think there may have been cross-textual pollination between the two sets of hadith, one involving a woman and the other a man. But note that Mālik is recorded to have said that he never heard anything about a convicted person needing to be placed in a hole before the stoning begins. See Saḥnūn, *al-Mudawwana*, 4:508. Mālik's comment raises important questions about the provenance of the particular element.

[127] Muslim, *Ṣaḥīḥ*, 1323f, no. 23.

[128] al-Bayhaqī, *al-Sunan al-kubrā*, 8:380f, no. 16,956. My emphasis.

attributable to the woman, such as being the primary caretaker of a child, took more time to develop. The second is that it may be a simple literary maneuver for those transmitters who are also aware of the Māʿiz story. Note that the Ḥanafī jurist al-Sarakhsī (d. 483/1090) writes that the Ghāmid woman's reference to Māʿiz "is hardly authentic."[129] He argues that in the Māʿiz case, the issue is strictly legal, whereas in the Ghāmidiyya account, it is about purification, that is, something nonlegal.[130] In whatever possible way(s) one may interpret the question posed by the self-confessing woman, al-Bayhaqī's remark (and Muslim's recension) serves as an example of how transmitters interlinked the Māʿiz and Ghāmid reports.

To determine the importance of other elements in the Ghāmid narrative on Burayda's authority, I provide here a chart comparing the detailed textual content on his authority with the recension circulated on the authority of ʿImrān b. Ḥuṣayn:

ʿImrān b. Ḥuṣayn	Burayda b. al-Ḥuṣayb
Juhayna woman confesses to *zinā* in the presence of the Prophet.	Ghāmid woman confesses to *zinā* in the presence of the Prophet and asks to be purified. *First confession.*
	Prophet sends her away.
	The woman returns and confesses. *Second confession.*
Says that she is pregnant.	Says that she is pregnant.
Prophet calls for her guardian and instructs him to take care of her until she gives birth.	Prophet tells her to go away until she gives birth.
	She returns and the Prophet tells her to go away until she weans the child. *Third confession.*
	She returns and the Prophet places the boy in the custody of a Muslim man. *Fourth confession.*
Bound up by her clothes.	Placed in a chest-high hole.
The Prophet orders her to be stoned.	The Prophet orders her to be stoned.
The Prophet prays for her.	
Conversation between the Prophet and ʿUmar.	Conversation between the Prophet and Khālid b. al-Walīd.

[129] Al-Sarakhsī, *al-Mabsūṭ*, 9:93.
[130] Al-Sarakhsī, *al-Mabsūṭ*, 9:93.

ʿImrān b. Ḥuṣayn	Burayda b. al-Ḥuṣayb
Repentance is equal to the repentance of 70 Medinans.	Repentance such that its spiritual effect would forgive a tax collector.
The Prophet prays over her.	The Prophet prays over her and she is buried.

Some variants on ʿImrān b. Ḥuṣayn's authority convey that the woman's single confession sufficed and, on the basis of this single confession, she was stoned on the order of the Prophet. For jurists like al-Shāfiʿī, who held that only a single confession was needed to secure a *zinā* conviction, such a report could stand as is.[131] Other jurists, however, demanded a higher threshold for conviction. Al-Māwardī (d. 450/1058), for instance, writes that some legal authorities assert that the number of confessions must be four in order to meet the Qur'ān's four-witness requirement.[132] The Ḥanafī al-Qudūrī (d. 428/1037) argues that four confessions are needed at four different times for conviction.[133] In the versions on the authority of Burayda, the Prophet sending her away reflects the four-witness requirement for conviction as per the Qur'ān. The first "witness" is established via the Qur'ānic notion of keeping one's own transgressions private: Q4:148 states, "God disdains making public [one's own] transgressions save the ones brought by those who have been wronged." The second confession is established based on the woman's presumable *voluntary* return after childbirth. But this is still a lower threshold than the Qur'ān's four-witness evidentiary requirement. The Burayda report mitigates the inconsistency by explicitly mentioning reasons necessitating the staying of the punishment, that is, childbirth (third confession) and the weaning of the child (fourth confession). In short, Burayda's version resolves the incongruity between the ʿImrān b. Ḥuṣayn recension and the Qur'ān four-witness requirement with an initial confession and the Prophet's staying of the punishment until certain events take place.

It is difficult to resolve why the tribe of Ghāmid appears in Burayda's version of the report. Note that in a version provided by Ibn Abī Shayba (mentioned above), the woman is recorded to belong to the tribe of Bāriq.[134]

[131] al-Shāfiʿī, *al-Umm*, 7:340.
[132] al-Māwardī, *al-Ḥāwī al-kabīr*, 13:207.
[133] al-Qudūrī, *al-Tajrīd*, 5885f, no. 28,410 and 5888, no. 28,424. He incorporates the Ghāmidiyya hadith to substantiate the four-confession requirement.
[134] Ibn Abī Shayba, *al-Muṣannaf* (2008 ed.), 9:361, no. 29,387.

This tribe falls under the Azd—the same tribe to whom the Ghāmids belong. In this case, a transmitter inadvertently changes the tribal reference. But Abū Dāwūd writes on the authority of Abū Bakr b. ʿAbd Allāh al-Ghassānī (d. 150/767, Ḥimṣ) that the woman from Juhayna, Ghāmid, and Bāriq is the same.[135] The Andalusian jurist, Ibn Ḥazm (d. 456/1064), conversely understands the Juhayna and the Ghāmid hadiths to be referencing two different women.[136] In my view, the tribal reference emerges after the hadith goes into circulation. In stabilizing the memory of the incident, transmitters fused a particular tribe name with the woman.[137]

It is noteworthy that, in the report, the Prophet entrusts the custody of the condemned woman's child specifically to a Muslim. Some legal authorities, such as Ibrāhīm al-Nakhaʿī (d. 96/717) and al-Thawrī (d. 161/778), opine that in the event a child is believed to have resulted from illicit sexual relations, the child's inheritance is given to the tribe of the mother after she receives her portion.[138] In other words, a legal relationship is recognized between an individual and the tribe to which the mother belongs. However, the textual content in Burayda's version states that the Prophet places the custody of the child in the hands of Muslims and *not* specifically someone from the tribe of Ghāmid. We must consider why the textual content is structured in such a way as to leave an important matter in doubt. One implication of the Prophet's order is that the pregnancy itself did not result from *zinā*. And from the standpoint of stabilizing a memory, the purpose of mentioning the religious affiliation of those who took custody of the child functions to solidify the Prophet's ordering of the stoning punishment upon a Muslim *zinā* offender.

There remains the possibility that the woman is not married and/or does not have *iḥṣān*. That she committed the more severe *zinā* has to be read into the report, since the report itself makes no mention of the particular elements, especially when the child's custody issue is taken into account. Taken at face value, the report itself fails to specify the type of *zinā* the woman is guilty of. This obscurity is likely why, in one Burayda recension, it is recorded:

[135] Abū Dāwūd, *Sunan*, 6:491.
[136] Ibn Ḥazm, *al-Muḥallā*, 12:97, 12:151, and 12:184.
[137] Noth and Conrad note that names of individuals can be used as a topos, that is, to elaborate on a particular incident. See Albrecht Noth and Lawrence I. Conrad, *The Early Arabic Historical Tradition*, 109f. It is possible that the tribal reference is a specific type of literary device, i.e., a topos.
[138] ʿAbd al-Razzāq, *al-Muṣannaf*, 7:123–6, nos. 12,475–90.

The Prophet asked the woman: Are you a non-virgin (*thayyib*)?
The woman replied: Yes.[139]
The woman's response, as it were, clarifies her status in a manner that would be satisfactory to the later legal tradition.

As I have previously discussed, non-virginity is a precursor to *iḥṣān* for *zinā*-stoning. That non-virginity eventually appears in the textual content and not *iḥṣān* is additional evidence for the early provenance of the hadith.

The conversation between Khālid b. al-Walīd (d. 21/642) and the Prophet in the Burayda variant is reminiscent of the dialogue between ʿUmar and the Prophet in the ʿImrān b. Ḥuṣayn report. The Prophet's censure of Ibn al-Wālid emphasizes a strong cause-and-effect relationship between punishment and forgiveness. The inclusion of a persona such as Khālid b. al-Walīd may have proved compelling. As "The Sword of God," he is known to have been an effective military leader who partially played a role in the conquest of ʿIrāq,[140] the place where most of the transmitters involved in the circulation of the Burayda recension come from.

Lastly, the woman's sacrificing her life in order to earn God's forgiveness—the spiritual effects of which are powerful enough to cleanse 70 Medinans of their sins in the ʿImrān b. Ḥusayn report—changes here to that of a tax collector. The variation appears to reflect certain socio-historical contexts. The abusive character of representatives of the Roman state in tax collection was notorious in late antiquity.[141] Moreover, Arabs belonging to the pre-Islamic period would impose a duty on goods carried for trade by the Arabs, Byzantines, and Sasanians.[142] The practice was curbed during the time of the Prophet but reinstated during the reign of ʿUmar b. al-Khaṭṭāb (r. 22–32/634–44).[143] The report also has echoes of the New Testament, in which Jesus proclaims that prostitutes, such as those who engage in illicit sexual relations

[139] al-Bayhaqī, *al-Sunan al-kubrā*, 8:399, no. 17,006; this line of question and answer tracks word-for-word with the textual content in the Māʿiz report on the authority of Burayda. See al-Bayhaqī, *al-Sunan al-kubrā*, 8:349f, no. 16,993.

[140] al-Mizzī, *Tahdhīb al-kamāl*, 8:188; al-Dhahabī, *Siyar aʿlām*, 1:366; *Encyclopaedia of Islam* 2nd ed., s.v. "K͟hālid b. al-Walīd."

[141] See generally, R. Morris Coats and Gary M. Pecquet, "The Calculus of Conquests."

[142] Ziauddin Ahmad, "Ushūr and Maks," 2; Hodgson states that by the advent of Islam, the Irano-Semitic cultural traditions were well entrenched in the process of shifting to a mercantile base. Accordingly, one of the distinguishing features of the expanding Islamicate civilization after the death of the Prophet is that it "grew largely from the special role in it of traditions linked to the mercantile class." See Hodgson, *Venture of Islam*, vol. 1, 43; Hodgson's observation about the socio-historical context is another consideration regarding the reference to a tax collector.

[143] Ahmad, "Ushūr and Maks," 4.

and tax collectors, that is, those who are greedy, shall have a place in paradise, that is, will be forgiven.[144] The mention of the forgiveness for the tax collector retains the same concept as the forgiveness for the people of Medina, namely, that the punishment is sufficient as expiation and for forgiveness.

The self-confessing woman hadith on the authority of ʿAbd Allāh b. Burayda shares a kindred relationship with the Juhayna version. Several of the elements/motifs in the latter are also found in the former. At the same time, the Ibn Burayda recension contains an important legal consideration: the number of self-confessions harmonizes with the four-witness requirement of the Qur'ān. But the similarities among the two groups of the hadith, as well as the independent attestations cited above, demonstrate that a report about a woman being stoned on the order of the Prophet emerges from a common source, one that is situated in the first/seventh century.

3.2.3. Reports on the authority of Sulaymān b. Burayda (d. 105/723, Baṣra and Marw)

Sulaymān is the identical twin brother of ʿAbd Allāh, and a detailed version on Sulaymān's authority is recorded by Muslim, al-Nasāʾī, and al-Bayhaqī. A comparative analysis of these versions is helpful in understanding the report's place in the broader context of the Ghāmidiyya narrative and to substantiate my claim that the hadith about the stoning of a self-confessing woman emerges in the first/seventh century. The textual contents recorded by the three collectors share undeniably high degrees of similarity with one another. Muslim's entry reads:

> Muḥammad b. al-ʿAlāʾ al-Hamdānī (d. 248/863, Hamdān and Kūfa) - Yaḥyā b. Yaʿlā b. al-Ḥārith al-Muḥāribī (d. 216/831, Kūfa) - Ghaylān b. Jāmiʿ al-Muḥāribī (d. 132/749, Bukhāra and Kūfa) - ʿAlqama b. Marthad (d. 120/737, Ḥaḍramawt and Kūfa) - Sulaymān b. Burayda (d. 105/723) - Burayda b. al-Ḥuṣayb (d. 63/683):
>
> A woman from Ghāmid of the al-Azd came to the Prophet and said: Messenger of God, cleanse me of my sin.

[144] Matt. 21:31; Richard B. Hays, *The Moral Vision of the New Testament*, 163.

The Prophet responded: Have mercy on yourself! Go away and seek forgiveness from God and repent to Him!

She replied: Are you sending me away just as you did Māʿiz?

The Prophet then asked: What is this?

The woman responded: I am pregnant as a result of *zinā*.

The Prophet asked her: Will you be delivering soon (*ānat*)?

She responded: Yes.

The Prophet said to her: Go and give birth.

A man from the Anṣār took care of her until she gave birth. Once the child was born, he went to the Prophet and said: The Ghāmid woman has given birth.

The Prophet said: We will not stone her. We will leave the small child with her because there is no one else to nurse him.

Right then a man from the Anṣār got up and said: I have someone who can nurse him, Prophet of God.

Upon hearing that the Prophet had her stoned.[145]

The transmission chain al-Nasāʾī furnishes is:

Ibrāhīm b. Yaʿqūb [b. Isḥāq] al-Jawzajānī (d. 259/872, Egypt, Baṣra, Mecca, and Syria) - Yaḥyā b. Yaʿlā b. al-Ḥārith (d. 216/831, Kūfa) - Yaʿlā b. al-Ḥārith (d. 168/784, Kūfa) - Ghaylān b. Jāmiʿ (d. 132/749) - ʿAlqama b. Marthad (d. 120/737) - Sulaymān b. Burayda - Burayda b. al-Ḥuṣayb.[146]

Al-Bayhaqī's textual content retains the same information found in reports provided by Muslim and al-Nasāʾī.[147]

As in the case with the versions disseminated on the authority of ʿAbd Allāh, the core elements remain intact in Sulaymān's recension:

[145] Muslim, *Ṣaḥīḥ*, 1321–3, no. 22.

[146] al-Nasāʾī, *al-Sunan al-kubrā*, 6:426, no. 7,148.

[147] The transmission chain provided by al-Bayhaqī is: Abū ʿAbd Allāh al-Ḥāfiẓ [Muḥammad b. ʿAbd Allāh] (d. 405/1014, ʿIrāq and Mecca) and Abū Bakr Aḥmad b. al-Ḥasan al-Qāḍī (d. 421/1030, Baghdād, Ḥijāz, Jurjān, and Nishapur) - Abū al-ʿAbbās Muḥammad b. Yaʿqūb (d. 346/957, Egypt, Nishapur, and Syria) - Jaʿfar b. Muḥammad [b. Shākir] al-Ṣāʾigh (d. 279/892, Baghdād) - Yaḥyā b. Yaʿlā b. al-Ḥārith al-Muḥāribī - Yaʿlā b. al-Ḥārith (d. 168/785, Kūfa) - Ghaylān b. Jāmiʿ - ʿAlqama b. Marthad - Sulaymān b. Burayda - Burayda. See al-Bayhaqī, *al-Sunan al-kubrā*, 8:372f, no. 16,928; al-Bayhaqī also provides the report from Yaḥyā b. Yaʿlā, who narrates it from his father, to al-ʿAbbās b. Muḥammad [b. Ḥātim b. Wāqid] b. al-Dūrī (d. 271, Baghdād and al-Dūr). See al-Bayhaqī, *al-Sunan al-kubrā*, 8:394f no. 16,993 and 8:399, no. 17,006.

1) A Ghāmid woman confesses to *zinā* in the presence of the Prophet and asks to be cleansed of her sin;
2) The Prophet attempts to dissuade her from said course of action, but she insists that the punishment be applied to her;
3) The Prophet stays the punishments until she gives birth;
4) The woman specifies that her pregnancy results from *zinā*. Recall that in ʿAbd Allāh's report, the woman does not specify that her commission of *zinā* culminated in a pregnancy;
4) The child is placed in the custody of someone other than her husband. Specifically, it is presumably given to the Azd, that is, the larger tribe to which the Ghāmid belongs. I noted above that, according to early legal opinions, a legal relationship is recognized between a tribe and a child that results from *zinā*. In ʿAbd Allāh's version, the custody is given to Muslims, not the tribe. Here, that the Anṣār are mentioned points to the tribal relationship with the Ghāmid and Azd;
5) The woman is stoned on the order of the Prophet.

Note that Sulaymān's and ʿAbd Allāh's recensions differ in the concluding part of their respective narratives. In Sulaymān's version, there is no mention of the Prophet's order to dig a chest-high hole for the woman, the conversation between Khālid b. al-Walīd and the Prophet, the Prophet's order to pray for her, or of her being buried. The absence of these concluding elements and, in connection with variances between the Juhayna and Ghāmid versions, reveals that the expressions of such elements as concepts developed over time and emphasized on a transmitter by transmitter basis. The overlap, however, between ʿAbd Allāh's and Sulaymān's respective versions means that the latter's was in circulation around the same time as the Juhayna and the Ghāmid (on ʿAbd Allāh's authority) variants—that is, by the turn of the first/seventh century.

Biographical information about the transmitters points to a historical transmission of Sulaymān's version. Yaḥyā b. Yaʿlā b. al-Ḥārith al-Muḥāribī (d. 216/831) is the earliest common source. While not much is written about him, he is thought of as a reliable transmitter.[148] Unlike the transmission chain provided by Muslim, both al-Nasāʾī and al-Bayhaqī note his father, Yaʿlā b. al-Ḥārith al-Muḥāribī (d. 168/784), as the person from whom his son narrates the report. This is more tenable on the basis of death dates alone. The gap between

[148] Ibn Ḥibbān, *al-Thiqāt*, 9:261, no. 16,327; al-Mizzī, *Tahdhīb al-kamāl*, 32:48; Ibn Ḥajar, *Tahdhīb al-tahdhīb*, 7:127.

Ghaylān b. Jāmiʿ al-Muḥāribī (d. 132/749) and Yaḥyā b. Yaʿlā is eighty-four years, meaning that even if we were to allow for the possibility that Yaḥyā b. Yaʿlā could have met and received the report from Ghaylān b. Jāmiʿ, he would have been quite young at the time. Hence, in Muslim's recension, perhaps by transmission error, excised Yaʿlā b. al-Ḥārith's name from the transmission chain.

As for Yaʿlā b. al-Ḥārith, he too has a favorable reputation as a transmitter, and many Kūfans narrated from him.[149] This last point is especially noteworthy because, as mentioned above, all of Bashīr b. al-Muhājir's students resided in or visited Kūfa, and some, in fact, are recorded to have acquired reports from Yaʿlā b. al-Ḥārith.[150] Yet none of them draws upon him as a source for the Ghāmid report. It may be that someone did, but the (extant) sources do not reflect it. Until evidence emerges that may indicate otherwise, we are only left to speculate as to why none of Bashīr b. al-Muhājir's students acquire the report from Yaʿlā b. al-Ḥārith.

There are other reasons that can help to explain the circulation of Sulaymān's transmission. First, the person from whom Yaḥyā b. Yaʿlā and his father transmit is Ghaylān b. Jāmiʿ al-Muḥāribī (d. 132/749), a Kūfan judge.[151] An authority based on legal expertise and as a fellow Muḥāribī explains why Yaḥyā b. Yaʿlā and his father would be in possession of hadith by Ghaylān b. Jāmiʿ. Second, Ghaylān b. Jāmiʿ's informant, ʿAlqama b. Marthad (d. 120/737), shares the same *nisba* as those below him in the transmission chain. He is also considered a respected transmitter.[152] Biographical entries specify that a number of legal authorities, including the famous Abū Ḥanīfa (d. 150/767), narrate from ʿAlqama. Similarly, ʿAlqama's informant, Sulaymān b. Burayda (d. 105/723), is held in high regard as a transmitter and as a legal authority. He served as a judge in Marw and was considered to be reliable.[153] Importantly, while ʿAbd Allāh is thought to be an acceptable transmitter, Sulaymān is considered to be more trustworthy and proficient in the transmission of reports.[154] Therefore, what is observable is that

[149] al-Bukhārī, *Tārīkh*, 8:418, no. 3,350; Ibn Abī Ḥātim, *al-Jarḥ wa al-taʿdīl*, 9:304; Ibn Ḥibbān, *al-Thiqāt*, 7:653, no. 11,916; Ibn Ḥajar, *Tahdhīb al-tahdhīb*, 7:224.

[150] E.g., Abū Nuʿaym (d. *c.* 215/830, Kūfa). See al-Ṭabarānī, *al-Muʿjam al-Kabīr*, 7:24, no. 6,257.

[151] Ibn Saʿd, *al-Ṭabaqāt*, 8:471; Ibn Abī Ḥātim, *al-Jarḥ wa al-taʿdīl*, 7:53; al-Mizzī, *Tahdhīb al-kamāl*, 23:128; Ibn Ḥajar, *al-Iṣāba*, 23:128.

[152] Ibn Abī Ḥātim, *al-Jarḥ wa al-taʿdīl*, 6:406; al-Mizzī, *Tahdhīb al-kamāl*, 20:310; al-Dhahabī, *Siyar aʿlām*, 5:206; Ibn Ḥajar, *Tahdhīb al-tahdhīb*, 4:560.

[153] Ibn Abī Ḥātim, *al-Jarḥ wa al-taʿdīl*, 4:102; al-Mizzī, *Tahdhīb al-kamāl*, 11:370 and 14:331; Ibn Ḥajar, *Tahdhīb al-tahdhīb*, 3:313 and 3:422.

[154] Ibn Saʿd, *al-Ṭabaqāt*, 9:220; Ibn Abī Ḥātim, *al-Jarḥ wa al-taʿdīl*, 4:102; al-Mizzī, *Tahdhīb al-kamāl*, 11:371; Ibn Ḥajar, *Tahdhīb al-tahdhīb*, 3:313.

throughout the transmission chain of Sulaymān's version, the transmitters garner more accolades, have a stronger affinity with one another, and are more consistently recognized as public legal authorities than the individuals recorded in ʿAbd Allāh's chains of transmission, save ʿAbd Allāh himself. Such characteristics shed light on the circulation of Sulaymān's version. Now, in theory someone could attempted to forge the transmission chain. But, with such high-profile figures, it is improbable that such a pursuit would not catch the eyes of other transmitters. Finally, recall that in ʿAbd Allāh's version, Bashīr al-Muhājir is a *murji*ʾ, meaning he believes that a sin does not affect a Muslim's faith. And it is in ʿAbd Allāh's version that we observe the framework that the punishment serves as expiation. In other words, we find a distinguishing "imprint" of a transmitter in the ʿAbd Allāh version. In sum, the overlapping motifs in ʿAbd Allāh's and Sulaymān's respective versions, along with an analysis of transmitters, point to the circulation of Sulaymān's recension as well as a common source in the first/seventh century.

We can conclude that the sons of Burayda played a role in the circulation of a report in which the Prophet ordered the stoning of a Muslim woman who confessed to *zinā*. Through the transmission process, the respective textual contents experience some changes. For instance, in ʿAbd Allāh's version, there is an alignment of the number of confessions with the Qur'ān's four-witness standard. In Sulaymān's recension, the report clarifies that the pregnancy is a result of *zinā*. In both reports, the primary function—to legitimize *zinā*-stoning on the authority of the Prophet—remains at the forefront. What remains to be explained is the Companion Burayda b. al-Ḥuṣayb's possible role, if any, in the dissemination of the report. As with ʿImrān b. Ḥuṣayn, comments about Burayda's involvement are deferred to Section 3.4 of this chapter. Presently, I turn my attention to one other version of the self-confessing woman's report, this time recorded on the authority of the Companion Abū Bakra.

3.3. Reports by the Companion Abū Bakra Nufayʿ b. al-Ḥārith al-Thaqafī (d. *c.* 55/674, Baṣra and Syria)

The Companion Abū Bakra, a manumitted slave from Ṭāʾif, is also recorded to have circulated a hadith, according to which the Prophet gave the order to stone a Muslim woman who confessed to *zinā*. In the sources, Zakariyyā Abī ʿImrān (d. second/eighth c., Baṣra) is the common source for the report. One of Zakariyyā's students, 'Abd al-Ṣamad b. 'Abd al-Wārith (d. 206–7, Baṣra), narrates a version that is provided by Ibn Ḥanbal. The entry reads:

> 'Abd al-Ṣamad [b. 'Abd al-Wārith] (d. *c.* 206/821, Baṣra) - Zakariyyā b. Sulaym al-Minqarī [Abū 'Imrān] (d. second/eighth c., Baṣra) - a man who narrated it to 'Amr b. 'Uthmān (unknown), and I was present - 'Abd al-Raḥmān b. Abī Bakra (d. *c.* 96/714, Baṣra and Syria) - Abū Bakra (d. *c.* 55/674):
>
> Abū Bakra saw the Messenger of God seated on a mare of his when a group of people brought a pregnant woman to him. She said that she committed *zinā* or some kind of illicit sexual act (*baghat*),[155] [and that he should] stone her. The Messenger of God replied: God has provided a safe haven for you. Make use of it. So she turned back.
>
> She then came back a second time while the Prophet was on his mare and said to the Prophet: Stone [me], Prophet of God.
>
> The Prophet replied: God has provided a safe haven for you. Make use of it. So she turned back again.
>
> She came back a third time while the Prophet was stock-sill. She then took hold of the mare's bridle and said: 'I implore you, by God's name! Will you not have [me] stoned?'
>
> The Prophet responded: Go, [and do not come back] until you have given birth.
>
> She left and gave birth to a boy. Thereafter she returned and spoke to the Messenger of God.
>
> The Prophet then said to her: Go, [and do not come back] until you are cleansed of your postpartum menses. She left again.
>
> She then returned to the Prophet and said she had cleansed herself [as instructed]. The Messenger of God ordered that some women be brought to physically examine the woman. Upon their return, they certified to the Messenger of God that she was ritually pure. Thereafter, the Prophet ordered that a chest-high hole be dug up for her. The Messenger of God then appeared, followed by the Muslim community. The Prophet picked up a stone the size of a chickpea and threw it at her.

[155] The term is derived from *b-gh-y*, which means to defile. It is used in Q19 and Q24:33. The use of *b-gh-y* should best be understood within the context of participating in illicit sexual relations, i.e., it is indicative of sexual defilement. See Bauer and Hamza, *Women, Households, and the Hereafter*, 204f.

> The Prophet stepped aside and ordered the Muslims to "strike her, but avoid her face!"
> Once she died, the Prophet ordered that she be removed from the hole. Then he led the congregation in reciting a funeral prayer for her. He then said: Were the spiritual effects (*ajr*) [of her repentance] to be distributed to everyone in the Ḥijāz, it would be enough [for all of them to be forgiven for their transgressions and be admitted into paradise].[156]

Al-Nasāʾī provides a version of the report on the authority of Muḥammad b. al-Muthannā (d. 252/866, Baghdād and Baṣra), who in turn narrates the report from ʿAbd al-Ṣamad (d. *c.* 206/821),[157] also the source of Ibn Ḥanbal's report. All of the elements in Ibn Ḥanbal's entry appear in al-Nasāʾī's version, which then points to ʿAbd al-Ṣamad's involvement.

Al-Nasāʾī provides another recension on the authority of ʿAbd Allāh b. al-Mubārak (d. 181, Baṣra, Kūfa, Khurāsān, Marw, Syria, and Yemen), also a student of Zakariyyā Abī ʿImrān. The transmission chain reads:

> Muḥammad b. Ḥātim b. Nuʿmān [al-Marwazī] (d. unknown, Egypt and Marw) - Ḥibbān b. Mūsā [al-Marwazī] (d. 233/847, Kushmayhan and Marw) - ʿAbd Allāh [b. al-Mubārak] (d. 181/797, Baṣra, Kūfa, Khurāsān, Marw, Syria, and Yemen) - Zakariyyā Abī ʿImrān (d. second/eighth c., Baṣra) - a *shaykh* - ʿAmr b. ʿUthmān - Ibn Abī Bakra (d. *c.* 96/714) - Abū Bakra (d. *c.* 55/674).[158]

With the exception of a few words, the textual content shares a high degree of similarity with the version recorded on ʿAbd al-Ṣamad's authority. The following is a comparison chart of the textual content of the versions on the respective authorities of ʿImrān b. Ḥuṣayn, Burayda b. al-Ḥuṣayb, and Abū Bakra:

ʿImrān b. Ḥuṣayn	Burayda b. al-Ḥuṣayb[159]	Abū Bakra
A woman confesses to *zinā* and states she is pregnant.	A woman confesses to *zinā* and asks the Prophet to cleanse her of her sin.	A woman confesses to *baghat* and asks the Prophet to have her stoned.

[156] Ibn Ḥanbal, *Musnad* (1995 ed.), 15:215f, no. 20,315f.
[157] al-Nasāʾī, *al-Sunan al-kubrā*, 6:439, no. 7,171.
[158] al-Nasāʾī, *al-Sunan al-kubrā*, 6:430f, no. 7,158.
[159] On ʿAbd Allāh b. Burayda's authority.

ʿImrān b. Ḥuṣayn	Burayda b. al-Ḥuṣayb[159]	Abū Bakra
Prophet calls for her guardian and instructs him to take care of her and to bring her back once she gives birth.	Prophet sends her away.	Prophet sends her away and instructs her to conceal her offense.
The guardian brings her back (equal to a second confession).	The woman returns, gives a second confession, and tells the Prophet she is pregnant.	The woman returns and gives a second confession.
	Prophet instructs her to go away until she gives birth.	Prophet instructs her to go away and to conceal her offense.
	She returns (equal to a third confession) and the Prophet instructs her to go away until the child is weaned.	She returns (equal to a third confession) and implores the Prophet, who then instructs her to go away until she gives birth.
	She returns (equal to a fourth confession) and the Prophet places the boy in the custody of a Muslim.	She returns (equal to a fourth confession) and the Prophet instructs her to go away until she is finished with her postpartum menses.
Prophet orders her to be bound up by her clothes.	Prophet orders a chest-high hole to be dug up for her.	Prophet orders a chest-high hole to be dug up for her.
She is stoned.	She is stoned.	She is stoned.
The Prophet prays for her.		The Prophet prays for her.
Conversation with ʿUmar.	Conversation with Khālid b. al-Walīd.	
Prophet states that the spiritual effects of her repentance would be enough to forgive the combined sins of 70 Medinans.	Prophet states that the spiritual effects of her repentance would be enough for God to forgive a tax collector.	Prophet states that the spiritual effects of her repentance would be enough to forgive the combined sins of the people of Ḥijāz.
	Prophet prays for her and she is buried.	

The thematic overlap between all three versions is undeniable. The following are noteworthy observations:

1) In all cases, the textual content functions to indicate that her offense merits the stoning punishment. And the spirit of willing, even enthusiastic, compliance, cements the legitimacy of *zinā*-stoning;

2) Note that in Abū Bakra's version provided by Ibn Ḥanbal, the woman is brought to the Prophet by a group of people (*jā'ū bi-imra'a*), that is, she does not come out of her own volition. But in the versions provided by al-Nasā'ī, Abū Bakr al-Bazzār (d. 292/905),[160] and Ibn Ḥazm (d. 456/1064),[161] the woman is recounted as coming to the Prophet (*jā'athu imra'a*) out of her own accord—as in the case of the 'Imrān b. Ḥuṣayn and Burayda recensions, respectively. The transition from being brought by someone to one on her own removes questions about who initiates the self-confession;
3) In Abū Bakra's hadith, the Prophet twice tells the woman to go away without expecting her to return. This harkens back to the Burayda variant in which, on the occasion of the first confession, the Prophet instructs the woman to go away. The occurrence of the initial double dissuasion in the Abū Bakra recension and the subsequent shift to an initial single dissuasion suggest a transition to a modified form. Why? The single counsel creates the opportunity for the woman to return after she weans the child, that is, the mother is situated as the immediate caretaker of the newborn, likely to account for instances if a wet nurse cannot be secured;
4) In Abū Bakra's recension, the Prophet is convinced of ordering the stoning punishment once the woman implores him to do so by an oath. This motif of using an oath to carry out the right/necessary/divinely directed course of action is in the hadith about the Prophet and the Jewish *zinā* offenders. Recall that the Prophet implores his Jewish interlocutors by an oath to reveal the correct form of punishment, that is, lapidation. To be sure, I am not suggesting that a transmitter borrowed the locution from one hadith and inserted it into another report. Rather, imploring someone to tell the truth on the basis of an oath in two hadith on the stoning punishment is a didactic concept to secure its place as a divine mandate. Another important point is that whereas the oath in the Jewish cases involves recourse to a scripture, in the self-confessing woman's case the focus remains on the Prophet. In other words, Abū Bakra's version functions to legitimize *zinā*-stoning on the authority of the Prophet during a time period when Muslims are rejecting the punishment on the basis of the Qur'ān;

[160] al-Bazzār, *Musnad*, 9:117, 3,665.
[161] Ibn Ḥazm, *al-Muḥallā*, 12:92f.

5) Unlike in the versions on the respective authorities of 'Imrān b. Ḥuṣayn and the Burayda b. al-Ḥuṣayb, the Abū Bakra narrative does not incorporate a conversation between the Prophet and some other key figure, that is, 'Umar b. al-Khaṭṭāb or Khālid b. al-Walīd. To firmly move in the direction of accepting the offender as a reformed Muslim, the Prophet's authority and precedent are cemented with Companions of such renown to serve as mouthpieces against opposing doctrinal groups. The silence on this particular motif in Abū Bakra's recension, combined with two different versions that represent and preserve the same concept, again points to Abū Bakra's hadith as the predecessor form.
6) The reference to the people of Ḥijāz in Abū Bakra's recension is reflected as 70 Medinans in the 'Imrān b. Ḥuṣayn version and the tax collector in the Burayda variant. The concept of repentance having both a material and spiritual impact is a recurring theme in these *zinā*-stoning hadith.

I now turn to the transmitters to understand the significance of their roles in the circulation of the different versions of the report. As noted above, Zakariyyā Abī 'Imrān's student, 'Abd al-Ṣamad (d. *c.* 206/821), appears in the respective transmission chains provided by Ibn Ḥanbal and al-Nasā'ī. The latter also includes a version on the authority of 'Abd Allāh b. al-Mubārak (d. 181/797), another student of Zakariyyā Abī 'Imrān. As for 'Abd al-Ṣamad, he is recorded to have been a trustworthy narrator.[162] He reportedly claimed that he was in the habit of preserving reports from certain teachers to writing.[163] It is not explicitly stated that he, in fact, made use of notes in his public sessions, but it is certainly the case their private use would not have raised suspicions.[164] In fact, no disparaging remarks are in the record about his taking written notes at one time or another. As for 'Abd Allāh b. al-Mubārak, he is recorded to be among the best transmitters and legal authorities of his time.[165] He was in the habit of writing down reports after having received them. He would then transmit them to others on the basis of these written notes.[166] During his time, there was no clear preference on the

[162] al-Mizzī, *Tahdhīb al-kamāl*, 18:102; al-Dhahabī, *Siyar a'lām*, 9:517; Ibn Ḥajar, *Tahdhīb al-tahdhīb*, 4:181.
[163] Ibn Ḥanbal, *Kitāb al-'ilal* (narrated by 'Abd Allāh), 1:524f, no. 1,229.
[164] Schoeler, *The Oral and the Written in Early Islam*, 114–6.
[165] Ibn Abī Ḥātim, *al-Jarḥ wa al-ta'dīl*, 1:262–81 and 5:179–81; Ibn Ḥibbān, *al-Thiqāt*, 7:8; al-Khaṭīb al-Baghdādī, *Tārīkh*, 11:391–3 and 11:397–405; al-Mizzī, *Tahdhīb al-kamāl*, 16:14–24.
[166] Ibn Abī Ḥātim, *al-Jarḥ wa al-ta'dīl*, 1:263 and 5:180; Ibn Ḥajar, *Tahdhīb al-tahdhīb*, 3:629.

part of hadith scholars about transmitters teaching from memory, written notes, or both.[167] Accordingly, transmissions could be made on the basis of either written records or from memory. Eventually, after his death, however, the balance shifted in favor of transmission on the basis of written notes. The biographical remark, then, stands as a compliment. Both ʿAbd al-Ṣamad's and Ibn al-Mubārak's employment of written material helps to explain the high degree of similarity in the textual content of their rather detailed narratives. It can be concluded, then, from a combination of comparative textual analysis and information from the biographical sources, that their involvement in their respective recensions is historical. This means that ʿAbd al-Ṣamad and Ibn al-Mubārak shared a common source: Zakariyyā Abī ʿImrān.

There exist other versions that are not as intricate but were nevertheless disseminated on the authority of Zakariyyā Abī ʿImrān. The *Muṣannaf* of Ibn Abī Shayba includes a much shorter version of the hadith which reads:

> Wakīʿ [b. al-Jarrāḥ] (197/813, Fayd and Kūfa) - Zakariyyā Abī ʿImrān (d. second/eighth c., Baṣra) - a *shaykh* - [ʿAbd al-Raḥmān] b. Abī Bakra - Abū Bakra:
>
> The Prophet had a woman stoned but, before [he did so], he had a hole dug up for her up to her chest.[168]

Ibn Ḥanbal also provides the same textual content on the authority of Wakīʿ.[169] Abū Dāwūd records two versions of the report. One transmission chain is on the authority of Ibn Abī Shayba's brother and also includes Wakīʿ. It reads: ʿUthmān b. Abī Shayba (d. 239/853, Kūfa) - Wakīʿ - Zakariyyā Abī ʿImrān who said: I heard a *shaykh* say from - Ibn Abī Bakra - Abū Bakra.[170] The one-line textual content is the same as in the versions by Ibn Abī Shayba and Ibn Ḥanbal. In the proceeding entry, Abū Dāwūd writes:

> The same is narrated by ʿAbd al-Ṣamad b. ʿAbd al-Wārith from Zakariyyā b. Sulaym, who added:
>
> The Prophet cast a stone the size of a chickpea and instructed: Cast your stones but avoid her face.

[167] Schoeler, *The Oral and the Written in Early Islam*, 114–6.
[168] Ibn Abī Shayba, *al-Muṣannaf* (2008 ed.), 9:360f, no. 29,374.
[169] Ibn Ḥanbal, *Musnad* (1995 ed.), 15:198, no. 20,257.
[170] Abū Dāwūd, *Sunan*, 6:490f, no. 4,443.

> Once she perished, she was taken out of the hole and he held the *jināza* prayer for her. He then commented about her repentance in a manner similar to that found in the Burayda report.[171]

All of these reports serve as an attestation to the involvement of Zakariyyā Abī ʿImrān. Biographical information on Zakariyyā Abī ʿImrān is scarce, and it appears that he is only known within the scope of the self-confessing woman's report. He is recorded to have only transmitted reports from a man, who in turn narrated from ʿAbd al-Raḥmān b. Abī Bakra.[172] Despite the lack of information on Zakariyyā Abī ʿImrān, he may very well have been a historical person who transmitted the report. Biographical entries on him do not convey any negative or neutral comments, tangentially or directly. In fact, he is not designated as an unknown or obscure (*majhūl*) transmitter. Even if early biographers wished to remain silent on the prospect of Zakariyyā Abī ʿImrān as a satisfactory transmitter, later biographers could have easily dismissed him. By the end of the third century, the standards of authentication were sufficiently developed, and there existed numerous recensions of the self-confessing woman's report with acceptable transmission chains. It would have been uncontroversial to reject Zakariyyā Abī ʿImrān while preserving the components of the detailed variant or by attributing the entire report to someone prominent. Therefore, Zakariyyā Abī ʿImrān cannot be dismissed, and his reference to a *shaykh* only points to his inability to remember his exact source or a lack of desire to name it.

That an unidentified transmitter appears in the transmission chain is, in fact, advantageous for the present analysis. It is unlikely that Ibn Abī Shayba, his brother ʿUthmān, Wakīʿ, or Zakariyyā fabricated the transmission chain. Ibn Abī Shayba prefers short or elevated (*ʿālī*) transmission chains because fewer links mean a shorter connection to the Prophet.[173] Having a "*shaykh*" in the chain of transmission would be counter to such a preference, not only because it adds another layer, but one that makes the transmission chain weak (by later standards) because of an unidentified person. Ibn Abī Shayba

[171] Abū Dāwūd, *Sunan*, 6:491, no. 4,444; al-Bayhaqī provides the report on the authority of Abū Dāwūd. See al-Bayhaqī, *al-Sunan al-kubrā*, 8:385, no. 16,967.

[172] E.g., see Ibn Ḥibbān, *al-Thiqāt*, 8:252:13,286; al-Mizzī, *Tahdhīb al-kamāl*, 9:363; al-Mizzī includes the self-confessing woman's report under the entry on Ibn Abī Bakra. The transmission chain is on the authority of Ibn Ḥanbal. See al-Mizzī, *Tahdhīb al-kamāl*, 9:364; Ibn Ḥajar, *Tahdhīb al-tahdhīb*, 3:483.

[173] On *ʿālī* transmission chains, see, e.g., Brown, Jonathan *Hadith*, 47; on the historical evolution regarding the desirability of elevated transmission chains, see Garrett A. Davidson, *Carrying on the Tradition*, 25–45 and 232–9.

would likely want to avoid such a "defective" chain of transmission. Indeed, if a placeholder was necessary to fill in a time gap between Zakariyyā and 'Abd al-Raḥmān b. Abī Bakra, then in lieu of an unidentifiable person, Ibn Abī Shayba, 'Uthmān, or Wakī' could have employed a name from the cadre of known 'Irāqi transmitters. In fact, a concern for a "reliable" *isnād* is why the detailed version provided by Ibn Ḥanbal, Abū Dāwūd, and al-Nasā'ī, respectively, contains the name 'Amr b. 'Uthmān alongside the *shaykh*. My attempts to determine who this 'Amr b. 'Uthmān could be in biographical dictionaries have not borne any fruit. While there are entries on individuals named 'Amr b. 'Uthmān, none provides any information that is helpful in pinning down the specific person in the transmission chains. Perhaps he was part of the transmission process, or his name was used by early transmitters. Indeed, it is difficult to establish the historical reasons for the inclusion of Amr b. 'Uthmān, but the presence of an unidentified *shaykh* affirms a historical transmission chain.

That a *shaykh* appears in the transmission chain points to 'Abd al-Raḥmān b. Abī Bakra's (d. *c.* 96/714) participation in the circulation of a report. To begin with, exchange of reports among family members should be expected. 'Abd al-Raḥmān was one of the more well-known sons of Abū Bakra. He was said to have been the first child to be born in Baṣra in 14/635, and he would later travel to Damascus to give allegiance to Mu'āwiya.[174] He served as governor in Sijistān and, at one time, oversaw the public treasury.[175] It is probable, then, that at the very least the short version of the report (as provided by Wakī' and 'Uthmān b. Abī Shayba) was disseminated with the help of 'Abd al-Raḥmān b. Abī Bakra near the end of the first/seventh century.

A short version of the report on Abū Bakra's authority can be found in the sources. It is a straightforward statement: "the Prophet had a woman stoned but before [he did so], he had a hole dug up for her up to her chest." The notably terse statement can lead one to believe that this is an early version of the self-confessing woman hadith. Ibn Abī Shayba provides this recension under the heading of "How to [properly] carry out the stoning punishment and how deep to dig the hole." It seems that he is providing a summary of the story to address the issue at hand. In other words, the report's brevity does not indicate an early provenance. Rather, it establishes Abū Bakra's involvement in the circulation of the report.

[174] Ibn Sa'd, *al-Ṭabaqāt*, 9:189; Ibn Ḥibbān, *al-Thiqāt*, 5:77, no. 3,935; Ibn 'Asākir, *Tārīkh*, 32:7f, 10, and 12; al-Mizzī, *Tahdhīb al-kamāl*, 17:5; al-Dhahabī, *Siyar a'lām*, 3:6 and 4:320.

[175] Ibn Ḥajar, *Tahdhīb al-tahdhīb*, 4:19.

In addition to ʿImrān b. Ḥuṣayn's, Burayda b. al-Ḥuṣayb's, and Abū Bakra's respective versions, several single-strand solitary reports indicate that many of the elements of a report about a self-confessing woman were in circulation by the end of the first/seventh century. Recall that the three narratives furnished earlier note the stoning of a woman who is pregnant:

1) [Sufyān] al-Thawrī (d. 161/778, Baṣra, Kūfa, and Ḥijāz) - Muḥammad b. Sālim [al-Hamdānī] (d. early second/eighth c., Hamdān, Kūfa, and Mecca) - [ʿĀmir] al-Shaʿbī (d. *c.* 105/723, Baghdād, Hamdān, Kūfa, and Syria):

The *ḥadd* is not applied to a pregnant woman until after she has given birth.[176]

2) Maʿmar [b. Rāshid] - Ayyūb [al-Sakhtiyānī] (d. 131/749, Baṣra and Medina) - ʿAṭāʾ b. Abī Rabāḥ (d. 115/733, Mecca):

A woman came to the Prophet and confessed to *zinā* and the Prophet sent her away four times. On the fourth confession, she asked him: Messenger of God, are you sending me away like you did Māʿiz b. Mālik?

The Prophet said: Take care of her until she gives birth. [Once she gave birth, she returned, and] then he said: [Go, and come back once] the child no longer needs nursing.

A man said: I can arrange for the child to have a wet nurse.

Then the Prophet sentenced her [to death] and she was stoned.[177]

3) Mālik - Yaʿqūb b. Zayd b. Ṭalḥa (d. *c.* 136/753, Mecca and Medina) - Zayd b. Ṭalḥa (d. unknown) - ʿAbd Allāh b. [ʿUbayd Allāh] b. Abī Mulayka (d. *c.* 117/735, Mecca, Medina, and Ṭāʾif):

A woman came to the Messenger of God and told him that she had committed *zinā* and that she was pregnant. The Messenger of God said to her: Go away until you give birth.

When she gave birth, she came back to the Prophet and he said: Go away until you are finished nursing him.

After she did that, she came back and the Prophet said: Go away so you can take care of him.

She did that and then came back again, at which point the Prophet gave the order and she was stoned.[178]

[176] ʿAbd al-Razzāq, *al-Muṣannaf,* 7:325, no. 13,346.
[177] ʿAbd al-Razzāq, *al-Muṣannaf,* 7:324f, no. 13,345.
[178] Mālik, *Muwaṭṭa'*, 1199, no. 3039/627.

The end of the first/seventh century provenance can be further attested to by a version Ibn Ḥanbal provides with a different transmission chain on the authority of a Companion other than those examined thus far:

> 4) Wakīʿ b. al-Jarrāḥ (d. 196–7, Fayd and Kūfa) - Isrāʾīl [b. Yūnus] (d. 160/777, Baghdād, Hamdan, and Kūfa) - Jābir [b. Yazīd al-Ḥārith] (d. *c.* 127/744, Kūfa) - Thābit b. Saʿd or Saʿīd [al-Ṭāʾī] (d. unknown, Syria) - Abū Dharr [Jundub b. ʿAbd Allāh b. Junāda b. Sufyān] (d. 32/652, Mecca, Medina, al-Rabadha):
>
> The Prophet had a woman stoned but, before [he did so], he had a hole dug up for her up to her chest.[179]

Given that the textual content is virtually the same as the recension on Abū Bakra's authority, it may be argued that Abū Dharr is the initial source of the story about a woman being stoned on the authority of the Prophet. My investigation into the transmission chain did not yield the kind of results that could lead to a non-speculative conclusion about the report on Abū Dharr's authority.[180] In addition to the recension on his authority, there are two reports furnished by al-Nasāʾī attributed to other Companions. They read:

> 5) Hilāl b. al-ʿAlāʾ b. Hilāl (d. 280/893, al-Raqqa) - al-ʿAlāʾ b. Hilāl (d. 215/830, al-Raqqa) - Hushaym [b. Bashīr al-Qāsim] (d. 183/799, Baṣra, Baghdād, and Wāsiṭ) - a man - [ʿAbd Allāh] b. Abī Najīḥ (d. *c.* 131/748, Mecca) - Mujāhid b. Jabr (d. *c.* 100/718, Mecca) - ʿAbd Allāh b. ʿAbbās (d. 68/687, Baṣra, Mecca, Medina, Syria, and Tāʾif):
>
> A woman who had committed a sexual transgression (*baghiyy^{in}*) was brought to the Messenger of God for the purpose of having the *ḥadd* applied to her. The Prophet said: Go away until your menses is finished.[181]

[179] Ibn Ḥanbal, *Musnad* (1995 ed.), 16:16f, no. 21,437.

[180] Abū Dharr was an early Muslim convert who witnessed the expansion of the Muslim polity after the death of the Prophet. On his biography, see for example, Ibn Saʿd, *al-Ṭabaqāt*, 4:205–23 and Ibn Ḥibbān, *al-Thiqāt*, 3:55f; al-Rabadha is in modern-day Saudi Arabia, northeast of Medina and, neither Thābit b. Saʿd nor Thābit b. Saʿīd are recorded to have traveled to al-Rabadha, though it is possible given the proximity to Syria, where both are recorded to have spent time. Neither Thābit Saʿd (or Saʿīd) is recorded to have visited Kūfa. See al-Mizzī, *Tahdhīb al-kamāl*, 16:352–5 and Ibn Ḥajar, *Tahdhīb al-tahdīb*, 1:489–90; given that their purported student is in Kūfa and Abū Dharr is in al-Rabadha, there may be a break in the transmission line due to an absence of regional overlap, thereby raising questions about its transmission veracity.

[181] al-Nasāʾī, *al-Sunan al-kubrā*, 6:459, no. 7,230.

6) Muḥammad b. ʿAlī b. al-Ḥasan b. Shaqīq (d. 250/864, Marw) - ʿAlī b. al-Ḥasan b. Shaqīq [al-Marwazī] (d. 215/830, Khurāsān and Marw) - Abū Ḥamza Muḥammad b. Maymūn al-Marwazī al-Sukkarī (d. *c.* 167/783, Marw) - [Abū Isḥāq] Ibrahīm [b. Maymūn] al-Ṣāʾigh (d. 131/748, Isfahan, Khurāsān and Marw) - Abū Zubayr [Muḥammad b. Muslim b. Tadrus] (d. 128/746, Mecca and Medina) - Jābir b. ʿAbd Allāh (d. 78/697, Baghdād, Egypt, Medina, and Syria):

> A woman came to the Prophet and said: I have committed *zinā* so apply the *ḥadd* to me.
>
> The Prophet responded: Go away until you have weaned your child.
>
> Once she weaned her child, she returned and said: Messenger of God, I have committed *zinā* so apply the *ḥadd* to me.
>
> The Prophet responded: Bring me someone who can take care of your child.
>
> A man got up and said: I can take care of her child, Messenger of God.
>
> Thereafter she was stoned.[182]

Version (5) expresses a legal and an implied theological discussion, and (6) retains clear legal considerations given that each time the woman returns, she confidently declares her situation in clear and legal terms: 'I have committed *zinā*, so apply the *ḥadd* to me.' These reports affirm procedural and substantive rules for a *zinā* conviction. The six single-strand solitary narratives serve as additional attestations of a hadith concerning a woman who is stoned on the Prophet's authority. Combined with the ʿImrān b. Ḥuṣayn, Burayda, and Abū Bakra variants, the provenance is in the first/seventh century. As I assert in this section and further contend in the next section, the common source must be Abū Bakra (d. *c.* 55/674). This means that the narrative—in one form or another—was in circulation by the second half of the first/seventh century.

[182] al-Nasāʾī, *al-Sunan al-kubrā*, 6:426, no. 7,149; Abū ʿAbd Allāh al-Ḥāfiẓ al-Nīsābūrī provides a report that begins with two different transmitters and then proceeds with Abū Ḥamza and the transmission chain provided by al-Nasāʾī. See Abū ʿAbd Allāh al-Ḥākim al-Nīsābūrī, *al-Mustadrak*, 4:404f, 61/8084.

3.4. The Companions ʿImrān b. Ḥuṣayn, Burada b. al-Ḥuṣayb, and Abū Bakra

In this section, I turn to an examination of the biographical data compiled on the three Companions associated with the report under investigation: ʿImrān b. Ḥuṣayn, Burayda, and Abū Bakra. As noted in the Introduction of this chapter, information on their backgrounds as well as on the reported relationships they had with one another helps to clarify efforts among early Muslims to stabilize their memories about the Prophet's role in ordering that members of his community to use lapidation as punishment for *zinā*.

As for ʿImrān b. Ḥuṣayn (d. 53/672), he converted to Islam during the latter part of the Prophet's life, most likely in the year 7/628.[183] He fought in several battles alongside the Prophet, including the conquest of Mecca, as did his father and his sister.[184] Following the conquest of ʿIrāq, ʿUmar sent ʿImrān to serve in a legal capacity in the newly established city of Baṣra, where he resided until his death.[185] It is also worth noting that ʿImrān b. Ḥuṣayn is recorded to have attended the funeral prayers of Abū Bakra.[186] Biographers go as far as to actually pair the two together as the best of the Prophet's Companions in Baṣra.[187]

The Companion Burayda b. al-Ḥuṣayb's (d. 63/683) role does not appear to be any more incidental than ʿImrān b. Ḥuṣayn's. Burayda participated in many battles alongside the Prophet, including the conquest of Khaybar (7/629).[188] With the rising conflicts during the caliphate of ʿUthmān, Burayda moved to Baṣra with his children and died either in Marw or Khurāsān.[189] He also had a number of descendants who eventually took residence in Baghdād.[190] The fact that he spent time in Baṣra may, in fact, help to explain how he became involved in the circulation of the self-confessing woman hadith. When he arrived in the city, ʿImrān b. Ḥuṣayn was already living there, and it is recorded that Burayda participated in auditions (*samāʿ*) of hadith

[183] Ibn ʿAbd al-Barr, *al-Istīʿāb*, 3:1208; al-Mizzī, *Tahdhīb al-kamāl*, 22:320.

[184] Ibn Saʿd, *al-Ṭabaqāt*, 5:190 and 9:10; Ibn Ḥajar, *Tahdhīb al-tahdhīb*, 5:116; al-Dhahabī, *Siyar aʿlām*, 2:509.

[185] Ibn Saʿd, *al-Ṭabaqāt*, 5:190 and 9:10; al-Khaṭīb al-Baghdādī, *Tārīkh*, 6:516; al-Mizzī, *Tahdhīb al-kamāl*, 22:321; al-Dhahabī, *Siyar aʿlām*, 2:508.

[186] Khayyāt, *Tārīkh*, 218.

[187] Ibn ʿAbd al-, *al-Istīʿāb*, 4:1531 and 4:1615; Ibn ʿAsākir, *Tārīkh*, 62:214; al-Dhahabī, *Siyar aʿlām*, 3:5.

[188] Ibn Saʿd, *al-Ṭabaqāt*, 4:228 and 9:8; Ibn ʿAsākir, *Tārīkh*, 71:379; Ibn Ḥajar, *Tahdhīb al-tahdhīb*, 1:406.

[189] Ibn Saʿd, *al-Ṭabaqāt*, 9:8; al-Mizzī, *Tahdhīb al-kamāl*, 4:55.

[190] Ibn Saʿd, *al-Ṭabaqāt*, 4:228 and 9:8.

led by 'Imrān.[191] Burayda's son, 'Abd Allāh, is also recorded to have narrated from 'Imrān b. Ḥuṣayn. It thus stands to reason that Burayda and/or his son 'Abd Allāh heard from 'Imrān b. Ḥuṣayn about an incident involving the stoning of a woman on the order of the Prophet and circulated it accordingly. During this process, the Burayda version underwent changes that led it to the final form that is collected in hadith compilations.

As for Abū Bakra (d. *c.* 55/674), as noted earlier, he was a slave from Ṭā'if. At the age of eighteen, he converted to Islam and was manumitted by the Prophet. He eventually moved to Baṣra, where he remained until his death.[192] Abū Bakra is infamous for having been flogged eighty lashes at the order of 'Umar b. al-Khaṭṭāb on charges of slander (*qadhf*). Significantly, his conviction on such charges was based on his being one of four witnesses whose collective testimonies 'Umar found insufficient to uphold a *zinā* conviction.[193] Per the Qur'ān, the wrongful accuser of *zinā* cannot be held in good public standing unless they repent.[194] Abū Bakra never demonstrated contrition, and this should have sullied his reputation in biographical dictionaries. However, early biographical works contain neutral descriptions of Abū Bakra.[195] Nonetheless, over time, a number of biographical authors would paint him in a positive light.[196] Also note that Abū Bakra had a reputation as a Companion renowned for his legal expertise.[197] Finally, Burayda and his sons traveled to Damascus to give allegiance to Mu'āwiya. Abū Bakra and his son did the same and could have spent time with Burayda.

Based on the biographical information discussed in this section, there is a web of connections between and among the Companions and, in two cases, their sons. The lives of 'Imrān b. Ḥuṣayn and Abū Bakra have a marked resemblance. Both are considered legal authorities, both moved to 'Irāqi cities where they became teachers of *fiqh*, and both died there. Burayda and his son 'Abd Allāh participated in the conquest of Khaybar with 'Imrān b. Ḥuṣayn

[191] Ibn 'Asākir, *Tārīkh*, 27:139.
[192] Ibn Sa'd, *al-Ṭabaqāt*, 9:16.
[193] Ibn Sa'd, *al-Ṭabaqāt*, 9:16; Ibn 'Abd al-Barr, *al-Istī'āb*, 4:1531 and 4:1,615; Ibn 'Asākir, *Tārīkh*, 62:216; for an informative summary of the event, see Abou El Fadl, *Speaking in God's Name*, 111f.
[194] Q25:5.
[195] Ibn Sa'd, *al-Ṭabaqāt*, 9:17; Ibn Abī Ḥātim, *al-Jarḥ wa al-ta'dīl*, 8:89; Ibn Ḥibbān, *al-Thiqāt*, 3:411f.
[196] My comment is partly based on Abou El Fadl's assessment of the positive ways in which Abū Bakra is perceived by hadith critics. See Abou El Fadl, *Speaking in God's Name*, 111; on biographical entries that speak favorably about Abū Bakra, see, e.g., Ibn 'Abd al-Barr, *al-Istī'āb*, 4:1531; Ibn 'Asākir, *Tārīkh*, 62:203, 205, 208, and 214f; al-Mizzī, *Tahdhīb al-kamāl*, 30:6f; al-Dhahabī, *Siyar a'lām*, 3:5 and 8; Ibn Ḥajar, *Tahdhīb al-tahdhīb*, 6:578.
[197] al-Dhahabī, *Siyar a'lām*, 3:6.

as well as attended study sessions with him after moving to Baṣra. Precisely because of the interfamilial relationships, it is far more likely that the three Companions and the sons discussed the hadith about the woman and *zinā*-stoning. Abū Bakra's legal expertise and involvement in a *zinā* case give credence to his being the initial source. This can also be substantiated by the text comparisons conducted in the previous sections. Given Abū Bakra's connection, the report involving the Prophet's order to stone a woman was in circulation by the second half of the first/seventh century.

Conclusion

In this chapter, I examined several recensions of a report in which the Prophet orders the stoning of a woman who confesses to *zinā*. In the case of the Jewish offenders and, as I demonstrate in the next chapter on ʿUmar b. al-Khaṭṭāb, scriptural authority plays a key role in legitimizing *zinā*-stoning. But here, in the case of the woman, it is the Prophet's authority that occupies the center of the source for the punishment's legitimacy. The absence of an explicit appeal to divine legislation and instead a narrow focus on the Prophet indicates a time period wherein Muslims claim that the Prophet did not, in fact, ever order death by lapidation for Muslim transgressors. It is in this context that the hadith involving the woman emerges.

The majority of the versions of the narrative are on the respective authorities of the three Companions ʿImrān b. Ḥuṣayn, Burayda b. al-Ḥuṣayb, and Abū Bakra. Biographical information brings into view that these three Companions had ties to the same general region and to one another. These connections helped to facilitate the initial circulation of the report. I have argued that Abū Bakra initiates the predecessor form. Among my reasons is that he is remembered to have accused an individual of *zinā* and this alleged offender is not convicted. Rather, Abū Bakra receives a punishment for false testimony, after which he does not repent so as to recover his public standing. There is also the version of the hadith on authority of Abū Bakra, which I presented above, wherein a woman who purportedly commits *zinā* is brought to the Prophet instead of her coming forward out of her own volition. While I cannot definitively psychoanalyze individuals who lived over a millennium ago, it is unsurprising that a person who sought out a *zinā* conviction and believed in the veracity of the accusation is tied to hadith according to which a woman is brought to the Prophet and is punished.

Now, it may be the case that Abū Bakra did not devise a story and instead had in mind the purported Jewish woman. But as I noted in Introduction of this chapter, the connection is tenuous on the basis of the extant sources. Whatever the case may have been, Abū Bakra is a key source of the report. Combined with the breadth of attestations, the report about a woman being stoned to death on the authority of the Prophet emerges during the second half of the first/seventh century.

Certain versions of the hadith include a tribal reference of either Juhayna, Ghāmid, or Bāriq. The inclusion of a tribal name reflects individual variations in recollection of the narrative. The instances in which the transmitters identify a particular tribe serve as mnemonic aids to facilitate the memorization and transmission of the hadith. The reference to a Muslim tribe as a concept helps to reinforce the woman's identity as a Muslim. Accordingly, a specific designation serves different functions in the substance of the report.

The evolution of the hadith demonstrates an effort to ground legal practices in Prophetic authority, among other things. The various textual iterations of the report play a pivotal role in the Islamic legal tradition by addressing key elements such as the lawfulness of *zinā*-stoning, the number of confessions required for conviction, and reasons for delaying the implementation of the punishments in cases involving women. These aspects become dispositive in shaping the manner in which *zinā* laws are applied. In short, certain details embedded in the different versions of the hadith help to secure procedural and substantive laws on *zinā*.

The recensions also express theological positions that are coming to fruition about *zinā*-stoning, specifically, and the *ḥudūd*, generally. The conversations between the Prophet and ʿUmar b. al-Khaṭṭāb or Khālid b. al-Walīd, waiting to enact the punishment until after the menses is completed (to signify ritual purity), the issue of performing the funeral prayer, and the spiritual effects of her repentance through the punishment, highlight theological motivations in shaping the jurisprudential discourse on *zinā*-stoning.

In my view, the circulation of the self-confessing woman hadith precedes the self-confessing man narrative. This chronology reflects broader cultural and theological shifts in early Islamic tradition. As I illustrated in the Introduction chapter of this book, in Mediterranean-Near Eastern cultures, the betrothed woman or wife often served as the locus for illicit sexual intercourse. In Chapter 1, I identified *zinā*-stoning in the sources, according to which a woman is portrayed as being brought to the Prophet. The depiction of the woman being brought to the Prophet by others emphasizes an external community role in her confession, which aligns with earlier cultural practices where women were often seen as the focal point of communal regulation of sexual infractions. This focus explains the earlier provenance of a narrative centered on a woman. Eventually, reports involving a woman depict her as approaching the Prophet entirely of her own volition. Narratives concerning the self-confessing man, identified as Māʿiz al-Aslamī, are almost entirely depicted as his acting independently and never as being brought forward by others. The male confessor's independent actions suggest a sharpening focus toward individual accountability regardless of sex. This fundamental point of personal responsibility irrespective of sex is observable in the concept of *iḥṣān*. Thus, the self-confessing woman hadith predates the self-confessing man version, as the former has echoes of older communal dynamics and early legal considerations that evolve in later accounts on *zinā*-stoning.

A critical issue remains with the hadith, which is the ambiguity surrounding the type of *zinā* the woman commits. Except for Sulaymān's recension, none of the versions identify certain legal elements—especially *iḥṣān*—required for a *zinā*-stoning conviction. While important for procedural laws, the reference to pregnancy is extraneous, as it could simply stem from an act of fornication. What we are left with in most of the versions is that the woman's *zinā* remains legally undefined. This ambiguity suggests that Muslim authorities and transmitters projected onto the account the notion that the self-confessing woman satisfied the criteria for the stoning punishment. In fact, the hadith itself reinforces this presumption. When the woman confesses before the Prophet and seeks absolution, the narrative implies that the logical remedy is the stoning punishment. There is no textual indication of deliberation or debate over the appropriate punishment. This absence underscores a presumption that stoning is the default consequence. This premise and, ostensibly, the provenance reflects a strategy to counter arguments about the Islamic legitimacy of the punishment, a time period that emerges after *zinā*-stoning was neither scripturally authorized nor practiced by the Prophet. In other words, the hadith is intended to demonstrate that *zinā*-stoning has always been the standard punishment. It is in this manner and others I summarized above that show the different ways in which the report serves as a foundational narrative for the beginnings of the process that helps to shape the emerging opinion on the lawfulness of the capital punishment.

4

The Islamization of the Stoning Punishment (Part 2): The Politics of ʿUmar b. al-Khaṭṭāb

Introduction

For Sunnī Muslims, ʿUmar b. al-Khaṭṭāb (r. 13–23/634–44) enjoys almost mythical status as an archetypal exemplar. He is documented as having used the nascent religio-political office of the caliphate to enact policies with lasting legal and ethical effects in the Islamic tradition.[1] For instance, in the area of social administration, he established the institution of the marketplace inspector (*muḥtasib*), who became the central face of law enforcement and public administration in the Islamic legal order.[2] Some reports suggest that he was a stalwart defender of what eventually would be accepted as the Prophetic *sunna*; other accounts indicate that he adopted alternative positions. Evidence reveals that ʿUmar's opinions and judgments[3] directly or indirectly influenced a number of what would become Sunnī Islamic legal positions along lines that, at times, may have been thought of as in contradistinction to those of the Prophet. ʿUmar's behavior in this respect can variously be described as either a major contributor to the *sunan*—that is, the set of normative practices or ideals considered to have been set as precedents by exemplary figures, beginning with Muḥammad, which Muslim society was expected to abide by—or, perhaps less charitably, as having diverged from and spurned Muḥammad's normative precedent (s. *sunna*).[4]

[1] Generally, Shīʿīs have a distinct, more overtly negative view of ʿUmar than Sunnīs. See, e.g., Hamid Mavani, "Sunni-Shi'i Rapprochement: Internal Contradictions," 133–47.

[2] Syed Ismail al-Qudsy and Asmak Al-Rahman, "Effective Governance in the Era of the Caliphate ʿUmar ibn al-Khattab (632–644)," 620; on the market inspector, see generally Stilt, *Islamic Law in Action*.

[3] Abraham Hakim, "Context: ʿUmar b. al-Khaṭṭāb," 205–20.

[4] See generally Linda Lee Kern, "The Riddle of ʿUmar ibn al-Khaṭṭāb in Bukhārī's *Kitāb al-Jāmiʿ aṣ-Ṣaḥīḥ*"; ʿUmar was not unique in establishing policies that could be interpreted as being either the same as or dissimilar to the practice(s) of the Prophet. E.g., on the customs of Abū Bakr, see Wilferd Madelung, *The Succession to Muḥammad*, 46–53.

Stoning as Punishment in Early Islam. Syed Atif Rizwan, Oxford University Press. © Oxford University Press 2026.
DOI: 10.1093/9780197823774.003.0005

ʿUmar's mixed record of seemingly abiding by Prophetic precedent at times and diverging from it at others raises important questions about the etiology of the record. In this chapter, I examine several reports that convey ʿUmar's support for the stoning punishment for certain types of *zinā* offenses as well as a report according to which he delivers a sermon about the lawfulness of *zinā*-stoning. The narrative is especially important because many Muslim jurists use ʿUmar's purported statement to help justify *zinā*-stoning.[5]

The chapter begins with a review of several reports on unlawful sexual intercourse (*zinā*) and the adjudicative authority of ʿUmar. In some reports, he expresses his moral abhorrence of certain forms of sexual relations and makes clear that had circumstances permitted, he would order the stoning punishment with little or no hesitation. Another set of reports has ʿUmar ordering and implementing the stoning punishment for *zinā*. Taken together, these reports demonstrate that the second caliph did consider *zinā*-stoning applicable to Muslims and that it was (or could be) enforced under the appropriate conditions.[6]

The remainder of the chapter is organized into the following sections. In Section 4.1, I present an analysis of a hadith in which ʿUmar delivers a public speech—in the form of a sermon—to deal with the rising discord over the selection of Abū Bakr as caliph following the Prophet's death. In Sections 4.2 and 4.3, I examine the transmission history of variants in which ʿUmar publicly asserts both that at one time a stoning existed and that the stoning of *zinā* offenders was at one time the practice of Abū Bakr and the Prophet.

I contend that a narrative in which ʿUmar publicly claiming the validity of Abū Bakr's caliphate constitutes the basis from which a memory—and a report—develops about ʿUmar publicly affirming the use of stoning upon Muslims. In other words, ʿUmar's endorsement of the capital punishment is remembered as a concept and gives rise to a report according to which he delivers a sermon about the irrefutable lawfulness of *zinā*-stoning. I further argue that ʿUmar's sermon on *zinā*-stoning stands as the "Islamic mirror" in front of the case involving the Prophet and the Jewish *zinā* offenders. As I demonstrate, ʿUmar's public speech reflects the same exact motifs found in the PJZO hadith. Whereas the PJZO hadith is instructive for Muslims

[5] E.g., see the Ḥanafī/Sunnī al-Sarakhsī, *al-Mabsūṭ*, 9:37.

[6] El Tantawi argues that it was an inclination to control female sexuality in general and, ʿUmar's sentiment that women in Medina were not as subservient to men as those in Mecca, along with his desire to regulate the movement and sexuality of women in particular, that informed his charge to make death by lapidation for sexual misconduct in Islam. See El Tantawi, "Mysterious Legislation," 291, 306, and 308.

using the case of the Jewish communities, 'Umar's hadith is instructive by using one of the most influential figures in Islam. It is in this way that 'Umar's sermon contributes to the beginnings of the process for legitimizing the stoning punishment in Islam. 'Umar making a public statement about Abū Bakr's caliphate and *zinā*-stoning points to the use of 'Umar's authority and his reputation for insulating the community against two internal crises: the contentious matters regarding the legitimacy of Abū Bakr's caliphate and *zinā*-stoning.

4.1. 'Umar, *Zinā*, and Stoning

Several reports describe 'Umar as wanting to order the stoning punishment upon individuals for what he considered to be unlawful sexual acts. The motif of 'Umar wanting to impose death by lapidation but refraining from doing so may indicate that, although the failure to meet the requisite elements for the imposition of punishment prevented application in a specific case, this form of capital punishment is otherwise considered valid when applied to Muslims. Conversely, the reports may simply point to 'Umar's immense displeasure with the act; his statement that the stoning punishment ought to have been implemented serves to convey to the reader as well as to the Muslim community at large the gravity of such an act, particularly coming from such an authoritative figure as 'Umar. In both cases, the narratives are compelling because, at a minimum, they are evidence of a correlation in the sources between the figure of 'Umar and *zinā*-stoning.

In some narratives, 'Umar expresses his objection to certain types of marriage contracts by invoking the stoning punishment.

(1) 'Umar b. al-Khaṭṭāb was presented with a case involving a marriage contract that no one witnessed except a man and a woman. 'Umar said: This is of the nature of a secret marriage (*nikāḥ al-sirr*) and I do not deem it lawful. If I had made the illegality of such a practice known beforehand (*law kuntu taqaddamtu*), I would have had them stoned to death.[7]

[7] Mālik, *Muwaṭṭa'*, narration of Yaḥyā b. Yaḥyā al-Laythī, 3:767, no. 1,960; al-Bayhaqī, *al-Sunan al-kubrā*, 7:204, no. 13,726.

(2) Khawla bt. Ḥakīm came to ʿUmar b. al-Khaṭṭāb and said: Rabīʿ b. Umayya had contracted a temporary marriage with a *muwallada*[8] and impregnated her. ʿUmar b. al-Khaṭṭāb marched forth angrily, dragging his robe, and said: This is [the] *mutʿa* [I've previously spoken about!] If I had made the illegality of such a practice known beforehand (*law kuntu taqaddamtu*), I would have had them stoned to death![9]

In these two reports, the statements attributed to ʿUmar are virtually identical. The primary difference relates to the specific type of marriage contract that draws ʿUmar's ire, a disparity that seems to reflect either uncertainty or manipulation on the part of the transmitter(s). It may be that either or both reports accurately reflect, in meaning if not in exact wording, ʿUmar's disapproval of what he regarded as irregular matrimonial agreements. In each case, we are dealing with a motif that points to ʿUmar's rationale for applying the stoning punishment. Note that during ʿUmar's lifetime, there may have been disagreements over what constituted legitimate *Muslim* unions. These two reports have as their main focus the nature of legitimate unions rather than the legitimacy of the stoning punishment. In other words, these two reports do not present stoning as the problem but instead what ʿUmar considers to be legitimate and illegitimate forms of sexual union: *nikāḥ al-sirr* and *mutʿa*. Thus, the reports signal that ʿUmar was prepared to implement stoning for *certain* forms of marriage that he considered illicit.

In another report, ʿUmar wants to implement the stoning punishment but waives it for exculpatory reasons. One variant of the report states:

(3) A man set out for travel, accompanied by his wife's slave, with whom he had sex during the trip. His wife became jealous and brought the matter to ʿUmar's attention. ʿUmar asked the husband about the wife's claim, and the husband argued: She gifted the slave to me.

ʿUmar threatened: Bring me proof or I will have you stoned to death (*armiyannaka*)!

[8] Muḥammad Zakariyyā al-Kāndhlawī (d. 1982 CE) provides two definitions for a *muwallada*: (1) "A [non-Arab] girl who was born among the Arabs, raised along with Arab children and taught Arab manners and customs; (2) an Arab girl of mixed ancestry." See *Awjaz al-masālik ilā muwaṭṭaʾ Mālik*, 10:531.

[9] Mālik, *Muwaṭṭaʾ*, 3:778f, no. 1,994; ʿAbd al-Razzāq, *al-Muṣannaf*, 7:503, no. 14,038; Ibn Abī Shayba, *al-Muṣannaf* (1989 ed.) 3:551, no. 17,069 and 3:552, no. 17,077; al-Bayhaqī, *al-Sunan al-kubrā*, 7:336, no. 14,172.

> The wife then acknowledged that she had gifted the female slave to her husband.[10]

In another narrative, ʿUmar makes the general proclamation: "If someone brings me a man who has had sex with his wife's female slave, I will have him stoned to death (*rajamtuhu*)."[11] The question of the legality of sex between a husband and his wife's slave merits further investigation. For the purposes of this study, what is important for us is the suggestion that ʿUmar would punish by stoning certain kinds of sexual relations that he regards as unlawful.

According to some reports, ʿUmar is ready to order stoning but is persuaded to delay or vacate the punishment. One narrative reads:

> (4) ʿUmar was once brought a woman who had committed a sexual transgression and he ordered her to be stoned. Coincidentally, on her way to where the punishment would take place, ʿAlī saw her and recognized her. He then had the woman released from custody. Someone went to ʿUmar and said to him that ʿAlī forcibly had them release her with his own hands. ʿUmar said, 'Bring him to me.' ʿAlī produced himself before ʿUmar, whereupon ʿUmar asked: Why did you let her go?
>
> ʿAlī responded: By God, Commander of the Faithful, are you not aware, as I am aware, that the Messenger of God said, "Sins are not recorded by God for acts committed by three types of people: one who is asleep, a child who has yet to undergo puberty, and an insane person." Indeed, this is so-and-so, the crazy woman of the tribe of such-and-such. It may well be that the man who had his obscene way with her did so while she was having one of her episodes?"[12]

Another report reads:

> (5) A case was brought before ʿUmar in which a woman whose husband had been absent for two years was found to be pregnant. ʿUmar had intended to have her stoned to death, but Muʿādh b. Jabal reprimanded

[10] Mālik, *Muwaṭṭaʾ*, 6:1213, no. 3,071.

[11] Ibn Abī Shayba, *al-Muṣannaf* (2008 ed.) 9:313, no. 29,119; al-Bayhaqī, *al-Sunan al-kubrā*, 8:420, no. 17,083.

[12] al-Mawṣilī, *Musnad*, 1:440f, no. 328 (578). For other versions of the report in which the woman is explicitly identified as insane at the outset, see: Abū Dāwūd, *Sunan*, 6:452, no. 4,399; al-Bayhaqī, *al-Sunan al-kubrā*, 8:459, no. 17,210; a similar story is reported by ʿAbd al-Razzāq. While some of the details differ, the central motifs are the same. See ʿAbd al-Razzāq, *al-Muṣannaf*, 7:350f, no. 13,444.

'Umar: Commander of the Faithful! Even assuming you have a right to punish her for this, do you have the right to punish the fetus in her stomach? 'Umar then let her be.

She later gave birth to a boy whose front teeth were already visible, and her husband recognized the boy's resemblance to him. 'Umar then said: 'Why do they not make them like Mu'ādh anymore! Were it not for Mu'ādh, 'Umar would have gone straight to Hell!'[13]

In all five of these reports, the central concern is the condition under which *zinā*-stoning can or cannot be enforced, not whether it is legitimate to begin with.

Recall the narrative from Chapter 1 (pp. 61–62) in which 'Umar dispatches one of his representatives to adjudicate a case. In that report, 'Umar's order to implement the stoning punishment was conditioned on his representative's finding that person in question had in fact been guilty of *zinā*:

(6a) A man brought a charge against his wife in the presence of 'Umar b. al-Khaṭṭāb, while in Syria, alleging that he discovered his wife with another man. 'Umar sent Abū Wāqid to the man's wife to ask her about the matter. When Abū Wāqid arrived at the accused's residence, he observed her socializing in the company of women. He told her about what her husband said to 'Umar b. al-Khaṭṭāb and that she would not be punished merely on his word. Abū Wāqid kept repeating this point, with the aim of getting her to say something of the nature that she was innocent. She refused and instead remained firm on her confession (*al-i'tirāf*). 'Umar then sentenced her to death by stoning, and she was stoned.[14]

In a different version of this report:

(6b) Abū Wāqid was with 'Umar b. al-Khaṭṭāb when a man came to the caliph and said: My slave has engaged in unlawful sexual intercourse with my wife and she has confessed to me about it.

Abū Wāqid said: 'Umar sent me to the accuser's wife but before I left, he said to me: Ask her about this matter. After receiving his instruction, I departed and when I arrived, I saw a young girl wearing a long gown sitting

[13] 'Abd al-Razzāq, *al-Muṣannaf*, 7:354, no. 13,454; Ibn Abī Shayba, *al-Muṣannaf* (2008 ed.), 9:363, no. 29,394.
[14] Mālik, *Muwaṭṭa'*, 6:1202, no. 4,043.

in the courtyard. I said to her: Your husband came to the Commander of the Faithful and told him that you committed adultery with his slave. The Commander of the Faithful sent me to ask you about the matter. If you did not do it, then you will not be harmed.

The girl remained silent for a while and eventually Abū Wāqid said to himself: God, make her say what You want her to say.

Immediately the wife spoke: By God I will not commit a sexual transgression (*fāḥisha*) and then lie about it. She then said: My husband told the truth.

Subsequently, ʿUmar sentenced her to death by stoning and she was stoned.[15]

In the later Sunnī Islamic legal tradition, Muslim jurists would rely on certain elements in these reports when developing *zinā* procedural laws, for example, the circumstances under which an executive authority's agent has the power to prosecute, find guilty, and/or order *zinā* punishments.[16] For our purposes, reports (6a) and (6b) indicate that stoning was an appropriate form of punishment for Muslims and that it was administered on the authority of the second caliph.

Accounts about ʿUmar and *zinā* are not limited to cases involving the stoning punishment. For example:

(7) A caravan of people from Yemen, which included a woman who had committed a sexual transgression (*fāḥisha*), arrived at *al-ḥarra*.[17] They departed for their journey and left her there. When ʿUmar learned about her offense, he asked her about it. She said: I am a poor woman, and no one has shown me generosity or kindness. I have nothing to use except my body.

Umar sent for the caravan and, when they returned, he asked them about the woman's situation. They confirmed her truthfulness, after which ʿUmar ordered that she be flogged 100 times, and then gave her rations and clothes. He then ordered the group to take her with them.[18]

[15] ʿAbd al-Razzāq, *al-Muṣannaf*, 7:349, no. 13,441; al-Bayhaqī, *al-Sunan al-kubrā*, 8:375, no. 16,934 and 8:383, no. 16,960.

[16] E.g., al-Shāfiʿī, *al-Umm*, 7:336.

[17] According to several opinions provided by Yāqūt, *ḥarra* is a stony tract made of black rocks, as if burned by fire. See Yāqūt, *Muʿjam al-buldān*, 2:245.

[18] ʿAbd al-Razzāq, *al-Muṣannaf*, 7:405, nos. 13,649–51.

In this narrative, the woman commits an unlawful sexual act out of necessity, but this exigency does *not* absolve her from being punished by ʿUmar. However, in another report involving hardship, he is recorded to have taken a different approach:

> (8) ʿUmar b. al-Khaṭṭāb presided over a case in which a woman, stranded in the middle of the desert and extremely thirsty, encountered a shepherd in the desert. When she asked the shepherd for water, he responded by saying that he would only give it to her if she would have sex with him. She invoked God and implored him not to make such a proposition, but the shepherd did not listen to her plea. At the point of dying from thirst, she gave in to him. ʿUmar dropped the fixed punishment (*ḥadd*) for her based on necessity (*ḍarūra*).[19]

In addition to adjudicating *zinā* cases involving free individuals, ʿUmar ruled in cases in which the *zinā* offenders were slaves:

> (9) A male slave belonging to ʿUmar raped a woman taken captive by the Muslims in war. ʿUmar issued a ruling that the male slave should be flogged but not banished. The female slave was not flogged on the grounds that she was raped.[20]

While reports 7, 8, and 9 do not mention *zinā*-stoning, the association between ʿUmar and rulings on *zinā* points to a communal memory about his involvement in the prosecution of Muslims accused of unlawful sexual intercourse. In other words, the sources present ʿUmar as one of the earliest authorities on *zinā* matters in general and on *zinā*-stoning in particular.

In addition to justifying *zinā*-stoning, there are other ways in which ʿUmar's support for the punishment served as an authoritative precedent for Muslim jurists. In Chapter 1, I discussed the debate among Muslim legal authorities about whether conviction for a *zinā* offense that triggers the enforcement of a single penalty (i.e., stoning only) or a dual penalty (i.e., flogging and stoning). Reports about ʿUmar and *zinā*-stoning came to serve as a precedent that only the single penalty applies. For instance, Ibrāhīm al-Nakhaʿī (d. 96/714) opines that "stoning is not applicable to someone who

[19] ʿAbd al-Razzāq, *al-Muṣannaf*, 7:407, no. 13,654.

[20] Mālik, *Muwaṭṭaʾ*, 6:1207f, no. 3,054; ʿAbd al-Razzāq, *al-Muṣannaf*, 7:358, no. 13,468 and 7:359, no. 13,470.

has been flogged. It has reached us that ʿUmar [ordered death by lapidation upon] someone but did not [instruct this same person to be flogged]."[21] Ibn Ḥanbal (d. 241/855) narrates a report which states that ʿUmar ordered the stoning punishment upon an offender, but did not have them flogged.[22] Al-Jaṣṣāṣ (d. 370/981) writes that because ʿUmar understood stoning alone to be the divine directive, flogging cannot and should not be used in the case of those stoned to death for *zinā*.[23] In sum, ʿUmar's position serves not only to legitimize *zinā*-stoning but also to contest the dual penalty of flogging and stoning.

In the reports reviewed above, ʿUmar presides over several cases involving charges of illicit sexual intercourse. In some situations, he advocates for lapidation and does so without explicitly invoking the Qurʾān or the authority of his predecessors (i.e., the Prophet or Abū Bakr). ʿUmar thus appears to be advocating for the capital punishment on his own or, at least, at his discretion. In my view, the link between ʿUmar and *zinā*-stoning becomes a concept that helps to shape a report about his proclamation that *zinā*-stoning is mandated by the Book of God and by the authority of the Prophet. It is to this hadith that I turn to in the next sections.

4.2. The Politics of ʿUmar

Abū Bakr's designation as the first caliph engendered discord over who was to be the rightful heir to the Prophet. ʿUmar's sworn allegiance to Abū Bakr as caliph deeply involved the former in the dynamics of this controversy about the legitimate stewardship of the Muslim community in the post-Prophetic era. This section focuses on versions of a report in which ʿUmar attempts to quell such public discord about the caliphal succession process. These narratives are relevant to the present inquiry for at least two reasons. First, most of the individuals who transmit ʿUmar's public speech about the legitimacy of Abū Bakr's caliphate are the same ones who circulate ʿUmar's declaration about *zinā*-stoning. Second, certain motifs found in ʿUmar's comments about Abū Bakr's selection as caliph can also be found in ʿUmar's remarks about *zinā*-stoning. The analysis in this section will be linked to

[21] ʿAbd al-Razzāq, *al-Muṣannaf*, 7:328, no. 13,357.

[22] Ibn Ḥanbal, *Masāʾil al-Imām Aḥmad b. Ḥanbal: riwāyat ibnihu Abī al-Faḍl Ṣāliḥ*, 3:119, no. 1,370.

[23] al-Jaṣṣāṣ, *Aḥkām*, 4:76f.

subsequent sections to substantiate my argument that 'Umar's sermon about governance contributes to the report in which he publicly states that *zinā*-stoning is valid.

Ibn Abī Shayba provides different versions of a report in which 'Umar comments on the selection of Abū Bakr as caliph. In one entry, the transmission chain and textual content read:

> Muḥammad b. Ja'far (d. 193/808) - Shu'ba b. al-Ḥajjāj (d. 160/776) - Sa'd b. Ibrāhīm (d. *c*. 126/743) - 'Ubayd Allāh b. 'Utba (d. *c*. 98/716) - Ibn 'Abbās (d. 68/687) - 'Abd al-Raḥmān b. 'Awf (d. *c*. 31/651):
>
> After 'Umar performed the *ḥajj*, he wanted to give a sermon. I [viz., 'Abd al-Raḥmān b. 'Awf] advised 'Umar: "The roughest and basest of people (*ra'ā' al-nās wa siflatuhum*) have assembled before you, so wait until you arrive in Medina to deliver your sermon." When I [viz., 'Abd al-Raḥmān b. 'Awf] arrived in Medina, I approached the pulpit and heard 'Umar say: "I am aware that many people are saying, Abū Bakr's caliphate was a *falta*.' Well, it was a *falta*, but God protected us from its harmful effects. Indeed, no caliphate should be established without consultation (*mashūra*)."[24]

Madelung glosses *falta* as "a precipitate and ill-considered deal."[25] Admittedly, this seems too technical of a translation for the pithy statement attributed to 'Umar. *Falta* signifies behavior that is animated, with zeal, an action taken quickly, or an event that occurs suddenly.[26] To be sure, none of these descriptions is intended in the negative. But 'Umar's comment leaves one wondering why God needs to protect people from the evil effects of something that is a *falta*.[27] As for *mashūra*, it is etymologically related to *shūrā*, which signifies counsel or consultation.[28] The use of the term should be taken as an explicit foreshadowing of 'Umar's appointment of the consultative council that elects 'Uthmān (r. 23/644–35/656).[29] It is also worth

[24] Ibn Abī Shayba, *al-Muṣannaf* (1989 ed.), 7:431, no. 27,042; al-Iṣbahānī, *Ḥilya al-awliyā'*, 2:453.

[25] Madelung, *The Succession to Muḥammad*, 22.

[26] Ibn Manẓūr, *Lisān*, 2:66f.

[27] Ibn al-Athīr (d. 630/1232) interprets 'Umar's statement regarding God's protection from the harmful effects of the *falta* as reflecting 'Umar's pledge to Abū Bakr. This pledge was of such significance and value that it had the potential to lead to evil and strife, which is why God felt it necessary to protect the Muslim community. See Ibn Manẓūr, *Lisān*, 2:67.

[28] See Lane, *An Arabic-English Lexicon*, 6:2,435f.

[29] 'Umar is generally portrayed as designating the council on his deathbed, after he was stabbed by the Persian slave Abū Lu'lu'a. See, e.g., Ibn Sa'd, *al-Ṭabaqāt*, 3:318f and 325; al-Tabarī, *Tārīkh*, 4:227f; for an overview about 'Umar discussing the creation of a council, see Madelung, *The Succession to Muḥammad*, 68–70.

stating that in the above report there is no mention of *zinā*-stoning, something that does happen in other versions that I review below.

In a longer version of the report, ʿUmar talks about both the designation of Abū Bakr as caliph and the legitimacy of *zinā*-stoning.[30] The transmission chain and the beginning of the textual content read:

> ʿAbd al-Aʿlā [b. ʿAbd al-Aʿlā al-Sāmī] (d. 189/804) - [Muḥammad] b. Isḥāq (d. 150/768) - ʿAbd al-Malik b. Abī Bakr [b. Muḥammad b. ʿAmr b. Ḥazm] (d. 177/793) - al-Zuhrī (d. 124/742) - ʿUbayd Allāh (d. *c*. 98/716) - Ibn ʿAbbās (d. 68/687):
>
> I used to spend a lot of time with ʿAbd al-Raḥmān b. ʿAwf. Once we were in Minā with ʿUmar b. al-Khaṭṭāb. I planned to give ʿAbd al-Raḥmān b. ʿAwf a Qur'ān lesson and, when I went to his residence, I did not find him there. Someone said, "He is with the Commander of the Faithful." I waited for his return.

The narrative goes on to say that upon ʿAbd al-Raḥmān's return, he tells Ibn ʿAbbās that he has never seen ʿUmar as upset as he was that day. Ibn ʿAbbās asks why and ʿAbd al-Raḥmān replies that ʿUmar had just learned about two men belonging to the Anṣār describing the selection of Abū Bakr as caliph as a *falta*.[31] The two men then discussed that, if "this one were to die (*in halaka hādhā*)," a reference to ʿUmar, what should stop them from approaching one of their members and declaring him to be the legitimate caliph. ʿAbd al-Raḥmān proceeds to tell Ibn ʿAbbās of his discussion with the second caliph, including the advice to ʿUmar to delay his public address until they return to Medina. When they all arrive in Medina, ʿAbd al-Raḥmān states that the caliph sat on the pulpit and, after praising God and the Prophet, declared:

> God allowed the Messenger of God to live amongst us for as long as God willed, sending divinely inspired revelations (*waḥy*) directly instructing him on what is permissible and what is forbidden. Then God took the Messenger's soul. God willed that some things fade while others persist. As a result, we held fast to some things and neglected others. Among the

[30] Ibn Abī Shayba, *al-Muṣannaf* (1989 ed.), 7:431f, no. 27,043; see also Madelung, *The Succession to Muḥammad*, pp. 28–30.

[31] The Anṣār ('the helpers') refers to the twin tribes of al-Aws and al-Khazraj, Arab residents of Medina who accepted Islam and supported Muḥammad against his enemies. On the Anṣār, see *Encyclopaedia of Islam* 2nd ed., s.v. "Al-Anṣār."

> things we used to read/recite as part of the Qur'ān was, "Do not seek to be a son to a man who is not your father, for it is an act of disbelief to do so." And the stoning was also sent down. The Prophet ordered the stoning punishment and we stoned after his death. I swear by God, the One in whose hand is the soul of Muḥammad, indeed I memorized it, taught it, and understood it! Were it not for the fact that people would say, "'Umar wrote something in the codex (*muṣḥaf*) that does not belong in it," I surely would have had it written down with my own hand! Stoning is mandatory under three conditions: pregnancy, a confession by the offender, or, as God has ordered, the testimony of upright individuals.[32] Now, I have learned that some men were saying that Abū Bakr's caliphate was a *falta*. I swear on my soul—even if it were (*in kānat kadhālik*), God favored us with good fortune in its aftermath and protected us from its potential harms.

Ibn Ḥanbal records a version of this report with the transmission chain: Mālik (d. 179/795) - al-Zuhrī (d. 124/742) - 'Ubayd Allāh (d. *c.* 98/716) - Ibn 'Abbās (d. 68/687).[33] Al-Bukhārī has two recensions. One chain of transmission is: Ṣāliḥ b. Kaysān (d. 140/757 or thereafter)[34] - al-Zuhrī - 'Ubayd Allāh - Ibn 'Abbās.[35] The second is Ma'mar b. Rāshid (d. 153/770) - al-Zuhrī - 'Ubayd Allāh - Ibn 'Abbās.[36] Lastly, al-Nasā'ī provides a version with the transmission chain: 'Uqayl [b. Khālid b. 'Aqīl] (d. *c.* 143/760) - al-Zuhrī - 'Ubayd Allāh - Ibn 'Abbās.[37] These versions help to reaffirm the transmission history of the textual content and the earlier part of the transmission chain encompassing al-Zuhrī - 'Ubayd Allāh - Ibn Abbās.

Al-Nasā'ī also provides three additional recensions that consist of the Abū Bakr-*cum-zinā*-stoning elements in which Sa'd b. Ibrāhīm replaces al-Zuhrī as 'Ubayd Allāh's student. This is the same Sa'd b. Ibrāhīm who circulates the report above in which 'Umar speaks only about Abū Bakr's caliphate. In two of al-Nasā'ī's variants, the textual contents retain most of the elements found in the longer versions provided above on the authority of al-Zuhrī.[38] In the

[32] Note that the conditions do not include *iḥṣān*. In the versions recorded by Ibn Ḥanbal and al-Bukhārī, 'Umar does mention *iḥṣān*. See next footnote for Ibn Ḥanbal's recension and footnote 35 on p. 261.
[33] Ibn Ḥanbal, *Musnad* (1992 ed.), 1:449–54, no. 391.
[34] Among hadith critics and biographers, Ṣāliḥ is considered to be one of al-Zuhrī's best students and, for some, second only to Mālik. See, e.g., al-Mizzī, *Tahdhīb al-kamāl*, 13:82.
[35] al-Bukhārī, *Ṣaḥīḥ* (1976 ed.), 6:2503–7, no. 6,442.
[36] al-Bukhārī, *Ṣaḥīḥ* (1976 ed.), 6:2670, no. 6,892.
[37] al-Nasā'ī, *al-Sunan al-kubrā*, 6:412f, no. 7,122.
[38] al-Nasā'ī, *al-Sunan al-kubrā*, 6:408, no. 7,113 and 6:410, no. 7,116.

third version, the report begins in the same fashion as the one in which 'Umar wishes to mollify grievances about the manner by which Abū Bakr becomes caliph. Again, 'Abd al-Raḥmān b. 'Awf advises 'Umar to delay the delivery of a sermon about Abū Bakr's caliphate until they arrive in Medina. When 'Umar does begin his sermon, the initial subject matter changes and unfolds along the same path as the version given above by Ibn Ḥanbal on al-Zuhrī's authority.[39] 'Umar discusses the stoning penalty, not the pledge of loyalty to Abū Bakr despite the latter being the motivating factor for delivering a sermon in Medina. The combination of al-Zuhrī's and Sa'd b. Ibrāhīm's respective attest to 'Ubayd Allāh's role in the transmission of a narrative in which 'Umar is depicted as having argued for the acceptability of the process by which Abū Bakr becomes caliph.

As for the sequence by which 'Umar addresses the issues, in some versions, 'Umar first talks about the legitimacy of stoning Muslim *zinā* offenders and then states his opinion about Abū Bakr's caliphate. In other recensions, the order is flipped, that is, he first discusses the selection of Abū Bakr and then death by lapidation. In an attempt to determine which version of the narrative emerges first, we must decide, then, whether the primary intent of the narrative in its predecessor form is to focus on *zinā*-stoning or, alternatively, to the pledge of fealty to Abū Bakr as the first caliph. In my view, the *zinā*-stoning elements emerge after the circulation of reports describing 'Umar's attempt to resolve disagreements about the process by which Abū Bakr becomes caliph.[40] The convergence of two issues signals a related underlying concern: the potential that communal disagreements will get dangerously get out of hand and risk tearing apart the Muslim community. In other words, my argument is that while 'Umar did approve of *zinā*-stoning, his endorsement is not recorded in the form of a normative report until there emerge sufficient intra-communal debates about the punishment's applicability upon Muslims. The motif of a sermon by 'Umar from the Prophet's pulpit—in which he attempts to set the record straight about a communal disagreement—would be a concept employed for establishing the lawfulness of stoning as a legitimately revealed punishment. The shared concept in all these recensions is a public address by 'Umar to establish normativity on an important issue about which there were divisions with potentially severe

[39] See al-Nasā'ī, *al-Sunan al-kubrā*, 6:409, no. 7,114.

[40] In Ibn Ḥanbal's *Musnad*, the report (including the stoning provisions) is listed under the heading, "Hadith of the Saqīfa." The Saqīfa is the assembly hall in Medina where Abū Bakr is proclaimed as caliph.

communal repercussions. Thus, two sets of issues are elaborated during the transmission process.

How are we to understand the significance of the appearance of 'Abd al-Raḥmān b. 'Awf, Ibn 'Abbās, and Sa'd b. Ibrāhīm in the transmission chains?[41] As for Ibn 'Awf, it is on his authority that Ibn 'Abbās narrates 'Umar's remarks about Abū Bakr's caliphate. Ibn 'Awf's high stature is reflected in biographical sources because he is identified as one of the ten Companions guaranteed entry into paradise.[42] In addition, he was present at the Saqīfa when Abū Bakr was selected as caliph. When the Anṣār submitted the names of candidates for leadership, it is Ibn 'Awf who reportedly says, "People of Anṣār, you are indeed meritorious, but there is no one among you as meritorious as Abū Bakr, 'Umar, or 'Alī."[43] Ibn 'Awf also serves as a member of the council (*shūrā*) established by 'Umar to select his successor.[44] It is hardly surprising, then, that 'Abd al-Raḥmān b. 'Awf's name appears in a report about successorship.

'Abd Allāh b. 'Abbās's involvement in the circulation of the report is unsurprising. To begin with, Ibn 'Abbās was the Prophet's cousin. He was present at the Farewell Pilgrimage and was between ten to fifteen years old when the Prophet died.[45] Ibn 'Abbās' method of deducing solutions to problems was first to consult the Qur'ān, then the Prophetic practice, then Abū Bakr's example, then 'Umar's enactments, and, finally, his own opinion (*ra'y*).[46] Ibn 'Abbās is considered highly proficient at transmitting reports, resolving legal matters, and interpreting the Qur'ān.[47] He taught religious sciences in Medina, and his expertise helped to facilitate his close relationship with 'Umar, who regularly sought Ibn 'Abbās' counsel. For instance, during a study session on the Qur'ān, community elders were deliberating with 'Umar about the meaning of several verses. 'Umar invited Ibn 'Abbās to participate, and the elders were surprised when 'Umar concurred with Ibn 'Abbās. They questioned his deference to the young man, but the teacher defended his pupil.[48] On another occasion, 'Umar is reported to have been asked about the interpretation of a verse. He then said that his understanding of the verse

[41] I leave an analysis regarding Sa'īd b. al-Musayyab and 'Ubayd Allāh to the subsequent sections.
[42] Ibn Sa'd, *al-Ṭabaqāt*, 2:294; Ibn Athīr, *Usd al-ghāba*, 779; *Encyclopaedia of Islam* 3rd ed. s.v. "'Abd al-Raḥmān b. 'Awf".
[43] Aḥmad b. Abī Ya'qūbī b. Ja'far b. Wahb, *Tārīkh al-Ya'qūbī*, 2:6; Ibn Isḥāq does not mention Ibn 'Awf when discussing the Saqīfa incident. See Ibn Isḥāq, *al-Sīra*, 2:714–7.
[44] Ibn Abī Athīr, *Usd al-ghāba*, 779.
[45] Ibn Sa'd, *al-Ṭabaqāt*, 6:321; al-Bukhārī, *Tārīkh*, 5:3; al-Mizzī, *Tahdhīb al-kamāl*, 15:161f.
[46] Ibn Sa'd, *al-Ṭabaqāt*, 2:316.
[47] Ibn Sa'd, *al-Ṭabaqāt*, 2:315ff and 6:335 (emphasis on Qur'ānic knowledge).
[48] Ibn Sa'd, *al-Ṭabaqāt*, 6:327–9.

was the same as that of Ibn ʿAbbās.[49] It is also recorded that ʿUmar and Ibn ʿAbbās once conversed about who would succeed ʿUmar.[50] In my view, the association between ʿUmar and Ibn ʿAbbās leaves little upon which to dismiss the reports about the former being circulated by the latter.

Recall that Saʿd b. Ibrāhīm is the student of ʿUbayd Allāh and helps to circulate the recensions in which ʿUmar exclusively discusses the political matter concerning the selection of Abū Bakr as caliph. It is worth highlighting that Saʿd b. Ibrāhīm is ʿAbd al-Raḥmān b. ʿAwf's grandson. Ibn ʿAwf is a senior Companion, who, as previously mentioned, was present at Abū Bakr's selection as caliph, and served as a member of the council of six put together by ʿUmar to select his successor, which would end up being ʿUthman. Ibn ʿAbbās, on the other hand, was a child of ten to fifteen years of age at the time ʿUmar delivers his sermon. With this in mind, it is far less likely that Saʿd b. Ibrāhīm fabricates the transmission chain and textual content involving his grandfather. Rather, it is far more likely that he seeks to preserve an episode in which ʿUmar represented for the early Muslim community two very different ways of electing a caliph, both of which involved his grandfather: (1) the pledge of fealty to Abū Bakr at the Saqīfa, and (2) ʿUmar's *shūrā*.

One intent of the narrative in which ʿUmar mentions the *falta* is to establish the legitimacy, necessity, and/or normativity of a *shūrā*. In other words, a purpose of the report about Abū Bakr's caliphate is to mitigate the unfolding discord (*fitna*, pl. *fitan*) over rightful leadership after the Prophet's death by explicitly warning against impulsive pledges of loyalty (i.e., the events that transpire at the Saqīfa in which ʿUmar was involved). It underscores the normativity of the ʿUmarian paradigm of succession as a way to ward off *fitna*. It is in this way that the concept of ʿUmar having endorsed *zinā*-stoning could be linked to a memory about ʿUmar's attempts to settle a communal crisis, that is, the *fitna* of all *fitan*. The interlink would eventually decouple to form an independent report about ʿUmar's public endorsement of *zinā*-stoning. The narrative would help to settle a legal *fitna* about *zinā*-stoning. It is to this specific report that I turn to in the next sections.

[49] Ibn Saʿd, *al-Ṭabaqāt*, 6:329.

[50] al-Māwardī, *al-Aḥkām*, 14–6; Madelung characterizes the story as a later fiction but remarks that ʿUmar's reservations about the six candidates, as portrayed in the report, may not have been too far from his actual state of mind. See Madelung, *The Succession to Muḥammad*, 72.

4.3. Reports On the Authority of the Companion ʿAbd Allāh b. ʿAbbās (d. 68/687)

According to the sources, the Companion ʿAbd Allāh b. ʿAbbās circulates a report according to which ʿUmar b. al-Khaṭṭāb declares that *zinā*-stoning is a divine directive and the practice of his authoritative predecessors, that is, the Prophet and Abū Bakr. In this section, I examine the transmission chains and the corresponding textual content of variants on the authority of Ibn ʿAbbās. I demonstrate that he helps to circulate the report, which means that it emerges during the second half of the first/seventh century. I also illustrate the significance of the textual content and how it helps to justify *zinā*-stoning in Islam. The section is divided into subsections 4.3.1 and 4.3.2, each representing the two Successors, ʿUbayd Allāh b. ʿAbd Allāh b. ʿUtba b. Masʿūd (d. *c.* 98/716) and Yūsuf b. Mihrān (d. *c.* 109/727) who, according to the sources, acquire the report from Ibn ʿAbbās.

4.3.1. Reports on the Authority of ʿUbayd Allāh b. ʿAbd Allāh b. ʿUtba b. Masʿūd

Ibn Shihāb al-Zuhrī (d. 124/742) is the most frequently recorded authority to have acquired Ibn ʿAbbās's report from ʿUbayd Allāh. An investigation into transmissions by the students of al-Zuhrī serves to shed light not only on the nature of al-Zuhrī's involvement in the dissemination of the report but also as to what he shared with his pupils. Establishing al-Zuhrī's participation provides the foundation upon which to assess the reference to both ʿUbayd Allāh and Ibn ʿAbbās as al-Zuhrī's putative sources.

Mālik b. Anas (d. 179/795) furnishes the narrative on al-Zuhrī's authority. The entry reads:

> Ibn Shihāb al-Zuhrī - ʿUbayd Allāh b. ʿAbd Allāh b. ʿUtba b. Masʿūd - ʿAbd Allāh b. ʿAbbās:
>
> I heard ʿUmar b. al-Khaṭṭāb say: Stoning is in the Book of God (*kitāb Allāh*). It is mandatory for any man or woman who commits *zinā* on the condition that they have *iḥṣān* and are convicted based on eyewitness testimony, confession, or pregnancy.[51]

[51] Mālik, *Muwaṭṭaʾ*, 6:1201f, no. 3,042.

This report has two motifs that convey the obligatory nature of *zinā*-stoning. The first is 'Umar's appeal to the Book of God, and the second is a delineation of the conditions under which *zinā*-stoning becomes obligatory.

By invoking the Book of God, does 'Umar intend that which eventually becomes the 'Uthmānī codex? In the Qur'ān, the phrase "the Book of God" refers to any divine text, including itself.[52] In the hadith literature, the Book of God, at times, is used to connote the Torah. Here is one example:

> A man asked Ka'b [b. al-Aḥbār (d. *c.* 33/653), a Jewish scholar/rabbi] regarding disobedience: What do you find in the Book of God (*kitāb Allāh*) about being undutiful to parents?
>
> [Ka'b] responded: If the person swears an oath to them and does not fulfill it, if the person is asked [for something] and the person does not provide it, or if the person is entrusted [with something] and the person betrays that trust. All of this is being undutiful.[53]

And in the *tafsīr* of al-Ṭabarī, regarding Chapter Three, *al-Āl 'Imrān* (The Family of 'Imrān):

> 23 Have you not seen [that when] those who have been given a portion of the Book (*kitāb*) are called to the Book of God (*kitāb Allāh*) to settle their disputes, some of them turn away? They are averse [to its rulings].

The exegete remarks that some understand *kitāb* to signify the Torah.[54] He then furnishes the following hadith:

> On the authority of the Companion Ibn 'Abbās (d. 68/687): The Messenger of God entered the house of study belonging to a Jewish group. There he called them to God. Na'īm b. 'Amr and al-Ḥārith b. Zayd asked the Prophet: What religion (*dīn*) do you practice, Muḥammad?
> The Prophet responded: The same as the one of Abraham.
> They remarked: Abraham was Jewish!
> The Prophet said: Bring the Torah since it stands between you and me.

[52] See, e.g., Q2:79; Q2:101, and Q3:23.
[53] al-Bayhaqī, *al-Jāmi'*, 10:292, no. 7,512.
[54] al-Ṭabarī, *al-Jāmi'*, 6:288.

> Ibn ʿAbbās said: They refused and God revealed [Q3:23].[55]

These reports indicate that some people, including ʿUmar, who belong to the first decades of Islam, could understand the Book of God to mean the Torah. Recall that in the PJZO hadith, the legitimacy of the stoning punishment is established on the basis of the Torah. Here, in ʿUmar's report, we have a Muslim portrayed as invoking scriptural authority to legitimize *zinā*-stoning. The pairing of the Book of God and the stoning punishment underscores the Qur'ānic notion of a book (*kitāb*) authorizing legal judgments (*ḥukm*).[56]

That the Book of God can signify the Torah additionally means ʿUmar is being portrayed as giving credence to scriptures before the Qur'ān or he believes such scriptures, or parts thereof, remain sources of authority. Certain reports portray ʿUmar as someone having a level of affinity for the Torah. According to one narrative:

> On the authority of ʿAbd Allāh b. Thābit (d. 1st/7th c.): ʿUmar b. al-Khaṭṭāb came to the Prophet and said: Messenger of God, I spent some time with my brother belonging to [the Jewish tribe] Qurayẓa and he wrote down for me a summary of the Torah. Shall I read to you what I have?
>
> ʿAbd Allāh b. Thābit: The Messenger of God's face changed color. I said to ʿUmar, "Do you not see what just happened to the face of the Messenger of God?"
>
> ʿUmar replied: I only seek God's pleasure, as God (*rabb*), and Islam, as [the expression] of religion (*dīn*), and Muḥammad, as a prophet.
>
> ʿAbd Allāh b. Thābit: [Upon hearing this] the Prophet's worries dissipated, who then said, "By the One in whose hand is the soul of Muḥammad, were Moses to appear before you and you were to follow him and leave me, then you would be the straying lot. You are my share among nations and I am your share from among the prophets.[57]

ʿUmar's position regarding the acceptability of *zinā*-stoning, along with his interest in the Torah as portrayed in the sources, means that he may have

[55] al-Ṭabarī, *al-Jāmiʿ*, 6:288f, no. 6,781; note the similarity between this hadith and the one involving the Prophet's order to stone the Jewish *zinā* offenders. In both scenarios, the Prophet asks his Jewish interlocutors to resolve the issue at hand by using the Torah.

[56] On *kitāb* as a focus-word, see Daniel A. Madigan, *The Qur'ān's Self-Image*, 90–6.

[57] ʿAbd al-Razzāq, *al-Muṣannaf*, 6:113, no. 10,165.

viewed scriptures before the Qur'ān as having some level of authority. During his lifetime and, perhaps, for a short while after his death, his views were common knowledge. The relationship between 'Umar and the Book of God formulates into a concept that finds expression in 'Umar's report about *zinā*-stoning, prior to the Book of God being primarily glossed as the Qur'ān. These connections are a reflection of the explicit one between the Torah and the stoning punishment in the PJZO hadith. 'Umar's appeal to the Book of God helps to establish an early first-/seventh-century provenance about certain elements of his *zinā*-stoning report.

The second motif from Mālik's recension comprises 'Umar's delineating a series of legal criteria for a *zinā*-stoning conviction. The first element is *iḥṣān*. Recall from Chapter 1 that *iḥṣān* is a necessary element for a *zinā* conviction. What we are observing in Mālik's report is that later transmitters interpolate the *term* to signify a legal concept regarding those Muslims who could potentially be subject to the stoning punishment. In the report, we also find 'Umar asserting that pregnancy is sufficient evidence for a *zinā* conviction. Muslim jurists contest the use of pregnancy as legal evidence. Medinans are transmitting the hadith that Mālik records and it is the Mālikīs, who emerge from Medina, that generally allow it as proof in *zinā* cases.[58] But for those belonging to other legal schools, pregnancy as a probative element is not a settled matter.[59] One possibility is that in the early period non-Medinans were unaware of 'Umar's position. Or, it may be that certain individuals interpreted 'Umar's precedent as time-bound and/or limited in scope. Perhaps others rejected it on the basis of the Qur'ān's instruction in Q24:4, "and if they do not bring four witnesses." Whatever the case may have been, there are no reasons to dispute that the second motif is a layered construction of the legal elements necessary for a *zinā* conviction.

Mālik's account is supported by other versions as cited by additional hadith collectors. Both al-Shāfi'ī (d. 204/820) and 'Abd Allāh b. al-Qa'nabī (d. 221/835) transmit the report from Mālik, and the respective textual content of their transmissions is strikingly similar to the report in the *Muwaṭṭa'*.[60]

[58] E.g., see Saḥnūn, *al-Mudawwana*, 4:514.

[59] See, e.g., al-Shāfi'ī, *al-Umm*, 8:110; the Ḥanafī jurist al-Qudūrī notes that pregnancy may result from sexual intercourse that is not consensual, which would make the act something other than *zinā*. See al-Qudūrī, *al-Tajrīd*, 10:5295, no. 25,369; the Shī'ī jurist al-Ṭūsī writes that one should ask a pregnant unmarried woman if the pregnancy resulted from *zinā*. If she says that the pregnancy is from intercourse other than *zinā* (e.g., rape), she is not subject to the fixed punishment (*ḥadd*). See al-Ṭūsī, *al-Mabsūṭ*, 8:7f; on the influence of 'Umar's statement about pregnancy on Mālikī legal discourses on rape, see Azam, *Sexual Violation in Islamic Law*, 204–9 and 216–9.

[60] al-Bayhaqī, *al-Sunan al-kubrā*, 8:369, no. 16,919 and 8:411, no. 16,053.

Moreover, the version of the *Muwaṭṭa'* redacted by the Iraqi jurist Muḥammad al-Shaybānī (d. 189/805) contains the same textual details as Yaḥyā's (d. 234/848) version cited above.[61] The overlap between and among the narratives indicates that Mālik transmitted the report on al-Zuhrī's authority.

Another version of 'Umar's *zinā*-stoning report is preserved in the *Muṣannaf* of 'Abd al-Razzāq. This version includes additional elements that emphasize the punishment's legitimacy. The chain of transmission and textual content are:

> Ma'mar b. Rāshid (d. 153/770) - al-Zuhrī (d. 124/742) - 'Ubayd Allāh (d. *c.* 98/716) - 'Abd Allāh b. 'Abbās (d. 68/687):
>
> I heard 'Umar say: Indeed, God Almighty sent Muḥammad with the Truth and the Book. One of the things that God revealed to him was the stoning verse. The Messenger of God ordered the stoning punishment, and we stoned after [his death]. I fear that a day will come when some people will say: "By God, we do not find stoning in the Book of God." These people will be lost, for they will have abandoned a religious duty that God has sent down. Indeed, stoning is mandatory for any man or woman who commits *zinā* on the condition that they have *iḥṣān* and are convicted based on eyewitness testimony, confession, or pregnancy.[62]

The following chart provides a comparison of the two versions of the hadith examined thus far.

[61] Mālik, *Muwaṭṭa'*, narration of al-Shaybānī, 220, no. 692. According to Motzki, the recensions of the *Muwaṭṭa'* transmitted by Yaḥyā and al-Shaybānī share a common source, namely, Mālik. See generally Motzki, "Der *Fiqh* des Zuhrī: die Quellenproblematik," 1–44; Schoeler provides a brief explanation for why there are different recensions of the *Muwaṭṭa'*. The primary reason is that it was Mālik's students who gave the work its final form, though at times Mālik "did read or recite the text himself in the presence of his students." See Schoeler, *The Genesis of Literature in Islam*, 73.

[62] 'Abd al-Razzāq, *al-Muṣannaf*, 7:315, no. 13,329; al-Ḥumaydī provides a version wherein the textual content is the same up to 'Umar's statement that the Prophet ordered the stoning punishment and that they did as well after his death. Al-Ḥumaydī does not record anything further. The transmission chain includes Ma'mar - al-Zuhrī - 'Ubayd Allāh - Ibn 'Abbās. See al-Ḥumaydī, *Musnad*, 1:161, no. 25; Ibn Ḥanbal records the report on 'Abd al-Razzāq's authority. The textual content is much shorter and similar to al-Ḥumaydī's version. It includes the following: (1) God sent the Prophet with the Truth, (2) God revealed the stoning verse, and (3) the Prophet ordered the stoning punishment and, after his death, Muslims stoned. Mālik's account, which appears to be a summary of the longer version of the report, identifies specific points that emphasize the legality of stoning Muslim *zinā* offenders. See Ibn Ḥanbal, *Musnad* (1992 ed.) 1:331, no. 414; al-Tirmidhī records the report on 'Abd al-Razzāq's authority. That the textual content is virtually identical to that given by 'Abd al-Razzāq suggests that al-Tirmidhī's version is likely based on a written source that goes back to 'Abd al-Razzāq. See al-Tirmidhī, *Jāmi'*, 3:101f, no. 1,432.

Mālik - **al-Zuhrī** - 'Ubayd Allāh - Ibn 'Abbās	'Abd al-Razzāq - Ma'mar - **al-Zuhrī** - 'Ubayd Allāh - Ibn 'Abbās
	God sent Muḥammad with the Truth and the Book.
Stoning is in the Book of God	God revealed the stoning verse.
	The Prophet ordered the stoning punishment and we stoned after his death.
	'Umar fears that a day will come when people will say: By God, we do not find stoning in God's Book.
	'Umar says people will abandon religious obligations sent down by God.
Conditions: *iḥṣān* plus eyewitness testimony, confession, or pregnancy	Conditions: *iḥṣān* plus eyewitness testimony, confession, or pregnancy.

Note the following:

(1) In Ma'mar's version, 'Umar states, "God Almighty sent Muḥammad with the Truth (*ḥaqq*) and the Book." The motif charts the authority of the Prophet and the Qur'ān. The phrase also brings to mind the several times in the Qur'ān that *ḥaqq* and *kitāb* appear together. As Madigan notes, "[*ḥ*]*aqq* is used to describe the way *kitāb* functions . . . to give judgment as well as form the basis for the judgment of the Prophet."[63] The expression uttered by 'Umar indicates a context in which the authority of the Qur'ān and the Prophet stand separate and apart. It represents broader currents wherein debates are occurring about the extent to which the hadith tradition can be a basis for establishing Islamic dogmas. The implication of emphasis also illuminates a dominant view that the practice of the Prophet did not support death by lapidation upon Muslim *zinā* offenders. Indeed, among the early players who focus primarily on the Qur'ān as the fount of knowledge include the *Shurāṭ* (*Khawārij*), who reject *zinā*-stoning and, eventually, the Mu'tazila.[64]

[63] Madigan, *Qur'ān's Self-Image*, 159.

[64] E.g., see Hassan Ansari, "Shī'ī Reception of Mu'tazilism;" *Encyclopaedia of Islam* 3rd ed., s.v. "Ḥadīth, Ibāḍism;" on the Mu'tazila, see, e.g., van Ess, "The Rise of the Mu'tazila," in *Theology and Society*, vol. 3, 33–99; for a discussion on Ibādī sources and the lawfulness of lapidation for certain types of *zinā* offenders, see Francesca, "Flogging, Banning, Lapidation," 177–80.

(2) As a way to emphasize the authority of the Prophet, in Maʿmar's version, we find ʿUmar claiming that the Prophet ordered the stoning punishment and that the practice continued after his death. Again, the phrase conveys that the stoning punishment is not only a divine directive but also a constituent element of the Prophetic practice. This has the double effect of (a) emphasizing the punishment's legitimacy and (b) intimating that people may forget a practice in certain matters of law without an explicit or extant mandate and/or reference to the Prophet's practice. In other words, this phrase functions to inform the reader/listener that the punishment was, in fact, implemented by the Prophet. Mālik's version, by contrast, is silent about what the Prophet did and did not do in this respect;[65]

(3) ʿUmar fears that Muslims will deny that a stoning verse ever existed. Given the short gap between the Prophet's death and ʿUmar's caliphate (two years), it is unlikely that ʿUmar laments that Muslims reject the stoning punishment shortly after his rise to power. During his caliphate, several Companions are still alive, meaning that some would remember the Prophet's involvement in the stoning of Muslim *zinā* offenders—a fact that is confirmed by ʿUmar's comment that Muslims stoned after the Prophet's demise. Hence, even with ʿUmar supporting *zinā*-stoning, the memory about him making a statement about its lawfulness emerges when a sufficient number of Muslims are questioning the punishment's applicability and when there are no living Companions who can confirm or deny the veracity of the claim that the Prophet practiced *zinā*-stoning.

In the PJZO hadith, the Jewish communities are accused of *taḥrīf* on the basis of denying the existence of a stoning verse. In ʿAbd al-Razzāq's recension, *Muslims* are implicitly being accused of *taḥrīf* because *they* are now denying the existence of a stoning verse. Both Jewish sages and Muslims are "abandon[ing] a religious duty that God has sent down to them." As for the overlapping clauses among the variants examined thus far, they point to al-Zuhrī as the common source. Mālik's version can be regarded as a summary of al-Zuhrī's transmission. According to the hadith critic Ibn Ṣalāḥ (d. 643/1245), transmitters did, at times, summarize narratives. The approach was

[65] This clause is absent from two other versions transmitted on Maʿmar's authority. See al-Ḥumaydī, *Musnad*, 1:161, no. 25; Ibn Ḥanbal, *Musnad* (1992 ed.), 1:414, no. 331. I consider the absence of these two motifs as a result of the transmission process.

supported by legal specialists because of their focus on the legal elements of a report.[66] Hence, Mālik's concise recension is explained as a byproduct of this practice.

Another version of 'Umar's *zinā*-stoning narrative can be found in Ibn Ḥanbal's *Musnad*. This recension is recorded on the authority of 'Abd al-Raḥmān b. Mahdī (d. 198/814), who relates it from Mālik.[67] The following is a comparison of the respective textual contents of Mālik's, 'Abd al-Razzāq's, and Ibn Ḥanbal's recorded versions:

'Abd al-Raḥmān b. Mahdī - Mālik - **al-Zuhrī**	'Abd al-Razzāq - Ma'mar - **al-Zuhrī** - 'Ubayd Allāh - Ibn 'Abbās	Mālik - **al-Zuhrī** - 'Ubayd Allāh - Ibn 'Abbās **(from the *Muwaṭṭa'*)**
God sent Muḥammad and with him the Book.	God sent Muḥammad with the Truth and the Book.	
God revealed the stoning verse.	God revealed the stoning verse.	Stoning is in the Book of God.
	The Prophet ordered the stoning punishment and we stoned after his death.	
'Umar says: . . . we read it/recited it (*qara'nā bi-hā*), we understood it (*'aqalnāhā*), and we memorized it (*wa'aynāhā*)		
'Umar fears that a day will come when people will say: By God, we do not find stoning in God's Book.	'Umar fears that a day will come when people will say: By God, we do not find stoning in God's Book.	'Umar fears that a day will come when people will say: By God, we do not find stoning in God's Book.
'Umar says people will thereby abandon religious obligations sent down by God.	'Umar says people will thereby abandon religious obligations sent down by God.	'Umar says people will thereby abandon religious obligations sent down by God.
Conditions: *iḥṣān* plus eyewitness testimony, confession, or pregnancy.	Conditions: *iḥṣān* plus eyewitness testimony, confession, or pregnancy.	Conditions: *iḥṣān* plus eyewitness testimony, confession, or pregnancy.

The textual content is strikingly similar to 'Abd al-Razzāq's report from Ma'mar. An important difference in Ibn Ḥanbal's version is that instead of 'Umar stating that "the Prophet ordered the stoning punishment and we

[66] On general debates about paraphrasing reports, see Ibn al-Ṣalāḥ, *'Ulūm al-ḥadīth*, 213–7, and esp. 216 on the permissibility of summary reports involving legal issues.
[67] Ibn Ḥanbal, *Musnad* (1992 ed.), 1:378, no. 276.

stoned after his death," he states, " . . . we read/recited it (*qara'nā bi-hā*), we understood it (*'aqalnāhā*), and we memorized it (*wa'aynāhā*)." The clause emphasizes the existence of a stoning verse and removes any ambiguity about its importance. What other than an actual verse could be the object of reading/recitation, comprehension, and memorization? The clause is intended to bring into light an actual stoning verse, just as it is brought into light in the PJZO hadith when a Jewish authority removes his hand that was covering it up. Note that the roots of the second verb (*'aqalnāhā*) and the third verb (*wa'aynāhā*) signify "to retain" and "to preserve," and are not synonyms for *ḥifẓ*, which signifies the preservation of something that is sacred or inviolable and cannot be lost. According to the Qur'ān, God will preserve the Qur'ān (Q15:9 and Q85:22) and a derivative of the verb *ḥafiẓa* is employed to convey this sense of preservation. That *ḥafiẓa* is not used in the reports indicates suspicion on the part of transmitters about the verse being part of the Qur'ān.

Although Ibn Ḥanbal's *Musnad* indicates that Mālik is Ibn Mahdī's teacher, there are notable differences between what Mālik states in his *Muwaṭṭa'* and what Ibn Mahdī claims to have received from Mālik. At face value, one could claim that it is difficult to imagine Mālik teaching some of his students (as found in redactions of the *Muwaṭṭa'*) an abridged version of the report he acquired from al-Zuhrī yet giving more details to Ibn Mahdī. It would follow that Ibn Mahdī acquires another version of the report from al-Zuhrī, since he is also a student of al-Zuhrī. But why would he lie? Besides, if he did receive the report from al-Zuhrī, then he could directly cite his famous teacher. Another possibility is that later redactors add elements to Ibn Mahdī's recension and preserve the transmission chain. But it seems highly unlikely that Ibn Mahdī or someone after his lifetime, that is, the third/ninth century, would risk getting caught by making such material amendments or, conversely, no one knowing about it. In fact, the sources cite other students who obtain the hadith from Ibn Mahdī with Mālik in the transmission chain, and have the same textual content as that provided by Ibn Ḥanbal.[68] The most reasonable explanation is, therefore, that the redactors of the *Muwaṭṭa'* are squarely focused on the legal considerations at hand and not the other details that Mālik is teaching. The similarities between the variants recorded by Mālik, 'Abd al-Razzāq, and Ibn Ḥanbal indicate that Mālik, Ma'mar, and 'Abd al-Raḥmān b. Mahdī helped to transmit a report about 'Umar's *zinā*-stoning

[68] al-Khaṭīb al-Baghdādī, *al-Faqīh wa al-mutafaqqih*, 1:247, no. 242.

proclamation. The common attributes—at a minimum—also support al-Zuhrī's involvement in the report's circulation.

An account recorded by Muslim further attests to al-Zuhrī's involvement. Reported by another of al-Zuhrī's pupils, Yūnus b. Yazīd al-Aylī (d. 160/776), the textual content overlaps with the recension narrated by Maʿmar as well as the one narrated by ʿAbd al-Raḥmān b. Mahdī. The transmission chain reads:

> Muslim - Ḥarmala b. Yaḥyā (d. *c.* 243/857) *and* Abū al-Ṭāhir [Aḥmad b. ʿAmr] (d. 250/864) - ʿAbd Allāh b. Wahb (d. 197/813) - Yūnus b. Yazīd al-Aylī - al-Zuhrī[69]

Al-Nasāʾī records the same version with Ibn Wahb in the transmission chain,[70] as does al-Bayhaqī.[71] The high degree of similarities among these two versions points to Ibn Wahb as a common source. The following chart provides a comparison of the textual contents narrated by Yūnus b. Yazīd al-Aylī, ʿAbd al-Raḥmān b. Mahdī, Maʿmar, and Mālik:

Yūnus b. Yazīd al-Aylī - al-Zuhrī	**ʿAbd al-Raḥmān b. Mahdī - (Mālik) - al-Zuhrī**	**Maʿmar - al-Zuhrī**	**Mālik - al-Zuhrī**
ʿUmar delivers the sermon from the pulpit of the Prophet.			
God sent Muḥammad with the Truth and the Book.	God sent Muḥammad and with him the Book.	God sent Muḥammad with the Truth and the Book.	
God revealed the stoning verse.	God revealed the stoning verse.	God revealed the stoning verse.	Stoning is in the Book of God.
The Prophet ordered the stoning punishment and we stoned after his death.		The Prophet ordered the stoning punishment and we stoned after his death.	

69 Muslim, *Ṣaḥīḥ*, 3:1317, no. 15(1,691).
70 al-Nasāʾī, *al-Sunan kubrā*, 6:411f, no. 7,120.
71 al-Bayhaqī, *al-Sunan al-kubrā*, 8:366, no. 16,909.

Yūnus b. Yazīd al-Aylī - al-Zuhrī	**'Abd al-Raḥmān b. Mahdī - (Mālik) - al-Zuhrī**	**Ma'mar - al-Zuhrī**	**Mālik - al-Zuhrī**
'Umar says: . . . we read it/recited it (*qara'nā bi-hā*), we understood it (*'aqalnāhā*), and we memorized it (*wa'aynāhā*).	'Umar says: . . . we read it/recited it (*qara'nā bi-hā*), we understood it (*'aqalnāhā*), and we memorized it (*wa'aynāhā*).		
'Umar fears that a day will come when people will say: By God, we do not find stoning in God's Book.	'Umar fears that a day will come when people will say: By God, we do not find stoning in God's Book.	'Umar fears that a day will come when people will say: By God, we do not find stoning in God's Book.	'Umar fears that a day will come when people will say: By God, we do not find stoning in God's Book.
'Umar says people will thereby abandon religious obligations sent down by God.	'Umar says people will thereby abandon religious obligations sent down by God.	'Umar says people will thereby abandon religious obligations sent down by God.	'Umar says people will thereby abandon religious obligations sent down by God.
Conditions: *iḥṣān* plus eyewitness testimony, confession, or pregnancy.	Conditions: *iḥṣān* plus eyewitness testimony, confession, or pregnancy.	Conditions: *iḥṣān* plus eyewitness testimony, confession, or pregnancy.	Conditions: *iḥṣān* plus eyewitness testimony, confession, or pregnancy.

In Mālik's, Ma'mar's, and Ibn Mahdī's respective versions, it is not entirely clear if 'Umar is talking in a public setting, unless we keep in mind his statement about Abū Bakr's caliphate. But in Yūnus al-Aylī's version, 'Umar delivers a sermon about *zinā*-stoning while standing on the Prophet's pulpit. One can hardly imagine, symbolically, a more appropriate platform for asserting one's authority on a matter of contention. .

Because Muslim provides a collective transmission chain, it is difficult to determine from whom he may have received specific details. Nevertheless, an analysis of the chain yields meaningful results. For instance, concerns existed about Ḥarmala b. Yaḥyā's reliability as a transmitter; yet, at the same time, in Egypt, he was considered among the most knowledgeable.[72] He reportedly narrated from written material, a remark likely made to counter allegations of weaknesses in his transmissions.[73] He is regarded as

[72] al-Mizzī, *Tahdhīb al-kamāl*, 5:550f; al-Dhahabī, *Siyar a'lām*, 11:389.
[73] al-Mizzī, *Tahdhīb al-kamāl*, 5:550–2; al-Dhahabī, *Siyar a'lām*, 11:390.

the most knowledgeable of Ibn Wahb's students, from whom he possessed a thematically arranged collection of Prophetic and non-Prophetic reports (*muṣannaf*).[74] Muslim's other source, Abū al-Ṭāhir, is widely acclaimed as both a transmitter and as a legal authority who wrote a commentary based on Ibn Wahb's collection of reports.[75] In all probability, Muslim records the recension as one report because of the closeness in content that he receives from his two informants and the two men's affiliation with Ibn Wahb. It could also be the case that Muslim wanted to compensate for Ibn Yaḥyā's reputation as a weak transmitter with the inclusion of Abū al-Ṭāhir, especially given the latter's laudatory stature as a reliable and legally authoritative source. Be that as it may, both Ibn Yaḥyā and Abū al-Ṭāhir received a version of the report from their teacher, Ibn Wahb.

ʿAbd Allāh b. Wahb is noted for the manner by which he secures narratives that he acquires from his teachers. Specifically, he distinguishes between reports he preserves through listening only and those he reviews with his teachers after writing them down; he uses both sources to produce *muṣannafs*.[76] It is also worth noting that he compiled a book consisting of al-Zuhrī - Saʿīd b. al-Musayyab transmission chains in which he substituted al-Zuhrī's name for his own.[77] He is also said to have transmitted reports that included al-Zuhrī's *ra'y*, or legal verdicts, and attributed them to Ibn al-Musayyab.[78] In my view, the distinctions noted about the different ways in which Ibn Wahb preserves his reports function to explain why there are inconsistencies in some of his transmissions. His manner of securing reports is to defend his reputation as a reliable narrator.

A few points are to be noted about Ibn Wahb's teacher, Yūnus b. Yazīd al-Aylī. He is accused of making errors when narrating reports that he receives from al-Zuhrī.[79] For instance, Yūnus al-Aylī teaches reports that he claims to have received from al-Zuhrī, when in fact he receives them from ʿUqayl b. Khālid (d. 144/761), also a student of al-Zuhrī's.[80] That Yūnus al-Aylī was known to have made these types of mistakes suggests that he could have received portions of the textual content from

[74] al-Mizzī, *Tahdhīb al-kamāl*, 5:550–2; al-Dhahabī, *Siyar aʿlām*, 11:390.
[75] al-Mizzī, *Tahdhīb al-kamāl*, 1:417; al-Dhahabī, *Siyar aʿlām*, 12:62.
[76] Ibn Ḥibbān, *al-Thiqāt*, 8:346; al-Mizzī, *Tahghīb al-kamāl*, 16:282f; al-Dhahabī, *Siyar aʿlām*, 9:226 and 233.
[77] Ibn Abī Ḥātim, *al-Jarḥ wa al-taʿdīl*, 9:248; al-Mizzī, *Tahdhīb al-kamāl*, 32:555; al-Dhahabī, *Siyar aʿlām*, 6:299; Ibn Ḥajar, *Tahdhīb al-tahdhīb*, 7:275.
[78] al-Mizzī, *Tahdhīb al-kamāl*, 32:555.
[79] al-Mizzī, *Tahdhīb al-kamāl*, 32:555; al-Dhahabī, *Siyar aʿlām*, 6:298.
[80] al-Mizzī, *Tahdhīb al-kamāl*, 32:555; al-Dhahabī, *Siyar aʿlām*, 6:298.

someone other than al-Zuhrī. However, Yūnus al-Aylī is also considered to be one of al-Zuhrī's best students—on par with Mālik and Maʿmar.[81] His relationship with al-Zuhrī is exemplified by a report which states that when al-Zuhrī visited Ayla,[82] he stayed with Yūnus al-Aylī. Yūnus also accompanied al-Zuhrī in some of the latter's travels to Medina.[83] This biographical information—coupled with the high degree of overlap between the versions transmitted by him, Maʿmar, and Ibn Mahdī—points to al-Zuhrī as Yūnus b. al-Aylī's source.

Abū Dāwūd records a version of ʿUmar's *zinā*-stoning report with al-Zuhrī in the transmission chain, which reads:

> ʿAbd Allāh b. Muḥammad al-Nufaylī (d. 234/848) - Hushaym [b. Bashīr al-Qāsim] (d. 183/799) - al-Zuhrī[84]

The following chart compares Hushaym's narrative with versions examined previously. I leave out Mālik's report due to its brevity:

Hushaym [b. Bashīr al-Qāsim] - al-Zuhrī	**Yūnus b. Yazīd al-Aylī - al-Zuhrī**	**ʿAbd al-Raḥmān b. Mahdī - (Mālik) - al-Zuhrī**	**Maʿmar - al-Zuhrī**
ʿUmar delivers a sermon.	ʿUmar delivers the sermon from the pulpit of the Prophet.		
God sent Muḥammad with the Truth and the Book.	God sent Muḥammad with the Truth and the Book.	God sent Muḥammad and with him the Book.	God sent Muḥammad with the Truth and the Book.
God revealed the stoning verse.	God revealed the stoning verse.	God revealed the stoning verse.	God revealed the stoning verse.
The Prophet ordered the stoning punishment and we stoned after his death.	The Prophet ordered the stoning punishment and we stoned after his death.		The Prophet ordered the stoning punishment and we stoned after his death.

[81] Ibn Abī Ḥātim, *al-Jarḥ wa al-taʿdīl*, 32:555f.
[82] Ayla is now known as al-ʿAqaba; see also Yāqūt, *Muʿjam al-buldān*, 1:292f.
[83] Ibn Abī Ḥātim, *al-Jarḥ wa al-taʿdīl*, 9:249; al-Mizzī, *Tahdhīb al-kamāl*, 32:556; al-Dhahabī, *Siyar aʿlām*, 6:300.
[84] Abū Dāwūd, 6:469, no. 4,418.

Hushaym [b. Bashīr al-Qāsim] - al-Zuhrī	**Yūnus b. Yazīd al-Aylī - al-Zuhrī**	**ʻAbd al-Raḥmān b. Mahdī - (Mālik) - al-Zuhrī**	**Maʻmar - al-Zuhrī**
ʻUmar says: . . . we read it/recited it (*qara'nā bi-hā*) and we memorized it (*waʻaynāhā*).	ʻUmar says: . . . we read it/recited it (*qara'nā bi-hā*), we understood it (*ʻaqalnāhā*), and we memorized it (*waʻaynāhā*).	ʻUmar says: . . . we read it/recited it (*qara'nā bi-hā*), we understood it (*ʻaqalnāhā*), and we memorized it (*waʻaynāhā*).	
ʻUmar fears that a day will come when people will say: By God, we do not find stoning in God's Book.	ʻUmar fears that a day will come when people will say: By God, we do not find stoning in God's Book.	ʻUmar fears that a day will come when people will say: By God, we do not find stoning in God's Book.	ʻUmar fears that a day will come when people will say: By God, we do not find stoning in God's Book.
ʻUmar says people will thereby abandon religious obligations sent down by God.	ʻUmar says people will thereby abandon religious obligations sent down by God.	ʻUmar says people will thereby abandon religious obligations sent down by God.	ʻUmar says people will thereby abandon religious obligations sent down by God.
Conditions: *iḥṣān* plus eyewitness testimony, confession, or pregnancy.	Conditions: *iḥṣān* plus eyewitness testimony, confession, or pregnancy.	Conditions: *iḥṣān* plus eyewitness testimony, confession, or pregnancy.	Conditions: *iḥṣān* plus eyewitness testimony, confession, or pregnancy.
ʻUmar asserts: By God, were it not that people would say ʻUmar added something to the Book of God, I surely would have written it down (*katabtuhā*).			

Generally, Hushaym's version strongly resembles the variants examined previously. However, his differs in the following ways:

(1) ʻUmar's statement is part of a sermon he delivers but without the reference to his standing on the Prophet's pulpit;
(2) The text reads, " . . . we read/recited it (*qara'nāhā*) and memorized it (*waʻaynāhā*)." The middle reference to "we understood it (*ʻaqalnāhā*)," as in two other versions, is dropped;
(3) In his closing remarks, ʻUmar asserts, "By God, were it not that people would say, ʻUmar added something to the Book of God, I surely would

> have written it down (*katabtuhā*)." From a jurisprudential standpoint, if indeed a stoning verse existed at one time, then, as noted in Chapter 1, why do some Muslim jurists claim that the Prophet's practice of stoning abrogates the Qur'ān directive of flogging?[85] And, as mentioned before, ʿAlī is remembered to have said that he flogs based on the Qur'ān and orders lapidation based on the Prophet's practice.[86] Setting aside the possible ways in which ʿUmar's statement about a stoning verse complicates certain jurisprudential methods, the provenance of his closing remark has to be in the first/seventh century of Islam. As I stated previously, the emphasis on the Prophet reflects a historical period in which there is a distinction between the Prophet's authority and the Qur'ān's authority. Moreover, ʿUmar's closing statement is a counter to arguments being made after the Qur'ān is standardized, wherein it is absent.

In light of comparative textual content analysis, Abū Dāwūd's version again attests to the pivotal role played by al-Zuhrī in the transmission of the report.

An investigation into the transmission chain recorded by Abū Dāwūd further supports al-Zuhrī's involvement. Abū Dāwūd cites ʿAbd Allāh b. Muḥammad al-Nufaylī, whom he holds in high regard.[87] As for Hushaym b. Bashīr al-Qāsim (d. 183/799), some biographers record that he is reliable,[88] produced *muṣannafs*,[89] and never transcribed reports he received during study sessions.[90] He supposedly possessed between 100 and 300 of al-Zuhrī's transmissions but lost his written copy when a strong gust of wind blew it out of his arms.[91] Much to his dismay, after this incident he could remember only nine of al-Zuhrī's reports.[92] To be sure, these biographical accounts are likely to be apocryphal, perhaps an attempt to explain why he recalls only a

[85] Recall that other jurists argue that *zinā*-stoning, i.e., the Prophetic practice, does not abrogate the Qur'ān but is rather a specificity (*takhṣīṣ*) to the general rule provided via the flogging directive (Q24:2). See Chapter 1, pp. 58–59.
[86] See also, e.g., ʿAbd al-Razzāq, *al-Muṣannaf*, 7:328, no. 13,354; al-Bukhārī, *Ṣaḥīḥ* (1976 ed.), 2498, no. 6,427.
[87] Ibn ʿAsākir, *Tārīkh*, 32:350; al-Mizzī, *Tahdhīb al-kamāl*, 16:90–2; al-Dhahabī, *Siyar aʿlām*, 10:636; Ibn Ḥajar, *Tahdhīb al-tahdhīb*, 3:650. Muḥammad al-Nufaylī is considered a reliable transmitter and a legal authority.
[88] Ibn Saʿd, *al-Ṭabaqāt*, 9:315 and 327; al-Mizzī, *Tahdhīb al-kamāl*, 30:280.
[89] al-Dhahabī, *Siyar aʿlām*, 8:289.
[90] Ibn Sahl, *Tārīkh al-wāsiṭ*, 138.
[91] al-Jurjānī, *al-Kāmil fī ḍuʿafāʾ al-rijāl*, 30:277.
[92] al-Mizzī, *Tahdhīb al-kamāl*, 30:278.

handful of narratives. Furthermore, Ibn Bashīr is alleged to have practiced *tadlīs* (improper citation), for which reason Sufyān al-Thawrī urged people not to record anything from him.[93] Additionally, it is also recorded that Ibn Bashīr narrated from several of al-Zuhrī's students,[94] including Yūnus and ʿAbd al-Raḥmān b. Mahdī, whose recensions are included in the chart above. Ibn Bashīr had a close relationship with ʿAbd al-Raḥmān b. Mahdī[95] and is also reported to have traveled often to Egypt, the primary residence of Yūnus b. al-Aylī, to acquire Prophetic and non-Prophetic reports.[96] The connection between Ibn Bashīr and al-Zuhrī's two students explains the high degree of similarity among their respective versions. On account of Ibn Bashīr being al-Zuhrī's student, I do not see any reason to dismiss his direct acquisition of the report from al-Zuhrī himself, even if Ibn Bashīr learned some details from other students of al-Zuhrī. The student–teacher relationship again points to the latter as someone who helped to circulate ʿUmar's *zinā*-stoning hadith.

Up to this point, I have reviewed the transmission chains and corresponding textual content of several versions of ʿUmar's *zinā*-stoning report on the authority of al-Zuhrī. His recorded students are:

Maʿmar b. Rāshid (d. 153/770);
Yūnus b. Yazīd al-Aylī (d. 160/776);
Mālik (d. 179/795);
Hushaym b. Bashīr al-Qāsim (d. 183/799);
ʿAbd al-Raḥmān b. Mahdī (d. 198/814).

The common textual elements in these versions (with the exception of Mālik's) are:

(1) ʿUmar's claim that stoning was at one time in the Book of God;
(2) ʿUmar's assertion that God sent Muḥammad with the Truth and revealed to him the Book, which included the stoning verse;

[93] Ibn Saʿd, *al-Ṭabaqāt*, 9:315 and 327; al-Jurjānī, *al-Kāmil*, 8:452f and 456; al-Mizzī, *Tahdhīb al-kamāl*, 30:283.
[94] al-Jurjānī, *al-Kāmil*, 8:452.
[95] Ibn Abī Ḥātim, *al-Jarḥ wa al-taʿdīl*, 9:115; al-Jurjānī, *al-Kāmil*, 8:453; al-Mizzī, *Tahdhīb al-kamāl*, 30:281f; al-Dhahabī, *Siyar aʿlām*, 8:290.
[96] Ibn Abī Ḥātim, *al-Jarḥ wa al-taʿdīl*, 9:115; al-Jurjānī, *al-Kāmil*, 8:453; al-Mizzī, *Tahdhīb al-kamāl*, 30:281f; al-Dhahabī, *Siyar aʿlām*, 8:290.

(3) ʿUmar's insistence that, "The Messenger of God ordered the stoning punishment and we stoned after [his death]";
(4) ʿUmar's fear that a time will come when people will deny the existence of the stoning verse;
(5) ʿUmar's fear that failure to stone will reflect the community's failure to fulfill a divinely revealed obligation;
(6) ʿUmar's enumeration of the necessary conditions for stoning: *iḥṣān,* in addition to testimony, confession.

Textual elements specific to one or another of the various versions of the report include:

(7) ʿUmar mentions *zinā*-stoning in a sermon;
(8) ʿUmar delivers this sermon from the Prophet's pulpit in Medina;
(9) ʿUmar's statement that the stoning verse was "read/recited, understood, and memorized" by the community;
(10) ʿUmar's explanation for why he made no effort to ensure that the stoning verse was included in the Qur'ān: "By God, were it not that people would say, ''Umar added something to the Book of God,' I surely would have written it down (*katabtuhā*)."

Other versions with al-Zuhrī in the transmission chains also exist in the sources that help with establishing the provenance of elements seven through ten. Al-Nasā'ī records three versions from three different pupils of al-Zuhrī's: Bishr b. ʿUmar (d. 206/821),[97] ʿAbd Allāh b. Abī Bakr [b. Ḥazm] (d. *c.* 135/752),[98] and ʿAbd Allāh b. Wahb (d. 197/813).[99] The textual content related by the first two are virtually identical to those transmitted by Maʿmar and ʿAbd al-Raḥmān b. Mahdī (via Mālik). Ibn Wahb, the third pupil, states that he received the report from both Mālik *and* Yūnus b. Yazīd al-Aylī. The fact that the textual content of Ibn Wahb's version is almost indistinguishable from that of Yūnus al-Aylī in Muslim's *Ṣaḥīḥ*[100] means that Ibn Wahb had access to a written source. In addition, Sufyān b. ʿUyayna transmits versions of the report once on the authority of Maʿmar and twice on the authority of al-Zuhrī. Each version has one of first six elements identified above and, when

[97] al-Nasā'ī, *al-Sunan al-kubrā*, 6:411, no. 7,119.
[98] al-Nasā'ī, *al-Sunan al-kubrā*, 6:412, no. 7,121.
[99] al-Nasā'ī, *al-Sunan al-kubrā*, 6:411f, no. 7,120.
[100] See above, p. 274.

taken together, we find all six elements. In my view, the transmission process led to the differences in the three versions disseminated on Ibn ʿUyayna's authority.[101] In sum, the analysis of several versions of the report on the authority of al-Zuhrī points to him as someone who narrated the ten elements identified above.

The presentation of Ibn Shihāb al-Zuhrī's relevant biographical notes in Chapter 2 and the connections brought out in this section establish al-Zuhrī's central role in disseminating the *zinā*-stoning narrative involving ʿUmar. The sources confirm that al-Zuhrī studied with, and transmitted several narratives from, ʿUbayd Allāh b. ʿUtba (d. c. 98/716), the source of al-Zuhrī for ʿUmar's report. In fact, a considerable amount of what we know about ʿUbayd Allāh's biography is due to al-Zuhrī,[102] which suggests that the two men knew one another. As for ʿUbayd Allāh, he is deemed to be one of the most proficient legal authorities of his time and is identified as one of the seven prominent jurists of Medina.[103] His concern about reports being incorrectly attributed to him prompted his demand that no one transmit anything in his name that was not specifically received in his presence, a rather surprising demand given the number of students a jurist of his caliber is likely to attract.[104] In addition to the considerations I mention about the textual content and how they help to date the provenance of the report, it follows from the transmission chain survey that ʿUmar's *zinā*-stoning report was in circulation by the end of the first/seventh century with Ibn ʿAbbās as the source—a point that I substantiate with additional reports in the proceeding sections.

4.3.2. Reports on the Authority of Yūsuf b. Mihrān (d. *c.* 109/727)

In this subsection, I present and examine variants circulated on the authority of Yūsuf b. Mihrān, a Persian *mawlā* of the Quraysh who, like ʿUbayd Allāh, is a student of Ibn ʿAbbās. The sources portray Ibn Mihrān as someone

[101] For his report from Maʿmar, see al-Ḥumaydī, *Musnad*, 1:161:25; for his reports on the direct authority of al-Zuhrī, see al-Bukhārī, *Ṣaḥīḥ* (1976 ed.), 6:2503, no. 6,441 and al-Mawṣilī, *Musnad*, 1:141, no. 12.

[102] E.g., see al-Dhahabī, *Siyar aʿlām*, 4:481f.

[103] *Encyclopaedia of Islam* 2nd ed., s.v. "Fuḳahāʾ"; al-Mizzī, *Tahdhīb al-kamal*, 19:73.

[104] Ibn Abī Ḥātim, *al-Jarḥ wa al-taʿdīl*, 5:320; al-Mizzī, *Tahdhīb al-kamāl*, 19:76; al-Dhahabī, *Siyar aʿlām*, 4:480.

not as well-known as 'Ubayd Allāh, which may explain why his version is not widely circulated.[105] Taken on its own merits, as well as in comparison to 'Ubayd Allāh's recension, Ibn Mihrān's version substantiates that 'Umar *zinā*-stoning report was circulating in the first/seventh century of Islam by Ibn 'Abbās.

The source material indicates that Ibn Mihrān's version circulated exclusively due to the efforts of 'Alī b. Zayd b. Jud'ān (d. *c.* 131/748). A recension of his transmission appears in the *Musnad* of al-Ṭayālisī (d. 204/819):

> Ḥammād b. Zayd (d. 179/795) - 'Alī b. Zayd b. Jud'ān - Yūsuf b. Mihrān:
>
> Ibn 'Abbās preached from the pulpit in Baṣra and said: People, indeed 'Umar b. al-Khaṭṭāb once stood before us and said, 'People, stoning is one of the fixed punishments (*ḥudūd*), so whatever you do, do not be deceived about it. It was in the Book of God and the practice of your Prophet. The Messenger of God ordered the stoning punishment, Abū Bakr stoned, and I stoned.'[106]

This version includes elements that have not been observed previously. The following is a comparison of Ibn Jud'ān's (d. *c.* 131/748) and Hushaym b. Bashīr's (d. 183/799) respective variants:[107]

Ḥammād b. Zayd - 'Alī b. Zayd b. Jud'ān - Yūsuf b. Mihrān	**Hushaym [b. Bashīr al-Qāsim] - al-Zuhrī - 'Ubayd Allāh**
Ibn 'Abbās delivers a sermon in Baṣra.	'Umar delivers a sermon.
	God sent Muḥammad with the Truth and the Book.
Stoning is one of the *ḥudūd* punishments.	
Stoning was in the Book of God.	Stoning was in the Book of God.

[105] Recall Motzki's point that, quantitatively, biographical dictionaries do not provide as much information on *mawlās*/non-Arabs as they do on Arabs. This phenomenon may explain the scarcity of information on Ibn Mihrān. See Chapter 2, pp. 150–151; on Yūsuf b. Mihrān's and the Mihrān family's impact on early Muslim dogma, see generally Parvaneh Pourshariati, "The Mihrāns and Their Articulation of Early Muslim Dogma."

[106] al-Ṭayālisī, *Musnad*, 1:29f, no. 25; Ibn Abī Shayba records a similar report in which Ibn Mihrān says, "Stoning is one of the *ḥudūd* of God, so do not be deceived about it. The Messenger of God ordered the stoning punishment, Abū Bakr stoned, and I stoned." This report does not have the motif about the punishment being in the Book of God. This is likely due to transmission error since it is found in the textual content of several other versions concerning 'Umar and his claim about *zinā*-stoning. See Ibn Abī Shayba, *al-Muṣannaf* (2008 ed.), 9:355, no. 29,358.

[107] I utilize Hushaym b. Bashīr's recension because of its comprehensiveness.

Ḥammād b. Zayd - ʿAlī b. Zayd b. Judʿān - Yūsuf b. Mihrān	**Hushaym [b. Bashīr al-Qāsim] - al-Zuhrī - ʿUbayd Allāh**
The Prophet ordered the stoning punishment, Abū Bakr stoned, and I stoned.	The Prophet ordered the stoning punishment and we stoned [after his death].
	ʿUmar says: . . . we read it/recited it (*qaraʾnā bi-hā*) and we memorized it (*waʿaynāhā*).
A warning not to be deceived about stoning.	ʿUmar fears that a day will come when people will say: "By God, we do not find stoning in God's Book."
	ʿUmar says people will thereby abandon religious obligations sent by God.
	Conditions: *iḥṣān* plus eyewitness testimony, confession, or pregnancy.
	ʿUmar asserts, By God, were it not that people would say ʿUmar added something to the Book of God, I surely would have written it down (*katabtuhā*).

Among other things, in Ibn Mihrān's version, we find:

(1) The assertion, " . . . stoning is one of the fixed punishments (*ḥudūd*)," which identifies *zinā*-stoning as a *ḥadd* punishment. Given that the *ḥudūd* came to be understood as the rights of God, transmitters are portraying ʿUmar's statement as an attempt to steer *zinā*-stoning toward divine legitimacy;

(2) There is also the presence of a warning, " . . . whatever you do, do not be deceived about it," which, in my view, represents other versions of the report in which ʿUmar fears that people will deny the existence of stoning in the Book of God, as well as stray and neglect their religious obligations.

(3) The declaration, "The Messenger of God ordered the stoning punishment, Abū Bakr stoned, and I stoned," is a clear reformulation of ʿUmar's remark in some other versions, "The Messenger of God ordered the stoning punishment, and we stoned after [after his death]."

Of consequential note is that in Ibn Mihrān's version, it is Ibn ʿAbbās who delivers the sermon. Indeed, the differences in Ibn Mihrān's variant may be explained by the fact that Ibn Abbās is speaking about something that happened approximately twenty years earlier, meaning, there would naturally be variations due to an oral transmission process. The broader point to note is that the report further establishes the role of Ibn ʿAbbās in the circulation of an account regarding ʿUmar's purported statement about *zinā*-stoning. This observation is important because, as I argue below, it is Ibn ʿAbbas who is the source of Saʿīd b. al-Musayyab's recension and not ʿUmar himself, as the transmission chain(s) indicate.

ʿAbd al-Razzāq preserves a recension on Maʿmar's authority that has Ibn Mihrān in the transmission chain and includes several elements found in the variant recorded by al-Ṭayālisī. The entry reads:

> Maʿmar b. Rāshid (d. 153/770) - ʿAlī b. Zayd b. Judʿān - Yūsuf b. Mihrān - Ibn ʿAbbās:
>
> ʿUmar b. al-Khattab instructed someone to make the call to prayer (*adhān*), which was then made. ʿUmar then climbed up on the pulpit, praised God, and said: "People, whatever you do, do not be deceived about the stoning verse for it was revealed in the Book of God. We read it/recited it but it perished (*dhahabat*) along with many other verses of the Qur'ān when Muḥammad died. One sign of the verse is that the Prophet ordered the stoning punishment, as did Abū Bakr, and as I did after them. However, a group of people from this Community will come (*sa-yajīʾu*) and lie about stoning, just as they will lie about the sun rising from the west,[108] intercession,[109] the watering trough (*al-ḥawḍ*),[110] the *dajjāl*,[111] torment in the grave,[112] and a people who exit the fire after having been placed in it."[113]

The Maʿmar-Ibn Judʿān-Ibn Mihrān line includes religio-ideological (eschatological) matters as a function of creedal dispositions. The particular

[108] This refers to one of the major signs that, in the hadith tradition, is supposed to precede the Day of Resurrection. On this, see *Encyclopaedia of Islam* 2nd ed., s.v. "Sāʿa."

[109] This refers to the Sunnī belief, established in the hadith tradition that, Muhammad will intercede on behalf of Muslim sinners, whereby they will be spared divine punishment. On this, see *Encyclopaedia of Islam* 2nd ed., s.v. "S̲h̲afāʿa;" W. Montgomery Watt, *The Formative Period*, 138.

[110] The basin at which on the day of the resurrection Muḥammad will meet his community. On this, see *Encyclopaedia of Islam* 2nd ed., s.v. "Ḥawḍ."

[111] This refers to the personage endowed with miraculous powers who will arrive before the end of time and rule the world with tyranny, following which Jesus will return to Earth, end his rule, and engineer a universal conversion to Islam. On this, see *Encyclopaedia of Islam* 2nd ed., s.v., "al-Dad̲j̲d̲j̲āl."

[112] This refers to the idea, once again, proposed in the Sunnī hadith tradition, in which human beings maintain a certain kind of existence after death in the grave. Unbelievers and sinners live a life of torment, whereas believers live a life of grace. On this, see *Encyclopaedia of Islam* 2nd ed., s.v. "ʿAd̲h̲āb al-Ḳabr."

[113] ʿAbd al-Razzāq, *al-Muṣannaf*, 7:330, no. 13,364.

elements in the textual content point to an environment in which such issues intertwine with identity politics. Among them is the point regarding the intercession of Muḥammad. Ḍirār b. ʿAmr (d. 215/745), a figure associated with the emerging Muʿtazilī movement, rejected the Prophet's intercession on the Day of Judgment.[114] Then there is the remark about "people who exit the fire after having been placed in it." This refers to the eventual Sunnī belief against those of certain groups, such as the Muʿtazila and the *Shurāt* (*Khawārij*), that Muslim sinners and heretics will, after a short internment in Hell, be allowed to enter into and enjoy Paradise.[115] As noted in the previous section, here the textual content infers ongoing debates about the acceptance and utilization of hadith in establishing theological positions. Both the versions by ʿAbd al-Razzāq and the one provided by al-Ṭayālisī, which includes a reference to *zinā*-stoning as a *ḥadd* punishment, illustrate how a previously established concept is being denied on "spurious" grounds, similar to the current denial of specific beliefs by certain groups. Also note that the intent undergirding the hadith should not come as a surprise, given that members of the Miḥrān family, such as Yūsuf b. Mihrān, are recorded to have played important roles to help establish Islamic dogmas.[116]

The following chart refers to the three reports, one on the authority of Ibn Judʿān and one on that of al-Zuhrī, both of which are transmitted by Maʿmar, and a version on the authority of Ḥammād b. Zayd (from al-Ṭayālisī):

Maʿmar - Ibn Judʿān - Ibn Mihrān	**Maʿmar - al-Zuhrī - ʿUbayd Allāh**	**Ḥammād b. Zayd - Ibn Judʿān - Yūsuf b. Mihrān**
ʿUmar delivers a sermon.	ʿUmar delivers a sermon.	Ibn ʿAbbās delivers a sermon.
	God sent Muḥammad with the Truth and the Book.	
		Stoning is one of the *ḥudūd* punishments.
Stoning was in the Book of God.	Stoning was in the Book of God.	Stoning was in the Book of God.

[114] van Ess, *Theology and Society*, vol. 3, 58; on the Muʿtazila, see, e.g., van Ess, "The Rise of the Muʿtazila," in *Theology and Society*, vol. 3, 33–99.

[115] On this, see *Encyclopaedia of Islam* 2nd ed., s.v. "al-Manzila Bayn al-Manzilatayn"; Watt, *The Formative Period*, 141.

[116] Pourshariati, "The Mihrāns and Their Articulation of Early Muslim Dogma," 15 and 17.

Ma'mar - Ibn Jud'ān - Ibn Mihrān	Ma'mar - al-Zuhrī - 'Ubayd Allāh	Ḥammād b. Zayd - Ibn Jud'ān - Yūsuf b. Mihrān
		Stoning was the practice of the Prophet.
We read it/recited it.		
The Prophet ordered the stoning punishment, Abū Bakr stoned, and I stoned.	The Prophet ordered the stoning punishment and we stoned [after his death].	The Prophet ordered the stoning punishment, Abū Bakr stoned, and I stoned.
'Umar claims that a day will come when people will lie about stoning just as they did about other theological matters.	'Umar fears that a day will come when people will say: By God, we do not find stoning in God's Book.	
A warning not to be deceived about stoning.	'Umar says people will abandon religious obligations sent by God.	A warning not to be deceived about stoning.
	Conditions: *iḥṣān* plus eyewitness testimony, confession, or pregnancy.	

Ma'mar transmits the report with two different transmission chains. His version from Ibn Jud'ān is not the same as that from al-Zuhrī. Had Ma'mar himself been responsible for the textual contents of the two respective reports, he could have amended them to mirror one another. The differences suggest that Ma'mar taught 'Abd al-Razzāq what he received from two different teachers. This, in turn, means that we have on our hands a historical transmission line between Ma'mar and 'Alī b. Zayd b. Jud'ān (d. c. 131/748).

Al-Mawṣilī (d. 307/919) records a version that is strikingly similar to the report transmitted by Ma'mar.[117] In this variant, Ḥammād b. Salama (d. 167/784), Ibn Jud'ān's pupil and a well-known transmitter, is in place of Ma'mar.[118] The transmission chain reads:

Ḥammād b. Salama - 'Alī b. Zayd al-Jud'ān - Yūsuf b. Mihrān - Ibn 'Abbās

The only noteworthy difference between Ibn Salama's and Ma'mar's respective versions is that in the former's account, 'Umar does not say that he and others read/recited the stoning verse. The reading/reciting clause is omitted

[117] al-Mawṣilī, *Musnad*, 1:136, no. 7/146.
[118] al-Mizzī, *Tahdhīb al-kamāl*, 7:259 and 262–5; al-Dhahabī, *Siyar a'lām*, 7:444ff.

by a narrator in Ibn Salama's transmission. Importantly, this version affirms Ibn Jud'ān as the common source.

As for 'Alī b. Zayd b. Jud'ān (d. *c.* 131/748), evidence points to his teaching of the report to his students. Some critics consider him to be a weak narrator and that his transmissions did not have any value, legal or otherwise.[119] But these comments may be linked to the fact that he was portrayed as an extremist Shī'ī.[120] By contrast, others acknowledged him as a reliable legal authority.[121] In fact, the well-known Sufyān b. 'Uyayna (d. 198/813) supposedly compiled a book of narratives based on Ibn Jud'ān's authority.[122] Ibn 'Uyayna receives high praise from al-Shāfi'ī, Ibn Ma'īn (d. 233/847), Ibn Ḥanbal,[123] and al-Dhahabī (d. 748/1348), who called him "Shaykh al-Islam."[124] For someone of Ibn 'Uyayna's stature to preserve a book by a transmitter who is possibly as weak as Ibn Jud'ān would have raised concerns among hadith critics, be they Ibn Uyayna's contemporaries or not. To the best of my knowledge, there is nothing in the sources to suggest that there is a controversy about Ibn 'Uyayna's endorsement of Ibn Jud'ān's transmissions. It is, therefore, reasonable to surmise that the transmission chain accurately portrays Ibn Jud'ān and his involvement.

Evidence points to Yūsuf b. Mihrān's (d. *c.* 109/727) teaching of 'Umar's *zinā*-stoning report on the authority of Ibn 'Abbās. In the biographical sources, it is noted that Ibn Mihrān's teaching methods prominently feature the use of written notes.[125] This remark should be viewed as a critique. During his lifetime, it was meritorious in Baṣra for transmitters to recite from memory.[126] Relevant to the present analysis, some biographers remark that no one other than Ibn Jud'ān transmits from Ibn Mihrān.[127] On the basis

[119] Ibn Sa'd, *al-Ṭabaqāt*, 9:251; Ibn Abī Ḥātim, *al-Jarḥ wa al-ta'dīl*, 6:186f; al-Mizzī, *Tahdhīb al-kamāl*, 20:437–9; Ibn Ḥajar, *Tahdhīb al-tahdhīb*, 4:599.

[120] al-Jurjānī, *Kāmil*, 6:335; al-Mizzī, *Tahdhīb al-kamāl*, 20:439; Ibn Ḥajar, *Tahdhīb al-tahdhīb*, 4:599; an investigation of Shī'ī extremism during Ibn Jud'ān's life time is a scholarly desideratum.

[121] al-Mizzī, *Tahdhīb al-kamāl*, 20:442f; Ibn Ḥajar, *Tahdhīb al-tahdhīb*, 4:599f.

[122] al-Mizzī, *Tahdhīb al-kamāl*, 20:441; Ibn Ḥajar, *Tahdhīb al-tahdhīb*, 4:600.

[123] al-Mizzī, *Tahdhīb al-kamāl*, 11:190; al-Dhahabī, *Siyar a'lām*, 8:457.

[124] al-Dhahabī, *Siyar a'lām*, 8:454. Al-Dhahabī uses "Shaykh al-Islam" conservatively to signify a specific group of elite scholars. The qualities shared by such scholars, in accordance with al-Dhahabī's standards, are (1) the person is a qualified Imām, (2) known for his overt rejection of *kalām* (commonly translated as speculative theology), (3) with expertise in at least two of the following disciplines: (a) Qur'ān readings, (b) *ḥadīth* textual criticism, (c) *ḥadīth*-transmitter criticism, or (d) jurisprudence; and finally, (4) a "moderate Sufi." See Lucas, *Constructive Critics*, 55–61.

[125] Ibn Abī Ḥātim, *al-Jarḥ wa al-ta'dīl*, 9:229; al-Mizzī, *Tahdhīb al-kamāl*, 32:463; Ibn Ḥajar, *Tahdhīb al-tahdhīb*, 7:249.

[126] Schoeler, *The Oral and Written in Early Islam*, 114f.

[127] Ibn Ma'īn, *al-Tārīkh*, 4:325, no. 4,614; Ibn Abī Ḥātim, *al-Jarḥ wa al-ta'dīl*, 9:229; al-Mizzī, *Tahdhīb al-kamāl*, 32:463; Ibn Ḥajar, *Tahdhīb al-tahdhīb*, 7:249.

of this student–teacher connection, one can argue that Ibn Mihrān's report is a neat forgery. If Ibn 'Abbās did in fact make such a public statement, we should find more attestations than a single pass through Ibn Mihrān and Ibn Jud'ān. This claim is questionable. The absence of several transmission lines is not indicative of a forgery. Furthermore, we have other works, such as that of al-Ṭabarī, which provide evidence of a historical connection between Ibn Jud'ān and Ibn Mihrān. In al-Ṭabarī's *History*, they appear in the transmission chains of reports provided by his immediate teachers.[128] Finally, there are some narratives with transmission chains affirming a connection between Ibn Mihrān and others, such as the Persian al-Ḥasan al-Baṣrī (d. 110/728).[129] Hence, the respective student–teacher links between Ibn Jud'ān, Ibn Mihrān, and Ibn 'Abbās point to Ibn 'Abbās' circulation of a report about 'Umar's public endorsement of *zinā*-stoning.

4.4. Reports On the Authority of Sa'īd b. al-Musayyab (d. *c.* 94/712)

In this section, I conduct an analysis of a version of the narrative transmitted on the authority of Sa'īd b. al-Musayyab. I explore the transmission chain and corresponding textual content of the variant put into circulation by his student, Yaḥyā b. Sa'īd al-Anṣārī (d. 143/760). I also examine a recension on the authority of another of Ibn al-Musayyab's students, Dāwūd b. Abī Hind (d. *c.* 139/756). In my estimation, while Ibn al-Musayyab did narrate 'Umar's *zinā*-stoning report, which affirms the provenance of the report in the first/seventh century, he did not directly hear—as suggested by the transmission chains—'Umar speak about the matter. His actual informant is Ibn 'Abbās.

Mālik (d. 179/795) provides a recension on Ibn al-Musayyab's authority. The transmission chain is: Yaḥyā b. Sa'īd - Sa'īd b. al-Musayyab. The textual content reads:

> After leaving Minā, 'Umar b. al-Khaṭṭāb made a stop at al-Abṭaḥ.[130] He then made a pile of pebbles and threw his cloak over it. He laid down and used

[128] E.g., see al-Ṭabarī, *Tārīkh* (History), 1:181 and 269; Pourshariati, "The Mihrāns and Their Articulation of Early Muslim Dogma," 8f.

[129] Ibn 'Asākir, *Tārīkh*, 64:193f; "The Mihrāns and Their Articulation of Early Muslim Dogma," 28.

[130] Also known as Wādī al-Muḥaṣṣab, al-Abṭaḥ is a valley that a pilgrim to Mecca encounters on the way back to the sacred city after fulfilling the pilgrimage rites at Minā, which lies some four miles to the east. The Prophet was known to have made a stop there during his final pilgrimage, following which he rendered his famous 'Farewell Sermon (*khuṭba al-wadā'*). For more information, see *Encyclopaedia Islamica*, s.v. "Al-Abṭaḥ."

> the pile to rest his head. He raised his hands to the sky and said: "God, I have grown old and weak, and my flock has expanded far and wide. Take me to Yourself as someone who has not wasted Your blessings or neglected his duties." 'Umar arrived in Medina near the end of Dhū al-Ḥijja and delivered the Friday sermon. He said: "People! You have before you the example set by the paragons of old (*sunan*). The onus is upon you to ensure that your duty to religion is fulfilled! The path forward has been made clear to you—it is your responsibility not to let others divert you from your destination!" He then clasped his hands together, as if to summon the congregation's attention. Then 'Umar said: "People, take heed! Do not fall into perdition by neglecting the stoning verse! Let not one of you say, 'We do not find two fixed punishments (*ḥaddayn*) in the Book of God, may God be blessed and exalted.' Indeed, the Messenger of God ordered the stoning punishment as did we [after his death]. I swear by God, in whose hand is my soul, were it not for the fact that people would say, "Umar b. al-Khaṭṭāb tampered with the Book of God,' I would have had written down: '*Al-shaykh* and *al-shaykha*, stone them both without wavering.' We had surely read it/recited it (*qara'nāhā*)."[131]

The opening section, wherein an aged 'Umar is portrayed as stopping at al-Abṭaḥ and praying to God, functions as a literary-mnemonic device that frames the sermon about the stoning punishment. It serves both to contextualize his purported public address and to ensure its memorability, consistent with the oral/aural tradition and rhetorical techniques of early Islamic literature.[132] The depiction of 'Umar's prayer highlights the culmination of his life struggles and as a leader burdened with responsibilities, setting the stage for the sermon's moral, theological, and legal significance. The scene at al-Abṭaḥ serves as a conceptual anchor, embedding the sermon's message within a vividly relatable moment of reflection and prayer.[133] For the remainder of the textual content, the following chart provides a comparison of Ibn al-Musayyab's version with other previously examined recensions:

[131] Mālik, *Muwaṭṭa'*, 5:1,203, no. 631; Ibn Ḥanbal records versions that focus on one aspect of Mālik's report in which 'Umar states, "People, take care not to ignore the stoning verse. And beware of those who say, 'We do not find two fixed punishments (*ḥaddayn*) in the Book of God, may God be blessed and exalted.' Indeed, the Messenger of God ordered the stoning punishment as did we [after his death]." See Ibn Ḥanbal, *Musnad* (1992 ed.), 1:362f, no. 249 and 1:394, no. 302.

[132] See generally Rashwan, "Hadith as Oral Literature."

[133] Rashwan, "Hadith as Oral Literature," 37.

Yaḥyā b. Saʿīd - Ibn al-Musayyab	**Maʿmar - Ibn Judʿān - Ibn Mihrān**	**Ḥammād b. Zayd - Ibn Judʿān - Yūsuf b. Mihrān**	**al-Zuhrī - ʿUbayd Allāh**
ʿUmar delivers a sermon.	ʿUmar delivers a sermon.	Ibn ʿAbbās delivers a sermon.	ʿUmar delivers a sermon.
			God sent Muḥammad with the Truth and the Book.
ʿUmar says that traditions have been established and religious obligations have been made compulsory.		Stoning was the practice of the Prophet.	
ʿUmar says: People, beware of straying from the stoning verse.	A warning not to be deceived about stoning.	A warning not to be deceived about stoning.	ʿUmar says people will abandon religious obligations sent by God.
ʿUmar warns about those who say: We do not find two fixed punishments (*ḥaddayn*) in the Book of God.	ʿUmar claims that a day will come when people will deny stoning just as they do about other theological matters.	Stoning is one of the *ḥudūd* punishments.	ʿUmar fears that a day will come when people will say: By God, we do not find stoning in God's Book.
The Messenger of God ordered the stoning punishment and we stoned [after his death].	The Prophet ordered the stoning punishment, Abū Bakr stoned, and I stoned.	The Prophet ordered the stoning punishment, Abū Bakr stoned, and I stoned.	The Messenger of God ordered the stoning punishment and we stoned [after his death].
"I have surely read it/recited it."	"We read it/recited it."		"We read it/recited it (*qaraʾnā bi-hā*), we understood it (*ʿaqalnāhā*), and we memorized it (*waʿaynāhā*)."
			Conditions: *iḥṣān* plus eyewitness testimony, confession, or pregnancy.

Yaḥyā b. Sa'īd - Ibn al-Musayyab	Ma'mar - Ibn Jud'ān - Ibn Mihrān	Ḥammād b. Zayd - Ibn Jud'ān - Yūsuf b. Mihrān	al-Zuhrī - 'Ubayd Allāh
'Umar asserts, "Were it not for the fact that people would say, "Umar b. al-khaṭṭāb added to the Book of God,' I would have written: 'Al-shakyh and *al-shaykha*, stone them both without wavering."			'Umar asserts, "By God, were it not that people would say 'Umar added something to the Book of God, I surely would have written it down (*katabtuhā*)."

Ibn al-Musayyab's narrative of 'Umar's *zinā*-stoning report has several elements found in the respective versions transmitted by al-Zuhrī, who is 'Ubayd Allāh's student, and Ibn Jud'ān, who is Ibn Mihrān's student. We are thus dealing with a common source. In my view, it is Ibn 'Abbās. The following transmission chain analysis supports my assertion.

Mālik's entry cited above is from the redaction of the *Muwaṭṭa'* on Yaḥyā's authority. It is reported that while he was living in Medina, Yaḥyā b. Sa'īd asked Mālik to bring him a compilation of reports that he could use to teach after moving to Baghdād.[134] This is indicative of the teacher–student relationship between the two transmitters. Their relationship can also be deduced by the fact that Mālik is one of the main sources of biographical information on Yaḥyā.[135] Some aspects about Yaḥyā may raise doubts about his version of the transmission chain and textual content. He reportedly transmitted between three hundred and three thousand Prophetic and non-Prophetic reports.[136] One might argue that the sheer size of his corpus increases the statistical probability of error. This argument, however, is diminished by the fact that other authorities corroborate Yaḥyā's transmissions. For instance, the same report is in the redaction of the *Muwaṭṭa'* on Muḥammad al-Shaybānī's authority.[137] The high degree of similarity between the two versions attest to Mālik being Yaḥyā's and al-Shaybānī's common source. Indeed, Yaḥyā b. Sa'īd was a respected transmitter and jurist, served as a judge,[138] and was

[134] Ibn Sa'd, *al-Ṭabaqāt*, 7:518.
[135] E.g., see al-Mizzī, *Tahdhīb al-kamāl*, 31:352.
[136] al-Dhahabī, *Siyar a'lām*, 5:475.
[137] Mālik, *Muwaṭṭa'*, narration of al-Shaybānī, 220, no. 693.
[138] Yaḥyā's judgeship was in Baghdād, Medina, or al-Hāshimiyya. For Medina, see Ibn Sa'd, *al-Ṭabaqāt*, 7:518; al-Bukhārī, *al-Tārīkh*, 8:275, no. 2,980; Ibn Abī Ḥātim, *al-Jarḥ wa al-ta'dīl*, 9:148;

considered by some to be on par with, or better than, al-Zuhrī.[139] Finally, it is also worth mentioning Ibn al-Musayyab himself supported *zinā*-stoning,[140] a fact that is verified by Yaḥyā b. Saʿīd.[141] Given Ibn al-Musayyab's stance on *zinā*-stoning, it is reasonable that Yaḥyā b. Saʿīd would transmit *zinā*-stoning reports to reinforce his own claim.

Certain comments in biographical dictionaries could raise questions about the reliability of transmissions by Yaḥyā b. Saʿīd, but I do not believe such remarks disqualify his accuracy in the general sense. Specifically, it is recorded that he had a reputation for providing an inaccurate account of his sources (*tadlīs*).[142] On the basis of *tadlīs*, it is possible that he could have received ʿUmar's stoning report from someone other than Ibn al-Musayyab even if Ibn al-Musayyab's name made its way into his transmission chain. This scenario is possible because he reportedly narrated from al-Zuhrī and from the seven jurists of Medina, including Ibn al-Musayyab and ʿUbayd Allāh, who is al-Zuhrī's source for ʿUmar's stoning report that I reviewed in the previous section.[143] That Yaḥyā b. Saʿīd could have practiced *tadlīs* with the report under investigation may be plausible given that he is recorded to have erroneously included Ibn al-Musayyab's name in the transmission chain of a report.[144] And in another case, he cited Ibn al-Musayyab as his source when he supposedly acquired the report from al-Zuhrī.[145] In my view, it need not follow from Yaḥyā's inaccuracy in two transmissions that *a priori* there are errors in many of the transmission chains he cites. On the basis of my analysis in this chapter, there is no reason to reject Ibn al-Musayyab as his source.

In recensions provided by Ibn Abī Shayba,[146] al-Tirmidhī,[147] and al-Bayhaqī,[148] Dāwūd b. Abī Hind (d. *c.* 139/756) is in place of Yaḥyā b. Saʿīd as Ibn al-Musayyab's student. All of the versions contain motifs found in the

for Baghdād and al-Hāshimiyya, see al-Baghdādī, *Tārīkh*, 16:155–8; al-Mizzī, *Tahdhīb al-kamāl*, 31:351.

[139] Ibn Saʿd, *al-Ṭabaqāt*, 7:518; al-Mizzī, *Tahdhīb al-kamāl*, 31:351; al-Dhahabī, *Siyar aʿlām*, 5:472 and 474f; Ibn Ḥajar, *Tahdhīb al-tahdhīb*, 7:49.

[140] Ibn Abī Shayba, *al-Muṣannaf* (2008 ed.), 9:347, no. 29,324 and 9:349, no. 29,334.

[141] ʿAbd al-Razzāq, *al-Muṣannaf*, 3:536, no. 6,621 and 7:323, no. 13,342 and 364, no. 13,489.

[142] Ibn Ḥajar, *Tahdhīb al-tahdhīb*, 7:50.

[143] Ibn Ḥajar, *Tahdhīb al-tadhīb*, 7:48; al-Dhahabī, *Siyar aʿlām*, 5:470.

[144] al-ʿUqaylī, *Kitāb al-ḍuʿafa'*, 2:36f, no. 461.

[145] Abū Muḥammad ʿAbd al-Raḥmān b. Abī Ḥātim, *Kitāb al-ʿilal*, Saʿd b. ʿAbd Allāh al-Ḥumaydī and khālid b. ʿAbd al-Raḥmān al-juraysī (eds.), 7 vols. (Riyāḍ: Maṭābiʿ al-juraysī, 2006) 3:83f, no. 708.

[146] Ibn Abī Shayba, *al-Muṣannaf* (2008 ed.), 9:355, no. 29,357.

[147] al-Tirmidhī, *al-Jāmiʿ*, 3:101, no. 1,431.

[148] al-Bayhaqī, *al-Sunan al-kubrā*, 8:370, no. 16,922.

textual contents of Yaḥyā's report, although at times using different language. For example, all three versions have ʿUmar stating that the Prophet ordered the stoning punishment just as Abū Bakr and himself. Neither al-Tirmidhī's nor al-Bayhaqī's respective versions have a reference to *zinā*-stoning being a *ḥadd*. The idiosyncrasies point to oral/aural teaching sessions rather than to transmissions based exclusively on written texts.

As for Dāwūd b. Abī Hind's transmission chain, some consider him to be a reliable narrator,[149] while others assert that when he taught from memory, he often misreported the correct transmitters. In addition, he reportedly had a habit of abbreviating transmission chains,[150] including ones that included Ibn al-Musayyab.[151] This practice related to Ibn al-Musayyab's narratives can help to explain why Ibn Abī Hind notes ʿUmar as Ibn al-Musayyab's direct source. In my estimation, on the basis of biographical information and comparative textual content analysis, we can proceed on the assumption that Ibn Abī Hind participated in the circulation of the report.

A reading of the sources implies that Saʿīd b. al-Musayyab directly hears from ʿUmar about *zinā*-stoning. However, there is disagreement about Ibn al-Musayyab's time of birth, which complicates the possibility of direct interaction between the two individuals.[152] The hadith scholar Ibn Maʿīn (d. 233/847) remarks that he is not aware of any evidence that Ibn al-Musayyab ever met ʿUmar.[153] According to one biographical entry, Ibn al-Musayyab denied having spent time with ʿUmar, though he confirmed that he was born during ʿUmar's caliphate.[154] Yet in a conversation between him and Iyās b. Muʿāwiya (d. 122/739), Ibn Muʿāwiya states that he descended from the tribe of Muzayna. Ibn al-Musayyab replies by noting that he remembers ʿUmar making a public announcement about the death of a well-known Muzanī.[155] It is entirely possible, then, that Ibn al-Musayyab was alive during the caliph's twelve-year caliphate. Nevertheless, the information in biographical sources raises doubts about whether he could have directly witnessed ʿUmar delivering sermons, especially one in which he advocate the validity of *zinā*-stoning.

[149] Ibn Saʿd, *al-Ṭabaqāt*, 9:255; al-Mizzī, *Tahdhīb al-kamāl*, 8:464f; Ibn Abī Hind was also a respected legal authority; see al-Dhahabī, *Siyar aʿlām*, 6:377 and Ibn Ḥajar, *Tahdhīb al-tahdhīb*, 3:370.
[150] al-Mizzī, *Tahdhīb al-kamāl*, 8:465; Ibn Ḥajar, *Tahdhīb al-tahdhīb*, 3:370.
[151] al-Dāraquṭnī, *al-ʿIlal*, 2:155f, no. 192 and 7:276–8, no. 1,349.
[152] al-Dāraquṭnī, *al-ʿIlal*, 7:120; Ibn Maʿīn, *al-Tārīkh*, 3:191, no. 858; Ibn Ḥibbān, *al-Thiqāt*, 4:273.
[153] Ibn Maʿīn, *al-Tārīkh*, 3:216, no. 999.
[154] al-Mizzī, *Tahdhīb al-kamāl*, 11:74.
[155] Ibn Saʿd, *al-Ṭabaqāt*, 8:141; al-Dhahabī, *Siyar aʿlām*, 1:404.

If Ibn al-Musayyab did not observe ʿUmar make a public declaration about the legitimacy of stoning, what then is to be made of the transmission chains suggesting otherwise? Biographical data and the examination of similarities among the relevant textual content provide the answer. There is noteworthy overlap between the recensions on the respective authorities of Ibn al-Musayyab and Ibn ʿAbbās, as well as the narrative about Abū Bakr's caliphate, which does not have Ibn al-Musayyab in the transmission chain but does have Ibn ʿAbbās. For instance, Ibn al-Musayyab's account opens with a journey by ʿUmar from Mecca to Medina, which harkens back to the Abū Bakr-*cum-zinā*-stoning hadith in which ʿUmar is portrayed as being in Mina after the pilgrimage and is advised to address the matter concerning Abū Bakr's caliphate in Medina. In both versions, ʿUmar states that were it not for people accusing him of adding something to the Qur'ān, he would have written down the stoning verse. Also worth highlighting is that Ibn al-Musayyab is recorded to have attended study sessions with Ibn ʿAbbās.[156] Ibn al-Musayyab remarks that he knows Ibn ʿAbbās well and that he considers this Companion to be the most knowledgeable of all people.[157] Owing to the information I just presented leads me to argue that Ibn ʿAbbās (d. 68/687) is Ibn al-Musayyab's source. As to why Ibn ʿAbbās's name is absent from the Ibn al-Musayyab transmission chain, it is because Ibn al-Musayyab is considered to be one of the best authorities for information about ʿUmar's rulings.[158] This means that early transmitters would have understood any mention of Ibn ʿAbbās to be superfluous.[159]

As for the textual content, ʿUmar's recitation of the stoning verse is instructive both in content and for the purpose of unearthing the narrative's provenance. In my opinion, the actual stoning verse in Ibn al-Musayyab's report reveals a limitation in its formulation and manifests attempts to parallel other verses from the Qur'ān. For instance, Q5:38 mandates amputation of the hands of "*al-sāriq wa-l-sāriqa*," or "the male or female thief." Q24:2 orders 100 lashes for "*al-zāniya wa-l-zānī*," or "as for the woman and man who commit illicit sexual intercourse." The active participles encompass the offense of theft or illicit sexual intercourse, respectively. On the other hand, the verse recited by ʿUmar gives us the terms *al-shaykh* and *al-shaykha*. A *shaykh*

[156] Ibn Saʿd, *al-Ṭabaqāt*, 7:121.
[157] Ibn Saʿd, *al-Ṭabaqāt*, 2:318.
[158] Ibn Saʿd, *al-Ṭabaqāt*, 7:121.
[159] Citing my dissertation and claim that Ibn ʿAbbās is Ibn al-Musayyab's source, Kara writes that "the linguistic distinction and textual evidence refute [my] thesis." See Kara, *The Integrity of the Qur'an*, 161, n. 69; I am unclear what he intends by "linguistic distinction." I cannot, therefore, address his comments.

(m.)/*shaykha* (f.) refers to an elderly person; in fact, the term often engenders a sense of reverence or respect to whom it is applied on account of their age. The term fails to connote *any* sort of offense. Now, it remains possible that the ambiguity is a result of something getting dropped during the transmission process. There are other versions according to which the stoning verse reads, "As for *al-shaykh* and *al-shaykha*, **when they commit *zinā*** [emphasis mine], stone them both without wavering."[160] The vagueness of *shaykh/a* as a standalone category and its connection to an offense is thrown into sharp relief by the conditional clause. Note, however, that even with the insertion of "when they commit *zinā*," it remains unclear which type of unlawful sexual transgression is intended. Is it fornication or adultery? The use of *shaykh/a* is likely designed to signify adultery. Regardless, transmitters already had the concept of *zinā*-stoning in mind and, therefore, did not need to include the conditional clause when referencing the purported verse.

The provenance of the stoning verse has a connection to another hadith. To help explain this further, let us recall Chapter 2, which focuses on an incident involving the Prophet and his order to stone Jewish *zinā* offenders on the basis of the Hebrew Bible. In some versions, the Jewish community explains why they do not implement the stoning punishment:

> The offense was common among our nobles but when we would catch one of them, we would let them go. But as to the poor, we would implement the fixed punishment (*ḥadd*). We eventually said to one another: Let us agree upon something. We will apply the same punishment to a noble person as to a poor person. So we agreed to blacken the face and flog.[161]

And in another version:

> A man, who had familial ties to our King, committed *zinā*. So the King imprisoned him and excused him from getting stoned. Thereafter, a commoner committed *zinā* and the King wanted to stone him. The offender's people intervened and protested by saying: 'By God, we will not be stoned until you stone those from among yourselves!' So we reformed the punishment for everyone.[162]

[160] Ibn Abī Shayba, *al-Muṣannaf* (2008 ed.), 9:354, no. 29,354; Ibn Mājah, *Sunan*, 2:853, no. 2553; al-Nasāʾī, *al-Sunan al-kubrā*, 6:410f, no. 7,118; al-Bayhaqī, *al-Sunan al-kubrā*, 8:366f, no. 16,920.
[161] See page 102.
[162] See page 155–156.

And finally:

> The Jews were loath to stone them on the account of their nobility and social position.[163]

The terms *al-shaykh* and *al-shaykha* as it appears in the stoning verse is partly used as a reference for social standing. The connection between the issue of social standing and the stoning verse is clearly expressed in one version found in al-Ṭabarī's exegetical work. Here I provide the relevant portions of the textual content:

> "And the Prophet said [to his Jewish interlocutor]: 'I bear witness to you by God and the Torah that God sent to Moses ... what do you find in the Torah?'
>
> [The Jewish interlocutor responded]: Abū Qāsim, '*Al-Shaykh* and *al-shaykha*, when they commit *zinā*, stone them both without wavering."[164]

In the context of the report about Jewish *zinā* offenders, the verse indicates that a person of seniority, whether due to age or social standing, is to be stoned when they commit *zinā*. It is a violation of a person's seniority—however defined—that warrants the kind of punishment they can receive. This concept is exemplified in the stoning verse as it is presented in the textual content of 'Umar's report. Moreover, the stoning verse in 'Umar's report is once again on the authority of a Muslim and, ostensibly, the Qur'ān. In the PJZO hadith, the verse is on the explicit authority of the Torah. This element—the stoning verse uttered by 'Umar—is another feature of the construction of his narrative as mirroring the PJZO hadith.

The terms *al-shaykh* and *al-shaykha* are also precursors to the category of persons upon whom later Muslim jurists would apply the label of *iḥṣān*. Partly due to concerns about the use of *shaykh* and *shaykha* in relation to *zinā*-stoning (e.g., can a virgin *shaykh* be stoned?), it comes as no surprise that we find divergent opinions about what *shaykh/a* actually means. For instance, Mālik remarks that the terms signify a male and a female non-virgin (*thayyib* and *thayyiba*), respectively.[165] If the stoning verse existed, then the

[163] See page 175.
[164] al-Ṭabarī, *Jāmi'*, 10:327f, no. 11,976 at 328.
[165] Mālik, *Muwaṭṭa'*, 5:1203f, no. 631; al-Bayhaqī, *Sunan al-kubrā*, 8:370, no. 16,921.

clarification necessitates that the Qur'ānic flogging mandate is directed toward virgin *zinā* offenders. But according to another report on the authority of Kathīr b. al-Ṣalt, ʿUmar states that a *shaykh* without *iḥṣān* is flogged, and a *shābb* (a youth)[166] with *iḥṣān* is stoned.[167] And a narrative transmitted on the authority of Ubayy b. Kaʿb reads:

> Ubayy b. Kaʿb said: [*Zinā* offenders are of three types: individuals of the first type] are flogged and stoned; [others] are stoned but not flogged, [while the third] are flogged but not stoned.
>
> Qatāda b. Diʿāma (d. 117/735) clarified: If a *muḥṣan* (someone with *iḥṣān*) *shaykh* commits *zinā*, he is flogged and stoned. If a *muḥṣan shābb* commits *zinā*, he is stoned. And if a *shābb* without *iḥṣān* (*lam yuḥṣan*) commits *zinā*, he is flogged.[168]

This report is transmitted by the Successor, Masrūq b. al-Ajdaʿ (d. 63/682), who is also noted to have given his own opinions about the conditions that make *zinā*-stoning mandatory. He asserts, for example, that two non-virgin offenders are punished with stoning but without flogging (*al-thayyibān yurjamān*), whereas two *shaykh*s are punished with flogging and stoning (*al-shaykhān yujladān wa yurjamān*).[169] Note that, in each of these circumstances, it is the person with the higher social standing who receives the greater punishment, rather than the reverse, as in the case of the Jewish *zinā* offenders. Circling back to the Ibn al-Musayyab report, what we have is an early provenance that can be situated in the first/seventh century, prior to Muslim jurists incorporating the use of *iḥṣān* as a legal element for *zinā*-stoning. The imputation of a stoning verse is designed to make it clear that *zinā*-stoning has been divinely revealed beyond a shadow of a doubt. It is an instruction based on Islamic theology whereas in the PJZO hadith it is based on Jewish theology. This can be gleaned from ʿUmar's comment, "We had surely read/recited it (*qara'nāhā*)."

[166] Lane provides the following meanings for *shābb*: in the state from puberty to the completion of thirty years; or from sixteen years to thirty-two; or in the state from the seventeenth year to the completion of fifty-one years. Lane, *An Arabic-English Lexicon*, 4:1,494.

[167] Ibn Ḥanbal, *Musnad* (1992 ed.), 35:472, no. 21,596; al-Nasāʾī, *al-Sunan al-kubrā*, 6:406, no. 7,107; in a third version, ʿUmar says, "*al-shābbayn al-thayyibayn* (the two young non-virgins)." See al-Nasāʾī, *al-Sunan al-kubrā*, 6:406, no. 7,110; this formulation appears to correct the cases in which a *shaykh* is a virgin or non-*shaykh* (*shābb*) is a non-virgin.

[168] al-Nasāʾī, *al-Sunan al-kubrā*, 6:407, no. 7,111.

[169] ʿAbd al-Razzāq, *al-Muṣannaf*, 7:329, no. 13,361; al-Bayhaqī, *Sunan al-kubrā*, 8:389, no. 16,980.

That 'Umar is remembered to have referenced the stoning verse may not have been deemed as an interpolation into the standardized Qur'ānic text if the stabilization of the memory is also occurring in a historical context when the Qur'ān's proposed standardization has yet to be fully accepted. Furthermore, the reference to the purportive stoning verse is to underscore 'Umar's anxiety about Muslims rejecting the capital punishment because of its absence from the Qur'ān. This context can be gleaned from reports about a stoning verse that circulate on the authority of other historical figures. For example, the Successor Kathīr b. al-Ṣalt (d. unknown) contends that one of the Prophet's scribes, Zayd b. Thābit (d. *c.* 49/669), said that he heard the Prophet recite the stoning verse:

> We used to write the *maṣāḥif* with Zayd b. Thābit (d. *c.* 50/670) and we came to a verse that we were supposed to record. Zayd b. Thābit commented: "I heard the Messenger of God say: 'As for the *shaykh* and the *shaykha*, when they commit *zinā*, stone them both as an exemplary punishment from God and God's Messenger.[170]' "

In this report, the verse includes, "As an exemplary punishment from God and God's Messenger (*nakāl*^{an} *min Allāh wa rasūlihī*)," a locution virtually identical to that found in the verse regarding theft, which stipulates amputation for the condemned "as an exemplary punishment from God, the Most Exalted, the Most Wise (*nakāl*^{an} *min Allāh wa Allāh 'azīz*^{un} *ḥakīm*^{un})." A third version of the stoning verse reportedly ended with, "stone them both without wavering for the [physical] pleasure they have engaged in (*bi-mā qaḍayā min al-ladhdha*)."[171] In another version of this report, Zayd b. Thābit remarks that after the stoning verse was revealed, 'Umar wanted the Prophet to let him write it down (*aktabnīhā*). The Prophet reportedly was not pleased by 'Umar's request and advised 'Umar not to write it down if it was possible.[172] The Prophet's wife, 'Ā'isha, remarks that after the stoning verse was revealed, a written copy of it was left in her house underneath her bed. While she and others were occupied with tending to the Prophet's health, a small animal entered her residence and ate the material upon which the verse was written.[173] The Companion Ubayy b. Ka'b (d. *c.* 32/652), a scribe of the

170 al-Ṭayālisī, *Musnad*, 1:503, no. 615; al-Bayhaqī, *Sunan al-kubrā*, 9:367, no. 16,912.

171 See al-Nasā'ī, *al-Sunan al-kubrā*, 6:406, no. 7,108.

172 Ibn Ḥanbal, *Musnad* (1992 ed.), 35:472f, no. 21,596; al-Nasā'ī, *al-Sunan al-kubrā*, 6:406, no. 7,107 and 407, no. 7,110; al-Bayhaqī, *al-Sunan al-kubrā*, 9:367, no. 16,913.

173 Ibn Ḥanbal, *Musnad* (1995 ed.), 18:188f, no. 26,194.

Prophet, is quoted as having said that, Chapter 33 *al-Aḥzāb* (The Combined Forces), at one time included the stoning verse:

> Ubayy said: Zirr b. Hubaysh, how many verses do you read in *Surat al-Aḥzāb*?
>
> Zirr responded: Such and such number of verses.
>
> Ubayy then remarked: At one time, the chapter was about the same length as *al-Baqara* (Chapter 2, The Cow). In fact, we used to read as part of *al-Aḥzāb*: "As for the *shaykh* and *shaykha*, when they commit *zinā*, stone them both as an exemplary punishment from God and God's Messenger."[174]

The remark by Ubayy b. Ka'b intimates that *al-Aḥzāb*, as it ultimately comes to stand, has been significantly downsized. It is at seventy-three verses whereas *al-Baqara* is at 286. The purported culling process excised the verse concerning the stoning punishment. It is not a coincidence, nor without significance, that the stoning verse supposedly existed in *al-Aḥzāb*. This chapter and *al-Nūr* (which contains the flogging directive for *zinā* offenders) have, among their major subjects, sexual ethics.[175] Moreover, individual piety and morality are connected to communal identity.[176] The intertwining of these themes can, therefore, be affirmed in a verse that provides regulation of sexual morality in relation to the distinguishing aspects of a community. Beyond this consideration, the plain purpose of the above reports is to explain why the stoning verse never makes it into the official 'Uthmānī codex.

In this section, I have examined the 'Umar *zinā*-stoning narrative circulated by two of Sa'īd b. al-Musayyab's students, Yaḥyā b. Sa'īd and Dāwūd b. Abī Hind. The evidence indicates that Yaḥyā b. Sa'īd and Dāwūd b. Abī Hind received 'Umar's *zinā*-stoning report from their teacher, Ibn al-Musayyab. I raised questions about 'Umar's status as Ibn al-Musayyab's direct source. As I have argued, Ibn 'Abbās is Ibn al-Musayyab's informant. From a textual content standpoint, the element according to which 'Umar is portrayed as citing a stoning verse emerges in a socio-historical context wherein it is necessary to stress scriptural authority—just as in the case of the PJZO hadith, for the justification of *zinā*-stoning. Moreover, the doctrines about the compilation and standardization of the Qur'ān are yet to be fully

174 al-Ṭayālisī, *Musnad*, 436f, no. 542; 'Abd al-Razzāq, *al-Muṣannaf*, 3:365, no. 5,990 and 7:329f, no. 13,363.
175 Bauer and Hamza, *Women, Households, and the Hereafter*, 30f and 163.
176 Bauer and Hamza, *Women, Households, and the Hereafter*, 163.

concretized and accepted. Accordingly, the stoning verse element, along with other aspects of the report, is indicative of a rather early first/seventh century provenance.

Conclusion

As the designated successor to the first caliph, ʿUmar lived at a time infused with numerous debates. Among the issues at hand was the political discord about the rightful communal leader after the Prophet's death. During his reign, ʿUmar also had the responsibility of guiding the growing Muslim community and, as a result, had to establish and uphold rules and regulations. In this chapter, I examined the respective variants of two reports that record ʿUmar's engagement with two communal matters: (1) the selection of Abū Bakr as leader and (2) the Islamic nature of death by lapidation for *zinā*. I have argued that the report about the legitimacy of Abū Bakr's caliphate plays a central role in providing the basis for another narrative in which ʿUmar makes a public statement—in the form of a sermon—about the obligatory nature of *zinā*-stoning.

I started by reviewing several reports about cases involving the manner in which ʿUmar is supposed to have passed judgment on members of the Muslim community accused of various kinds of sexual impropriety. In some instances, he invokes the stoning punishment to convey his strong dislike for certain practices, such as temporary marriage. In other instances, he is recorded to have ordered the implementation of the punishment. These reports create a nexus between the authority of ʿUmar and *zinā*-related issues in general and, in several cases, *zinā*-stoning in particular. This association, I argue, reflects ʿUmar's likely endorsement of this form of capital punishment. But ʿUmar's endorsement of *zinā*-stoning was not widely accepted or, at least, not on his own authority. Consequently, advocates of *zinā*-stoning, including ʿUmar, had to seek alternative justifications. The Book of God and the purported practice of the Prophet served as the foundation of the justifications.

The connection between ʿUmar's Abū Bakr-*cum*-*zinā*-stoning hadith and ʿUmar's independent *zinā*-stoning is undeniable. Many of the same transmitters are part of the respective chains of transmission. The following summary of the respective textual contents helps to corroborate the relationship:

(1) In several variants on the authority of al-Zuhrī, we find that ʿUmar states that he read/recited and memorized the stoning verse and that he would have added it to the Qurʾān were it not for people accusing him of modifying the Book of God. These elements also appear in the speech by ʿUmar regarding Abū Bakr's caliphate;

(2) In versions on al-Zuhrī's authority, ʿUmar fears that Muslims will deny that a stoning verse ever existed. Though not expressed as fear, in the report about Abū Bakr's caliphate and *zinā*-stoning, ʿUmar is recorded to have said Muslims will absolve themselves of the stoning mandate as they do other obligations;

(3) In the ʿAbd al-Razzāq - Maʿmar - al-Zuhrī - ʿUbayd Allāh - Ibn ʿAbbās version, ʿUmar reportedly states that people will say: "By God, we do not find stoning in God's Book." In the Yūsuf b. Mihrān account, ʿUmar says, "People, stoning is one of the fixed punishments (*ḥudūd*)." And in Ibn al-Musayyab's recension, ʿUmar remarks, "Let not one of you say, 'We do not find two fixed punishments (*ḥaddayn*) in the Book of God.'" These expressions parallel the statement attributed to ʿUmar in the version about Abū Bakr's caliphate and *zinā*-stoning, where he purportedly claims, "The stoning verse was sent down";

(4) In one of al-Zuhrī's versions, ʿUmar asserts, "By God, were it not that people would say, ʿUmar added something to the Book of God, I surely would have written it down (*katabtuhā*)." In Ibn al-Musayyab's recension, ʿUmar bemoans, "Were it not for the fact that people would say, 'ʿUmar b. al-Khaṭṭāb tampered with the Book of God,' I would have had written down." The same statement appears in the report on ʿUmar's discussion about Abū Bakr's caliphate and *zinā*-stoning. There, ʿUmar is remembered to have said, "Were it not for the fact that people would say, 'ʿUmar wrote something in the codex (*muṣḥaf*) that does not belong in it,' I surely would have had it written with my own hand."

As I note in the previous sections, some of ʿUmar's statements serve as countermeasures to theological disputes in early Islamic history. Such responses and the circulation of the *zinā*-stoning elements with remarks about Abū Bakr's selection mean that most of elements found in ʿUmar's report about *zinā*-stoning can be traced back to the second half of the first/seventh century.

As the sources plainly indicate, there is a crucial link between Ibn ʿAbbās and the spread of ʿUmar's account regarding *zinā*-stoning. Indeed, one can argue that someone after Ibn ʿAbbās is responsible for the content of the report, that Ibn ʿAbbās is not involved whatsoever. But recall (from Section 4.3.2) that Yūsuf b. Mihrān circulates a narrative in which Ibn ʿAbbās himself delivers a sermon in Baṣra, asserting that ʿUmar made a public statement about *zinā*-stoning. Ibn Mihrān's recension, then, corroborates the involvement of Ibn ʿAbbās. As I demonstrate in the previous section, Ibn ʿAbbās is Ibn al-Musayyab's source for the latter's transmission of the speech given by ʿUmar on the question of *zinā*-stoning despite being unidentified as such. This is attested to by the fact that the parallels in the Abū Bakr-*cum-zinā*-stoning hadith and Ibn al-Musayyab's report are striking and much too uniform to allow for the possibility that the similarities in the two reports are a result of sheer coincidence. For instance, in the respective versions, Ibn ʿAwf and Ibn ʿAbbās both say that ʿUmar was in Minā—returning from the *ḥājj*—when people began to ask questions about the process by which Abū Bakr became caliph. Ibn ʿAwf advises ʿUmar to delay his response until they arrive in Medina, which he does. ʿUmar's travel from Mecca to Medina is also included in Ibn al-Musayyab's version of the report. There is also the overlap of concepts in ʿUmar's hadith on the authority of Ibn ʿAbbās and Ibn al-Musayyab. ʿUmar's warning to Muslims to not abandon their religious obligations, the existence of a stoning verse, and the practice of the Prophet, among others, find expressions in the respective versions of Ibn al-Musayyab and Ibn ʿAbbās. Hence, the combination of transmission chain and textual content analysis points to Ibn ʿAbbās based on three independent attestations: Ibn al-Musayyab, Yūsuf b. Mihrān, and ʿUbayd Allāh.

In my view, Ibn ʿAbbās did not actually hear ʿUmar deliver a sermon about *zinā*-stoning. As reviewed in Section 4.1, there are several versions of the report in which the transmission chains include Saʿd b. Ibrāhīm, ʿAbd al-Raḥmān b. ʿAwf, and Ibn ʿAbbās. I presented a version according to which ʿUmar delivers a sermon about Abū Bakr's caliphate without any mention of *zinā*-stoning. In this variant, ʿAbd al-Raḥmān b. ʿAwf narrates to Ibn ʿAbbās the entirety of the account: from what was discussed with ʿUmar in Mecca to what was proclaimed publicly by ʿUmar in Medina. Here, it is Ibn ʿAwf, not Ibn ʿAbbās, who is with ʿUmar in Mecca and who witnesses him deliver a sermon in Medina about the legitimacy of Abū Bakr's caliphate. In all versions of the *zinā*-stoning report I examined in the sources that feature Saʿd b. Ibrahīm in the transmission chain, it is Ibn ʿAwf who recounts to Ibn

ʿAbbās the events leading up to, and the contents of, ʿUmar's sermon.[177] And then there is a report provided by Ibn Ḥanbal with the earlier part of the transmission chain being al-Zuhrī - ʿUbayd Allāh - Ibn ʿAbbās. The textual content reads:

> ʿAbd al-Raḥmān b. ʿAwf *told me* [viz. Ibn ʿAbbās] *that he heard* ʿ*Umar b. al-Khaṭṭāb say* [my emphasis]: "People have been wondering: 'What is this about stoning, when the Book of God stipulates flogging?' Indeed, the Messenger of God stoned and we stoned after his death! Were it not that people would say [or, 'declare'] that ʿUmar added something to the Book of God that does not belong in it, I would have kept it[178] exactly as it was revealed."[179]

ʿAbd al-Raḥmān b. ʿAwf is the source for Ibn ʿAbbās. But with the transmission process, Ibn ʿAbbās (a highly favored student of ʿUmar's) is remembered as having been present when ʿUmar delivered a sermon about his predecessor's selection as caliph.

The connection between ʿUmar b. al-Khaṭṭāb and the stoning punishment, coupled with his involvement in the ascension of Abū Bakr as caliph following the death of the Prophet, culminates in a report according to which the second caliph publicly declares the divine legitimacy of *zinā*-stoning. ʿUmar's considerable influence over much of the early Muslim community, and subsequently among Sunnī Muslims, positions him as an instrumental figure in the process of stabilizing and institutionalizing a practice that was not originally intrinsic to Islam. During this process, his persona, specifically, and the report, generally, is shaped to mirror the Islamic image of the PJZO hadith. If early Muslims were not convinced about *zinā*-stoning from the Jewish case, then they surely must be from an influential figure like ʿUmar b. al-Khaṭṭāb.

[177] al-Nasāʾī, *al-Sunan al-kubrā*, 6:408–10: nos. 7113–7; al-Ṭaḥāwī, *Sharḥ mushkil*, 5:303, no. 2,060.
[178] Undoubtedly, the pronoun "it" refers to the stoning verse.
[179] Ibn Ḥanbal, *Musnad* (1992 ed.), 1:327, no. 197.

Conclusion

When did *zinā*-stoning become part of the Islamic dogma? My answer is that it was not during the revelatory period. Among the evidence I presented to support my claim is that, on the eve of Islam, cultures belonging to the Near Eastern-Mediterranean milieu had by and large replaced capital punishments with corporal ones for hetero sexual transgressions. This socio-historical context is reflected in the Qur'ān, which explicitly provides corporal punishments for such kinds of infractions. As for the Prophet, it may be argued that he ordered the stoning punishment either because the Qur'ān was silent on the matter or that he could have done so before Q24:2 (the flogging verse). My examination of the transmission history of particular *zinā*-stoning hadith, which are critical for justifying the punishment, demonstrates that such reports cannot be situated to his lifetime. As for 'Umar b. al-Khaṭṭāb, while he supported the capital punishment, I have argued that he did not deliver a sermon justifying its religious legitimacy. Finally, the jurisprudence utilized to create procedural and substantive *zinā*-stoning laws, such as the legal formulation of *iḥṣān* as a necessary contingency for conviction, reveals gaps and slippages that indicate an uncertainty around the normativity of *zinā*-stoning. All of this indicates that death by lapidation for certain Muslims who commit illicit sexual intercourse became part of the Islamic legal tradition after the Qur'ān and outside the practice of the Prophet.

In Chapter 1, I examined both the widely cited and less commonly mentioned reports that support *zinā*-stoning. I illustrated the different ways in which certain narratives interplay with the Islamic exegetical and legal traditions. As for hadith that do not garner wide circulation, it would appear they are early iterations of attempts to justify the capital punishment on the authority of the Prophet. Take for example the account on the authority of the Companion al-Lajlāj [Abū al-'Alā' al-'Āmirī] (d. first/seventh century). In this report, a woman with a child passes by the Prophet. Impromptu, he asks her about the paternity of the child. The subsequent chain of events leads him to order the stoning punishment upon the child's father. In another

Stoning as Punishment in Early Islam. Syed Atif Rizwan, Oxford University Press. © Oxford University Press 2026.
DOI: 10.1093/9780197823774.003.0006

narrative on the authority of the Companion Abū Hunayda Wā'il b. Ḥujr (d. unknown), an accused rapist is brought to the Prophet who, without any investigation, orders the stoning punishment upon the culprit. These narratives stand diametrically in contradiction to hadith in which purported Muslims self-confess and the Prophet provides exculpating mechanisms to avoid a conviction. The reports on the respective authorities of al-Lajlāj and Abū Hunayda Wā'il b. Ḥujr are also irreconcilable with Islamic *zinā*-stoning laws, which have strict procedures for passing a guilty verdict. It would thus appear that such uncommon reports reflect additional efforts by which the Prophet is portrayed as approving the stoning punishment.

Jurisprudence around legitimizing *zinā*-stoning reveals irregularities, the kinds that ostensibly indicate juristic struggles to legitimize a practice that did not have an Islamic basis. For instance, recall al-Ḥārith b. Asad al-Muḥāsibī (d. 243/857), who writes that while the stoning verse is abrogated the punishment itself is not. This assertion conflicts with the report involving ʿAlī, who is recorded to have claimed that he ordered the flogging punishment based on the Qur'ān and the stoning punishment based on the practice of the Prophet—a narrative used to justify the dual punishment of flogging and stoning. The al-Muḥāsibī and ʿAlī hadith reveal the different ways in which memories about the order to implement death by lapidation for *zinā* developed and how purported practices of the Prophet and other Companions were used to naturalize the stoning punishment into the Islamic legal tradition.

In Chapter 2, I examined a report according to which the Prophet orders death by lapidation upon Jewish *zinā* offenders. Taking the Qur'ān to be contemporaneous with the life of the Prophet indicates that individuals from Jewish communities sought out his rulings. This leaves open the possibility that some Jewish members approached him to ask about his stance on individuals who commit illicit sexual intercourse. But in my view, the broader scenario depicted in the Qur'ān does not substantiate the specific events illustrated in the PJZO hadith. The report's beginnings could represent any number of actual encounters between the Prophet and Jewish community members. Reports about these encounters would eventually be circulated and functioned to partly reflect intra- and inter-communal polemic, that is, to highlight theological and/or legal points. The PJZO hadith emerges within this context.

To reiterate, the PJZO hadith is not directed at Jewish communities generally but rather specifically at the rabbis and their supposed *taḥrīf*—the willful distortion and/or concealment of divine law. As I discussed in Chapter 2, both the Mishnaic and the Talmudic rabbinic authorities maintain fidelity to the stoning punishment. Whether it was actually implemented is a different matter. Indeed, several factors, including the establishment of high evidentiary burdens for execution, ostensibly rendered it inoperable. Regardless, Muslim transmitter(s) familiar with rabbinic law cast rabbinic authorities as being unfaithful to divine laws. They portrayed the non-use of lapidation by Jewish religio-legal authorities as evidence of *taḥrīf*—an accusation that served to underpin broader claims about the untrustworthiness of the Jewish interpretative traditions. The basis for such incrimination is likely to be the Qur'ān. Zellentin notes that the Qur'ān does not universally challenge rabbinic authority. Rather, it criticizes specific interpretations, particularly regarding the perceived independence of rabbinic exegesis.[1] Verses such as Q5:41–4 hint at these disagreements, reflecting the Qur'ān's (re)imagining of rabbinic Judaism.[2] In my view, Muslims belonging to the early communities drew upon the Qur'ānic critiques by focusing on the issue of the stoning punishment. The implications of *taḥrīf* extended further. If the authoritative members belonging to the Jewish communities of Medina could obscure or distort a commandment as explicit as stoning, then they could distort the Torah's purported announcement of Muḥammad's prophethood. Then there is a third layer of the report. It is used to emphasize the Prophet's authority and his ruling on the stoning punishment as aligning with divine law. Finally, and the most important assessment, is that the PJZO hadith functions as a teaching device for Muslims, ones belonging to early Islam who reject *zinā*-stoning. Thus, the PJZO hadith highlights how early Muslims engaged with and imagined Jewish legal practices to articulate why Muslims should not be like their Jewish contemporaries, who ignore the Prophet's legitimacy and scriptural authority in cases involving illicit sexual intercourse and the stoning punishment. Accordingly, this report is critical for the beginnings of the process by which *zinā*-stoning is justified in the Islamic legal tradition because it is an early attempt by supporters of *zinā*-stoning to convince their co-religionists about why it is necessary for them to accept it.

Even if the PJZO hadith could succeed in impressing upon Muslims that the Prophet ordered a Torah punishment upon Jewish *zinā* offenders and even if the act forged a relationship between the Prophet's authority and the

[1] Zellentin, "What Falls Within Judaism," 286.
[2] Zellentin, "What Falls Within Judaism," 285.

stoning punishment, it remained vital to explicitly link his endorsement of the punishment upon Muslim *zinā* offenders. For advocates of *zinā*-stoning, the hadith, according to which the Prophet orders death by lapidation upon a woman, serves such a purpose. As I argue in Chapter 3, the narrative's development strategically incorporates specific elements to establish the woman's religious identity as Muslim. These include things like the Prophet's participation in her *jināza* (Muslim burial prayer). Different versions of the report also function to affirm certain aspects of *zinā* laws, such as four self-confessions or the conditions under which the punishment must be delayed, for example, pregnancy and child rearing. Finally, the hadith makes clear that the punishment is the ultimate form of expiation for the transgressor—a move that helps to frame *zinā*-stoning as part of the *ḥudūd*, which in turn come to be conceived formally as the "rights of God." Ultimately, as part of the beginnings of the process by which to defend *zinā*-stoning as Islamic, the self-confessing hadith operates to cement the Prophetic authority in relation to death by lapidation upon Muslim *zinā* offenders.

The shift from the Prophet being portrayed as delivering a ruling for Jewish *zinā* offenders to Muslim *zinā* offenders reveals an evolving theological and legal relationship to the stoning punishment. This connection becomes exceptionally clear through the role of ʿUmar b. al-Khaṭṭāb. Given his impact on the early Muslim communities, an impact that would translate later into an iconic status for most latter-day Sunni Muslims, ʿUmar's *logia* on *zinā*-stoning must be viewed as a critical element for stabilizing the punishment in the Islamic legal tradition.

The communal memory of ʿUmar's attempts to quell political discord among the early Muslim communities helps to explain the circulation of the narrative involving his purported delivery of the *zinā*-stoning sermon. I showed that the key individuals who helped to circulate the report in which ʿUmar legitimizes Abū Bakr's successorship are also cited in the transmission chains of ʿUmar's *zinā*-stoning narrative. I also illustrated how some of the literary composition of ʿUmar's account about the validity of Abū Bakr's caliphate share parallels with the versions involving his *zinā*-stoning proclamation. What exactly ʿUmar may have said during his purported sermon may be lost to history. But on the basis of the record that demonstrates his strong endorsement of the capital punishment, memories about his role in trying to resolve communal disputes are preserved as concepts and expressed through reports that exhibit intermixing. ʿUmar's sermon addresses two significant controversies among early Muslim communities, with one that challenges the Islamic basis for a punishment constructed as normative in the eventual Islamic legal tradition.

'Umar's supposed claim that stoning was revealed in the Book of God and a practice of the Prophet points directly to the non-normativity of *zinā*-stoning. To begin with, his reference to the Book of God is ambiguous. Given 'Umar's own interest in the Judaic tradition, it is entirely possible that he intends the Torah. To be sure, the phrase is also indicative of divine revelation of any kind, whether received by Muḥammad or anyone else. The upshot to the ambiguity with the term Book of God is that it means 'Umar's report is of an early provenance, a period when the phrase's interpretation is not yet firmly established to signify the Qur'ān. Importantly, 'Umar's recourse to the Book of God and the *sunna* of Muḥammad implies their acceptance as authoritative sources. His appeal reflects the echo of a socio-historical context involving debates about the need to ascertain the correct locus of authority for theological and legal disputes. In other words, those who were rejecting *zinā*-stoning were doing so precisely because of its absence from the Qur'ān and the Prophet's practice.

As I have argued in Chapters 2 and 4, 'Umar's hadith is the Islamic expression of the PJZO hadith. For example, the Torah in the PJZO hadith is the Book of God/Qur'ān in the 'Umar report. Obscuring divine law, *taḥrīf*, by rejecting *zinā*-stoning on the part of the Jewish communities mirrors *taḥrīf* on the part of Muslims for doing the same. 'Umar's chastisement of Muslims for not maintaining fidelity to *zinā*-stoning—portrayed as an almost unconscionable attempt to subvert the implementation of a clear-cut divine directive—parallels the criticism leveled against the Prophet's rabbinic contemporaries for likewise not maintaining fidelity to *their* clear-cut divine directives. Hiding the stoning verse by Jewish sages is the same as Muslims denying the existence of a stoning verse. Revealing the stoning verse in the Torah is akin to 'Umar stating that he read/recited it. Whereas the Jewish communities admit that they were not applying the punishment to those belonging to the upper class of society, 'Umar's recitation of the stoning verse addresses exactly such types of individuals (*shaykh*/*shaykha*). And of course, the emphasis in both accounts is on the participation of the Prophet and his ordering of death by lapidation. In consideration of the ways in which certain Muslims attempted to substantiate *zinā*-stoning in early Islam, the PJZO hadith represents a non-Islamic way to teach a lesson. Since it may have not been sufficiently convincing, an Islamic version emerges in the form of 'Umar's purported sermon.

Comparing the PJZO and self-confessing woman hadith reveals an evolution in the different ways in which early Muslims construct the prosecution of *zinā*-stoning. In the self-confessing woman report, the Prophet is never portrayed as eliciting a confession. Instead, he is shown to give the Muslim offender ample opportunity to avoid the punishment through dissuasion and delay tactics. In the Jewish *zinā* case, the Prophet is depicted as going out of his way to elicit an admission by his Jewish interlocutors about the lawfulness of the stoning punishment. Once the rabbis "confess," the stoning takes place immediately. His demand for the punishment's implementation overcomes the very schemes he encourages to avoid its application in the report about the Muslim offender. Teleologically, the Jewish *zinā* case establishes a link between the Prophet's authority and death by stoning, and the self-confessing woman's story legitimizes this link.

Recall that I began this book by citing a report involving the Companion Ibn Abī Awfā and his inability to remember whether the Prophet ordered the punishment before or after the flogging directive in the Qur'ān. Setting aside the chronological issue, the report conveys a certainty on the part of the Companion that the Prophet did, in fact, order the punishment. It would be reasonable to extrapolate that Ibn Abī Awfā had a *zinā*-stoning case in mind. If so, it would mean that the provenance of such an account could be situated to the time of the Prophet—a counter to my argument. But Ibn Abī 'Awfā's report, in my view, does not indicate firsthand knowledge. Rather, his familiarity could very well be secondhand, that is, he heard about the purported incident. Moreover, Ibn Abī Awfā's report focuses on the general application of the stoning punishment that is tied to early Islamic legal development. His report does not independently verify any of the *zinā*-stoning hadith. If Ibn Abī Awfā's affirmation is based on hearing about the same reports, it creates a circular validation: (1) the reports depend on Ibn Abī Awfā for credibility and (2) Ibn Abī Awfā's testimony depends on the *zinā*-stoning reports for substance. In short, Ibn Abī Awfā's report cannot be used to independently affirm the provenance of *zinā*-stoning narratives.

In my analysis of hadith, I have attempted to build on existing methods, such as ICMA. I broadened its scope by accounting for single-strand transmission chains, including those that appear to be "defective." Admittedly, the task demands a certain level of intuition, such as deciding when a particular single-strand report belongs to one set of hadith versus another. My approach also does not *a priori* discard transmissions based on *ex silentio* arguments. Rather, I consider the relevance of the narratives on a case-by-case basis. The hadith complexes I constructed are, in my opinion, defensible and yielded salient results. An important one is that I am able to situate all three hadith in the middle of the first/seventh Islamic century.

For the purpose of analyzing hadith, my use of memory studies to examine the possible ways humans understand, preserve, and stabilize their knowledge of the world is propaedeutic. That my wife can comingle and speak about our basement refrigerator as a garage refrigerator because of her childhood association of a second refrigerator with the garage is not, despite appearances, significantly different from how transmitters could inadvertently obfuscate the exact way ʿUmar b. al-Khaṭṭāb spoke in public settings and how that could help to shape a sermon about *zinā*-stoning. My limited engagement demonstrates that there are additional ways to think about transmission history. That humans remember through concepts involves a convoluted process of contraction, expansion, and/or substitution of details. This is the case both in oral/aural and non-oral/aural traditions. Can individuals deliberately amend certain aspects of stories or create them outright? Of course. I have shown some of the ways in which this is possible. However, emendations do not—more than often—have to be viewed as premeditated attempts to deceive. By examining the process of how concepts develop and can shape our experiences of and attitudes about the world, we gain valuable insights into the ways in which beliefs are created and reinforced. Such considerations can help us to understand how the concept of the Qurʾān's charge of *taḥrīf* can inform a story about the Prophet's interaction with his Jewish contemporaries can become a lesson for Muslims. Drawing on memory studies that shed light on how people remember and *understand* their world can enrich the ways in which we explore history. In this regard, we can do more work to incorporate such insights into hadith studies.

There remain areas for additional research on the subject matter of *zinā*-stoning. To state the obvious, the punishment for certain Muslims of *zinā* was made more severe in the post-Qurʾānic period by the introduction of death by lapidation. It would be helpful to explore who, among the early Muslims after the Prophet's death, could have advocated for the capital punishment. ʿUmar b. al-Khaṭṭāb is one proponent. However, I do not believe that he alone caused this major shift in Islamic criminal law. In addition to exploring early supporters of *zinā*-stoning, it would be worthwhile to explore the contingencies that helped to naturalize it into Shīʿī law.[3] This research will

[3] For instance, to justify *zinā*-stoning a hadith is cited on the authority of Jaʿfar al-Ṣādiq (d. 148/765), the sixth Imām in Twelver Shīʿī Islam. He supposedly stated that the stoning punishment was

shed further light on the broader process by which *zinā*-stoning is situated in the Islamic legal tradition.

Insights from *zinā*-stoning reports that I did not fully engage with can also propel the present study forward. Such narratives can elucidate the different ways in which various factors helped to stabilize stoning as a lawful punishment for certain Muslim transgressors of *zinā*. For instance, according to an entry in al-Bukhārī's *Ṣaḥīḥ*:

> The Companion ʿAmr b. Maymūn is recorded to have said: During the days of Jāhiliyya, I saw a group of monkeys gather around one of their members who had committed *zinā*. They began to stone her and I joined in the stoning myself.[4]

Whatever reasons al-Bukhārī may have had to include this report, at some level, it may represent efforts to employ a natural law strategy to justify stoning for *zinā* offenders.[5] If monkeys stone their *zinā* offenders, then surely humans must at least live up to the same moral rectitude that monkeys hold themselves to. How could they not? After all, what would it say about humans—particularly the community of humans who are supposed to be a beacon unto other nations as recipients of the final divine revelation to humankind—when they fail to uphold the virtues of monkeys?[6] The point is especially driven home when we consider that monkeys were often castigated in Arab cultural memory for their perceived tendency toward moral malleability.[7] A closer examination of this narrative and other *zinā*-stoning reports

in the Qur'ān on the basis of a stoning verse. The verse cited in the report is the same as the one recorded on the authority of ʿUmar b. al-Khaṭṭāb. See al-Kulaynī, *al-Kāfī*, 7:114, no. 3.

[4] al-Bukhārī, *Ṣaḥīḥ* (2002 ed.), 942, no. 3,849.

[5] Michael Cook, "Ibn Qutayba and the Monkeys," 54f and 57.

[6] Though speculative at the moment, it is worth noting a possible relationship between the hadith, the Qur'ān, and rabbinic law. Specifically, the Qur'ān states that God turns into monkeys those who violate the sabbath (Q2:65). According to the Mishna, the "one who profanes the Sabbath" is subject to the stoning punishment. See Cohen et al., *The Oxford Annotated Mishnah*, vol. 2, Sanhedrin 7:4, 527; this hadith could represent a symbolic intra-/inter-communal challenge. The members of Jewish communities are portrayed as breaking their covenant with God, which serves as a lesson for early Muslims to remain committed to their religious obligations.

[7] See also, e.g., Q5:60:

> "Say: Should I tell you about the unjust behavior deserving a worse recompense from God? It is the kind that God has cursed, the kind that makes God angry, the kind that makes God turn them into monkeys and pigs, the kind of behavior exhibited by those who worship idols. Those who exhibit such behaviors are the worst and have strayed far from the ethical path."

would provide further insights into the theological, historical, and sociopolitical factors that contributed to the establishment of the capital punishment in the Islamic legal tradition.

As Alon Confino notes, "Every society sets up images of the past. Yet to make a difference . . . it must steer emotions, motivate people to act, be received; in short, it must become a socio-cultural mode of action."[8] Reports about certain Muslims from early Islamic history and their purported endorsement of *zinā*-stoning are set up to steer emotions, to motivate people to action, and to convey that fidelity to Islam means fidelity to a strict moral code—to upholding *zinā*-stoning. Coincidentally, these narratives, laws, and jurisprudence associated with *zinā* point toward a specific historical moment when *zinā*-stoning was not Islamic.

[8] Alon Confino, "Collective Memory and Cultural History: Problems of Method," 1,390.

Bibliography

PRIMARY SOURCES

'Abd al-Razzāq b. Hammām al-Ṣan'ānī al-Himyarī. *al-Muṣannaf fī al-ḥadīth*. Edited by Ḥabīb al-Raḥmān al-A'ẓamī. 12 vols. Beirut: Dār al-Kutub al-'Ilmiyya, 1972.

Abū 'Awāna, Ya'qūb b. Isḥāq al-Isfarāyīnī. *al-Musnad al-ṣaḥīḥ al-mukhraj 'alā ṣaḥīḥ Muslim*. Edited by 'Abbās b. Ṣafākhān b. Shihāb al-Dīn. 20 vols. Medina: al-Jāmi'a al-Islāmiyya, 2014.

Abū 'Awāna, Ya'qūb b. Isḥāq al-Isfarāyīnī. *Musnad Abī 'Awāna*. Edited by Ayman b. 'Ārif al-Dimashqī. 5 vols. Beirut, Dār al-Ma'rifa, 1998.

Abū Dāwūd, Sulaymān b. al-Ash'āth al-Azdī al-Sijistnānī. *Sunan Abī Dāwūd*. Edited by Shu'ayb al-Arna'ūt and Muḥammad Kāmil Qarah Balilī. 7 vols. Damascus: Dār al-Risāla al-'Ālamiyya, 2009.

Abū Sa'īd al-Barādhi'ī, Khalaf b. Alī al-Qāsim. *al-Tahdhīb fī ikhtiṣār al-mudawwana*. Edited by Muḥammad al-Amīn Walad Muḥammad Sālim b. al-Shaykh. 4 vols. Dubai: Dār al-Buḥūth lī al-Dirāsāt al-Islāmiyya wa Iḥyā' al-Turāth, 2002.

Abū Ya'lā, Muḥammad b. al-Ḥusayn b. al-Farrā'. *al-Masā'il li-fiqhiyya min kitāb al-riwāyatayn wa al-wajhayn*. Edited by 'Abd al-Karīm b. Muḥammad Lāḥim. 3 vols. Riyāḍ: Maktaba al-Ma'ārifa, 1985.

Abū Yūsuf, Abū al-Ḥajjāj Ya'qūb b. Ibrāhīm al-Anṣārī. *Kitāb al-kharāj*. Beirut: Dār al-Ma'rifa lil-Ṭabā'a wa al-Nashr, 1979.

'Ayyāshī, Abū al-Naṣr Muḥammad b. Mas'ūd b. (al-). *Tafsīr al-'Ayyāshī*. Edited by Hāshim al-Rasūlī al-Maḥallātī. 2 vols. Beirut: Mu'assasa al-A'lamī, 1991.

Bayhaqī, Abū Bakr Aḥmad b. al-Ḥusayn b. 'Alī al-. *al-Jāmi' al-shu'ab al-īmān*. Edited by 'Abd al-'Alī 'Abd al-Ḥamīd. 14 vols. Riyāḍ: Maktaba al-Rushd lil-Nashr wa al-Tawzī', 2003.

Bayhaqī, Abū Bakr Aḥmad b. al-Ḥusayn b. 'Alī al-. *al-Sunan al-kubrā*. Third Edition. Edited by Muḥammad 'Abd al-Qādir 'Aṭā'. 11 vols. Beirut: Dār al-Kutub al-'Ilmiyya, 2003.

Bazzār, Abū Bakr Aḥmad b. 'Amr b. 'Abd al-Khāliq al-'Atakī al-. al-Baḥr al-zakhkhār al-ma'rūf bi-musnad al-Bazzār. Edited by Maḥfūẓ al-Raḥmān Zayn Allāh. 20 vols. Beirut: Maktaba al-'Ulūm wa al-Ḥikam, 1988.

Bukhārī, Abū 'Abd Allāh Muḥammad. Ismā'īl al-. *Kitāb al-tārīkh al-kabīr*. Edited by Muḥammad 'Abd al-Mu'īd Khān. 9 vols. Hyderabad: Maṭba'a Jamī'a Dā'ira al-Ma'ārif, 1942–79.

Bukhārī, Abū 'Abd Allāh Muḥammad. Ismā'īl al-. *Ṣaḥīḥ al-Bukhārī*. Edited by Muṣṭafa Dīb al-Bughā. Damascus: Dār b. Kathīr, 1976.

Bukhārī, Abū 'Abd Allāh Muḥammad. Ismā'īl al-. *Ṣaḥīḥ al-Bukhārī*. Damascus: Dār b. Kathīr, 2002.

Ḍaḥḥāk, b. Muzāḥim al-. *Tafsīr al-Ḍaḥḥāk*. Edited by Muḥammad Shukrī Aḥmad Zāwītī. Cairo: Dār al-Salām, 1999.

Dāraquṭnī, al-Ḥasan 'Alī b. 'Umar al-. *al-'Ilal al-wārida fī al-ḥadīth al-nabawīya*. 16 vols. Riyāḍ: Dār Ṭayba, 1985.

Dārimī, 'Abd Allāh b. 'Abd al-Raḥmān al-. *Sunan al-Dārimī*. Edited by Fawāz Aḥmad Zimrlī and Khālid al-Sab' al-'Alamī. 2 vols. Karachi: Qadīma Kutub Khāna, 1986.

Dhahabī, 'Abū 'Abd Allāh Shams al-Dīn Muḥammad b. Aḥmad b. 'Uthmān al-. *Kitāb Tadhkira al-ḥuffāẓ*. Edited by 'Abd al-Raḥmān b. Yaḥyā al-Mu'allimī. Beirut: Dār al-Kutub al-'Ilmiyya, n.d.

Dhahabī, ʿAbū ʿAbd Allāh Shams al-Dīn Muḥammad b. Aḥmad b. ʿUthmān al-. *Mīzān al-iʿtidāl fī naqd al-rijāl.* Edited by ʿAlī Muḥammad al-Bajāwī. 4 vols. Beirut: Dār al-Maʿrifa, 1963.

Dhahabī, ʿAbū ʿAbd Allāh Shams al-Dīn Muḥammad b. Aḥmad b. ʿUthmān al-. *Siyar aʿlām al-nubalāʾ.* Eleventh Edition. Edited by Bashshār ʿAwwād Maʿrūf. 25 vols. Beirut: Muʾassasa al-Risāla, 1996.

Ḥumaydī, Abū Bakr ʿAbd Allāh b. al-Zubayr al-Qurishī al-. *Musnad.* Edited by Ḥusayn Salīm Asad. Damascus: Dār al-Saqqā, 1996.

Ibn ʿAbbās, ʿAbd Allāh. *Tanwīr al-miqbās min tafsīr Ibn ʿAbbās.* Beirut: Dār al-Kutub al-ʿIlmiyya, 1992.

Ibn ʿAbd al-Barr, Abū ʿUmar Yūsuf b. ʿAbd Allāh b. Muḥammad. *al-Istīʿāb fī maʿrifa al-aṣḥāb.* Edited by ʿAlī Muḥammad al-Bajjāwī. Beirut: Dār al-Jīl, 1992.

Ibn Abī Ḥātim, Abū Muḥammad ʿAbd al-Raḥmān. *Kitāb al-ʿilal.* Edited by Saʿd b. ʿAbd Allāh al-Ḥumaydī and Khālid b. ʿAbd al-Raḥmān al-Juraysī. 7 vols. Riyāḍ: Maṭābiʿ al-Juraysī, 2006.

Ibn Abī Ḥātim, Abū Muḥammad ʿAbd al-Raḥmān. *Kitāb al-jarḥ wa al-taʿdīl.* 9 vols. Beirut: Dār al-Kutub al-ʿIlmiyya, 1953.

Ibn Abī Shayba, Abū Bakr ʿAbd Allāh b. Muḥammad b. Ibrāhīm. *al-Muṣannaf.* Edited by Abū Muḥammad Usāma b. Ibrāhīm b. Muḥammad. 15 vols. Cairo: al-Fārūq al-Ḥadīth lil-Ṭabāʿa wa al-Nashr, 2008.

Ibn Abī Shayba, Abū Bakr ʿAbd Allāh b. Muḥammad b. Ibrāhīm. *al-Kitāb al-Muṣannaf al-aḥādīth wa al-āthār.* 7 vols. Edited by Kamāl Yūsuf al-Ḥūt. Beirūt: Dār al-Tāj, 1989.

Ibn Abī Zamanīn, Abū ʿAbd Allāh Muḥammad b. ʿAbd Allāh. *Tafsīr al-qurʾān al-ʿazīz.* 5 vols. Edited by Abū ʿAbd Allāh Ḥusayn b. ʿUkāsha and Muḥammad b. Musṭafā al-Kanz. Cairo: al-Fārūq al-Ḥadītha lil-Ṭibāʿa wa al-Nashr, 2002.

Ibn Abī Zayd, Abū Muḥammad ʿAbd Allāh b. ʿAbd al-Raḥmān. *al-Nawādir wa al-ziyādāt ʿalā mā fī al-mudawwana min ghayrihā min al-ummahāt.* Edited by ʿAbd al-Fattāḥ Muḥammad al-Ḥulw. 15 vols. Beirut: Dār al-Gharb al-Islāmī, 1999.

Ibn al-Athīr, ʿIzz al-Dīn Abī al-Ḥasan ʿAlī b. Muḥammad al-Jazarī. *Usd al-ghāba fī maʿrifa al-ṣaḥāba.* Beirut: Dār Ibn Ḥazm, 2012.

Ibn ʿAmmār al-Shahīd, Muḥammad b. al-Ḥusayn, *ʿIlal al-aḥādīth fī kitāb al-Ṣaḥīḥ li-Muslim b. al-Ḥajjāj.* Edited by ʿAlī b. Ḥasan ʿAlī b. ʿAbd al-Ḥamīd al-Ḥalbī al-Asharī. Riyad: Dār al-Hijra lil-Nashr wa al-Tawzīʿ, 1991.

Ibn ʿAsākir, Abū Qāsim ʿAlī b. al-Ḥasan b. Hiba Allāh b. ʿAbd Allāh al-Shāfiʿī. *Tārīkh madīna dimashq.* 80 vols. Edited by Muḥammad al-Dīn ʿUmar b. Gharāma al-ʿAmrawī. Beirut: Dār al-Fikr, 1995.

Ibn Ḥajar Shihāb al-Dīn al-ʿAsqalānī, Aḥmad b. ʿAlī. *al-Iṣāba fī tamīz al-ṣaḥaba.* Edited by ʿĀdil Aḥmad ʿAbd al-Mawjūd et al. 8 vols. Beirut: Dār al-Kubut al-ʿIlmiyya, 1995.

Ibn Ḥajar Shihāb al-Dīn al-ʿAsqalānī, Aḥmad b. ʿAlī. *Nuzha al-naẓar fī tawḍīḥ nukhba al-fikr fī muṣṭalaḥ ahl al-athar.* Third edition. Edited by ʿAbd Allāh b. Ḍayf Allāh al-Ruḥaylī. Medina, 2021.

Ibn Ḥajar Shihāb al-Dīn al-ʿAsqalānī, Aḥmad b. ʿAlī. *Tahdhīb al-tahdhīb.* Edited by ʿĀdil Aḥmad ʿAbd al-Mawjūd and ʿAlī Muḥammad Maʿūd. 7 vols. Beirut: Dār al-Kutub al-Ilmiyya, 2004.

Ibn Ḥanbal, Aḥmad b. Muḥammad. *Kitāb al-ʿilal wa maʿrifa fī al-rijāl.* Second Edition. Edited by Waṣī Allāh b. Muḥammad ʿAbbās. 4 vols. Riyāḍ: Dār al-Khānī, 2001.

Ibn Ḥanbal, Aḥmad b. Muḥammad. *Masāʾil al-Imām Aḥmad b. Ḥanbal: riwāya ibnuhu Abī al-Faḍl Ṣāliḥ.* Edited by Faḍl al-Raḥmān Dīn Muḥammad. 3 vols. Delhi: al-Dār al-ʿIlmiyya, 1988.

Ibn Ḥanbal, Aḥmad b. Muḥammad. *Musnad.* Edited by Shuʿayb al-Arnaʾūṭ and ʿĀdil Murshid. 50 vols. Beirut: Muʾassasa al-Risāla, 1992.

Ibn Ḥanbal, Aḥmad b. Muḥammad. *Musnad.* Edited by Ahmad Muḥammad b. Shākir. 20 vols. Cairo: Dār al-Ḥadīth, 1995.

Ibn Ḥazm, ʿAlī b. Aḥmad. *al-Muḥallā.* 12 vols. Edited by Hishām al-Mannān. ʿAmmān: Bayt al-Ifkār al-Dawliyya, 2009.

Ibn Ḥibbān, Muḥammad. *Kitāb al-thiqāt*. Edited by Muḥammad 'Abd al-Mu'īd Khān. 10 vols. Hyderabād: Dā'ira al-Ma'ārif al-'Uthmāniyya, 1973.

Ibn Isḥāq, Muḥammad. *al-Sīrat al-nabawīya*. Beirut: Dār al-'Ilmiyya, 2004.

Ibn Ma'īn, Yaḥyā. *Yāḥyā b. Ma'īn wa-kitābuhu al-tārīkh: dirāsa wa tartīb wa taḥqīq*. Edited by Aḥmad Muḥammad Nūr Sayf. 4 vols. Mecca: Markaz al-Baḥth al-Ilmī wa Iḥyā' al-Turāth al-Islāmī, 1979.

Ibn Mājah, Abū 'Abd Allāh Muḥammad b. Yazīd al-Qazwīnī. *Sunan*. Edited by Muḥammad Fu'ād 'Abd al-Bāqī. Beirut: Dār al-Iḥyā' al-Kutub al-'Arabiyya, 1952–53.

Ibn Manẓūr, Abū al-Fuḍayl Jamāl al-Dīn b. Mukarram. *Lisān al-'arab*. 15 vols. Beirut: Dār al-Ṣādir, 1968.

Ibn Qudāma, Muwaffaq al-Dīn 'Abd Allāh. *al-Mughnī sharḥ mukhtaṣar al-khiraqī fī al-fiqh al-Ḥanbalī*. Edited by 'Abbās b. 'Abd al-Raḥmān al-Turkī and 'Abd al-Fatāḥ Muḥammad. 15 vols. Riyāḍ: Dār al-'Ālam al-Kutub, 1986.

Ibn Sa'd, Muḥammad. *Kitāb al-ṭabaqāt al-kubrā*. Edited by 'Alī Muḥammad 'Amr. 11 vols. Cairo: al-Nāshir Maktaba al-Khānjī, 2001.

Ibn Sahl, Aslam. *Tārīkh al-wāsiṭ*. Edited by Georgis 'Awwād. Beirut: Maktaba al-'Ulūm wa al-Ḥikma, 1986.

Ibn Ṣalāḥ, Abū 'Amr 'Uthmān b. 'Abd al-Raḥmān al-Shahrazūrī. *'Ulūm al-ḥadīth li-Ibn al-Ṣalāḥ (Ma'rifa awwā' 'ilm al-ḥadīth)*. Edited by Nūr al-Dīn 'Itr. Damascus: Dār al-Fikr, 1986.

Ibn Sallām, Yaḥyā. *Tafsīr Yaḥyā b. Sallām*. 7 vols. Edited by Hind Shalabī. Beirut: Dār al-Kutub al-'Illmiyya, 2004.

Ibn Wahb, 'Abd Allāh. *al-Jāmi' tafsīr al-qur'ān*. Edited by Mīklow Mawrānī. 3 vols. Beirut: Dār al-Gharb al-Islāmī, 2003.

Ibn Yūnus, Abū Bakr Muḥammad b. 'Abd Allāh. *al-Jāmi' li-masā'il al-mudawwana*. 24 vols. Beirut: Dār al-Fikr, 2013.

Iṣbahānī, Abū Na'īm al-. *Ḥilya al-awliyā' wa ṭabaqāt al-aṣfiyā'*. Edited by Sāmī Anwar Jāhīn. 8 vols. Cairo: Dār al-Ḥadīth, 2009.

Jabr, Mujāhid bin-. *Tafsīr al-Imām Mujāhid b. Jabr*. Edited by Muḥammad 'Abd al-Salām Abī al-Nīl. Madīna Naṣr: Dār al-Fikr al-Islāmī al-Ḥadītha, 1989.

Jaṣṣāṣ, Abū Bakr Aḥmad b. 'Alī al-Rāzī al-. *Aḥkām al-qur'ān*. Edited by Muḥammad al-Ṣādiq Qamḥāwī. 5 vols. Beirut: Dār Iḥyā' al-Turāth al-'Arabī, 1996.

Jurjānī, Abū Aḥmad 'Abd Allāh b. 'Adī al-. *al-Kāmil fī ḍu'afā' al-rijāl*. Edited by 'Ādil Aḥmad 'Abd al-Mawjūd and 'Alī Muḥammad Ma'ūd. 9 vols. Beirut: Dār al-Kutub al-Ilmiyya, 1997.

Kāndhlawī, Muḥammad Zakarīyya al-. *Awjaz al-masālik ilā muwaṭṭa' Mālik*. Edited by Taqī al-Dīn al-Nadwī. 17 vols. Damascus: Dār al-Qalam, 2003.

Khaṭīb al-Baghdādī, Abū Bakr Aḥmad b. 'Alī b. Thābit al-. *al-Kifāya fī ma'rifa uṣūl 'alā al-riwāya*. Edited by Abū Isḥāq Ibrāhīm Muṣṭafa al-Dimyāṭī. 2 vols. Mīt Ghamr: Dār al-Hudā, 2002.

Khaṭīb al-Baghdādī, Abū Bakr Aḥmad b. 'Alī b. Thābit al-. *Kitāb al-faqīh wa al-mutafaqqih*. Edited by Abū 'Abd al-Raḥmān and 'Ādil b. Yūsuf al-'Azāzī. 2 vols. Jedda: Dār Ibn al-Jawzī, 1996.

Khaṭīb al-Baghdādī, Abū Bakr Aḥmad b. 'Alī b. Thābit al-. *Tārīkh madīna al-salām*. Edited by Bashshār 'Awwād Ma'rūf. 17 vols. Beirut: Dār al-Gharb al-Islāmī, 2001.

Khayyāṭ, Khalīfa bin-. *Tārīkh Khalīfa b. Khayyāt*. Second Edition. Edited by Akram Ḍiyā' al-'Amrī. Riyāḍ: Dār Tayuba, 1985.

Khiraqī, Abū Qāsim 'Umar b. al-Ḥusayn al-. *Mukhtaṣar al-Khiraqī*. Edited by Muḥammad Zuhayr al-Shāwīsh. Damascus: Dār al-Salām, 1958.

Kulaynī, Muḥammad b. Ya'qūb al-. *Uṣūl al-kāfī*. 7 vols. Beirut: Manshūrāt al-Fajr, 2007.

Mālik, Mālik b. Anas al-Aṣbaḥī al-Ḥimyarī. *al-Muwaṭṭa'*. Narrated by Muḥammad b. al-Ḥasan al-Shaybānī. Edited by 'Abd al-Wahhāb 'Abd al-Laṭīf. Cairo: Wizāra al-Awqāf al-Majlis al-'Ālā lil-Shu'ūn al-Islāmiyya, 1994.

Mālik, Mālik b. Anas al-Aṣbaḥī al-Ḥimyarī. *al-Muwaṭṭa'*. Narrated by Yaḥyā b. Yaḥyā al-Laythī. Edited by Muḥammad Muṣṭafa al-A'ẓamī. 5 vols. Abū Ẓabī: The Zayed Charitable Foundation, 2004.

Marwazī, Muḥammad b. Naṣr. *al-Sunna*. Edited by Abū Muḥammad Sālim b. Aḥmad al-Salafī. Beirut: Mu'assasa al-Kutub al-Thaqāfiyya, 1988.

Māwardī, Abū al-Ḥasan 'Alī b. Muḥammad b. Ḥabīb al-. *al-Aḥkām al-sulṭāniyya wa al-wilāyāt al-dīniyya*. Kuwait: Maktaba Dār ibn Qutayba, 1989.

Māwardī, Abū al-Ḥasan 'Alī b. Muḥammad b. Ḥabīb al-. *al-Ḥāwī al-kabīr fī fiqh madhhab li-imām al-Shāfi'ī wa hu wa sharḥ mukhtaṣar al-Muzanī*. Edited by 'Alī Muḥammad Ma'awwaḍ and 'Ādil Aḥmad 'Abd al-Mawjūd. 18 vols. Beirut: Dār al-Kutub al-'Ilmiyya, 1994.

Mawṣilī, Abū Ya'lā Aḥmad b. 'Alī b. al-Muthannā al-Tamīmī al-. *Musnad Abī Ya'lā al-Mawṣilī*. Edited by Ḥusayn Salīm Asad. 16 vols. Beirut: Dār al-Ma'mūn al-Thurāt, 1971.

Mizzī, Jamāl al-Dīn Abī al-Ḥajjāj Yūsuf al-. *Tahdhīb al-kamāl fī asmā' al-rijāl*. Third Edition. Edited by Bashshār 'Awwād Ma'rūf. 35 vols. Beirut: Mu'assasa al-Risāla, 1983.

Muḥāsibī, al-Ḥārith b. Asad. *al-'Aql fahm al-qur'ān*. Edited by Ḥusayn al-Quwwatlī. Beirut: Dār al-Fikr, 1971.

Muslim b. Ḥajjāj, Abū al-Ḥusayn. *Ṣaḥīḥ al-Muslim*. Edited by Muḥammad Fu'ād 'Abd al-Bāqī. Beirut: Dār al-Ḥadīth, 1991.

Najafī, Muḥammad Ḥasan al-. *Jawāhir al-kalām fī sharḥ sharī'i al-Islām*. Edited by Ḥaydar al-Dabbagh. 44 vols. Qom: Mu'assisat al-Nashr al-Islāmī, 2012.

Nasā'ī, Abū 'Abd al-Raḥmān Aḥmad b. Shu'ayb al-. *Kitāb al-sunan al-kubrā*. Edited by Ḥasan 'Abd al-Mu'min Shalabī. 12 vols. Beirut: Mu'assasāt al-Risāla, 2001.

Qudūrī, Abū al-Ḥasan Aḥmad b. Ja'far al-Baghdādī al-. *Mukhtaṣar al-Qudūrī fī al-fiqh al-ḥanafī*. Edited by Kāmil Muḥammad Muḥmmad 'Uwayḍah. Beirut: Dār al-Kutub al-Ilmiyya, 1997.

Qummī, 'Abbās b. Muḥammad Riḍā al-. *al-Kunā wa al-aqlāb*. Fifth Edition. 3 vols. Tehran: Maktaba al-Ṣadr, 1929.

Qummī, Abū al-Ḥasan 'Alī b. Ibrāhīm al-. *Tafsīr al-Qummī*. Third Edition. Edited by al-Sayyid Ṭayyib al-Mūsawī al-Jazā'irī. 2 vols. Qom: Mu'assasa Dār al-Kitāb, 1885.

Sahl, Aslam bin-. *Tārīkh al-wāsiṭ*. Edited by Georgis 'Awwād. Beirut: Maktaba al-'Ulūm wa al-Ḥikma, 1986.

Saḥnūn b. Sa'īd al-Tanūkhī. *al-Mudawwana al-kubrā*. 5 vols. Beirut: Dār al-Kitāb al-'Ilmiyya, 1993.

Sam'ānī, Abū Sa'd 'Abd al-Karīm b. Muḥammad b. Manṣūr al-Yamanī al-. *al-Ansāb*. Edited by 'Abd al-Raḥmān b. Yaḥyā al-Mu'allamī al-Yamanī. 13 vols. Hyderabad: Dār al-Ma'ārifa al-'Uthmāniyya, 1977.

Sarakhsī, Shams al-A'imma Muḥammad b. Aḥmad b. Sahl al-. *Kitāb al-mabsūṭ*. Edited by Abū 'Abd Allāh Muḥammad Ḥasan. 31 vols. Beirut: Dār al-Kutub al-'Ilmiyya, 2001.

Shāfi'ī, Muḥammad b. Idrīs al-. *al-Umm*. Edited by Rif'at Fawzī 'Abd al-Muṭṭalib. 11 vols. Alexandria: Dār al-Wafā', 2001.

Shaybānī, Abū 'Abd Allāh Muḥammad b. al-Ḥasan al-. *al-Aṣl*. Edited by Mehmet Boynukalın, 13 vols. Beirut: Dār Ibn Ḥazm, 2012.

Shaybānī, Abū 'Abd Allāh Muḥammad b. al-Ḥasan al-. *Jāmi' al-saghīr, ma'a sharḥ-hi al-nāfi' al-kabīr*. Edited by 'Abd al-Ḥayy. Karachi: Idārat al-Qur'ān wa al-'Ulūm al-Islāmiyya, 1990.

Shaybānī, Abū 'Abd Allāh Muḥammad b. al-Ḥasan al-. *Kitāb al-āthār*. Edited by Khālid al-'Awwād. Beirut: Dār al-Nawādir, 2008.

Sulaymān, Muqātil bin-. *Tafsīr Muqātil b. Sulaymān*. Edited by 'Abd Allāh Maḥmūd Shihāta. 5 vols. Beirut: Mu'assasa al-Tārīkh al-'Arabī, 2002.

Ṭabarānī, Sulaymān b. Aḥmad al-. *al-Mu'jam al-kabīr*. Edited by Ḥamdī 'Abd al-Majīd al-Salafī. 25 vols. Cairo: Maktaba Ibn Taymiyya, 1983.

Ṭabarī, Abū Ja'far Muḥammad b. Jarīr al-. *Tafsīr al-Ṭabarī: Jāmi' al-bayān 'an ta'wīl āy al-qur'ān*. Second Edition. Edited by Maḥmūd Muḥammad Shākir and Aḥmad Muḥammad Shākir. 16 vols. Cairo: Maktaba b. Taymiyya, n.d.

Ṭabarī, Abū Ja'far Muḥammad b. Jarīr al-. *Tafsīr al-Ṭabarī: Jāmiʿ al-bayān ʿan taʾwīl āy al-qurʾān.* Edited by ʿAbd Allāh b. ʿAbd al-Muḥsin al-Turkī. 26 vols. Cairo: Dār al-Hajr, n.d.
Ṭabarī, Abū Jaʿfar Muḥammad b. Jarīr al-. *Tārīkh al-Ṭabarī: tārīkh al-rusul wa al-mamlūk.* 11 vols. Second Edition. Edited by Muḥammad Abū al-Faḍl Ibrāhīm. Cairo: Dār al-Maʿrifa, 1967.
Ṭaḥāwī, Aḥmad b. Muḥammad b. Salāma al-. *Sharḥ mushkil al-āthār.* Edited by Shuʿayb al-Arnāʾūt. 16 vols. Beirut: Muʾassassa al-Risāla, 1994.
Ṭayālisī, Sulaymān b. Dāwūd b. al-Jārūd al-. *Musnad Abī Dāwūd al-Ṭayālisī.* Edited by Muḥammad b. ʿAbd al-Muḥsin al-Turkī. 4 vols. Jīza: Hajr lil-Ṭabāʿā wa al-Nashr wa al-Tazīʿa wa al-Aʿlām, 1999.
Tirmidhī, Abū ʿĪsā Muḥammad b. ʿĪsā al-. *al-Jāmiʿ al-kabīr.* Edited by Bashshār ʿAwwād Maʿrūf. 6 vols. Beirut: Dār al-Gharb al-Islāmī, 1996.
Ṭūsī, Muḥammad b. al-Ḥasan b. ʿAlī al-. *al-Mabsūṭ fī fiqh al-imāmiyya.* Edited by Muḥammad Taqī al-Kashfī, 8 vols. Tehran: al-Maṭbaʿa al-Ḥaydariyya, 19671968.
Ṭūsī, Muḥammad b. al-Ḥasan b. ʿAlī al-. *Al-Tibyān fī tafsīr al-qurʾān.* 10 vols. Edited by Āghā Buzruq al-Ṭihrānī. Beirut: Dār Iḥyāʾ al-Turāth al-ʿArabī, 1999.
ʿUqaylī, Abū Jaʿfar Muḥammad b. ʿAmr b. Mūsā b. Ḥammād al-. *Kitāb al-ḍuʿafāʾ al-kabīr.* Edited by ʿAbd al-Muʿtī Amīn Qalʿajī. 4 vols. Beirut: Dār al-Kutub al-ʿIlmiyya, 1984.
Wakīʿ, Muḥammad b. Khalaf b. Ḥayyān. *Akhbār al-quḍāt.* 3 vols. Beirut: ʿĀlam al-Kutub, n.d.
Yaʿqūbī b. Jaʿfar b. Wahb, Aḥmad b. Abī-. *Tārīkh al-Yaʿqūbī.* Edited by ʿAbd al-Amīr Muhannā. 2 vols. Beirut: Sharkat al-ʿĀlamī, 2010.
Yāqūt b. ʿAbd Allāh, Shihāb al-Dīn Abī ʿAbd Allāh. *Muʿjam al-Buldān.* 5 vols. Beirut: Dār al-Ṣādr, 1977.
Zamakhsharī, Abū al-Qāsim Jābir Allāh Maḥmūd b. ʿUmar al-. *Tafsīr al-kashshāf ʿan ḥaqāʾiq al-tanzīl wa ʿuyūn al-aqāwīl fī wujūh al-taʾwīl.* Edited by Khalīl Maʾmūm Shīḥā. Beirut: Dār al-Maʿrifa, 2009.

SECONDARY SOURCES

Abbott, Nabia. "*Ḥadīth* Literature—II: Collection and Transmission of *Ḥadīth*." In *Arabic Literature to the End of the Umayyad Period*, edited by A.F.L. Beeston et al., 289–98. Cambridge: Cambridge University Press, 1983.
Abel, Armand. "al-Dad̲j̲d̲j̲āl." In Encyclopaedia of Islam New Edition Online (EI-2 English). Edited by Peri Bearman et al., Brill, 2012. doi: https://doi-org.proxy.uchicago.edu/10.1163/1573-3912_islam_SIM_1654.
Abou El Fadl, Khaled. *Rebellion & Violence in Islamic Law.* Cambridge: Cambridge University Press, 2001.
Abou El Fadl, Khaled. *Speaking in God's Name: Islamic Law, Authority, and Women.* Oxford: Oneworld Publications Ltd., 2001.
Abou El Fadl, Khaled. "The Shariʿah." In *The Oxford Handbook of Islam and Politics*, edited by John L. Esposito and Emad El-Din Shahin, 7–26. Oxford: Oxford University Press, 2013.
Abdullah, Arif Kemil. *The Qurʾan and Normative Religious Pluralism: A Thematic Study of the Qurʾan.* Herndon: The International Institute of Islamic Thought, 2014.
Abdullah, Faisal Z. "Pre-Muḥammadan Law and the Muḥammadan Sharīʿah: Muslim Theories and Implementation of Biblical Law and the Laws of Prior Religious Communities." PhD diss., University of California, Los Angeles, 2020.
Abu-Alabbas, Bilal, Michael Dann, Christopher Melchert. *Modern Hadith Studies: Continued Debates and New Approaches.* Edinburgh: Edinburgh University Press, 2020.
Adang, Camilla. *Muslim Writers on Judaism and the Hebrew Bible: From Ibn Rabban to Ibn Hazm.* New York: Brill, 1996.
Ahmad, Ziauddin. "Ushūr and Maks in Early Islam." *Journal of Islamic Studies* 27, no. 1 (Spring 1988): 1–11.

Ahmed, Mohammed Shahab. "The Satanic Verses Incident in the Memory of the Early Muslim Community: An Analysis of the Early *Riwāyah*s and Their *Isnād*s." PhD diss., Princeton University, 1999.

Aghaei, Ali. "The Common Link and Its Relation to Hadith Terminology." In *Modern Hadith Studies: Continued Debates and New Approaches*, edited by Belal Abu-Alabbas et al., 97–128. Edinburgh: Edinburgh University Press, 2020.

Ali, Kecia. *Sexual Ethics and Islam: Feminist Reflections on Qur'an, Hadith, and Jurisprudence*, expanded and revised edition. London: One World Publications, 2016.

Ansari, Hassan. "The Shi'i Reception of Mu'tazilism (II): Twelver Shiis." In *The Oxford Handbook of Islamic Theology*. Edited by Sabine Schmidtke, 196–214. Oxford: Oxford University Press, 2016.

Anthony, Sean W. "Crime and Punishment in Early Medina: The Origins of a *Maghāzī*-Tradition." In *Analysing Muslim Traditions: Studies in Legal, Exegetical and Maghāzī Ḥadīth*. Edited by Harald Motzki et al., 385–466. Leiden: Brill, 2013.

Asad, Talal. *Genealogies of Religion: Discipline and Reasons of Power in Christianity and Islam*. Baltimore: The John Hopkins University Press, 1993.

Azam, Hina. *Sexual Violation in Islamic Law: Substance, Evidence, and Procedure*. New York: Cambridge University Press, 2015.

Azami, M. Mustafa. *Studies in Hadith Methodology and Approaches*. Oakbrook: American Trust Publications, 1978.

Bauer, Karen and Feras Hamza. *Women, Households, and the Hereafter in the Qur'an: A Patronage of Piety*. Oxford: Oxford University Press, 2024.

Becker, Jürgen. *Jesus of Nazareth*, trans. James E. Crouch. Berlin: Walter De Gruyter, 1998.

Bergsma, John Sietze and Scott Walker Hahn, eds. "Noah's Nakedness and the Curse of Canaan (Genesis 9:20–27), *Journal of Biblical Literature* 124, no. 1 (2005): 25–40.

Berkey, Jonathan. *The Formation of Islam: Religion and Society in the Near East, 600-1800*. New York: Cambridge University Press, 2003.

Berkowitz, Beth H. *Execution and Invention: Death Penalty Discourse in Early Rabbinic and Christian Cultures*. Oxford: Oxford University Press, 2006.

Berg, Herbert, editor. *Method and Theory in the Study of Islamic Origins*. Leiden: Brill, 2003.

Bevir, Mark. "Why Historical Distance Is Not a Problem." *History and Theory* 50, no. 4 (2011): 24–37.

Biale, Rachel. *Women and Jewish Law: An Exploration of Women's Issues in Halakhic Sources*. New York: Schocken Books Inc., 1984.

Boekhoff-van der Voort, Nicolet. "Untangling the 'Unwritten Documents' of the Prophet Muḥammad. An *Isnād-cum-Matn* Analysis of Interwoven Traditions." *Religions* 12 (2021): 1–32.

Brown, Jonathan. "Did the Prophet Say It or Not? The Literal, Historical, and Effective Truth of Ḥadīths in Early Sunnism." *Journal of the American Oriental Society* 129, no. 2 (Apr.–Jun. 2009): 259–85.

Brown, Jonathan. *Ḥadīth: Muhammad's Legacy in the Medieval and Modern World*. London: OneWorld Publications, 2009.

Brown, Jonathan. *Misquoting Muhammad: The Challenge and Choices of Interpreting the Prophet's Legacy*. London: Oneworld Publications, 2014.

Brown, Jonathan. "The Rules of Matn Criticism: There Are No Rules." *Islamic Law and Society* 19, no. 4 (2012): 356–96.

Brundage, James A. *Law, Sex, and Christian Society in Medieval Europe*. Chicago: The University of Chicago Press, 1987.

Brunner, Rainer. "The Role of Ḥadīth as Cultural Memory in Shīʿī History." *Jerusalem Studies in Arabic and Islam* 30 (2005): 318–60.

Burton, John. "Law and Exegesis: The Penalty for Adultery in Islam." In *Approaches to the Qur'ān*, edited by G.R. Hawting and Abdul-Kader A. Shareef, 269–84. New York: Routledge, 1993.

Burton, John. *The Collection of the Qur'ān*. Cambridge: Cambridge University Press, 1977.

Burton, John. "The Meaning of 'IHSAN.'" *Journal of Semitic Studies* 19 (1974): 47–75.
Burton, John. "The Origin of the Islamic Penalty for Adultery." Lecture at Glasgow University. Glasgow, UK, 1978.
Burton, John. *The Sources of Islamic Law: Islamic Theories of Abrogation.* Edinburgh: Edinburgh University Press, 1990.
Butler, Thomas. "Memory: A Mixed Blessing." In *Memory: History, Culture and the Mind*, edited by Thomas Butler. Oxford: Basil Blackwell Ltd., 1989.
Cantarella, Eva. "Gender, Sexuality, and Law." In *The Cambridge Companion to Ancient Greek Law*, edited by Michael Gagarin and David Cohen, 236–53. Cambridge: Cambridge University Press, 2005.
Coats, R. Morris and Gary M. Pecquet. "The Calculus of Conquests: The Decline and Fall of the Returns to Roman Expansion." *The Independent Review* 17, no. 4 (Spring 2013): 517–40.
Cohen Shaye J.D., Robert Goldenberg, and Hayim Lapid eds. *The Oxford Annotated Mishnah.* 2 Vols. Oxford: Oxford University Press, 2022.
Cole, Juan. "Late Roman Law and the Quranic Punishments for Adultery." *The Muslim World* 112 (Spring 2022): 207–24.
Confino, Alon. "Collective Memory and Cultural History: Problems of Method." *The American Historical Review* 102, no. 5 (1997): 1386–403.
Cook, Michael. *Early Muslim Dogma: A Source-Critical Study.* Cambridge: Cambridge University Press, 1981.
Cook, Michael. "Ibn Qutayba and the Monkeys." *Studia Islamica* 89 (1999): 43–74.
Crone, Patricia. "Two Legal Problems Bearing on the Early History of the Qur'ān." *Jerusalem Studies in Arabic and Islam* 18 (1994): 1–37.
Davidson, Garrett A. Carrying on the Tradition: A Social and Intellectual History of Hadith Transmission Across a Thousand Years. Boston: Brill, 2020.
Donner, Fred. Muhammad and the Believers: At the Origins of Islam. Cambridge, MA: The Belknap Press of Harvard University Press, 2010.
Donner, Fred. *Narratives of Islamic Origins: The Beginnings of Islamic Historical Writing.* Princeton: The Darwin Press, 1998.
Driver, G.R., and John C. Miles. *The Babylonian Laws.* Oxford: Clarendon Press, 1952.
du Plessis, Paul. *Borkowski's Textbook on Roman Law.* Fifth Edition. Oxford: Oxford University Press, 2015.
El Shamsy, Ahmed. "The Curious Case of Early Muslim Hair Dyeing." In *Islam at 250: Studies in Memory of G.H.A. Juynboll*, edited by Petra M. Sijpesteijn and Camilla Adang, 187–206. Leiden: Brill, 2020.
El Tantawi, Sarah. "Mysterious Legislation: 'Umar ibn al-Khaṭṭāb's Role in the Legalization of the Stoning Punishment in the Sunni Islamic Tradition." In *Islamic Interpretative Tradition and Gender Justice: Processes of Canonization, Subversion, and Change*, edited by Nevin Reda and Yasmin Amin, 288–313. Montreal & Kingston: McGill-Queen's University Press, 2020.
El Tantawi, Sarah. *Shari'ah on Trial: Northern Nigeria's Islamic Revolution.* Oakland, California: The University of California Press, 2017.
Epp, Eldon Jay. "The Multivalence of the Term 'Original Text' in New Testament Textual Criticism." *The Harvard Theological Review* 92, no. 3 (Jul. 1999): 245–81.
Epstein, Louis M. *Sex Laws and Customs in Judaism.* New York: Ktav Publishing House, 1967.
Erhart, Victoria. "The Development of Syriac Christian Canon Law in the Sasanian Empire," in *Law, Society, and Authority in Late Antiquity*, edited by Ralph W. Mathisen, 115–32. New York: Oxford University Press Inc., 2001.
Eyre, C.J. "Crime and Adultery in Ancient Egypt." *The Journal of Egyptian Archaeology* 70 (1984): 92–105.
Faizer, Rizwi S. "Muhammad and The Medinan Jews: A Comparison of the Texts of Ibn Ishaq's Kitab Sirat Rasul Allah With al-Waqidi's Kitab al-Maghazi." *International Journal of Middle East Studies* 28, no. 4 (Nov. 1996): 463–89.

Francesca, Ersilia, "Flogging, Banning, and Lapidation: What Was the Punishment for Fornication and Adultery in Early Islam?" *Journal of Jerusalem and Arabic and Islam* 52 (2022): 165–210.

Friedman, Shamma. "Sorting Out the Wages of Adultery: Execution, Ordeal or Divorce." In *Jewish and Iranian Studies in Honor of Yaakov Elman*, edited by Shoshannat Yaakov, 77–109. Leiden: Brill, 2012.

Gaiser Adam R. "Ḥadīth, Ibāḍism." In *Encyclopaedia of Islam*. Third Edition. Edited by Kate Fleet et al., 2:140–44. Leiden: Brill, 2016.

Gaiser Adam R. Shurāt *Legends Ibāḍī Identities: Martyrdom, Ascetism, and the Marking of an Early Islamic Community*. Columbia: The University of South Carolina Press, 2016.

Galpaz-Feller, Pnina. "Private Lives and Public Censure: Adultery in Ancient Egypt and Biblical Israel." *Near Eastern Archaeology* 67, no. 3 (2004): 153–61.

Gerhardsson, Birger. *The Reliability of the Gospel Tradition*. Grand Rapids: Baker Publishing Group, 2001.

Gil, Moshe. "The Origin of the Jews of Yathrib." In *The Arabs and Arabia on the Eve of Islam*, edited by F.E. Peters, 145–66. Brookfield: Ashgate/Variorum, 1999.

Goldin, Hyman E. *Hebrew Criminal Law and Procedure: Mishnah: Sanhedrin—Makkot*. New York: Twayne Publishing, Inc., 1952.

Goldziher, Ignaz. *Muslim Studies*. Vol. 2. Translated by C.R. Barber and S.M. Stern. London: George Allen & Unwin Ltd., 1971. Edited by Majid Daneshgar and Walih Saleh. Leiden: Brill, 2016.

Görke, Andreas. "Eschatology, History, and the Common Link: A Study In Methodology." In Method and Theory in the Study of Islamic Origins. Edited by Herbert Berg, 179–208. Leiden: Brill, 2003.

Görke, Andreas. "Remnants of an Old *Tafsīr* Tradition: The Exegetical Accounts of 'Urwa b. al-Zubayr." In *Islamic Studies Today: Essays in Honor of Andrew Rippin*, edited by Majid Daneshgar and Walid Saleh, 22–42. Leiden: Brill, 2017.

Görke, Andreas, Harald Motzki, and Gregor Schoeler. "First Century Sources for the Life of Muḥammad? A Debate." *Der Islam* 80, no. 2 (2012): 2–59.

Grubbs, Judith Evans. *Law and Family in Late Antiquity: The Emperor Constantine's Marriage Legislations*. Oxford: Clarendon Press, 1995.

Grubbs, Judith Evans. *Women and The Law in the Roman Empire: A Sourcebook on Marriage, Divorce and Widowhood*. New York: Routledge, 2002.

Günther, Sebastian. "Fictional narration and imagination within an authoritative framework. Towards a new understanding of Ḥadīth." In *Story-telling in the framework of non-fictional Arabic literature*, edited by Stefan Leder, 433–72. Wiesbaden: Harrassowitz, 1998.

Haider, Najam. *The Rebel and the Imām in Early Islam: Explorations in Muslim Historiography*. Cambridge: Cambridge University Press, 2019.

Hakim, Abraham. "Conflicting Images of the Lawgivers: The Caliph and the Prophet: Sunnat 'Umar and Sunnat Muhammad." In *Method and Theory in the Study of Islamic Origins*, edited by Herbert Berg, 159–78. Leiden: Brill, 2003.

Hakim, Abraham. "Context: 'Umar b. Al-Khaṭṭāb." In *The Blackwell Companion to the Qur'an*, edited by Andrew Rippin, 205–20. Oxford: Oxford University Press, 2009.

Haleem, M.A.S. Abdel. *The Qur'an*. Oxford: Oxford University Press, 2005.

Hall, Stuart. *Representations:* Cultural Representations and Signifying Practices. Edited by Stuart Hall. London: Sage Publications, 1997.

Hallaq, Wael. *An Introduction to Islamic Law*. Cambridge: Cambridge University Press, 2009.

Hagler, Aaron M. "Repurposed Narratives: The Battle of Ṣiffīn and the Historical Memory of the Umayyad Dynasty." *Mathal* 3, no. 1 (2013): 1–27.

Hagler, Aaron M. Sapping the Narrative: Ibn Kathir's Account of the *Shūrā* of 'Uthmān in *Kitab al-Bidaya wa-l-Nihaya*." *International J. of Middle East Studies* 47 (2015): 303–21.

Hasan Elahi-zadeh, Mohammad, and Translated by Alexander Khaleeli. "Bilāl b. Ḥārith." In Encyclopaedia Islamica Online. Edited by Wilferd Madelung et al., Brill, 2015. doi: https://doi.org/10.1163/1875-9831_isla_SIM_000000131.

Hawting, G.R. *The Idea of Idolatry and the Emergence of Islam: From Polemic to History*. New York: Cambridge University Press, 1999.

Hayes, Christine. The Emergence of Judaism: Classical Traditions in Contemporary Perspective. Minneapolis: Fortress Press, 2007.

Hayes, Christine. "Rabbinic Contestations of Authority," *Cardozo Law Review* 28, no. 1 (2006): 123–41.

Hays, Richard B. *The Moral Vision of the New Testament: Community, Cross, New Creation: A Contemporary Introduction to New Testament Ethics*. San Francisco: Harper San Francisco, 1996.

Hibri, Tayeb El-. *Reinterpreting Islamic Historiography: Hārūn al-Rashīd and the Narrative of the 'Abbāsid Caliphate*. Cambridge: Cambridge University Press, 2004.

Hirschfeld, Hartwig. "Historical and Legendary Controversies Between Mohammed and the Rabbis." *The Jewish Quarterly Review* 10 (1897): 100–16.

Hirschfeld, Hartwig. New Researches into the Composition and Exegesis of the Qoran. London: Royal Asiatic Society, 1902.

Hodgson, Marshall G.S. *The Venture of Islam: Conscience and History in a World Civilization*. Vol. 1. Chicago: University of Chicago Press, 1974.

Humphreys, R. Stephen. *Islamic History: A Framework for Inquiry*. Minneapolis: Bibliotheca Islamica, Inc., 1988.

Ibrahim, Ayman S. *Conversion to Islam: Competing Themes in Early Islamic Historiography*. New York: Oxford University Press, 2021.

Juynboll, Gautier H.A. *Encyclopedia of Canonical Ḥadīth*. Boston: Brill, 2007.

Juynboll, Gautier H.A. "The *Man Kadhaba* Tradition and the Prohibition of Lamenting the Dead. An Investigation Into *Mutawātir* Traditions." In *Muslim Tradition: Studies in Chronology, Provenance and Authorship of Early Hadīth*, 96–133. Cambridge: Cambridge University Press, 1983.

Juynboll, Gautier H.A. "Nāfi', the *mawlā* of Ibn 'Umar, and his position in the Muslim *Ḥadīth* Literature." *Der Islam* (Jan. 1993): 207–44.

Juynboll, Gautier H.A. "The Role of Mu'ammarūn in the Early Development of the Isnād." *Wiener Zeitschrift fur die Kunde des Morgenlandes* 81 (1991): 155–75.

Juynboll, Gautier H.A. "S̲h̲u'ba b. al-Ḥad̲j̲d̲j̲ād̲j̲." In *Encyclopaedia of Islam*, Second Edition. Edited by Peri Bearman et al., 9:491–2. Leiden: Brill, 1997.

Juynboll, Gautier H.A. "Some *Isnād*-Analytical Methods Illustrated on the Basis of Several Women-Demeaning Sayings from *Ḥadīth* Literature." *Al-Qanṭara* 10, no. 2 (1989): 343–84.

Kamali, Mohammad Hashim. *A Textbook of Ḥadīth Studies: Authenticity, Compilation, Classification and Criticism of Ḥadīth*. Leicestershire: The Islamic Foundation, 2016.

Kansteiner, Wulf. "Finding Meaning in Memory: A Methodological Critique of Collective Memory Studies." *Journal of History and Theory* 41, no. 2 (May 2002): 179–97.

Kara, Seyfeddin. *The Integrity of the Qur'an: Sunni and Shi'i Historical Narratives*. Edinburgh: Edinburgh University Press, 2024.

Kern, Linda L. "The Riddle of 'Umar ibn al-Khaṭṭāb in Bukhārī's *Kitāb al-Jāmi' aṣ-Ṣaḥīḥ*." PhD diss., Harvard University, 1996.

Khalek, Nancy. *Damascus After the Muslim Conquest: Text and Image in Early Islam*. New York: Oxford University Press, 2011.

Khalidi, Tarif. *Arabic Historical Thought in the Classical Period*. Cambridge: Cambridge University Press, 1994.

Lane, Edward William. *An Arabic-English Lexicon*. Beirut: Librairie du Liban, 1968.

Lange, Christian. "Sins, Expiation and Non-Rationality in Ḥanafī and Shāfi'ī *Fiqh*." In *Islamic Law in Theory. Studies on Jurisprudence in Honor of Bernard Weiss*. Edited by A. Kevin Reinhart and Robert Gleave, 143–75. Leiden: Brill, 2014.

Lassner, Jacob. *Islamic Revolution and Historical Memory: An Inquiry Into the Art of ʿAbbāsid Apologetics*. New Haven: American Oriental Society, 1986.

Lazarus-Yafeh, Have. "Taḥrīf." In Encyclopaedia of Islam. Second Edition. Edited by Peri Bearman et al., 10:111–2. Leiden: Brill, 2000.

Lecker, Michael. "Biographical Notes on Ibn Shihāb al-Zuhrī." *Journal of Semitic Studies* 41 (1996): 21–63.

Lindstedt, Ilkka. *Muḥammad and His Followers in Context: The Religious Map of Late Antique Arabia*. Leiden; Boston: Brill, 2024.

Lowin, Shari. "Kaʿb al-Aḥbār." In Encyclopedia of Jews in the Islamic World. Edited by Norman A. Stillman et al., 83. Leiden: Brill, 2010.

Lowry, Joseph E. *Early Islamic Legal Theory: The Risāla of Muḥammad ibn Idrīs al-Shāfiʿī*. Boston: Brill, 2007.

Lucas, Scott C. *Constructive Critics, Ḥadīth Literature, and the Articulation of Sunnī Islam: The Legacy of the Generations of Ibn Saʿd, Ibn Maʿīn, and Ibn Ḥanbal*. Boston: Brill, 2004.

Lucas, Scott C. "Perhaps You Only Kissed Her: A Contrapuntal Reading of the Penalties for Illicit Sex in the Sunni *Hadith* Literation." *Journal of Religious Ethics* 39, no. 3 (2011): 399–415.

Madigan, Daniel A. *The Qur'ān's Self-Image: Writing and Authority in Islam's Scripture*. Princeton: Princeton University Press, 2001.

Madelung, Wilferd. *The Succession to Muḥammad: A Study of the Early Caliphate*. Cambridge: Cambridge University Press, 1997.

Mavani, Hamid. "Sunni-Shi'i Rapprochement: Internal Contradictions." *The American Journal of Islamic Social Sciences* 33, no. 1 (2016): 133–47.

Mazuz, Haggai. *The Religious and Spiritual Life of the Jews of Medina*. Leiden: Brill, 2014.

Meeks, Wayne A. *The Moral World of the First Christians*. Philadelphia: Westminster Press, 1986.

Meeks, Wayne A. *The HarperCollins Study Bible: New Revised Standard Version*. New York: HarperCollins Publishers, 1997.

Melchert, Christopher. "Qur'ānic Abrogation Across the Ninth Century: Shāfiʿī Abū ʿUbayd, Muḥāsibī, and Ibn Qutaybah." In *Studies in Islamic Legal Theory*, edited by Bernard G. Weiss, 75–98. Leiden: Brill, 2002.

Mendelsohn, S. *Criminal Jurisprudence of The Ancient Hebrews*. Union: The Lawbook Exchange, Ltd., 2001.

Mesoudi, Alex and Andrew Whiten. "The Multiple Roles of Cultural Transmission Experiments in Understanding Human Cultural Evolution." *Philosophical Transactions of The Royal Society B* 363 (2008): 3489–501.

Miller, David J. D., and Peter Sarris, eds and trans. *The Novels of Justinian*. 2 vols. Cambridge: Cambridge University Press, 2018.

Modarressi, Hossein. "Early Debates on the Integrity of the Qur'ān: A Brief Survey." *Studia Islamica* 77 (1993): 5–39.

Mottahedeh, Roy. "Oaths and Public Vows in the Middle East of the Tenth and Eleventh Centuries." In *Oralité et lien social au Moyen Âge (Occident, Byzance, Islam): parole donnée, foi jurée, serment*, edited by Marie-France Auzépy and Guillaume Saint-Gullain, 117–22. Paris: Association des amis du Centre d'histoire et civilisation de Byzance, 2008.

Motzki, Harald. *Analysing Muslim Traditions: Studies in Legal, Exegetical and Maghāzī Ḥadīth*. Edited by Harald Motzki, Nicolet Boekhoff-van der Voort, and Sean W. Anthony. Leiden: Brill, 2013.

Motzki, Harald. "Dating Muslim Traditions: A Survey." *Arabica*, no. T. 52, Fasc. 2 (Apr. 2005): 204–53.

Motzki, Harald. "The Jurisprudence of Ibn Shihāb az-Zuhrī. A Source-critical Study." Translated by Barbara Paoli and Vivien Reid. Originally published as "Der Fiqh des Zuhrī: die Quellenproblematik" *Der Islam* 68 (1991a): 1–44.

Motzki, Harald. "The Muṣannaf of ʿAbd al-Razzāq al-Sanʿānī as a Source of Authentic Aḥādīth of the First Century A.H." *Journal of Near Eastern Studies* 50, no. 1 (Jan. 1991b): 1–21.

Motzki, Harald. *The Origins of Islamic Jurisprudence: Meccan Fiqh Before the Classical Schools.* Translated by Marion H. Katz. Boston: Brill, 2002.

Motzki, Harald. "The Prophet and the Cat: On Dating Mālik's *Muwaṭṭa'* and Legal Tradition." *Journal of Jerusalem Studies in Arabic and Islam* 22 (1998): 18–83.

Motzki, Harald. "Wal-muhsanātu mina n-nisā'i illā mā malakat aimānukum (Koran 4:24) und die Koranische Sexualethik." *Der Islam* 63 (1986): 192–218.

Mourad, Suleiman. *Early Islam Between Myth and History: Al-Ḥasan al-Baṣrī (d. 110H/728CE) and the Formation of His Legacy in Classical Islamic Scholarship.* Leiden: Brill, 2005.

Nanko-Fernández, Carmen. "Held Hostage by Method? Interrupting Pedagogical Assumptions—Latinamente." *Theological Education* 48, no. 1 (2013): 35–46.

Neusner, Jacob. *The Talmud of the Land of Israel: A Preliminary Translation and Explanation.* 35 vols. Chicago: University of Chicago Press, 1982.

Newby, Gordon Darnell. *A History of the Jews of Arabia: From Ancient Times to Their Eclipse Under Islam.* South Carolina: University of South Carolina Press, 2009.

Nickel, Gordon. *Narratives of Tampering in the Earliest Commentaries of the Qur'ān.* Boston: Brill, 2011.

Nöldeke, Theodor and Friedrich Schwally. *Geschichte des Qorâns.* Göttin-gen: Dieterichschen Buchhandlung, 1860.

Noth, Albrecht and Lawrence I. Conrad. *The Early Arabic Historical Tradition: A Source-Critical Study.* Princeton: Darwin Press, 1994.

Parsons, Mikeal. "'Exegesis By the Numbers': Numerology and the New Testament." Perspectives in Religious Studies 35 (2008): 25–43.

Pavlovitch, Pavel. "Early Development of the Tradition of the Self-Confessed Adulterer in Islam. An *Isnād* and *Matn* Analysis." *Al-Qanṭara*, no. 31 (Jul.–Dec. 2010): 371–410.

Pavlovitch, Pavel. "*Kunnā nakrahu al-kitāb*: Scripture, Transmission of Knowledge, and Politics in the Second Century AH (719–816 CE)." In *Modern Hadith Studies: Continued Debates and New Approaches*, edited by Belal Abu-Alabbas et al., 9–26. Edinburgh: Edinburgh University Press, 2020.

Pavlovitch, Pavel. *The Formation of the Islamic Understanding of Kalāla in the Second Century AH (718-816 CE): Between Scripture and Canon.* Boston: Brill, 2016.

Pavlovitch, Pavel. "The Islamic Penalty for Adultery in the Third Century AH and Al-Shāfiʿī's *Risāla*." *Bulletin of the School of Oriental and African Studies* 74, no. 3 (Oct. 2012): 473–97.

Pavlovitch, Pavel. "The Origin of the *Isnād* and al-Mukhtār b. Abī ʿUbayd's Revolt in Kūfa (66–7/685–7)." *Al-Qanṭara* 39 no. 1 (2018): 17–48.

Pavlovitch, Pavel. "The ʿUbāda b. al-Ṣāmit Tradition at the Crossroads of Methodology." *Journal of Arabic and Islamic Studies*, no. 11 (2011): 137–235.

Pavlovitch, Pavel. "Juynboll, al-Zuhrī, and *al-Kitāb*: About the Historicity of Transmission below the Common Link Level." In *Islam at 250: Studies in Memory of G.H.A. Juynboll*, edited by Petra M. Sijpesteijn and Camilla Adang, 103–32. Leiden: Brill, 2020.

Pavlovitch, Pavel. "The Stoning of a Pregnant Adulteress from Juhayna: The Early Evolution of a Muslim Tradition." *Islamic Law and Society*, no. 17 (2010): 1–62.

Pellat, Charles. "Fuḳahā' al-Madīna al-Sabʿa." In Encyclopaedia of Islam. Second Edition. Edited by Peri Bearman et al., S:310b–312b. Leiden: Brill, 1997.

Perikhanian, Anahit. *The Book of a Thousand Judgements (A Sasanian Law-Book).* Translated by Nina Garsoïan. Costa Mesa: Mazda Publishers, 1997.

Peters, Rudolph, *Crime and Punishment in Islamic Law: Theory and Practice from the Sixteenth to the Twenty-first Century.* Cambridge: Cambridge University Press, 2005.

Pourshariati, Parvaneh. "The Mihrāns and the Articulation of Early Islamic Dogma: A Preliminary Prosopographical Analysis." *Cahiers de Studia Iranica* 42 (2009): 1–33.

Qudsy, Syed Ismail al- and Asmak al-Rahman. "Effective Governance in the Era of Caliphate 'Umar Ibn Al-Khattab (632–644)." *European Journal of Social Sciences* 18, no. 4 (2011): 612–24.

Quiroga, Rodrigo Quian. *The Forgetting Machine: Memory, Perception, and the "Jennifer Aniston Neuron."* Dallas: BenBella Books, 2017.

Rabb, Intisar. "Crime and Punishment in Medieval Islamic Societies." In *Cultural History of Crime and Punishment in the Medieval Age*, edited by Sarah McDougall and Karl Shoemaker. New York: Bloomsbury Press, 2023.

Rabb, Intisar. *Doubt in Islamic Law: A History of Legal Maxims, Interpretation, and Islamic Criminal Law.* New York: Cambridge University Press, 2015.

Rafi`i, Ali, and Translated by Hassan Lahouti. "Al-Abṭaḥ." Encyclopaedia Islamica Online. Edited by Wilferd Madelung. Brill, 2015. doi: https://doi.org/10.1163/1875-9831_isla_COM_0031.

Rahman, Fazlur. "The Concept of Ḥadd in Islamic Law." Journal of Islamic Studies 4 (1965): 237–51.

Rashwan, Hany. "Hadith as Oral Literature through Early Islamic Literary Criticism." *Studia Islamica* 119 (2024): 34–69.

Reinhart, A. Kevin. "Review: Juynbolliana, Gradualism, the Big Bang, and Ḥadīth Study in the Twenty-First Century." *Journal of the American Oriental Society* 130, no. 3 (Jul.–Sept. 2010): 413–44.

"Revision and Alteration." In *Encyclopedia of the Qur'ān*. Edited by Jane Dammen McAuliffe. 4:448f. Leiden: Brill, 2004.

Ricoeur, Paul. "The Hermeneutical Function of Distanciation." In *Hermeneutics and the Human Sciences: Essays on Language, Action and Interpretation*, edited and translated by John B. Thompson, 93–106. Cambridge, Cambridge University Press, 1981.

Rigney, Ann. "Scales of Postmemory: Six of Six Million." In *Probing the Ethics of Holocaust Culture*, edited by Claudio Fogu et al. Cambridge: Harvard University Press, 2016.

Rippin, Andrew. *The Qur'an and Its Interpretative Tradition.* Farnham: Ashgate Publishing, 2001.

Robinson, Chase F. *Islamic Historiography*. New York: Cambridge University Press, 2003.

Rose, Steven P.R. "How Brains Make Memories." In *Memory*, edited by Patricia Fara and Karalyn Patterson, 134–61. Cambridge: Cambridge University Press, 1998.

Roth, Martha T. Law Collections from Mesopotamia and Asia Minor. Atlanta: Scholars Press, 1995.

Rubin, Uri. "'al-Walad li-l-Firāsh' on the Islamic Campaign Against 'Zinā.'" *Studia Islamic* 78 (1993): 5–26.

Rubin, Uri. *The Eye of the Beholder: The Life of Muhammad as Viewed by the Early Muslims, a Textual Analysis*, Studies in Late Antiquity and Early Islam. vol. 5. Princeton: The Darwin Press, Inc., 1995.

Sadeghi, Behnam. "The Traveling Tradition Test: A Method for Dating Traditions." *Der Islam* 85, no. 1 (2010): 203–42.

Sadeghi, Behnam. *The Logic of Law Making: Women and Prayer in the Legal Tradition.* New York: Cambridge University Press, 2013.

Saeed, Abdullah. *Interpreting the Qur'an: Towards a Contemporary Approach.* New York: Routledge, 2006.

Salaymeh, Lena. *The Beginnings of Islamic Law: Late Antique Islamicate Legal Traditions.* Cambridge: Cambridge University Press, 2016.

Saleh, Walid A. *The Formation of the Classical Tafsīr Tradition: The Qur'ān Commentary al al-Tha'labī (d. 427/1035).* Leiden: Boston, 2003.

Saleh, Walid A. "Preliminary Remarks on the Historiography of Tafsir in Arabic: A History of the Book Approach." *Journal of Qur'anic Studies* 12, no. 1–2 (2010): 6–40.

Satlow, Michael L. "Defining Judaism: Accounting for 'Religions' in the Study of Religion." *Journal* of the American Academy of Religion 74, no. 4 (Dec. 2006): 837–60.

Satlow, Michael L. *Tasting the Dish: Rabbinic Rhetorics of Sexuality*. Atlanta: Scholars Press, 2020.

Schacht, Joseph. *The Origins of Muhammadan Jurisprudence*. Oxford: The Clarendon Press, 1958.

Schoeler, Gregor. "Die Frage der schriftlichen oder mündlichen Überlieferung der Wissenschaften im frühen Islam." *Der Islam* 62, no. 2 (1985): 201–30.

Schoeler, Gregor. *The Biography of Muḥammad: Nature and Authenticity*. Edited by James E. Montgomery. Translated by Uwe Vagelphol. New York and London: Routledge, 2011.

Schoeler, Gregor. *The Genesis of Literature in Islam: From the Aural to the Read, Revised Edition*. Translated by Shawkat M. Toorawa. Edinburgh: Edinburgh University Press, 2009.

Schoeler, Gregor. *The Oral and the Written in Early Islam*. Edited by James E. Montgomery. Translated by Uwe Vagelpohl. New York and London: Routledge, 2006.

Schoeler, Gregor. "The Relationship of Literacy and Memory in the Second/Eighth Century." In *The Development of Arabic as a Written Language* (Supplement to the Proceedings of the Seminar of Arabic Studies 40), edited by M.C.A. Macdonald, 121–30. Oxford: Archaeopress, 2010.

Shah, Mustafa, ed. *Tafsīr: Interpreting the Qur'ān*. New York: Routledge, 2013.

Spohn, William. *Go and Do Likewise: Jesus and Ethics*. New York: The Continuum International Publishing Group, Inc., 2007.

Stafford, Samuel A. "Constructing Muḥammad's Legitimacy: Arabic Literary Biography and the Jewish Pedigree of the Companion 'Abd Allāh b. Salām (d. 43/633)." *Journal of Jerusalem Studies in Arabic and Islam* 47 (2019): 133–86.

Steinsaltz, Adin, Tzvi Hersh Weinreb, Shalom Zvi Berger, Joshua Schreier, and Hotsa'at Ḳoren, eds. *Talmud Bavli: Koren Talmud Bavli*. First Hebrew/English Edition. 42 vols. Jerusalem: Koren Publishers, 2012.

Stidwell, Richard et al., eds. "Mopsuestia." In *The Princeton Encyclopedia of Classical Sites*, 593–94. Princeton: Princeton University Press, 1976.

Stilt, Kristen. *Islamic Law in Action: Authority, Discretion, and Everyday Experiences in Mamluk Egypt*. Oxford: Oxford University Press, 2011.

Takim, Liyakat. "The Origins of and Authentications in Shi'i Biographical Literature." *The American Journal of Islamic Social Sciences* 24, no. 4 (2007): 26–49.

Tantawi, Sarah El. "Ṭūsī Did Not 'Opt Out': Shiite Jurisprudence and the Solidification of the Stoning Punishment in the Islamic Legal Tradition." In *Essays in Islamic Philosophy, History, and Philosophy*, edited by Alireza Korangy et al., 312–32. Boston: De Gruyter, 2016.

The Digest of Justinian. Vol. IV. Latin text edited by Theodor Mommsen with the aid of Paul Krueger. English translation edited by Alan Watson. Philadelphia: University of Pennsylvania Press, 1985.

Thompson, Alistair. "Memory and Remembering in Oral History." In *The Oxford Handbook of Oral History*, edited by Donald A. Ritchie, 77–95. Oxford: Oxford University Press, 2010.

Umbach, Maiken. "Memory and Historicism: Reading Between the Lines of the Built Environment, Germany c. 1990." *Representations* 88, no. 1 (Fall 2004): 26–54.

Umbach, Maiken, and Mathew Humphrey. *Authenticity: The Cultural History of a Political Concept*. Cham: Palgrave Macmillan, 2018.

van Ess, Joseph. "al-Manzila Bayn al-Manzilatayn." In *Encyclopaedia of Islam New Edition Online (EI-2 English)*. Edited by Peri Bearman et at. Brill, 2012. doi: https://doi-org.proxy.uchicago.edu/10.1163/1573-3912_islam_SIM_4949.

van Ess, Joseph. *Theology and Society in the Second and Third Centuries of the Hijra: A History of Religious Thought in Early Islam*. Vol. 1. Translated by John O'Kane. Leiden: Brill, 2016.

van Ess, Joseph. *Theology and Society in the Second and Third Centuries of the Hijra: A History of Religious Thought in Early Islam*. Vol. 2. Translated by Gwendolin Goldbloom. Leiden: Brill, 2017.

van Ess, Joseph. *Theology and Society in the Second and Third Centuries of the Hijra: A History of Religious Thought in Early Islam*. Vol. 3. Translated by Gwendolin Goldbloom. Leiden: Brill, 2018.

Vansina, Jan. Oral Tradition: A Study in Historical Methodology. Translated by H.M. Wright. New Brunswick, NJ: Transaction Publishers, 2006.

Vidal, F.S. "G̲h̲āmid." *Encyclopaedia of Islam New Edition Online (EI-2 English)*. Edited by Peri Bearman et al., Brill, 2012. doi: https://doi-org.proxy.uchicago.edu/10.1163/1573-3912_islam_SIM_2454.

Wansbrough, John. *Quranic Studies: Sources and Methods of Scriptural Interpretation*. Oxford: Oxford University Press, 1977.

Wasserstrom, Steven M. *Between Muslim and Jew: The Problem of Symbiosis Under Early Islam*. Princeton: Princeton University Press, 1995.

Watt, W. Montgomery. *Muhammad in Medina*. Oxford: Oxford University Press, 1956.

Watt, W. Montgomery. *The Formative Period in Islamic Thought*. Oxford: Oneworld Publications, 1998.

Wensinck, Arent Jan. "Ḥawḍ." In Encyclopaedia of Islam, Second Edition. Edited by Bernard Lewis et al., 3:286. Leiden: Brill, 1971.

Wensinck, Arent Jan. "Shafāʿa." In Encyclopaedia of Islam, Second Edition. Edited by P.J. Bearman et al., 9:177–9. Leiden: Brill, 1997.

Wensinck, Arent Jan and A.S. Tritton. "ʿAd̲h̲āb al-Ḳabr." In Encyclopaedia of Islam New Edition Online (EI-2 English). Edited by Peri Bearman. Brill, 2012. doi: https://doi-org.proxy.uchicago.edu/10.1163/1573-3912_islam_SIM_0301.

Westbrook, Raymond. "Adultery in Ancient Near Eastern Law." *Revue Bilbique* 97, no. 4 (Oct. 1990): 542–80.

White, Cynthia. *The Emergence of Christianity*. Westport: Greenwood Press, 2007.

White, Hayden. *Tropics of Discourse: Essays in Cultural Criticism*. Baltimore: Johns Hopkins University Press, 1978.

Witztum, Joseph. "Q 4:24 Revisited." *Islamic Law and Society* 16, no. 1 (2009): 1–33.

Yanagihashi, Hiroyuki. *Studies in Legal Hadith*. Leiden: Brill, 2019.

Yerushalmi, Yosef Hayim. *Zakhor: Jewish History and Jewish Memory*. New York: Schocken Books, 1989.

Young, Walter. "Stoning and Hand-Amputation: The Pre-Islamic Origins of the Hadd Penalties for *Zinā* and *Sariqa*." Master's thesis, Institute of Islamic Studies at McGill University, 2005.

Yusoff, Muhammad Fawwaz bin Muhammad. "On Biographical Dictionaries of Ḥadīṯ Transmitters: Rethinking Development in the Islamic Literature." *Al-Bayān—Journal of Qur'ān and Ḥadīth Studies* 17 (2019): 125–46.

Zellentin, Holger Michael. *The Qur'ān's Legal Culture: The Didascalia Apostolorum as a Point of Departure*. Tübingen: Mohr Siebeck, 2013.

Zellentin, Holger Michael. "Aḥbār and Ruhbān." In *Qur'ānic Studies Today*, edited by Angelika Neuwirth and Michael Sells, 262–93. London: Routledge, 2016.

Zellentin, Holger Michael. *Law Beyond Israel: From the Bible to the Qur'an*. Oxford: Oxford University Press, 2022.

Zellentin, Holger Michael. "What Falls Within Judaism According to the Quran?" In Within Judaism? Interpretive Trajectories in Judaism, Christianity, and Islam from the First to the Twenty-First Century. Edited by Karin Hedner and Anders Runesson, 282–308. Lanham, MD: Lexington Books/Fortress Academic, 2023.

Index of Hadith Transmitters and Other Historical Figures

For the benefit of digital users, indexed terms that span two pages (e.g., 52–53) may, on occasion, appear on only one of those pages.

General Subject Index

For the benefit of digital users, indexed terms that span two pages (e.g., 52–53) may, on occasion, appear on only one of those pages.

www.ingramcontent.com/pod-product-compliance
Ingram Content Group UK Ltd.
Pitfield, Milton Keynes, MK11 3LW, UK
UKHW020842150926
475595UK00010B/189/J